M000276041

LOVE AND LET DIE

Also by John Higgs

I Have America Surrounded

The KLF

Stranger than We Can Imagine

Watling Street

The Future Starts Here

William Blake Now

William Blake vs the World

LOVE AND LET DIE

JAMES BOND, THE BEATLES, AND THE BRITISH PSYCHE

JOHN HIGGS

PEGASUS BOOKS

NEW YORK LONDON

LOVE AND LET DIE

Pegasus Books, Ltd.
148 West 37th Street, 13th Floor
New York, NY 10018

ISBN: 978-1-63936-330-8

10 9 8 7 6 5 4 3 2 1

Printed in the United States of America
Distributed by Simon & Schuster
www.pegasusbooks.com

This book is dedicated to Jon Smith

'Without Contraries is no progression'
—William Blake

'They've got a lot to answer for, those James Bond films'
—Paul McCartney

CONTENTS

INTRODUCTION

A TURNING POINT IN BRITISH HISTORY. That was the dramatic front-page headline of the *Daily Mirror* on Friday, 5 October 1962. This was a bold claim, even by tabloid standards, and readers may have felt that the accompanying story didn't live up to the hyperbole. It concerned a speech about the European Common Market which the Labour leader Hugh Gaitskell had given at a party conference in Brighton. This is the nature of tabloid journalism – hysterical about the surface froth of events, but blind to genuinely historical changes occurring in the depths.

Elsewhere in the world, significant events were unfolding. In France, it looked like President De Gaulle's government was about to collapse, and the United States was calling on European countries to join it in a planned blockade of Cuba. In contrast to all this drama, the UK appeared to be having an otherwise unremarkable day. Princess Anne had gone down a coal mine in County Durham and, after a 35-minute tour of the 1,200ft deep coal face, had remarked, 'It's a wonderful place.' Four masked bandits had ambushed a mail van near Dungeness in Kent and escaped with nearly £5,000. An Admiralty clerk called William Vassall was due on trial for passing 'secret information to an enemy'. It was a warm, dry October day, although very windy in the south. It did not in any way seem to be 'a turning point in British history'.

Or at least, it didn't on the political level. Culturally, things were being born for which there was no precedent. In the world of the British imagination, the *Daily Mirror*'s hyperbolic headline would prove to be surprisingly apt. Friday, 5 October 1962, saw the release of 'Love Me Do', the first record by the Beatles, and *Dr. No*, the first James Bond film. The Beatles were about to become the most successful and important band in history. Not to be outdone, James Bond would go on to become the single most successful movie character ever. The music industry and the film industry would be entirely changed by these new arrivals. So too would the international reputation of Britain, which was suddenly giving the world spy thrillers and mop-tops rather than redcoats and cannons. Most countries can only dream of a cultural export becoming a worldwide phenomenon on this scale. For Britain to produce two on the same windy October afternoon was, by anyone's standards, unusual.

There are those who will argue, of course, that culture is ultimately trivial. They will say that a few films and songs, in the face of great national narratives, are neither here nor there. The correct focus for telling the story of a nation, according to this position, is power. Indeed, the history of Britain is almost always told from a perspective focused on power – be that military power, symbolic power such as monarchy, or financial power such as the story of the East India Company. The problem with this approach is that the history of power is not something the vast majority of people in Britain connect with. We do not have power, so we are not hugely invested in stories about it. From what we know of it, it is something to be suspicious of, not something to be admired. As a result, we are presented with a national story which could be about Martians for all that we can identify with it.

There are, however, other ways to tell the story of an island people, and one of them is by focusing on the imagination. This is the story of our internal lives – the tales that people are drawn to and share, and what they reveal about our dreams, beliefs and attitudes. To focus on imagination rather than power offers a deeper portrait of a population. It is also one which those who live there can actually recognise, and that must count for something.

Those who focus on power often do so in the belief that imagination is an ephemeral, weak, unimportant thing. This is not true, but imagination does influence the world in a different way to brute force. Water can be just as destructive as fire, even though its nature is to behave in an entirely different way. Imagination matters because ideas alter beliefs, beliefs shape attitudes, and attitudes decide actions. In this way does the story of the mind play out in the material world.

The Romantic poet Samuel Taylor Coleridge was fascinated by imagination, and the power it had to alter reality. Imagination was a different thing, he argued, to simple fantasy. As Coleridge defined the term, imagination was the arrival of something truly new. This had a significant impact on the world because things had to adjust and rearrange themselves to make way for this new arrival. What he defined as fantasy, in contrast, was the simple rearranging of things that already existed. This could be entertaining and diverting, but it did not change the world like imagination did. Had Coleridge been around in 1962, he would have classified most of the new songs and films being created then as mere fantasy. They were still of value, of course, but the world was not made noticeably different by them. The events of Friday, 5 October, with hindsight, would have given him a perfect example of why

3

true imagination, in all its world-changing power, was different to fantasy.

The world of the imagination is a wild ecosystem stuffed with an uncountable number of plays and paintings, sitcoms and orchestras, comics and operas. Creation is ongoing and constant, and trying to make sense of this seemingly infinite landscape can be overwhelming. Not everything, however, is equal. There are oversized monsters in this landscape. As with shipwrecked explorers who make it to an island only to find it inhabited by King Kong and Godzilla, the presence of two cultural monsters in the ecosystem does tend to bring a particular focus. Yes, insect life and fungal life are important and worthy of study. But first – it's probably best to pay attention to the monsters.

The Beatles and the Bond films are our monsters in the cultural ecosystem. Neither make any sense when viewed from the perspective of the regular entertainment industry. The idea that a film series based on a single character could continue uninterrupted for sixty years or more, always remaining successful and making money during twenty-five sequels, is in no way plausible. There has been no shortage of film producers who have tried and failed to create something that reliable and profitable. If it was possible, everyone would be doing it. And likewise, the idea that a band of musicians could produce a body of work as large, ambitious, original and varied as the Beatles – in a little over eight years – is not something that any other musicians would consider plausible. No band can realistically hope to do what the Beatles did, and you would be considered crazy for suggesting otherwise. None of this, clearly, is normal. It may be more instructive to look at these two monsters together, because in a number of ways the Beatles and the Bond films have more in common with each other than they do their peers in their own industries. As we shall see, they are also two stories which are often interlinked.

Bond films and Beatles records arrived at a pivotal time. At stake was how the British would come to define themselves. Britain's sense of identity was then being torn up by profound global change, something which had happened several times before. In medieval times, the stories which defined the country were known as the Matter of Britain. These were stories of monarchy, chivalry and the moral justification of aristocracy, featuring such noble heroes as King Arthur, Galahad and Lancelot – and of course the wily trickster Merlin. At the heart of these stories was the belief that our rulers, in their quest for the Holy Grail, were pure and spiritually devout.

Around 400 years ago the country began to grow into a global empire and the narrative of Britain had to change. Our story became one about Britannia ruling the waves, and how the sun would never set on the largest empire the world had ever known. In this new narrative, the pursuit of earthly power replaced spiritual attainment as our great goal. At the heart of these stories was the belief that the British were, inherently, superior to people from other parts of the world. This sense of history-defining grandeur framed British thinking for centuries.

After the end of the Second World War, however, the bulk of this empire was handed back, wrestled away or otherwise disposed of. This significant historical event occurred with remarkably little fuss – or at least, that was how it appeared in Britain to the readers of the *Daily Mirror*. It was a story about power, after all, so most of the population were largely detached from it. But despite how little these changes impacted British people, they were still confusing. Hadn't Britain just won the war? We had been on the same side as America and the Soviet Union, and we celebrated that hard-won victory. Yet we now found ourselves much smaller and less influential than before. Had it not been for VE day and the defeat of Hitler, it might have seemed as if we were one of the war's great losers. This situation left us with a tricky question – if we were not a big, globally important country anymore, then who were we? What story would a modern Matter of Britain tell?

Beneath the *Daily Mirror*'s headline about 'a turning point in British history' was a second headline: THE BRICKIE'S MATE AND THE DAUGHTER OF A BRIGADIER. This story revealed much about how the country was questioning things it had previously accepted. It told how Jeanette, the daughter of Brigadier C.A.L. Suther (retired), had eloped with a man who was, shockingly, her social inferior. Her new husband David Miller was not even a fully trained bricklayer – he was only a lowly bricklayer's mate! To modern eyes, it is not so much the events that are fascinating, but the fact that it was considered front-page material. The worldview of British people back in 1962, clearly, was very different.

The story also made the front page of the *Daily Herald*. The *Herald* was a left-wing newspaper known for its pro-worker views; two years later it would be relaunched as the *Sun*. That day their front page included photos of both Jeanette and David. They appeared to make a handsome and likeable couple who would probably be a little surprised to see themselves on the front page of the national papers. The *Herald* included a quote from Brigadier Suther, who insisted that his concern about his daughter's marriage wasn't a matter of class. 'I don't object to young people from different spheres seeing each other if they are in love,' he said. 'I was angry because of the underhand way we parents have been treated. I want them both to come back and discuss this sensibly.'

Brigadier Suther had asked Greenock Police to look out for the couple in case they had gone to Scotland to get married. As he explained, 'I want to do all I can to stop my daughter doing something that she may regret.' The mother of the bricklayer's mate, Mrs Ivy Miller, was also against the marriage, but for different reasons. 'I knew about the friendship and I tried to stop it,' she told the *Daily Mirror*. 'That was not because of any class barriers but because I thought they were too young to be thinking about marrying.'

That both sets of parents felt the need to deny that their concern was class-based illustrates the extent to which Britain in 1962 was riddled with class consciousness. Class was the reason why the marriage of these two otherwise unnewsworthy young people was considered front-page news. Believers in a class-based hierarchical society thought that this young couple should not get married because the wealth and status of Jeanette's father made her – in some strange and ill-defined way – 'better' than David. By thinking he had the right to marry the woman he had fallen in love with, David had 'ideas above his station' and needed to 'know his place'. From this perspective, a loveless marriage to a more suitable husband would have been better for Jeanette than spending her life with the man she loved.

By the 1960s, this deferential class-based worldview was built around ideas that were no longer as convincing as they once were. The shared delusion of class superiority was rubbing up against reality – in this case, the love of Jeanette and David – and generating a great deal of cognitive dissonance. It was people's attempts to process this cognitive dissonance that created the compulsion among the newspaper-buying public to read stories about events like a brigadier's daughter falling in love with a bricklayer's mate. The strange obsessions of the British press, then as now, are often a sign that long-held beliefs are being reassessed, or are starting to fail.

If the question that post-imperial Britain needed to answer was when we should hold on to the traditional, and when we should embrace the new, then Bond and the Beatles gave us very different answers. James Bond celebrated the modern – sports cars, international travel, all the latest gadgets and so on. His desire for the new, however, was limited to the material world of things. In terms of attitudes – to women, to class, to non-British people – he remained resolutely traditional. We could have exciting new things, he suggests, but we shouldn't change the way we see the world. The answer that the Beatles gave was the exact opposite. They embraced new ways of thinking, on topics such as sex, drugs, male identity and religion, because they thought the old ways were flawed and were holding us back. In the world of things, however, they often found value in the traditional, from the faux-Victoriana of *Sgt. Pepper's Lonely Hearts Club Band*, to mystery coach tours and the childhood nostalgia of songs like 'Penny Lane'. The subject of which aspects of the old traditions still had value is only one of the ways that Bond and the Beatles were arguing for futures that were entirely contradictory.

In the strange world of particle physics, it is normal for something brand new to pop into existence from out of nothing. It will then have an impact on the existing world, in a way that Coleridge would have understood. Physicists, however, know that when a particle appears like this, an equal and opposite particle must also appear to keep the universe in balance. If a particle like a quark was to ping into existence, for example, then an opposite particle called an anti-quark would also be created. As the James Bond film series and the music of the Beatles both popped into existence on the exact same afternoon, it is tempting to see a similar process at play. This would mean that Bond and the Beatles were, in the world of the mind, in some way opposites. Astrologers will tell you that, being born on 5 October, Beatles records and Bond films are Libra, the scales, and that they represent balance.

When Paul McCartney was asked to sum up the Beatles in the mid-1990s, he said they were about love. 'It was all done in the name of love, and about love, and I'm very proud of that,' he explained. From first single 'Love Me Do' to their posthumous final single 'Real Love', through songs such as 'All You Need Is Love', which was the soundtrack to the 1967 Summer of Love, McCartney's assessment is hard to dispute. But while the Beatles represent love, James Bond represents death. What makes Bond different from other spies is that he has a licence to kill. From films such as *Live and Let Die* to *A View to a Kill*, *Die Another Day* or his most recent adventure *No Time to Die*, Bond is an assassin with official permission to kill anyone he wants.

According to Freudian psychologists, love and death are the two central opposing drives in the human psyche. Freud's thoughts on these drives are complex and they evolved over his career, but Freudians now typically refer to them as *Eros* and *Thanatos*. Love or *Eros* was the instinct towards life, co-operation and pro-social behaviour, and the desire to open yourself up and become part of something larger. The death drive or *Thanatos*, in contrast, was the self-destructive pull towards aggression, cruelty and risky behaviour. Although this drive is sometimes directed internally, leading to self-harm or suicide, it is usually directed outwards as a desire to harm others. The respective pull between *Eros* and *Thanatos*, Freud believed, was one of the most fundamental struggles in the human psyche.

The Britain of 1962 was a country starting to emerge from the human trauma and financial devastation of the Second World War. The old Britain of crippling class hierarchies and global empire was on its way out, although this was perhaps more apparent to the younger generation than to their parents and grandparents. The character of the new country that would emerge was unknown. The future, as always, was up for grabs. If Freudians were correct, the competing drives towards love and death would help shape this new world. They would play out in the minds of the people as this new country appeared and be apparent in the culture that they created.

Our attraction to the *Thanatos* death drive is, obviously, a dangerous thing, but there are ways in which it can be channelled in order to minimise the damage it would otherwise do to society. One of the best examples of this is action cinema, which allows people to enjoy the visceral thrill of car crashes, shoot-outs and explosions without anyone actually getting hurt. Although there may be a danger that spectacle such as this desensitises us to violence, it is probably healthier to enjoy screen-based action than it is to deny that we are drawn to it in the first place. In a similar way, our desire for *Eros* can attract us to music, because we can lose ourselves in music and surrender ourselves to something larger. Action cinema and music, then, were the ideal mediums to express *Thanatos* and *Eros*, and it is hard to imagine more perfect cultural expressions of those drives than James Bond films or the Beatles. Given the astonishing global success they would enjoy, this must surely be the most public struggle for the soul of a culture ever. Never before had one country's psychic laundry been washed in front of an audience of the whole planet.

There are not many outsized cultural monsters like Bond or the Beatles – or at least, not which come from Britain. *Doctor Who* arrived a year later and is still going strong, but it didn't make a global impact in the way Bond and the Beatles did. *Harry Potter* has had similar global success, but it is still too early to say if this will sustain over time. Given how modern teenagers often mock members of the Millennial generation for their love of *Harry Potter*, it may well be that its audience remains focused in that one demographic group, in a similar way to how the devotees of Bob Dylan are predominantly Baby Boomers. Global hits that maintain over generations are rare things indeed.

After sixty years, Bond and the Beatles still hold dominant

roles in British culture. There has been little that has come along since that has been able to compete with them, and the differing perspectives they offered on what being British means are still being processed. They are so familiar that it is easy to overlook the extent to which they operate outside of the regular way of things – if it were not for the fact that they actually happened, no one would believe a word of this.

This, then, is the story of the irrational clash of these two cultural monsters, and the impact they had on these damp but sparky Atlantic islands.

PART 1: INITIATE COUNTDOWN

1945: THERE'S NOBODY TO TALK TO WHEN IT'S RAINING

One of Ringo Starr's earliest memories is sitting in the back of a removal van when he was about five years old. The World War that he had been born into had ended, and he and his mother were about to start life in a new home, in peacetime. They were not going far, however. The journey was about 300 yards across the Welsh Streets area of the Dingle, Liverpool. It was so short that the removal men didn't bother putting the back flap of the van up. This meant that Ringo could sit with his legs dangling out of the back of the vehicle, as he watched the streets of his childhood pass by, aware that something significant was happening but not entirely sure what. As a child he was always watching. His mother said that when he was born, a week late, he had his eyes open and was looking around. The German bombing of Liverpool began a week after his birth.

He wasn't called Ringo Starr then, of course. He was Richard Starkey, a first son named after his father in the established working-class tradition. His father became known as Big Richy, to differentiate the pair. His grandparents would refer to him as 'that bloody Noddler'.

Big Richy abandoned his wife and son before the end of war, walking out of Little Richy's life. This left his mother Elsie, despite working multiple jobs, unable to afford the rent on their small, terraced house. Her only option was to move to somewhere even smaller, and cheaper. Her next house at 10 Admiral Grove had been condemned a decade earlier, yet Elsie would live there for the next twenty years. It lacked many of the amenities we now take for granted – central heating, hot running water, a telephone, a bath. Elsie loaded up her possessions and her young son into a van and headed to her new home, only two minutes' walk away on the opposite side of High Park Street. It is perhaps an indication of how little Ringo's mother owned that he was able to sit in the back of the van, rather than having to walk to his new home.

To visit those streets in the Dingle now is to find them relatively unchanged. The roads have been tarmacked, of course, and the most striking difference is the presence of cars. As Ringo's childhood friend Davy Patterson recalled, 'The first car that came onto our street must have been when I was about twelve. The first person to own a car was a fellow called Mr Kraft, and he was a builder, so he had a van. You were lucky if you saw a taxi coming down the street.' The excitement of seeing a rare taxi or other vehicle may explain why Ringo's ride in the removal van remains such a powerful memory. Concrete traffic bollards now block access to Admiral Grove, and Madryn Street, where Ringo was born, has been renovated with smart new windows and doors on all the houses. The wartime craters and bombed-out houses that Richy used to play in as a child have long since gone. Yet the streets and houses that he watched from the van are still present, untroubled by the years.

If anything, it is the immaterial aspect of life in those streets that changed more radically during the following sixty years. Couples living together before marriage was considered scandalous then, and most people would expect to be married by their early twenties. Homosexuality was illegal and no one would have believed that gay marriage would occur in their lifetime. The media consumed was limited to radio, newspapers and cinema – the idea of TVs in every home was unthinkable then, let alone the internet, smartphones or social media. The *Windrush* had not yet arrived at Tilbury Docks with workers from Jamaica and other Caribbean countries, and Britain did not see itself as a multicultural country. Attitudes to everything from Empire and sex to single mothers and the importance of the church would be torn up and rewritten during Little Richy's lifetime.

The war changed everything. Working men who previously had little reason or opportunity to leave their local area suddenly found themselves touring the globe, from the deserts of North Africa to the tropical heat of Southeast Asia. People from around the country were mixing in a way they had never done before. The regular 'Tommies' came into contact with officer-class 'Ruperts'. Horizons were being stretched, unquestioned assumptions were crumbling, and the limitations of the pre-war system were impossible to ignore. There was no chance that people would go back to the old way of things.

Liverpool was always different to other cities in England. This difference of character was often most apparent when compared to Manchester, its industrious, Protestant near-neighbour. Liverpool sometimes seemed like an Irish city that woke one morning nestled up to Lancashire, quite unable to explain how it got there. This sense of Liverpool being a culture apart has intensified since 1989, when the population of the city effectively rejected the *Sun*, Rupert Murdoch's bestselling English tabloid newspaper. This was a reaction to coverage of the Hillsborough Stadium tragedy in

Sheffield, in which ninety-seven Liverpool fans lost their lives. The *Sun*'s front-page coverage lied repeatedly in order to blame the victims, and the paper has effectively been boycotted by the people of Liverpool ever since. The personality of the city compared to other parts of England, as a result, now offers a unique insight into the question of whether newspapers just give their readers what they want, or actively shape how they think. In 2004, Boris Johnson published an article in *The Spectator* which argued that the continuing boycott of Murdoch's *Sun* was down to Liverpool's 'victim culture'. To Liverpudlian eyes, such a criticism was baffling. Surely standing up and rejecting the paper was refusing to be a victim? The wayward spiky confidence which characterises the city would be evident in the personalities of all four Beatles.

Little Richy was a sickly child who was not expected to live to adulthood. Just before his seventh birthday he was rushed to hospital with suspected appendicitis. On the operating table it was found that his appendix had burst and caused peritonitis, an infection that resulted in him being in a coma for ten weeks. His mother was told on three occasions that he would not survive the night. Even after he awoke, he slipped in and out of consciousness during the following four months. To help his stiches heal, he was advised not to move, so the most difficult aspect of those months in hospital was the utter boredom he endured. He loved cowboy stories, with the freedom and excitement they offered, and always longed for friends or brothers to play with. His mother remembered him once saying, 'I wish I had brothers and sisters. There's nobody to talk to when it's raining.'

Richy eventually returned home, hopelessly behind in school but with a new nickname – Lazarus – to show for his brushes with death. When he reached the age of eleven it was thought that there was no point in entering him for the eleven-plus exam. This could have given him the opportunities of a better education, which Paul

McCartney, John Lennon and George Harrison all received. At the age of thirteen, he contracted first pleurisy and then tuberculosis, those classic diseases of poverty. Had this been only a few years earlier it seems unlikely that he would have survived to adulthood, unless he had been lucky enough to receive long-term medical care from a religious or philanthropic charity. Fortunately, the National Health Service had just been established by Clement Attlee's post-war government. Richy was able to spend an extended period in a convalescent hospital in Heswall on the Wirral, despite his mother's financial hardship.

Richy eventually spent two whole years in hospital, killing off any hope of achieving a reasonable education. During those long, painful, boring years, however, he and his fellow patients were visited by a music teacher. There was only one thing this teacher had which Richy wanted – a drum, like the one he had previously stood and stared at in the window of his local music shop. No other instrument held any interest. And so, in the Wirral sanatorium away from school and family, he first took a drumstick, started pounding, and found the thing that he loved.

After Richy recovered and returned home, his paternal grand-father Johnny Starkey borrowed money to buy him a drum kit. He started playing with any skiffle or rock band that would have him, soon joining a promising young group then called Al Storm and the Hurricanes. No one in his family or close circle owned a car, so he had to lug his drumkit across town on buses to get to gigs. Getting home from gigs was worse, because of the risk of missing the last bus, or being attacked by gangs of Teddy Boys. Richy's world was a violent one, and it's hard to make a run for it when you're carrying a full drum kit. He was beaten up a few times but he considered himself lucky, because he saw other people beaten with hammers, being stabbed, or losing an eye.

Shortly after paying off the loan for Ringo's drums, his

grandfather died. Johnny had helped to fill the void in Richy's life that was left when his dad had walked out, and his death introduced his young grandson to grief and loss. Granny Starkey gave him Johnny's wedding ring, which he immediately put on his finger and said he would never remove. This gave him a total of three rings on his fingers, along with one his mother gave him on his sixteenth birthday and one from his then girlfriend. Three rings on a teenage boy in the 1950s was unusual and it gave him a distinctive gimmick. It would not be long before this led to another name. Here was Ringo, the cowboy drummer.

This was not the only thing Granny Starkey gave him. When Ringo was a little boy, she had been horrified that he was left-handed. To her, it signalled that he was possessed by witches, so she attempted to save her grandson by forcing him to favour his right hand. Granny Starkey, Ringo would later claim, was 'the voodoo queen of Liverpool'. Ringo became a drummer who played a right-handed kit but who led with his left hand, giving him a unique playing style that would become a vital part of the Beatles' sound and success. When his granny gave him his granddad's wedding ring, she gave him what we would now call his brand. When she forbade him from being left-handed, she gave him his uniqueness. Powerful voodoo indeed.

Thanks to his hound-dog eyes and hapless everyman persona, it used to be the case that Ringo's talent as a drummer was the butt of jokes. A popular joke in the 1980s was, 'Is Ringo the best drummer in the world? He isn't even the best drummer in the Beatles!' Anti-Ringo jokes like this now mark people out as being of a certain age. For musicians and younger fans, listening in particular to his drumming in the period between 'Tomorrow Never Knows' in 1966 and John Lennon's *Plastic Ono Band* album in 1970, such jokes are baffling. Ringo's playing, clearly, is amazing. His skill comes from an almost egoless approach, in which the drummer is there to serve the song, never to overpower it. He had a knack of coming up with completely unexpected but entirely perfect drum parts, which hugely elevated songs like 'Come Together' or 'Rain'. In the words of ex-Nirvana drummer and Foo Fighters frontman Dave Grohl, 'Ringo was the king of feel.' According to Elvis Presley's legendary drummer D.J. Fontana, Ringo 'had the greatest conception of tempo I've ever heard in my life'. In 2011, *Rolling Stone* magazine voted him the fifth greatest drummer of all time. The jokes of the late twentieth century are a reminder that there was a lot of resistance to acknowledging talent which came from areas like the Dingle.

Looking back, Ringo's childhood can seem almost Dickensian – a harsh tale of poverty, violence, ill health and paternal abandonment, set in years of post-war austerity, during which he longed for brothers and friends more than material possessions. He came from nothing, and nothing was expected for him. No one could ever have imagined the wealth and success that was in store for that 'bloody Noddler'. Of course, no one could have imagined what the future had in store for the country, either, or how the coming changes in the culture would impact on this one, sickly, Liverpudlian boy.

It was time to leave Dickensian sagas behind. A new story was about to be written.

1952: ALL OF HIS OWN DARKNESS

After five years of procrastination, Ian Fleming sat down at the typewriter.

He began to write not for the joy of creating, but as a way to avoid reality. He was forty-three years old and troubled by thoughts of the future. At the typewriter, he could escape reality and dream about the person he would rather be.

On the surface, Fleming's life looked idyllic. It was 1952, and he was wintering in Goldeneye, a simple one-storey house near Oracabessa on the north shore of Jamaica. He had had this house built after the end of the Second World War, with the intention of using it as a winter writing retreat. It was quite an ugly, sparse building, to the eyes of those used to beauty and luxury, and it lacked basic amenities like cupboards, hot water and even glass in the windows. It did include a separate garage which served as staff quarters, however; although he saw it as a rough, rugged, masculine retreat, Fleming still wanted servants.

Outside Goldeneye, the views and the weather were as close to paradise as you will find on this earth. So too was the act of walking through the rough garden and taking the steps down to the beach, entering the warm clear water and snorkelling among the coral of the Caribbean. Fleming left London and came to stay at Goldeneye for three months every winter. His life, clearly, was markedly different to that of his fellow Englishmen who were born in the Dingle. It was not hard to see why it took him five years to start his novel.

Fleming was depressed and drinking heavily. He was also about to get married. His fiancée, Ann, was the love of his life and pregnant with his child, but this didn't mean that he wanted to be married to her. He began writing, he later admitted, to take his mind off the 'hideous spectre of matrimony'. A committed relationship requires a level of emotional maturity which he did not possess. Mutual friends suspected from the start that the marriage would be a disaster. As the playwright Noël Coward noted in his diary, 'I have doubts about their happiness if [Ann] and Ian were to be married.'

When the pair first began their affair, Ann was married to an aristocrat and had the title Lady O'Neill. After Lord O'Neill was killed in action in the Second World War, she considered continuing her relationship with Ian, but decided against it. Instead she married Viscount Rothermere, the owner of the *Daily Mail*. In Ann's opinion, Rothermere's title and wealth made him a more attractive husband. The marriage was not a fulfilling one, however, so Ann and Ian resumed their affair. Their physical relationship was a BDSM one, in which Ian inflicted pain on Ann. As she wrote to him after a liaison in Dublin in 1947, 'I loved cooking for you and sleeping beside you and being whipped by you and I don't think I have ever loved like this before [...] I love being hurt by you and kissed afterwards.' In a letter Ian wrote to Ann during the war, which was sold by Sothebys in 2009, he told her that 'I love whipping you & squeezing you & pulling your black hair, and then we are happy together & stick pins into each other & like each other & don't behave too grownup & don't pretend much.'

Although Ann and Ian's stormy relationship was an open secret in the social circles they moved in, Ann and Viscount Rothermere didn't divorce until after she fell pregnant with Ian's child. This left the pair finally free to marry. As Ian wrote in a letter to Ann's brother ahead of their wedding, 'We are of course totally unsuited ... I'm a non-communicator, a symmetrist, of a bilious and melancholic temperament ... Ann is a sanguine anarchist/traditionalist. So china will fly and there will be rage and tears. But I think we will survive as there is no bitterness in either of us and we are both optimists – and I shall never hurt her except with a slipper.'

Most of Fleming's biographers link his fear of marriage with his lack of healthy emotional relationships in his formative years. His grandfather was Robert Fleming, who developed the concept of investment trusts and who founded the merchant bank Robert Fleming & Co. Robert Fleming has been called 'one of the pioneers of investment capitalism'; he made his family extremely wealthy. Robert's son and Ian's father was Valentine, a Conservative Member of Parliament who was killed in action at the Battle of the Somme in the First World War. His obituary in *The Times* was written by his friend Winston Churchill.

Ian was only nine when Valentine died. He was brought up to see his father as the epitome of male virtue – brave, successful in worldly affairs, incredibly rich, and entirely absent. As paternal figures go, Valentine was impossible to live up to. Fleming and his siblings used to end their nightly prayers with the words, 'and please, dear God, help me grow up to be more like Mokie' – their nickname for their late father, a child's variation on 'smokey', because of Valentine's love of pipe smoking. The family nickname for Fleming's mother Eve, curiously, was 'M'.

Eve was less admired than her late husband. She was beautiful but could be domineering and was, according to her granddaughter, 'a quite frightening woman'. She was aware that young Ian was sensitive, but she liked to humiliate him in public regardless. A cruel clause in her husband's will meant that she would be cut off from his family's wealth if she ever remarried, so Eve chose wealth over love and remained single for the rest of her life. When she later became pregnant by the painter Augustus John, she went away for the rest of the year and returned with a baby she claimed was adopted. Later, when Ian was in his early twenties, he became engaged to an Austrian girl he had fallen in love with, who Eve didn't approve of. His mother made him an ultimatum: either Ian split from his fiancée or she would cut him off from the family money. Ian also chose wealth over love and ended his engagement. Had he made a different choice, like the brigadier's daughter Jeanette, his life may have been very different.

Ian was sent away to a series of elite boarding schools. His first, Durnford, was described by Fleming's friend and biographer Andrew Lycett as 'a harsh and often cruel establishment [...] If it existed today, it would certainly be closed down.' Durnford led to Eton, where his housemaster was bluntly described, in Tim Card's official history of Eton, as a sadist. Interviewed for a 2006 documentary, his friend Tina Beal recalled how at Eton, Fleming 'was scheduled to be beaten and he was going to run in a cross-country race, so he applied to be beaten early so that he would be in time to run in this race'. At Eton, it was the tradition that boys were beaten at noon. 'They beat him so savagely that blood came through his trousers and he ran the race with blood coming through his pants,' Beal continued. 'He finished second!' As Lycett described the incident, Fleming ran the steeplechase with 'his shanks and running shorts stained with his own gore'.

To modern eyes, the delight and amusement with which

Beal recounts this story is disturbing. Beating children was then accepted as normal. There was little awareness that such trauma could leave lifelong psychological scars. As his friend Robert Harling has argued, it was Fleming's time in English boarding schools that forged his 'imprisonment of emotions'. As Harling observed, 'the English upper crust wants and needs affection as deeply as any other crust, but impulses towards this important emotional release are frequently stifled for them [...] the boys grow up, professing to hate what they so need.'

Faced with an imminent wedding and a pregnant fiancée, with all the responsibility, commitment and emotional understanding that this entailed, Fleming struggled with his innate desire to escape. It was this that finally pushed him into sitting down at his typewriter and starting his long-threatened novel. He would create a hero who was an avatar of himself, with the same tastes, background, opinions and prejudices, but with none of the troubles that weighed so heavily on him – an unashamedly unemotional masculine fantasy. Fleming could then set that avatar free to live the life he fantasised about, but could not have himself. He stole the name of the author of *Birds of the West Indies*, a book he had on his desk, and called the hero of this novel James Bond.

Fleming was growing into middle age at the time, and he had a long list of complaints about both himself and the direction that the world was going. In the real world these were things that he had no control over, and they made him feel weak and insignificant. In the world of the imagination, however, they were things that he could change, or simply deny, whichever he preferred. There was no end, he would discover, to the liberation found in fiction.

The first of these complaints was his health, which had already started to deteriorate. Suffering from chest pains, Fleming had been advised to cut back on alcohol and cigarettes. The problem was that he didn't want to. Like a spoiled child, Fleming clung to the idea that he should be able to live as unhealthily as he liked while still remaining virile and energetic. His James Bond avatar, then, would be younger, smoke as much as he wanted, and drink like a fish. Research published in the Christmas 2013 edition of the *British Medical Journal* reported that, across all of Fleming's novels, Bond drinks an average of ninety-two units of alcohol a week, significantly more than the recommended fourteen. In *Casino Royale*, Fleming refers to Bond smoking his 'seventieth cigarette of the day'. Even in fiction, this takes a toll. In the novel *Thunderball*, Bond's blood pressure is revealed to be a frightening 160/90.

The issue of Fleming's coming marriage was obviously another concern. Fleming wanted to sleep with glamorous, exciting women, and he wanted them to fall for him in the same way they used to when he was younger. Then he just wanted them to disappear afterwards, and not talk about marriage. Fleming had previously had a girlfriend who was killed during the war. This was a tragedy, but to Fleming it was also a neat solution. The idea that women would die after falling into bed with Bond entered the novels. It quickly became a recurring pattern in the secret agent's relationships.

Then there was the issue of his war record. Fleming had been in Naval Intelligence and had held the mid-ranking title of commander. He was proud of this title and insisted that his Jamaican servants called him by it. The war had taken him twice around the world and there is no question that he had served his country with honour, but the reality of his service embarrassed him. He had been the personal assistant to the Director of Naval Intelligence, a cushy desk job he had been handed through family contacts, and he had never seen action or been exposed to any danger. He was the man who sent other men into battle while he lived a secure and comfortable life a long way from the front. He was referred to as a 'chocolate sailor', a nickname that defined him as not a 'real' member of the navy. Bond, in contrast, would also be a commander in Naval Intelligence, but he would lead from the front, fighting the enemy face to face like Fleming's father had. Bond would refer to himself as 'strictly a chocolate sailor' on board an American submarine in the novel *Thunderball*, but he did so in a charmingly self-deprecating way. There were no question marks about Bond's bravery.

Another issue was Britain and its standing in the world. Fleming's education and upbringing had taught him to unquestioningly believe in British exceptionalism – that Britain was automatically 'better' than other places, and that the British Empire had been a force for good. Like many, he saw the world as it had been during his childhood as right and proper, and any changes that occurred later as terrible mistakes. The thought that the British Empire was ending, unloved and unwanted, was too horrible to contemplate. He remained in denial for as long as he could. Like many of his class, he never really understood why Winston Churchill was defeated in the 1945 general election. Fleming was firmly against the post-war welfare state and the creation of the NHS which saved Ringo's life.

In Fleming's eyes, Jamaica was one of the last places on earth that preserved all that he admired about the Empire. Here a British gentleman could enjoy an exotic but civilised life, where the climate was agreeable and the servants weren't too rebellious. It was a place where he could fool himself that the sun would never set on the British Empire. This image of Jamaica was delusional, of course. It was certainly not shared by the Jamaican people themselves. Ending ties with Britain dominated local politics and within a decade, Jamaica gained its independence.

A key moment in the end of the British Empire was the Suez Crisis of 1956. This was a moment of clarity for those who still saw Britain as a global power. As the Deputy Cabinet Secretary

Burke Trend explained, Suez was 'the psychological watershed, the moment when it became apparent that Britain was no longer capable of being a great imperial power'. In the aftermath of this ill-fated attack on Egypt, Prime Minister Anthony Eden fell ill. He decided that a holiday in Jamaica would help him recover, and he chose to recuperate at Fleming's Goldeneye. His Conservative Party colleagues plotted against him in his absence, and he was removed from office three weeks after his return. Goldeneye, the house where James Bond was born, was the last refuge for those still in denial about Britain's place in the world.

An unquestioning belief in Britain was vital to the character of Bond. It was the source of another thing that Fleming desired, which was an ethical and moral excuse to be above the law and to do whatever he wanted. Bond famously has a licence to kill, which raises the question of who has the right to grant someone permission to murder. The answer, as Fleming and Bond saw it, was the British crown. Bond's enemies also killed and destroyed, of course, but they did so without the correct paperwork and authority. This made them bad. His licence to kill and the freedom it offered has proved to be a major part of James Bond's appeal.

Last but certainly not least, Fleming gave Bond absolute mastery of the physical world. He was a skilled pilot, marksman, driver, gambler, skier, linguist, bomb disposal expert, diver, lover, or any other skill that the plot demanded. He knew exactly what food, drinks, clothes or cars were the best available. More importantly, he would always triumph. He could suffer, but whatever scheme or plot he attempted, no matter how implausible, would always succeed. This was aspirational fantasy at its most alluring. Wherever he went and whatever he did, the material world bowed in his presence, subservient to its master. The spiritual or immaterial world, on the other hand, was almost entirely ignored.

Fleming's first novel, in which the character of James Bond

was born, was *Casino Royale*. It is a brutal, cold and sadistic book that sets the tone of the Bond universe. It was initially published on 13 April 1953, about six weeks before the coronation of Queen Elizabeth II, making the arrival of Bond the harbinger of the second Elizabethan Age. The book's villain is Le Chiffre, the paymaster of a trade union secretly controlled by the Soviet counterespionage agency SMERSH. Like almost all of Fleming's villains, Le Chiffre is dual heritage, in this instance a mixture of 'Mediterranean with Prussian or Polish strains'. Purity of race is often an indicator of who is good and who is bad in Fleming's books.

Bond's mission is not regular espionage. Instead, he must bankrupt Le Chiffre by beating him at cards. This would force him to defect to British Intelligence in order to seek protection from SMERSH. If a thriller contains a card game, Fleming understood, then the stakes needed to be high. He later claimed that the inspiration for the plot came from a trip to Portugal during the war, in which he had attempted to bankrupt a leading Nazi at baccarat. This did not go well, Fleming claimed, and he was beaten and financially wiped out. His avatar Bond, on the other hand, was certain to win the game. On that trip to Portugal, Fleming was accompanying the Director of Naval Intelligence, Vice-Admiral Godfrey. Godfrey's recollection of the trip was that Fleming had only played against Portuguese businessmen, but that he had fantasised about playing against German agents.

Before the game, Bond is told that another agent will be present to support him – a female agent. He does not take this news well: 'What the hell do they want to send me a woman for?' As he saw it, 'Women were for recreation. On a job, they got in the way and fogged things up with sex and hurt feelings and all the emotional baggage they carried around.' The dialogue Fleming gives to Bond to express his feelings about working with a woman is typically disturbing: ' "Bitch," said Bond.'

From the perspective of the twenty-first century, the misogyny displayed by both Fleming and Bond in *Casino Royale* is quite a sight to behold. Bond complains about 'These blithering women who thought they could do a man's work. Why the hell couldn't they stay at home and mind their pots and pans and stick to their frocks and gossip and leave men's work to the men.' After Bond meets the agent sent to assist him, Vesper Lynd, he decides that he does want to sleep with her, but only after the job is done. Sex with Vesper would be 'excitingly sensual', he decides, because it would have 'the sweet tang of rape'. That was a sentence which Fleming thought reasonable to type, and a publisher thought fine to publish. The 1950s were a very different time. Here were the 'traditional' attitudes that Fleming thought needed to be maintained in the new, technological future.

For those familiar with the character of Bond from the films, encountering him in the books can be difficult. The films spare you from the interiority of Bond, and the coldness and cruelty of his thoughts are largely missing from the on-screen action. Once you encounter them in print it is hard to see Bond in the same light again.

Casual violence against women had been a common theme in Fleming's creative writing throughout his life. As a student in Austria, for example, he wrote stories about the villainous Count Max von Lamberg, and included graphic details of the elaborate tortures the Count devised. Consider this limerick he wrote around the time:

There once was a girl called Asoka,
Who played three young fellows at poker.
Having won all their money,
She thought it so funny,
They calmly decided to choke her.

31

Casino Royale is not really a spy story, for all that its main character is employed by British Intelligence. Although Bond's prime motivation is to defeat Russian Intelligence, the plot has little in the way of actual espionage or intrigue. Bond defeats Le Chiffre at baccarat through skill and luck rather than spycraft. This is to be expected, of course, due to Bond's aforementioned mastery of the physical world. Instead, *Casino Royale* slowly reveals itself to be structured as a love story, albeit a deeply dark and disturbing one.

In the second act Le Chiffre gets his revenge. Bond and Vesper are kidnapped, and Bond is subjected to a lengthy sequence of genital torture. Here we perhaps glimpse Fleming's burgeoning love for his alter ego, given his habit of demonstrating desire by inflicting pain. According to Fleming's biographer Henry Chancellor, Le Chiffre is physically modelled on the English occultist Aleister Crowley, so that 'when Le Chiffre goes to work on Bond's testicles with a carpet-beater and a carving knife, the sinister figure of Aleister Crowley is there lurking in the background'.

Fortunately for what remains of Bond's testicles, Russian SMERSH agents arrive. They kill Le Chiffre and foolishly set Bond free – an act they will come to regret in later books. Now we enter the third act, in which Bond decides he is in love with Vesper. It is this lengthy final section of the book that structurally makes it a love story, albeit a highly disturbing one. Vesper nurses Bond while they wait to see if his genitals heal (spoiler: all is well). Bond asks Vesper to marry him. Unfortunately, Vesper notices a sinister figure from her earlier life as a double agent and commits suicide. Bond reacts to this as well as can be expected. 'The bitch is dead now,' he says, and the book ends.

Vesper Lynd becomes the first woman to sleep with Bond and then die. The template for his future relationships has been set. You can see why Ann was not keen on Fleming's novels, which she used to dismiss as his 'horror comics'. Fleming offered to dedicate *Casino Royale* to her, but she told him not to.

In the novel, Fleming gave Vesper a piece of philosophical dialogue which was a clear statement of his own worldview. 'People are islands,' Vesper says. 'They don't really touch. However close they are, they're really quite separate. Even if they've been married for fifty years.' Here Fleming is explicitly denying the seventeenth-century Christian poet John Donne, who wrote that 'No man is an island'. All islands are connected under the water, as Donne knew, but Fleming and the Bond novels are only concerned with the surface.

This then was the character of James Bond, an avatar sculpted from his creator's history and desires. Bond was the escapist fantasy of a privileged but damaged soul, but one sketched so vividly, honestly and unashamedly that he outlived his creator and went on to forge a globally successful life of his own. Bond was escapism and aspiration in human form, but as icons go he was a dark one. Here Bond differs from other British folk heroes, such as King Arthur, Robin Hood or Sherlock Holmes. Inside, he is damaged and rotten to the core. He only does good because it is his job, and if you took away that job, the character would collapse. His creator's wounds were so integral to the character that any attempt to try and fix or redeem him could break the spell.

And yet Fleming had also created a character who was, from certain angles, undeniably attractive. Fleming was ultimately a good thriller writer, and his journalist's eye for detail helped make the exotic locations of his books feel real and believable. The world of conspicuous consumption and international travel was still an unattainable dream for most readers in austerity Britain, but Fleming dangled the promise of it, tantalisingly just out of reach. In this vivid world is placed the character of James Bond himself – Fleming's greatest achievement. Almost from the beginning, this damaged antihero seemed to have the ability to step out of the page and into people's minds, where he came alive and lived outside the books. Many novelists spend their entire careers trying to create characters who can do this.

Here it might be helpful to compare Fleming's creation with the character of Jinx, from the 2002 Bond movie *Die Another Day*. Jinx is a Black, female, American version of Bond, who was every bit as skilled, brave and heroic as he was. She too is hard-drinking, sexually promiscuous and has absolute mastery of the material world. Like Bond, she would make heartless puns after killing enemies, to show how little emotion she felt. Even better, she was played by the talented, charismatic and strikingly beautiful Halle Berry, who had just won the Best Actress Oscar for her performance in *Monster's Ball*. In December 2002 it was announced that Jinx would star in her own spin-off movie, which was scripted and allocated a budget of $80–90m.

On paper, Jinx was every inch the escapist fantasy that Bond was. And yet, after the spin-off film was announced, it became apparent that nobody was really interested. The project was quietly shelved. Jinx may have ticked all the boxes that Bond did on paper, but she never felt like anything more than another two-dimensional cartoon. The same goes for the great majority of the Bond clones who have arrived regularly in cinemas since the mid-sixties, before disappearing due to dwindling interest. At one point it seemed that every European country was trying to create their own Bond, but few of these super-spies are remembered now.

The character of 007 was born from the cauldron of Fleming's damaged psyche, and his psychological wounds brought the character to life in a way that Jinx and the other Bond clones never achieved. The creation of Bond was, ultimately, a mid-life crisis put to good use. Fleming thought he was creating a hero, but through the strange alchemy of the novelist's craft he unconsciously poured

all of his own darkness into his avatar. This was partly because of
the speed at which he wrote, and because his books didn't always
receive as much editing as perhaps they should have. The novel
Thunderball, to give one example, includes the sentence, 'It was
a room-shaped room with furniture-shaped furniture.' In these
circumstances, Fleming's ideas and opinions slipped unfiltered into
Bond. Like Dr Frankenstein, Fleming believed that he was creating
something good. As Frankenstein reasoned, surely there was no
higher goal than creating life? This thought blinded him to the
macabre nature of the limbs he stitched together, or the horror of
the monster he was building.

Fleming's brutally honest writing revealed an uncomfortable
truth, which was that the dark side and the light side of Fleming's
idealised masculinity appeared to be intractably linked, and perhaps inseparable. To be brave and protect others in this dangerous
world was noble, but to do so required emotional numbness and
the cruelty needed to kill. This emotional numbness then prevented Bond from ever having a long-lasting loving relationship.
Vesper Lynd had to die, in other words, because Bond would not
be able make the sacrifices needed to protect the world if he found
happiness. The alternative was to make Bond asexual, but that was
clearly no fun. The idea that the women who Bond touches die, by
this logic, became an unavoidable aspect of the character.

From this perspective, Bond was an honest, fully realised
depiction of the masculine paradox. All the other knights in shin-
ing armour, in contrast, were little more than two-dimensional
sketches. It was this mix of good and bad, and the uncensored
honesty of the character's depiction, which elevated him above so
many other fictional heroes. It was this that granted Bond those
mysterious qualities which enabled him to escape the racks of
paperback thrillers and become a global icon.

Fleming seems to have been only dimly aware of how

emotionally damaged he was, or how much of his dark side he was pouring into his creation. Jungian psychologists refer to psychological blind spots like this as our 'shadow'. They argue that we should work to understand and accept our dark shadow, rather than deny or destroy it. The aim is to bring it into the light of awareness, because to ignore or hide from our darkness only makes it stronger. Aptly for Bond, William Blake referred to the same concept as our 'Spectre'.

Over the decades that followed, the character of James Bond would slowly – sometimes almost imperceptibly – become aware of its own darkness. This process would not be quick, because a cultural concept as deeply ingrained as masculinity is not an easy thing to change. To the progressively minded, of course, Bond is always behind the curve. He is misogynistic and imperialistic now, just as he was in the 1950s or the 1970s. Being always wrong, the progressive argument goes, he is beyond saving. In a similar way, to the conservative or reactionary minded, the changes in Bond that would follow were always too much, too soon, and must inevitably lead to the loss of all that is good. The territory between these two positions is messy and it is not ideologically pure – but it is the terrain where change actually happens.

From the moment James Bond appeared out of Fleming's typewriter, he embarked on a long, slow quest to face down his Spectre.

1956: I WOULD HAVE LIKED TO HAVE SEEN THE BOYS GROWING UP

Paul McCartney was born in 1942, in the dark middle years of the Second World War. He grew up, with his younger brother Mike, in a council house in Allerton, Liverpool. His mother Mary was a hard-working midwife and the principal breadwinner of the family. In later life he retained a crystal-clear memory of her going out to work one night. 'The streets were thick with snow, it was about three in the morning, and she got up and went out on her bike with the little brown wicker basket on the front, into the dark, just with her little light, in her navy-blue uniform and hat, cycling off down the estate to deliver a baby somewhere.'

Mary McCartney died on Hallowe'en 1956, following complications arising from surgery for breast cancer. Paul was fourteen at the time. The severity of his mother's illness had been kept from him and his brother, and they had been sent to stay with their uncle. They did see her one last time in hospital, however. 'We didn't really know what was happening. We were shielded from it all by our aunties and our dad and everything,' Paul recalled.

'I remember one horrible day me and my brother going to the hospital. They must have known she was dying. It turned out to be our last visit and it was terrible because there was blood on the sheets somewhere, and seeing that, and your mother, it was like "Holy cow!".' One of the last things she said was, 'I would have liked to have seen the boys growing up.'

When the boys were informed that she had died, Paul's immediate response was, 'What are we going to do without her money?' Throughout his life, Paul has repeatedly been criticised for how he has reacted to the news of the death of loved ones. Approached by a reporter in the street on the day of John Lennon's murder, for example, he was only able to mumble, 'Drag, isn't it?' This response struck many grieving Beatle fans as insensitive and inadequate, but with hindsight it is clear that he was still in shock. Asked about it two years later, he attempted to explain. 'How did I feel? I can't remember. I can't express it. I can't believe it. It was crazy. It was anger. It was fear. It was madness. It was the world coming to an end. And it was, "Will it happen to me next?" I just felt everything. I still can't put into words. Shocking. And I ended up saying, "It's a drag," and that doesn't really sum it up.'

Paul's initially emotionless reaction to the news of his mother's death was the product of many factors. He had had no warning that she was about to die and did not know at the time she had been suffering with cancer, so he'd had no time to process the situation. He had no prior experience of death or grief on this scale. He was also a fourteen-year-old boy, and fourteen-year-old boys are not known for their emotional sophistication. Yet his reaction does illustrate one way in which his personality differed from that of John Lennon.

McCartney's emotions were not always on the surface, but that doesn't mean they don't exist. They are buried within layers of his psyche and may be filtered through other, more rational parts of his personality before they emerge. McCartney's ability to keep his emotions in check and act more rationally sometimes struck people as cunning or manipulative – even when he was making decisions which, with hindsight, were good ones. It was a trait that would cause friction between the Beatles in the later years.

It should be noted, of course, that his reaction was a valid one. It is easy to criticise if you have not lost a parent as a child and are in a more financially secure position than the post-war Liverpudlian working class. The question of what they were going to do for money when the wage-earning parent suddenly died was a very real one, and it is a luxury to pretend otherwise.

A child who loses a parent is marked out as different. Grief and loss are typically seen as adult emotions, which should play no part in a happy, carefree childhood. A bereaved child, then, has aspects of both childhood and adulthood mixed together in their perspective on the world. They understand very early that death is real, and that they too will one day die. A child who has lost one parent is also acutely aware that they are halfway to becoming an orphan, and they view themselves and their world accordingly. This sense of being different can put the child on unexpected paths through life. In the prehistoric nomadic tribes of northern Europe, it was not unusual for a child who had lost a parent to become a shaman – a healer who looks after a tribe by interacting with the spirit world. As Rogan Taylor notes in *The Death and Resurrection Show*, his exploration of the links between ancient shamanism and modern showbiz, 'amongst the psychological disturbances frequently associated with a young shaman-to-be, the experience of partial or total orphanhood seems to be quite common'.

The Jamaican historian Lucille Iremonger has noted that 67 per cent of British prime ministers, from the start of the nineteenth century to the start of the Second World War, lost a parent as a child. Twelve US Presidents lost their fathers, including George

Washington, Thomas Jefferson and Barack Obama. The list of famous people who lost a parent or were adopted as a child is incredibly long, and includes such notables as Madonna, Bono, Barbra Streisand, P. Diddy, Steve Jobs, 50 Cent, Larry Ellison and Malcolm X. The Canadian writer Malcom Gladwell has coined the term 'eminent orphans' to describe the phenomenon in which people who lose a parent in childhood are overly represented among high-achieving adults. Of course, the loss of a parent does not automatically mean that a successful life will follow. Prisons are full of people who grew up without both parents.

In the world of myth, folklore and fiction, heroes who lost one or both parents as a child are common. They include Snow White, Harry Potter, Superman, Cinderella, Luke Skywalker, Simba in *The Lion King*, Hansel and Gretel, Batman, Spider-Man and, of course, James Bond. The theme is so prevalent in the James Bond universe that, in 2021's *No Time to Die*, both the arch villain Safin and Bond's love interest Madeleine Swann lost parents at a young age. In one scene, they discuss the impact that this had on them. 'It's difficult to lose a parent. Especially at a young age,' Swann tells Safin. 'Death has a particular effect on children, doesn't it?' he replies. When questioned about the effect that it had on him, he replies simply, 'Profound.' In the film, Swann's mother was killed by Safin, because her father killed Safin's parents for Blofeld, who killed his own father, who was also Bond's father-figure. The story then ends with Swann's young daughter losing her father. This is a film that doubles down on its theme to an almost obsessive degree.

In the Beatles story, it is striking that the only major characters to have been raised by both parents are George Harrison and George Martin. Of the early Beatles, Pete Best's father was killed in the war and Stu Sutcliffe's father was away at sea during his early years. Manager Brian Epstein was largely raised by nannies, and their later manager Allen Klein's mother died of cancer when he was two. His father, unable to cope, placed Klein and two of his three older sisters in an orphanage. Yoko Ono's mother was distant and Yoko didn't meet her father until she was two and a half years old. Like Epstein, she was largely raised by nannies. Billy Preston was raised without a father and Linda McCartney's mother was killed in a plane crash when Linda was a teenager. As the American psychologist Arthur Janov has observed, 'With the actors and rock stars that I've seen, they've almost all been rejected in childhood. Most of them are very deprived as children. We all [have a need for love and acceptance] and it never goes away. It gets transformed, but it never goes away.'

In later years, when Ringo Starr underwent therapy for his alcohol problems, he came to recognise the anger caused by his father abandoning the family. During his childhood, however, he simply accepted the situation. 'I felt really angry later on,' he said, 'going through therapy in rehab, when I came to look at myself and get to know my feelings, instead of blocking them all out. For me, I felt I'd dealt with it when I was little. I didn't understand that really I had been blocking my anger out. You get on with it; that's how we were brought up.'

Like Paul McCartney, Ringo still had the support of a loving family around him, albeit a smaller one. The death of Mary McCartney was a tragedy, but there was no blame involved. It produced the understanding, years too early, that life can be unfair and painful. Ringo being abandoned by his father was equally straightforward. His father didn't want him in his life and that was that. It is tempting to see Ringo's later persona of the runt of the band, with his hound-dog eyes and put-upon demeanour, as a reaction to this. For John Lennon however, as for Ian Fleming, their childhood loss was more complicated to process.

John Lennon's parents split when he was four years old, although his merchant seaman father had been mostly absent before this. His mother Julia then had a second child out of marriage, a girl called Victoria, who was given up for adoption. Later, Julia would move in with a man called Bobby Dykins, with whom she had two daughters. This was despite never being able to legally divorce John's father Alf, whose whereabouts were frequently unknown. In the eyes of John's uptight and proper Aunt Mimi, this made her sister an unfit mother. Mimi contacted Liverpool social services about the situation. Shortly afterwards it was decided that John would live with his Aunt Mimi, who was otherwise childless, rather than with his mother.

The idea that Julia was an unfit mother is a hard one to square with the account of her from Julia Baird, John's younger half-sister from his mother's relationship with Dykins. Baird describes her mother as a wonderful parent and concludes, 'My mother was a beautiful, vibrant and loving woman. And she was wronged.' Julia Lennon's friend and neighbour Hannah Starkey – no relation to Ringo – has spoken about Julia's distress at having her son taken from her, and how she came to her crying, 'They've taken my son from me. They won't let me have him. We've got to get him back.'

It is true that Julia had problems and needed more support, especially after the adoption of her second child, but ultimately John was taken from Julia not because she had an absence of love, but because she had an absence of respectability. Mimi was operating under the same class-based awareness of respectability that considered the relationship between a brigadier's daughter and a brickie's mate to be worthy of the front page. As Mimi saw it, she was doing what she thought was best for John. Many a wound is well intentioned.

A common family story about Lennon's childhood was that John was taken to Blackpool when he was only six years old and asked who he wanted to live with, his father or his mother. Beatle historians are nowadays suspicious of this story, but the sense that it suggests of him being an unwanted problem rather than a loved child does fit with Lennon's view of himself. As he later said, 'The worst pain is that of not being wanted, of realising your parents do not need you in the way that you need them. When I was a child I experienced moments of not wanting to see the ugliness, not wanting to see not being wanted. The lack of love went into my eyes and into my mind. I was never really wanted. The only reason I am a star is because of my repression. Nothing would have driven me through all that if I was "normal".'

John's experience of being sent away, and the impact that this had on his adult life, is similar in many ways to what Ian Fleming experienced when he was sent away by his parents to boarding school. In both cases, the child trying to understand why they have been sent away from their parents is told that it's for their own good. They then must deal with the cognitive dissonance that this creates.

Psychologists now refer to the cluster of emotional problems and unhealthy behaviours that are common among children sent away by their parents as Boarding School Syndrome. Difficulties with attachment and trust in adult life are common, along with an inability to ever feel at home, especially if the child was sent to a place which not only lacked love, but which offered bullying and cruelty. The study of Boarding School Syndrome recognises that what is often dismissed as homesickness in children who have been sent away is often far more serious, and that it should be thought of as closer to a form of undiagnosed bereavement.

In 2021, the author Louis de Bernières wrote a painful account of his time at boarding school for the *Sunday Times* entitled 'Aged 8, I was sent to hell'. The editors were shocked by the number of letters from readers – nearly a thousand – that followed its publication, with the majority telling of their own experiences in similar schools. These letters detailed rape and other forms of abuse at around five hundred schools over a period from the 1930s to the twenty-first century. After analysing these accounts, they reported that 54 per cent described physical abuse, 27 per cent mentioned sexual abuse and 18 per cent concerned emotional abuse. In contrast, 19 per cent of the letters told of a positive experience at boarding school, and there are many who were sent to a British boarding school who insist that it did them no harm. They often make a point of sending their children to the same schools, as if to prove the point.

When John Lennon was in his early teens, he learned from his cousin Stanley that his absent mother actually lived near to him. Bravely, he went round and knocked on her door. The reunion went well, and his mother once again became part of his life. Julia was fun and acted more like a friend than a mother. Where Mimi refused to have a record player in the house, Julia taught John how to play the banjo and bought him his first guitar. It seemed that the growing relationship between John and his mother, and her new family, was starting to heal his childhood wounds – even if John was still unable to explain to people at school why he lived with his aunt, rather than his mother.

In July 1958 Julia left Mimi's house on a summer's evening and was headed for the bus stop when she was hit by a car. She was killed instantly. The driver was a police constable who had not passed his test. He was acquitted of all charges but given a short suspension from duty. John, naturally, was devastated. There were no McCartney-esque rational comments about practical matters when Lennon was told the news. Instead, he wept. He could not bring himself to look at her body when he was taken to the hospital, and he buried his head in his aunt's lap during the funeral. As he later told *Playboy*, 'I lost her twice. Once as a five-year-old when I was moved in with my auntie. And once again at seventeen when she actually physically died [...] That was a really hard time for me. It just absolutely made me very, very bitter. The underlying chip on my shoulder that I had as a youth got really big then.'

By this time, Lennon had become friends with Paul McCartney, even though McCartney was two years younger, which was a significant gap during teenage years. That Paul had also lost his mother brought the pair closer – they had been marked as different, but now they were not alone. They would both go on to write songs about their late mothers, and both named their first child after them.

When you see early film of Lennon and McCartney, it is striking how close they are, ending each other's sentences and delighting in each other's company. Lennon would later talk about how he felt they had a psychic connection, able to communicate without words. They referred to their relationship as being as close as brothers, but it is perhaps more accurate to describe their bond as being like a marriage. They joined their names together, after all, when they decided that all the songs they wrote would be credited to Lennon/McCartney. When the time came to end their song-writing partnership, both referred to it as a 'divorce'.

As teenagers, the pair bonded despite the disapproval of their remaining guardian. Aunt Mimi thought that McCartney was common because he lived in a council house. She wouldn't let him use the front door. Paul's dad Jim McCartney thought, probably correctly, that Lennon was trouble. But as in all the best romances, parental disapproval could do nothing to break the close connection between those two grieving boys. For all the undeniable importance of George and Ringo, the relationship between Paul and John would become the engine that powered the Beatles. There is an argument to be made that this was one of the most important relationships between two men in the post-war Western world.

Beatles biographers have often treated John's loss as more significant than Paul's, because John always appeared more damaged.

Lennon struggled with anger and issues of abandonment for the rest of his life while Paul, in contrast, was able to just get on with things. Although young Paul had experienced real grief, like Ringo he still had a loving family around him to help him process it. Lennon's situation, in contrast, was closer to that of Ian Fleming, whose father had died after Ian had already been exiled from the family home. Fleming's parents, of course, thought that by sending him away to boarding school they were doing the best for him. It is perhaps an important question as to what has the greater positive impact on a child's adult life – being sent to elite schools or knowing that they are loved.

The damage caused by being sent away from their mothers was the initial wound to Lennon's and Fleming's sense of themselves, and how they fitted into the world. They were already damaged children when they had to process the death of their parents, so it should not be too surprising if they never managed it. There was further loss in Lennon's early life, including Aunt Mimi's husband George, who was the closest thing young John had to a father, and his close art-school friend Stu Sutcliffe. But it was the double-loss of his mother that all biographers see as the most significant.

Lennon and McCartney's different reactions to their loss illustrates something that, as they grew to adulthood, became a significant difference in their personalities. Paul's intelligence could sometimes seem cold, while John's anger could burn bridges. As Paul described their differing personalities: 'that was the balance between us: John was caustic and witty out of necessity and, underneath, quite a warm character when you got to know him. I was the opposite, easy-going, friendly, no necessity to be caustic or biting or acerbic but I could be tough if I needed to be.'

Of course, their differences were part of what drew them to-gether and made their friendship so special. They had complement-ary personalities, and each seemed to offer what the other lacked.

But in time – after their relationship was put through unheard-of pressures – what were once complementary differences would become incompatibility, and the fault line between them would give. From the very beginning, as the two teenage rock 'n' rollers and aspiring songwriters found and inspired each other, the seed that would bring about the end of the Beatles was already planted.

1960: A NOTORIOUS CENTRE
FOR PROSTITUTION

When the fledgling Beatles were offered a residency in the clubs of
Hamburg, their parents and guardians were far from happy. On
the one hand this was much-needed paid work for the young band,
who by then consisted of guitarists and vocalists John Lennon,
Paul McCartney and George Harrison, along with Pete Best on
drums and Stu Sutcliffe on bass. The St Pauli area of Hamburg was
a notorious centre for prostitution, however, and its main street,
Reeperbahn, was known as *die sündigste Meile*, or the most sinful
mile. The thought of the teenaged boys leaving home to live in
such a sleazy environment gave their families pause, especially
given the anti-German sentiment of those post-war years.

Lennon's Aunt Mimi had initially not wanted John to go, but
he persuaded her by explaining how much more they would be
paid compared to gigging in England. Paul McCartney's dad Jim
was also reluctant, but he was talked into it by the band's booking
agent, Allan Williams. On 16 August 1960 the band left Liverpool
to write the first chapter in their legend.

Had the Lennon and McCartney families been readers of the *Sunday Times*, they may have stood their ground more firmly. A couple of weeks earlier, on 31 July 1960, the paper had included an article which was essentially a review of the area's sex clubs. It was written by Ian Fleming.

Fleming's article began, 'She was a big girl with a good figure,' before going on to describe a bout of topless mud-wrestling he very much enjoyed in a Hamburg club at two in the morning. It was written as part of a 'Thrilling Cities' series of articles, which were later published in a book of the same name. After describing the various striptease and sex shows he encountered, Fleming explained, 'In Hamburg, normal heterosexual "vice" is permitted to exist in appropriate "reservations" and on condition that it remains open and light-hearted. How very different from the prudish and hypocritical manner in which we so disgracefully mismanage these things in England!' In Fleming's eyes, the Hamburg sex industry was a decent, cheerful, civilised affair. 'Now all this may sound pretty devilish in cold print on a Sunday morning in England,' he wrote, 'but in fact, except to the exceedingly chaste, it is all good clean German fun.' The extent to which Fleming is blind to the darker side of the scene can be occasionally glimpsed in his report, such as light-hearted remarks about how 'the waitresses scream dramatically when they get pinched'. He then provides directions to the main area of prostitution, in which 'girls of varying ages' are 'to put it bluntly, "for sale" at a price, I am reliably informed, of twenty Reichsmarks'. All of this meets Fleming's approval. 'I was altogether immensely impressed by Hamburg, which is now one of my favourite cities in the world,' he wrote. Favourable references to sex work appear in many of his Bond novels.

Fleming's editor at the *Sunday Times* had not been happy about this article. He did not think that it was the role of the paper to promote sex tourism. As he wrote to its author, 'We must remember that for a great many of our readers, probably the majority, prostitution is not even a necessary evil, but something immoral and degrading. Again, striptease acts may be all right for callow youths and frustrated middle-aged men but are a vulgar and debased form of entertainment for balanced people.' Fleming was not convinced by this argument. 'It is clear from your letter that our views on public morals are at variance,' he wrote back.

The fledgling Beatles encountered Hamburg not as sex tourists, but as residents. This was their home for long months of playing up to eight hours a night, fuelled by beer and speed. Their accommodation was squalid. 'We lived backstage in the Bambi Kino [nightclub],' McCartney recalled, 'next to the toilets, and you could always smell them. The room had been an old storeroom, and there were just concrete walls and nothing else. No heat, no wallpaper, not a lick of paint, and two sets of bunkbeds, like little camp beds, with not many covers. We were frozen.' If Fleming had seen this side of Hamburg, he might have been considerably less impressed.

Hamburg was, ultimately, exactly what their parents feared and exactly what those young men hoped for. As Lennon remarked, 'I grew up in Hamburg, not Liverpool.'

'It was a sex shock,' McCartney has said. 'Suddenly, you'd have a girlfriend who was a stripper. If you had hardly ever had sex in your life before, this was fairly formidable. Here was somebody who obviously knew something about it, and you didn't. So we got a fairly swift baptism of fire into the sex scene. There was a lot of it about and we were off the leash [...] It was quite something.'

The Beatles saw the women of Hamburg in a different light to Ian Fleming, for whom they were commodities to be bought and then discarded. As young employees of the Hamburg night-time pleasure industry, the Beatles and the sex workers of the Reeperbahn encountered each other as essentially equals. Hanging out and having fun together, in this context, was natural. This is not to suggest, of course, that the Beatles didn't also view these women primarily as sex objects. They were a bunch of teenage lads who suddenly found themselves away from home in a promiscuous culture and they reacted as you would expect. But they did form friendships with some of the strippers and sex workers which seemed genuine, and which sustained over time, in a way that Fleming never would.

Squashed together in these surroundings, the Beatles had no privacy and would always 'be walking in on each other and things', as McCartney has recalled. 'I'd walk in on John and see a little bottom bobbing up and down with a girl underneath him.' This level of intimacy was normal for the band, even if the arrival of girls was new. 'We used to have wanking sessions when we were young at [ex-Quarrymen manager] Nigel Walley's house in Woolton,' McCartney has said, telling a story that might be too much information for some, but which does at least show how close and intimate the lives of this gang of boys was. 'We'd stay overnight and we'd all sit in armchairs and we'd put all the lights out and being teenage pubescent boys we'd all wank. What we used to do, someone would say, "Bridgette Bardot." "Oooh!" That would keep everyone on par, then somebody, probably John, would say, "Winston Churchill." "Oh no!" And it would completely ruin everyone's concentration.'

Lennon and McCartney may have been young to experience the world of Hamburg, but their lead guitarist, George Harrison, was the youngest of the lot. Their first stint in the clubs of the Reeperbahn was cut short when Harrison was deported for being underage, but this didn't darken his memories of the town. 'The city of Hamburg was brilliant,' he later said, 'A big lake, and then the dirty part. The Reeperbahn and Grosse Freiheit were the best things we'd ever seen, clubs and neon lights everywhere and lots of restaurants and entertainment. It looked really good. There were seedy things about it, obviously.' Harrison's sexual education also began in these circumstances. 'My first shag was in Hamburg – with Paul and John and Pete Best all watching. We were in bunkbeds. They couldn't really see anything because I was under the covers, but after I'd finished they all applauded and cheered. At least they kept quiet whilst I was doing it.'

The hundreds of hours spent playing on the stages of Hamburg, while drunk, crazed or exhausted, bonded Lennon, McCartney and Harrison as musicians in a unique and profound way. They came to intuitively understand each other musically, knowing what the others would play and when, and knowing how much they could rely on each other. As Lennon later admitted, after the band had split, 'In spite of all the things, the Beatles really could play music together when they weren't uptight [...] That's the only thing I sometimes miss is, is being able to just sort of blink or make a certain noise and I know they'll all know where we're going on an ad lib thing.' This was not just with their guitars, but with their singing as well. The three young men's harmonies were forged during this experience and would become the band's secret weapon. Their voices would come to fit together effortlessly into a sound which was exceptionally beautiful. Despite how many decades have passed and how much recording technology has advanced over the years, the musical connection they shared is undeniable and timeless.

To the young, a few years' age difference can seem hugely significant. Lennon was able to shrug this off sufficiently to hang out with Paul McCartney, and introduce him to his art-school friends, even though Paul was nearly two years younger. McCartney, however, was always conscious that Harrison was younger than he was – even though the gap was only a little over eight months. It was McCartney who introduced Harrison to Lennon, in the hope that Lennon would allow him to join their band. In Paul's eyes, though, the issue of age gave Harrison a lower standing in the band. That Harrison did not initially write songs also served to make him less important in the band dynamic. In time, the issue of his status in McCartney's eyes would become a source of great resentment for Harrison. Even as their story began, the seed of a second reason for their eventual demise was once again already present.

During those days in Hamburg, however, the band were too distracted to worry about whether George was receiving the respect he deserved. They had been initiated into a sensual world of adult sexual relations, and they did not find it dirty or shameful as British society back home insisted. Like Fleming, they saw it as a desirable part of the future, which they would be fools not to fully embrace. This is one of the few areas where Fleming and the Beatles were in agreement.

In 1959 a new obscenity law was introduced, which made it possible to publish work previously declared obscene provided it showed 'literary merit'. This led to the famous 'Lady Chatterley Trial', in which D.H. Lawrence's novel *Lady Chatterley's Lover* was deemed to indeed have literary merit, and hence could be published by Penguin Books. This book was shocking to many in the establishment because it graphically detailed Lady Chatterley's affair with a working-class groundskeeper, and the extent to which this enriched her life. Then in December 1961, the Minister of Health Enoch Powell announced that the oral contraceptive pill would be prescribed via the NHS. This is not perhaps what Powell is best remembered for, but it may be the most significant thing he did.

As the sixties progressed, Britain underwent a period of sexual liberation to an extent unthinkable in the 1950s. The Beatles and Ian Fleming were already ahead of the curve. Sexual liberation would be a central part of the work of both band and author – but in ways that were significantly different. Their differing relations with the sex workers of Hamburg proved to be a blueprint for their attitudes in the years ahead.

1961: UNASHAMEDLY, FOR PLEASURE AND MONEY

Ian Fleming placed an order for a bespoke gold-plated typewriter while he was still writing his first novel *Casino Royale*. It was an act of sympathetic magic from an author who took up writing to become rich. As he openly admitted, he wrote 'unashamedly, for pleasure and money'. The gold-plated typewriter prefigured perhaps the key image of the Bond franchise – a beautiful naked woman on a bed, covered in gold and quite dead.

As Fleming explained, 'You don't make a great deal of money from royalties and translation rights and so forth and, unless you are very industrious and successful, you could only just about live on these profits, but if you sell the serial rights and film rights, you do very well.' After he finished the book, he bought a small theatrical agency called Glidrose Production to which he assigned the literary copyright of his novels. He did this to limit the amount of tax he would be expected to pay on his expected forthcoming Bond wealth. This was Fleming's plan from the very start: to put

Bond on screen and get rich. But it would not prove to be as easy as he hoped.

Most writers struggle with the problem of securing a publisher after they finish their first manuscript. This was not a concern for Fleming. As a privileged member of society, he could expect wonderful opportunities to regularly appear, regardless of how much he screwed up or how little he deserved them. That, at least, had been the pattern of his life up until then.

After being removed from Eton due to his attitude and his womanising, Fleming was accepted at Sandhurst Royal Military College. He was kicked out after a year, however, after contracting gonorrhoea from a sex worker. This did not prevent him from later landing the plum position of personal assistant to the Director of Naval Intelligence during the war. Despite his disgrace at Sandhurst, an interview for the Foreign Office's diplomatic service was arranged for him, thanks to personal references from the Archdeacon of London and Lord D'Abernon, the former British Ambassador to Berlin. When his performance in the entrance exams was insufficient to gain him a job, his mother told him to write to Sir Roderick Jones, head of Reuters and a family friend. Despite the spelling mistakes in his letter, he was soon working at Reuters, where he did in fact show great promise as a journalist. Writing, it turned out, was the one thing he was good at. He quit after three years, however, because he considered a journalist's salary to be beneath him. Instead, he decided to become wealthy by working in the City. Unfortunately, he had no head for figures – he has been described by friends as the 'world's worst stockbroker' – so his career in finance was not a success. After the war he worked as the foreign-news manager for the *Sunday Times* after being offered the job by Lord Kemsley, the newspaper's proprietor, whom Fleming played bridge with. He accepted on the condition he could have a few months off every winter to spend in Jamaica – not the sort of condition every job seeker can demand.

For those outside Fleming's privileged circle, the steady stream of golden opportunities that he was offered and squandered seems unbelievable. So too does the lack of consequences he faced for his failures. Here perhaps we can see the source of Bond's ability to always succeed, no matter how rash or foolish his course of action. The manuscript for *Casino Royale* was submitted to the publishers Jonathan Cape, who were unenthusiastic and rejected it, until a member of Fleming's family had a word, and they were persuaded to publish.

Casino Royale was published in April 1953 and did well in the UK, if not the US. The UK hardback sold out of its first print run within a month, and on the back of this Jonathan Cape offered Fleming a three-book deal. Although James Bond as a literary character got off to a solid start, it took the best part of a decade before he made it to the cinema screen. On one level, the novels appeared ideal for film adaptations. They were pacy, thrilling and glamorous. They took their audience to far-off locations which, in the years before mass-market air travel and package holidays, seemed almost impossibly exotic. There were beautiful women, fights, excitement, danger and a brave masculine hero. Fleming consciously ticked all the boxes required to attract the movie money he craved.

It was Bond himself who was the problem. The sadism, cruelty and coldness which Fleming brought to the character were, for many, a reason to reject him. A good film producer with an eye on the box office can often solve problems like these, of course, by tweaking characters and plots to give them a more universal appeal. Stories can be rewritten, and Bond's emotional cruelty and psychological damage could be cleaned up for the screen. The misogyny could be dialled down, as could the overt racism that became apparent in Fleming's second novel *Live and Let Die*. But there remained the issue of the character being part of the British establishment.

Fleming saw Bond as an urbane, charming, sophisticated English gentleman, a natural part of the ruling classes – just like him. He wrote a memo about adapting the character for the screen in which he opposed 'too much stage Englishness. There should, I think, be no monocles, moustaches, bowler hats, bobbies or other "Limey" gimmicks. There should be no blatant English slang, [and] a minimum of public school ties and accents.' Despite this, Fleming's view of the character was still far more privileged than Hollywood was comfortable with. His preferred actor for the role was David Niven, who he knew from frequenting the exclusive London gentleman's club Boodles. Outside of Fleming's social circles, however, the particular English archetype that Niven represented was not as universally appealing as Fleming thought. In the eyes of the eventual producer of the Bond films Albert R. 'Cubby' Broccoli, Niven just wasn't tough enough for the part. When Columbia Pictures turned down Broccoli's initial approach to make Bond movies, they did so in part because they thought the character of Bond was a sub-par Mike Hammer and 'too English to boot'. For Fleming, Bond was in part an attempt to insist that Britain still mattered on the global stage, and that the English elite was capable of running things as it had in the eighteenth and nineteenth centuries. Hollywood, however, had a more realistic appraisal.

Fleming was still clinging to a view of geopolitical power epitomised by the Yalta Conference in the Crimea, towards the end of the Second World War. This was a meeting between Churchill, Stalin and Roosevelt. The United Kingdom, United States and Soviet Union were called the 'Big Three' of the Allied powers, and it was natural that between them they should define the structure of the post-war world. Throughout the 1950s and 1960s, however, as the British Empire was wound down and President de Gaulle vetoed British membership of the European Common Market, Britain's standing and influence dropped considerably. The 'Big Three' became the 'Big Two', and Britain was no longer important enough to be invited to the Kennedy–Khrushchev Vienna Conference in 1961. Fleming's novels are often seen as an attempt to deny this reality, and to insist that Britain was still a major player on the world stage. As late as 1967, the film of *You Only Live Twice* included a tripartite conference between America, Britain and the Soviet Union, in which Britain was confident enough to chide the rash Americans. Thanks to memories of the Yalta Conference, the sight of Britain acting as an equal to Russia and the US still seemed natural to many British viewers. To the rest of the world, however, it was easy to assume this was a joke.

The first attempt to film Bond was an adaptation of *Casino Royale* in the American television anthology series *Climax!* in 1954. This solved the issue of Bond's English establishment character by turning him into a CIA spy called Jimmy Bond, played by the all-American actor Barry Nelson. The programme is now mainly remembered for the casting of Peter Lorre as Le Chiffre. There was hope that it would lead to a TV series, but nothing came of it and the show was quickly forgotten.

A further opportunity for growing the Bond brand came in 1958, when Fleming's friend Lord Beaverbrook, the owner of the *Daily Express*, suggested using the character in a daily newspaper cartoon. Fleming was initially unsure, aware that his wife already dismissed his books by describing them as a comic strip. But business sense won out over pride, and apart from a two-year period from 1962–64, when Fleming and Beaverbrook fell out, the James Bond comic strip ran first in the *Daily Express* and then later in the *Sunday Express* until the mid-eighties. When work on the script began, Fleming commissioned an artist to draw a portrait of Bond as he saw him – refined and elegant, and not unlike the actor Basil Rathbone. The illustrator of the script, John McLusky, felt that he looked 'outdated' and 'pre-war'. He used his own idea of Bond in the strip, and drew a harder, more rugged character. Once again it had been necessary to move away from Fleming's idea of the character when adapting him for popular media.

After the comic strip began, Fleming decided he needed to take a more proactive approach to getting his avatar hero onto the big screen. He began work on a screenplay for an original Bond movie called *Thunderball*, working in collaboration with the Irish director Kevin McClory and the screenwriter Jack Whittingham. When no immediate interest from film studios followed, Fleming began adapting the script into the next of his yearly Bond novels. He did so without crediting McClory or Whittingham for their work or ideas, a decision that would spawn lawsuits for decades to come.

The question of how Bond could be made to work as a film was finally solved in 1959, when Alfred Hitchcock made his classic spy thriller *North by Northwest*. The hero, Roger Thornhill, was an American everyman played by Cary Grant who was humanised by his relationship with his mother. Other than this, *North by Northwest* contained everything we would come to think of as the ingredients of a Bond film, including its striking title sequence designed by Saul Bass and a dramatic score by Bernard Herrmann. From the perspective of the 1950s, it was unashamedly modern.

Throughout the film, Cary Grant was dressed amazingly. In 2006, a panel of fashion experts brought together by *GQ* magazine declared that the suit he wore for most of the film was the best suit in movie history. The American novelist Todd McEwen even wrote a short story called 'Cary Grant's Suit', which told the story of the film from the suit's perspective. It was indeed a great suit, and Grant looked immaculate. Style like that, alongside Grant's martini-drinking cosmopolitan confidence, made it easier to accept his age-inappropriate relationship with a beautiful, and twenty years younger, female double agent.

The structure of *North by Northwest* is both the reason why Bond films are so successful, and also why their plots are so readily criticised. It is essentially a collection of set pieces that make very little sense from a story perspective, but which nevertheless entertain because of their confidence and visual flair. For example, when a mysterious evil organisation decided to kill Thornhill, they didn't just shoot him or kidnap him. Instead, they passed on a message via a glamorous female double agent that he needed to travel to a remote rural location. Once there, the villains buzz him in a low-flying crop-duster plane. It's a thrilling, visually memorable sequence – which the Bond movies would recreate in 1963's *From Russia with Love* – but it is not a particularly rational or effective way to kill someone. Or to give another example, the villain's lair is a stylish, glamorous modern house of which any Bond villain would be proud. It sits, somewhat implausibly, on top of Mount Rushmore. This leads to a thrilling chase in which the hero and heroine must climb down the giant granite faces of the great American Presidents to escape. Again, a visually unforgettable sequence that doesn't make a huge amount of sense should you stop and think about it.

North by Northwest had a lead character who was brave, charming and fantastically dressed. It had an evil secret organisation led by a sinister figure in an impressively stylish building, protected by their chief henchman and army of goons. It had thrilling, visually striking action sequences in original and memorable locations. It had twists, deceptions and beautiful female agents who betray their evil employers when they fall in love with our dashing hero, and it made the whole thing work through style, confidence and bravado rather than a plausible plot. Like much of Hitchcock's greatest work, it was not just a film but a template which less-original filmmakers could return to over and over again.

Fleming's long struggle to get Bond on the cinema screen eventually paid off in 1961, when the Canadian film producer Harry Saltzman optioned the rights and went into partnership with 'Cubby' Broccoli. Watching Grant in *North by Northwest*, it is easy to see why he was Cubby Broccoli's first choice for the role of Bond. Grant had been the best man at Broccoli's wedding, and the way his likeable charm undercut his handsome features perfectly solved the problem of Fleming's establishment vision of the character. Grant would not sign for more than one film, however, and at fifty-eight was considerably older than the character, so Cubby had to look elsewhere. But Grant had already, unwittingly, provided the blueprints for the future of James Bond. It took Fleming a decade, but 007 would make it to the silver screen.

1962: GLUTTED WITH THE
OVERLOAD OF STUFF

On 22 August 1962, a notice was put up outside one of the ware-houses that lined Mathew Street in Liverpool:

AT THE CAVERN CLUB WEDNESDAY LUNCHTIME
THE SHOW WILL BE FILMED BY GRANADA TV CAMERAS
FEATURING THE NORTH'S TOP GROUP:
THE BEATLES

When the Granada TV crew arrived, they found a queue of hundreds of young, mostly female fans stretched along the narrow, cobblestoned street, waiting to enter. The steep steps that led from street level were the only way in or out of the former underground fruit cellar. The Cavern was usually hot, with perspiration running down the brick walls, but the heat from the TV lights turned it into a sauna. The venue was noted for its distinctive smell, a combination of damp, sweat, cigarettes, food, the often-overflowing toilets, the fruit in the neighbouring warehouses and the disinfectant liberally applied during morning cleaning. This smell would stick to the Cavernites, so that when they went home their parents would always know where they had been. Even decades later, a mention of the Cavern smell can push old Cavernites into reveries of nostalgia.

As the camera rolled, and the single microphone recorded the sound from the stage at one end of the middle of the three vaulted brick tunnels, the Beatles performed cover versions of the songs 'Kansas City' and 'Some Other Guy'. They had returned from Hamburg, and the influence of their new manager Brian Epstein was already apparent in the professional, smart outfits they now wore; white shirts, black ties, dark tank-top vests and 'Beatle boots' – essentially, tight Chelsea boots with Cuban heels – which Epstein had specially commissioned from a London bootmaker. Even Lennon was on his best behaviour, and he managed to perform the songs without his usual gurning or mocking of disabled people. The footage captures almost the very beginning of the Fab Four story. Ringo had played his first gig with the band four days earlier. Their audience had still not come to terms with his arrival, and fans can be heard shouting, 'We want Pete!' on the recording.

Still an unsigned band at the time, this film of the Beatles playing in the Cavern is now regarded as priceless. It is the first film of the Beatles ever made. The Beatles had been photographed before, of course, by friends and family – most notably the black-and-white photographs taken by Astrid Kirchherr in Hamburg and the candid images taken by Paul's brother Mike McCartney – but the Cavern filming marked the first time that the regular media trained their cameras on them.

It was the start of one of the most intense periods of media attention that anyone has ever experienced. Once the number-one hits started coming, the Beatles were filmed and photographed by the world's press on an almost daily basis for the rest of the decade. The workload of the band over the next eight years has often been marvelled at – it leaves most modern bands agog with horror – and it all took place in front of swarms of cameras. One of the strange moments that Beatle fans experience is the realisation that they will never stop encountering new images or photos of the band. While most historic subjects are recorded by a set number of images which aficionados soon become overly familiar with, the number of Beatles images appears to approach infinity.

Over the past half-century, information about the band has evolved away from fan scrapbooks and into the realm of academic historians, where it has been analysed, cross-checked and debated. There is so much information about the band now that leading Beatles scholar Mark Lewisohn released a 1,728-page biography of the group that only went up to the release of their first single. Because of their unprecedented global success in a technological era awash with film, tape and newsprint, it is possible that we know more about the career of the Beatles than about any other individuals in history. In terms of the moving image, that began in the heat and smell of this summer lunchtime Cavern gig.

The filming was the idea of Leslie Woodhead, a young researcher on *People and Places,* an early-evening magazine pro-gramme broadcast in the northwest of England. Woodhead was then at the beginning of his TV career. After leaving school he had worked as a junior intelligence officer during his national service, an experience he would later detail in his memoir *My Life as a Spy.* After graduating from a secret spy school in Scotland, where he was taught Russian, he had been posted to a former Luftwaffe base in Berlin where he intercepted and recorded Soviet transmis-sions. During long, lonely night shifts at the listening post, he would abandon his work and instead tune in to *Jazz Hour* on the American Forces Network. Jazz was Woodhead's great love, and he never forgot how that music melted away the grim reality of

Cold War espionage and let him escape into an entirely new and better world. This was the reason why Western nations broadcast radio like this behind the Iron Curtain – to let communist citizens know that a different life was possible.

This message was heard. Woodhead recalled an incident when a pair of bedraggled Russian defectors arrived at his Berlin barracks. 'It was a scary moment,' he later wrote, as he and his fellow junior spies 'crowded round the soldiers, trying to work out if they were the vanguard of an invasion'. They asked the frightened soldiers why they had risked climbing over the fence from the Soviet Zone of Berlin to defect. The answer was 'Because our officer won't let us listen to Elvis Presley.'

With his life of espionage behind him, Woodhead began a career that would eventually lead to him becoming an award-winning documentary director. At the time he was working on *Know Your North*, a series of short films which showcased the different people and events occurring in the Granada TV region – an example of how even independent TV had a strong public-service remit in the 1960s. Woodhead had already shot footage of the Brighouse and Rastrick Brass Band in a village hall, and he needed a second subject to complement this. Such was the excitement about the Beatles in their home town that word had spread as far as the Granada TV studios in Manchester. Woodhead contacted Brian Epstein and shortly afterwards found himself in a hot, smelly cellar. For all that Woodhead's great love was jazz, he was instantly converted. He began following the band around the northwest as a fan, catching whatever performance he could.

That evening in the Cavern making the first recorded film of the Beatles had a disorientating effect on Woodhead. Perhaps it was the music itself, or perhaps it was the noise, smell and atmosphere of that hot cellar concert that affected him so deeply. But those factors alone didn't seem to be enough to fully explain the impact the performance had on him. It was as if this ex-spy with an understanding of the international political importance of music felt a sense of foreboding about the enormity of what was about to happen – and what he had unwittingly played a part in unleashing on the world. Something unprecedented was about to be born, and there was nothing anyone could do to stop it.

As he later wrote about returning home after the filming, 'Driving back to Manchester down the East Lancashire Road, I felt glutted with the overload of stuff the Beatles had served up in the Cavern. Abruptly, I had to stop the car and be sick in a ditch.'

PART 2: DETONATE

1962: BIGGER THAN THE BEATLES

On 5 October 1962 a new seven-inch single was placed in the racks of record shops across the land. Nestled among the rest of the new releases was 'Love Me Do', the first single by the Beatles. It was just one of ten new singles that EMI released that day. There were no picture sleeves on singles in 1962, so it did not look significantly different to any of the others. The standard Parlophone paper sleeve featured an angular pattern of primary colours, the Parlophone logo and the message 'This record must be played at 45 R.P.M.' The only indication of what was on the disc was the red label on the record, revealed through the circle cut-out on the sleeve.

Despite the efforts of Parlophone's in-house plugger Alma Warren, no BBC radio programme was interested in playing the record. Neither were TV programmes like *Juke Box Jury* or *Thank Your Lucky Stars*. There was nothing like the song in the charts at the time, which were dominated by solo artists, along with a few groups playing instrumentals. DJs and producers presented with the record frequently dismissed it on the grounds that the Beatles had a weird and unappealing name. The record was played on Radio Luxembourg, however, and thirty years later George Harrison still considered hearing 'Love Me Do' coming through his mono radio speaker on this crackling medium-wave station to be one of the greatest moments of his life.

The London music press barely noticed. *Melody Maker* and the *NME* didn't review it. There was a full-page ad for the single in *Record Retailer*, but this was paid for by Brian Epstein, not EMI. The reaction was very different in Liverpool, however, and in other areas of the northwest where the band had built an audience through relentless gigging. As the leading Beatles historian Mark Lewisohn writes, 'The Beatles were the first recording artists post-war (and probably pre-war as well) launched with an already thriving sales base. The business had never been geared this way – singers were always discovered and then promoted in the usual clichéd ways.' Thanks to their existing fan base, and to the surprise of the industry in London, the single climbed to the respectable heights of number seventeen in the charts.

As catchy and likeable as 'Love Me Do' was, it was extremely simple. Written in 1958 when McCartney was sixteen, it was one of the first songs he had ever written, back when he was playing truant from school. There was little there which hinted at the artistic growth that he or the band would undergo, let alone the cultural legitimisation of pop music they would herald. The personality of the band, however, was already evident. The A-side showcased John Lennon demanding to be loved, while the B-side, 'P.S. I Love You', featured Paul promising to love – a template which immediately established the core personalities of the Lennon–McCartney partnership.

'Love Me Do' was the first in a string of twenty-two Beatles singles. They arrived like postcards from the band, typically every three or four months, gradually increasing in confidence and originality. These records still shape the folk memory of the Beatles to this day, as such well-known songs as 'She Loves You', 'Strawberry Fields Forever' or 'Hey Jude' were only released as singles – they were not included on any album during the band's lifetime. The Beatles were never content to repeat themselves, and the competitive rivalry between John and Paul saw them always trying to top what they had done before. As McCartney has explained, 'We always tried to make every song different because we figured, why write something like the last one? We've done that. We were always on a staircase to heaven, we were on a ladder so there was never any sense of stepping down a rung, or even staying on the same rung, it was better to move one rung ahead.' This attitude of constant evolution is in marked contrast to most modern bands, who develop a style and then largely stick to it, in order to give their audience what they want and expect.

The evolution of the Beatles began gradually, with the boy-meets-girl love songs of the early years slowly becoming more complex and surprising. By the band's middle years all bets were off, and the singles became entirely unpredictable – who could have expected August 1966's double-A sided single 'Yellow Submarine' backed with 'Eleanor Rigby'? One song is a moving and deeply empathetic depiction of loneliness accompanied by a string quartet, and the other a riotous silly children's singalong. What other band could come up with songs as utterly different and yet equally classic as these? To put them out on the same single, and expect their audience to understand, showed unprecedented confidence.

Musically, the Beatles are credited with pioneering the use of the studio as a creative instrument, popularising the idea that bands could and indeed should write their own material, and gigging in huge venues like sports stadiums. They were constantly exploring and trying new things, such as being the first to intentionally record feedback, print lyrics on album sleeves or release double-A-sided singles. Their influence on rock, pop and songwriting hardly needs mentioning, but even musicians in genres that were not influenced by their music, such as hip-hop or electronic dance music, are still operating in a music industry that was shaped by them.

Judging the size and importance of the Beatles is a strangely disorientating task. They are like a Lovecraftian monster whose proportions and immensity are somehow beyond our perception. We know, rationally, that they are the biggest band in history and that, in terms of influence and record sales, they will probably never lose that position. We know that the phrase used to describe the ultimate in musical success is to say that someone will become 'bigger than the Beatles'. Yet the Beatles have always felt homely and approachable, rather than enormous and untouchable. Their level of success was and is unthinkable, but they wore it so casually. They have always been part of the family, so familiar as to be unremarkable.

Measuring their success in terms of sales is one thing, defining their impact on society is quite another. As the classical historian Tom Holland has noted, the rate of social change in the 1960s was almost historically unprecedented: 'the transformation in values and ethics and assumptions about sexuality [has] been as rapid as any period in history anywhere'. He went on, 'The Reformation is the only parallel that I can think of. I think that maybe in a hundred years' time, the Sixties will be seen as equivalent to the 1520s – a period where touch papers were lit that just explode and explode and transform.'

The Beatles were, of course, a key factor in this transformation. They were the most popular and best-loved entertainers in the world and, when countless millions of eyes were on them, they sucked up every idea that excited them in the counterculture and the *avant garde*, transformed them into gold, and sprayed them all over the mainstream. There had never been a transmission vector for evolutionary ideas like the Beatles. 'Changing the lifestyle and appearance of youth throughout the world didn't just happen,' John Lennon said in 1972, 'We set out to do it; we knew what we were doing.' You might argue about the extent to which Lennon is using hindsight here, and how deliberate all this really was, but the fact that it happened is clear. In the 1960s the psychology professor and LSD evangelist Timothy Leary wrote, 'I declare that John Lennon, George Harrison, Paul McCartney and Ringo Starr are mutants. Evolutionary agents sent by God, endowed with mysterious powers to create a new human species.' Histrionic stuff, but you can see what he's getting at.

This is not to claim, of course, that the Beatles were the sole catalyst of all the social changes that characterised the 1960s. There were many factors which fed into these, such as the demographic boom in young people, the arrival of the contraceptive pill, and a period of economic growth. Change was inevitable, and the Beatles were just one aspect of this historic period. But it is also fair to say that what happened in the 1960s could not have occurred in exactly the same way if they had not been there. There still would have been interest in subjects like psychedelic drugs and Eastern thought, for example, but it's hard to imagine how these ideas could have become quite so mainstream without the Beatles. Over the course of the decade, the Beatles managed to bend society to their own image, in a way that other mega-selling artists such as Coldplay, Ed Sheeran or Adele are unable to do. Life was different, after the Beatles. It's hard to say that about any other band.

The extent to which the Beatles changed Western society can be glimpsed when you compare the four fresh-faced young boys on the cover of their first album *Please Please Me* to the four strange, hairy men on the cover of *Abbey Road*, their last recorded album. Only six and a half years separate these two photographs, and yet the older men on the zebra crossing are unrecognisable as the former lads on the stairwell. The change runs much deeper than haircuts or clothes; at the time when the first photograph was taken, there was nobody like those older men in existence. In that earlier, innocent world of 1963, people with the ideas, opinions and perspectives that the 1969 Beatles had not only didn't exist – they were simply unimaginable. Viewers watching Peter Jackson's eight-hour docuseries *Get Back* soon feel very comfortable with the four Beatles, because the way they relate, joke and discuss problems feels entirely normal and modern. It is not until the end of the series, when the cameras go outside into the streets of London, that you are hit by how far back in history all this was. The flat caps and bowler hats, along with the clipped accents and headscarves, plunge you into a very different, long-gone world. The four Beatles then appear like modern people marooned in the distant past, waiting for society to catch up with them.

Collectively, the Beatles changed the world, but it's interesting how all four members of the band were also changed over the course of their career. Their individual journeys mirror what happened in the wider world. John Lennon began as an angry and damaged young man who hit his girlfriend and constantly mocked disabled people. He was the product of a violent world where war was always patriotically supported – his parents even gave him the middle name 'Winston'. He ended his career as a Beatle as one of the world's most high-profile pacifists and peace activists, in a society that saw millions of people take to the streets to protest against war.

Paul McCartney started out as the most naturally talented musician of his generation, but his working-class background meant that his genius was not expected to be recognised. The band would be a bit of fun, his family thought, but he would eventually have to get a regular job because only the privileged could become artists.

By the end of the 1960s, working-class creativity was recognised as vital and important, and seen as a way to escape impoverished backgrounds.

George Harrison entered the Beatles as a materially minded young kid and left deeply devoted to meditation and Indian religion, filling a spiritual void that his Catholic upbringing failed to satisfy. In the wider culture, the rise of alternative religions that he championed and popularised led to the 'New Age' spirituality of the 1970s and beyond.

Ringo Starr was the poorest and most underprivileged of the four. As we've noted, he was an only child who was confined to bed due to ill health during his formative childhood years, and he was not expected to reach adulthood. Ringo used to dream of having friends and money in those long, lonely days on his sickbed in a hospital on the Wirral. The Beatles proved to be the brothers that he always longed for, and the band brought him luxuries unimaginable to his childhood self. This unexpected wealth was mirrored in the wider society, as the boom in consumer products and economic growth made life in the 1970s unrecognisable from life in the 1950s. The Beatles were not the reason for this change, of course, but in embodying those changes publicly they helped the country come to terms with the idea of increasing material wealth.

As we get further and further away from their time, we gain more and more perspective on the importance of the band. It was not so long ago that people used to talk of 'the Beatles and the Stones', as if those bands were on a similar level or could be considered equivalent. That is no longer the case. Just as the footprint of Shakespeare is culturally far larger than the footprint of sixteenth-century theatre, so too have the Beatles become larger than 1960s pop music. Should you ask Google about the United Kingdom it will display its own 'factbox' about the country. It begins, 'The United Kingdom, made up of England, Scotland, Wales and Northern Ireland, is an island nation in northwestern Europe. England – birthplace of Shakespeare and The Beatles – is home to the capital, London.' In the eyes of the American data giant, the Beatles deserve to be mentioned in the second sentence of an account of the United Kingdom. As the passing of time allows us to slowly grasp just how profound their influence was, we realise that the only band who have proved to be bigger than the Beatles are the Beatles themselves.

On that windy October Friday in 1962, you would think, none of this would apply. On the day the record came out, it should have been possible to listen to the band without the epic baggage that would follow. And yet, even then in those early days, the absurd sense that the Beatles were historically important was already in circulation. The music-shop owner Brian Epstein sensed it when he descended the steps into Liverpool's underground Cavern Club one lunchtime in November 1961 and first saw the band play. It was present in the sleeve notes on *The Beatles' Hits*, an EP released less than a year after 'Love Me Do'. These requested the listener 'preserve this sleeve for ten years [and] exhume it from your collection somewhere around the middle of 1973', in order to confirm its belief that people would still be admiring Lennon and McCartney songs a whole decade later. In 1963, this was a bold claim indeed. Pop music was then viewed in much the same way that we now view memes or Snapchat filters. It was ephemeral and not expected to last – certainly not a whole ten years.

The sleeve notes for the album *Beatles for Sale*, released a year later, took this bold idea further, suggesting that 'in a generation or so' you might be asked about the Beatles by 'a radio-active, cigar-smoking child, picnicking on Saturn [...] The kids of AD 2000 will draw from the music much the same sense of well being and warmth as we do today.' Reading this over fifty years later, it is the idea that children will be smoking cigars that seems most outrageous, with the notion of picnics on Saturn coming in a close second. In 1964, however, it was the notion that the Beatles would be listened to in the year 2000 that was truly wild.

Only six months later, the idea the Beatles may be remembered in 1973 or even 2000 didn't seem extreme enough. We now find them being spoken about as still being culturally important centuries in the future. In a 1965 episode of the BBC science-fiction series *Doctor Who*, William Hartnell's original time-travelling Doctor was experimenting with a machine called a Space-Time Visualiser, which could show any event in history on a screen. After watching Abraham Lincoln deliver the Gettysburg Address and William Shakespeare converse with Queen Elizabeth I, he uses the machine to watch the Beatles on *Top of the Pops*. This was hugely exciting for his companion Vicki, an orphan girl from the twenty-fifth century. Vicki knew all about the Beatles. She explained that they play classical music, and that she has visited the Beatles' Memorial Theatre in Liverpool. This comment seems unremarkable now, at a time when there are two Beatles museums in Liverpool. In 1965, it was very much intended as a joke. And yet it was a joke that only worked because, deep down, people felt that the Beatles might well be remembered in the twenty-fifth century. It was not a joke that would have worked with Cliff Richard and the Shadows, or Gerry and the Pacemakers, or any other of the popular bands of the time. The music of the Beatles is currently stored in a bomb-proof doomsday vault on an island near the North Pole, so it should make it to Vicki's time, regardless of what humanity does to itself before then.

That first seven-inch single, then, was a strangely charged thing as it sat in the record racks on that October Friday. It was brand new, simultaneously innocuous and world-changing, with no past to speak of but a great weight from the future bestowed upon it. How strange it would have been to have listened to it on that first day, when it was nothing more than just a simple and innocent song, rather than the end of the old world and the start of the new.

1962: SEAN CONNERY (1930-2020)

At the same time that 'Love Me Do' was released, the first James Bond film *Dr. No* opened in British cinemas. Audiences were immediately attracted to this glossy, modern adventure and the film did good business, eventually becoming the fifth-highest grossing film of the year in the UK. With hindsight, this does not appear surprising. The film is now seen as a combination of rare talents, most notably production designer Ken Adam, title designer Maurice Binder, director Terence Young and musician John Barry, who came together in a perfect cocktail that defines the Bond formula to this day. Most importantly, there was also Sean Connery. It might not have been apparent from *Dr. No* that the character of James Bond was going to be quite so prominent in the decades ahead, but it was clear to audiences that Sean Connery was going to be a major star. Critics, however, didn't quite know what to make of the film, or of him.

Many critics recognised that the character of Bond had been changed from that found in Fleming's novels, but oddly they thought Sean Connery was playing the part as an Irishman, or possibly an Irish-American. 'At last Mr. Ian Fleming's James Bond makes his bow on the screen, and it is doubtful whether either his admirers or his detractors will recognize him,' said *The Times*, explaining that 'there is that about him, a faint Irish-American look and sound, which somehow spoils the image'. The *Guardian* thought that 'Sean Connery, though he very nearly looks right, sounds all wrong (with his slightly Irish, slightly American accent)'. The *Daily Mail* mentioned Connery's 'dark brown Irish voice'. Connery's accent is indeed unusual, but to think that he sounds Irish illustrates just how parochial the London press were in the early 1960s. Being of a similar class to Fleming, they had expected a hero who spoke with their own Received Pronunciation accent.

Reviews of the film were generally mixed, with perhaps the most perceptive comment coming from Penelope Gilliatt in the *Observer*. 'It is easy to get angry about Ian Fleming's James Bond. He is snobbish, brutal and sneering, and his rapacious little character is full of the new upper-class thuggishness: he is a vile man to be given as a hero,' she began, before admitting that 'the first of what is obviously going to be a series of James Bond films, takes the wind out of one's rage: it makes him seem funny. Instead of admiring his vodka martinis and his idle grabs at girls and his cool way of dumping a corpse on Government House, it gently sends him up. "Dr. No" is full of submerged self-parody.' That crucial ingredient in the Bond formula, its strange ability to take itself seriously and not take itself seriously at the same time, was something that Sean Connery played beautifully.

On paper, Connery could not have been more wrong for the part. Bond was an Eton-educated English snob familiar with the privileges of the establishment. Connery was from the Fountainbridge area of Edinburgh and left school at thirteen to work at a dairy. His parents were a lorry driver and a cleaning woman, and the poverty of the depression-era 1930s made childhood education a luxury for many. Connery started working at the age of nine, getting up early to deliver milk before school.

The role which brought him to the attention of the Bond team was the 1959 Disney fantasy *Darby O'Gill and the Little People*, a children's story about leprechauns. It was a light, comedic part in which Connery attempted a broad Disney 'Oirish' accent. Critics didn't mistake him for an actual Irishman in this film. The role was about as far as you could get from Fleming's Bond, and Connery also did not appear very Bond-like when he came in to audition. In person he was every inch the scruffy working-class brawler, with a 'Scotland Forever' tattoo on his arm. Yet the producers weren't looking for Fleming's Bond. They wanted an actor who would appeal outside of Fleming's social circles. After Connery left, they watched him walk away through the office window and marvelled at how he moved. He was so assured and graceful, walking with the utter confidence of a cat. As wrong as he may have seemed for the role, they would never find another actor with that masculine mastery of the physical world. As Broccoli said, 'We were very lucky in finding the type we thought Americans would like as Bond when we came across Sean.'

Fleming's conception of Bond, ultimately, wilted in front of the blazing power of Connery's charisma. In response, the character was forever changed in the eyes of the public. It was Connery who realised that Bond needed a sense of humour that was absent in the novels. As Saltzman remembered, 'Fleming didn't like Sean Connery because he spoke with a Scottish accent. Fleming saw James Bond as himself, high-born, very educated, very English, posh public-school accent.' But Fleming was not blind to the appeal of Connery, and he was quite prepared to rewrite his character if that was what the general public wanted. In his next Bond novel, he gave the character a Scottish background for the first time. James Bond, it was now said, attended the prestigious public school Fettes in Edinburgh. Connery knew Fettes well. He used to deliver milk there.

That Connery was physically right to play Bond is shown by an incident that happened in 1958, after he had landed his first major Hollywood role in the film *Another Time, Another Place*. He had been personally chosen by the film's star Lana Turner to play her love interest, and the chemistry between the pair angered Turner's jealous and possessive boyfriend, Johnny Stompanato, a bodyguard and enforcer for Mickey Cohen of the Cohen crime family. Stompanato visited the film set and, after seeing Turner with her handsome co-star, threatened Connery with a gun. Connery responded by knocking the gun out of Stompanato's hand and flattening him to the ground with one punch. This was a brave, skilful, impressive and also incredibly stupid move. It was also perfectly Bond-like. Connery had reacted in a similar way back in Edinburgh when he had been threatened by the violent Valdor gang in a billiard hall. That incident gave Connery the reputation as a hard man back home in Scotland, and it serves as a reminder that the world Connery came from was a more violent and lawless place than today. The incident with Stompanato occurred shortly before he was killed by Turner's teenage daughter, who stabbed him when he was attacking her mother. A court would later rule that it was justifiable homicide. It was thought that other mobsters believed Connery was responsible, however, causing him to go into hiding.

Stompanato would not be the only man jealous of their partner's reaction to Connery. He was, in the opinion of his girlfriend Julie Hamilton, the most beautiful thing she'd ever seen. According to his *Goldfinger* co-star Honor Blackman he was 'the sexiest devil in the world [...] There's no question there was a great attraction between the two of us. I was married at the time so I had to rein in my horses.' This was a common reaction among his female co-stars. Although Roger Moore's 'Bond Girls' are complimentary, they don't have quite the same look in their eyes when they speak of him. If Bond was intended as an idealised masculine icon, then casting Sean Connery in 1962 was as close to perfection as casting gets.

For all that a large part of Connery's appeal was his 'real man' reputation, his familiarity with violence came at a cost. According to his first wife Diane Cilento, Connery was physically abusive during their eleven-year marriage, a period which covered his years as Bond. 'I don't think there is anything particularly wrong in hitting a woman, though I don't recommend you do it in the same way you hit a man,' he said in a 1965 *Playboy* interview. This quote was raised in a 1987 TV interview by a deeply unimpressed Barbara Walters. 'I haven't changed my opinion,' he told her. In 1993, he told *Vanity Fair* that there were women who 'want a slap'.

Like many domestic abusers, Connery argued that it was often the woman's fault she was beaten. As the historian and writer Hallie Rubenhold has noted, Victorian working-class sentiments about domestic violence 'frequently placed the onus for a beating on the woman herself. A certain degree of violence within the home was felt to serve a disciplinary function. Husbands felt no remorse for administering a chastising slap, while wives were often made to feel that they had "asked for it".' Connery, however, was still making this argument at the end of the twentieth century, after second-wave feminism had helped to change mainstream attitudes. He eventually recanted in 2006, shortly after the publication of Cilento's autobiography detailing the abuse she received. He then told *The Times*, 'My view is I don't believe that any level of abuse against women is ever justified under any circumstances. Full stop.'

It had taken a long time for Connery to change his views. It was apparent in his interview with Barbara Walters that he was considerably behind the curve of public opinion in the 1980s. This is a reminder that although cultural changes wash through populations, they don't do so smoothly. As the sci-fi author William Gibson famously said, 'The future is already here – it's just not evenly distributed.' This applies as much to attitudes as it does to technology.

Following the success of *Dr. No*, Connery returned to the role of Bond in a series of films that became increasingly successful as the sixties rolled on. By the time his third Bond film *Goldfinger* arrived in cinemas, he was uncomfortable with the level of global fame the part had brought him. When the following film *Thunderball* was released, he was regularly complaining publicly about the role. 'I find that fame tends to turn one from an actor and a human being into a piece of merchandise,' he said. 'Well, I don't intend to undergo that metamorphosis.' In a 1996 documentary he recalled being mobbed by fans: 'It was around the same time as the Beatles. The difference was that they had four of them to deal with it.'

For all that Bond made Connery wealthy, he didn't see how the formulaic franchise could continue to interest him as an actor. 'All the gimmicks now have been done. And they are expected. What is needed now is a change of course – more attention to character and better dialogue.' Although persuaded to continue for a fifth film, he then quit the series. In the years that followed he would twice be tempted back into the role by phenomenally large salaries.

For all his fear of being typecast, Connery's non-Bond film career was one that most actors would envy. He proved his talent as an actor in films like *The Name of the Rose* (1986), *The Hill* (1965) and *The Man Who Would Be King* (1975). In 1988 he won an Oscar for his role in Brian De Palma's *The Untouchables*, and he received a knighthood in 2000. Almost uniquely among actors, he made no attempt to adopt accents for the characters he played, from *Dr. No* onwards, even when his own was entirely inappropriate. It is tempting to see this as a reaction to his much-mocked Irish accent in *Darby O'Gill and the Little People*. His natural Scottish voice was used for English secret agents, Russian submarine captains, Chicago Irish cops, mythological Greek kings and even Spanish-based Egyptian immortals. It's hard to think of another actor who could have made this approach work. But then, which other actor had a voice like his?

Having once been Bond, Connery was happy to avoid the standard leading-man life choices. He made no attempt to hide his ageing and was happy to take elder mentor roles. His natural gravitas may have made him unsuitable to play the everyman, but there were more than enough mythological figures to keep him busy – including King Arthur, Robin Hood, King Agamemnon and Indiana Jones's dad. His final role was as Allan Quatermain in the disappointing *The League of Extraordinary Gentlemen* (2003). The experience of making the film prompted him to retire, citing the 'idiots now making films in Hollywood'. His life was rich enough without needing to act. He was a skilled golfer and was active politically. He was a lifelong advocate of Scottish independence, even if his love for the country did not extend to living or paying taxes there.

None of his illustrious career, however, could separate him from James Bond in the public's mind. This was the role that dominated his obituaries when he died in the Bahamas in 2020 at the age of ninety. Roger Moore always graciously insisted that Connery was the best James Bond, and in doing so established the practice of all future Bonds deferring to Connery as the greatest. It was Connery, after all, who added humour to the character, and warped the portrayal of the spy in Fleming's later books to better match his own template. The archetype of James Bond is as much Sean Connery as it is Ian Fleming's idealised self.

Connery's Bond was strong, confident and wilful. He was also charming, relaxed and funny. He was brave, made an effort to dress well, and made time to enjoy the finer things in life. He was also violent and abusive, in a way that, like Fleming's Bond, suggested that the dark and light sides of masculinity may not easily be separated. For all that the flaws of masculinity are readily apparent in his portrayal of Bond, Connery showed that masculinity could also have an extraordinary appeal. This was not a quality that came from Fleming's background or his imagination, however. It came from Sean Connery, and it was acquired as he grew to manhood in the streets of 1930s Edinburgh.

1963: THERE ARE TRUTHS
IN THAT SCREAMING

James Bond embodied an idealised version of male identity that was common after the Second World War: he was a man who could fight. He was brave, skilled and willing to risk his life to defeat an oppressor. In the less wealthy areas of the country like Connery's Fountainbridge or Ringo's Liverpool 8, the ability to fight was often necessary for survival.

To the post-war generation of boys, raised on a diet of war comics that depicted combat in heroic and moral terms, being good at fighting bad guys looked like an admirable and desirable vision of masculinity. It offered competitiveness and excitement, and excused the violence through the greater moral good of protecting the innocent and vulnerable – and, in particular, the saving of girls. Their parents who had lived through the war knew that things weren't quite that simple, and that the psychological cost of grief, loss and trauma caused by violence was a heavy one. But who wanted to hear boring true-life war stories from old people when the adventures in comics and films were so thrilling?

Although Bond was initially aimed at adults – and, in Ian Fleming's mind at least, quite sophisticated adults – it soon found a following among young boys. Watching Bond films was like watching football – one of those rare bonding activities that dads and their sons could enjoy doing together. Boys claimed to find the glamorous women boring, but there was more than enough in the Bond films to grab their attention, not least the fights, explosions and gadgets. And those gadgets were ideally suited to the toy market. Chief among the Bond toys was the 007 Aston Martin DB5 toy car – four inches long and painted gold instead of silver, on the highly Bondian grounds that things painted gold looked great. This was the bestselling boys' toy of 1965 and also the first of the 'blockbuster' toys, for which demand outstrips supply and parents desperately hunt stock in the weeks before Christmas. By 1970, over 4 million of these cars had been sold in the UK alone.

It was not just a nice car. It had a bulletproof shield that popped up to protect the rear windscreen, machine guns that emerged out of the front bumper and, best of all, a working ejector seat. The fact that the Aston Martin was such a stylish car helped, but it was these modifications that made it such a successful toy. According to *Classic and Sports Car* magazine, it was 'the greatest toy ever'. Growing up with ace toys like this, it's easy to see the appeal of James Bond to post-war boys.

While the Beatles were also raised after the war, they embodied a very different version of male identity. They were jokers rather than fighters, quick-witted and unpredictable. This was, of course, another survival technique in deprived areas. They were also emotionally direct, talking to teenage girls about love and romance. Their willingness to display what were then thought of as feminine qualities was visually symbolised by their 'mop-top' hair, which seems entirely unremarkable now but appeared shockingly feminine to those who had fought in the war and worn army regulation haircuts.

Early Beatles singles acted as a conversation between the band and their female teenage audience. Those seven-inch singles were cheap, democratic and readily available, and the songs on both sides of the vinyl were a powerfully direct form of communication. The words sung by John, Paul and George might appear simple, but this was a feature rather than a bug – those simple phrases bypassed the nets of the intellect and, propelled by the confidence of the music, arrived undiluted in the heart. The boys sang of wanting to hold a hand or asked the listener to please please him – words which held enormous emotional power. They would only have been weakened by the kind of literary ambitions that better-educated songwriters believed were necessary. For teenage girls who owned a Dansette or other portable record player, they could take the singles into the privacy of their own bedroom, where they would be alone with those voices. It was a type of intimacy unknown to earlier generations. The Beatles spoke directly to the emotional part of their audience, a part of them that the rest of the world failed to recognise or acknowledge.

Being unobtainable, the Fab Four were imagined as both perfect and non-threatening. What real-life boys at school could compete with them? There were four to choose from, which provoked endless conversations and complicated shifting allegiances between groups of friends. They came into the lives of teenage girls with all the force and purity of first love – that period after the heart has opened, but before experience has taught us to build walls around it for our own protection. The love these first fans felt for the Beatles could be almost overwhelming. And so, the screaming started.

There had been screaming before, of course. Throughout history, figures as diverse as Lord Byron or Frank Sinatra had become huge celebrities, as had less well-remembered figures such as Sarah Bernhardt and Vesta Tilley. But television had brought the Beatles into homes in a way that was entirely new. They became so familiar that they were almost part of the family. When girls got together, they recognised the same depths of feeling in each other, and that recognition acted as a confirmation that what they were feeling was real. This created a feedback loop of escalating emotion, an energy that had to be vented somehow. How could they not scream? No one can keep all that inside.

This level of emotion meant that it was no longer possible for the Beatles to remain living at home with their parents, at addresses that were widely shared among their fans. Ringo's mum Elsie realised the extent of her son's fame when bus-loads of fans began turning up at their house, some having come all the way from London. Elsie did the polite thing, which was to invite them in and offer them sandwiches. 'They never ate anything,' she recalled. 'They just wrapped them up to take back as souvenirs [...] They'd ask "which is his chair?" I'd say, "Sit on them all, love, he has." They always wanted to go up to see his bed as well. They'd lie on it, moaning.' Elsie's friend Marie Maguire recalled that Elsie's house in 'Admiral Grove was surrounded by fans twenty-four hours a day, which was awkward, particularly as the toilet was still in the yard'.

There are different types of screaming crowds. At rock concerts, the screams are low and guttural and show approval and tribal allegiance. At sports events, the crowd noise fluctuates with the events on the pitch, a model of the game in audio form. When girls scream at boybands, the sound is at a higher pitch, simultaneously constant yet out of control. Screams in those quantities have qualities that no other sound possesses. Air becomes noise. Screams become something you breathe as much as hear. Paul McCartney has described them as sounding like 'a million seagulls'. We are a long way from screaming as approval here. We have crossed over into territory somewhere between hysteria and ecstasy.

If you listen to the recordings of Beatles concerts now, you would be forgiven for thinking there was an oversized jet engine somewhere nearby. It is not clear how long a human can survive in that soundscape, but there is definitely something addictive about being inside it. The more you listen, the more you need it. You can imagine new forms of life evolving inside that sound. It is easy to assume that it is the ultimate in noise, and the pinnacle of what human voices can achieve. But then John or Paul will announce that the next song is going to be sung by Ringo and the idea crumbles into hubris as the screams escalate exponentially. The earlier shrieks, you realise, were nothing more than a whisper.

In the midst of communal screaming, there is only the present moment. The past and the future have dissolved away, nothing more than illusions. When the past disappears, it takes with it the possibility of regret or shame. When the future vanishes, gone are any feelings of worry, stress and our capability to experience fear. There was no sense, watching a theatre performance by the Beatles, that it took place in linear time – of the type that can be measured on a watch. The concert was over as soon as it had begun, yet it happened outside of time and it was eternal. There are truths in that screaming that many religions have yet to grasp.

There have been countless boybands who have experienced similar screams, from the Bay City Rollers to Bros, Westlife or Take That. The press always likens this to Beatlemania, a practice that shows no sign of stopping as the decades pass. You will never read of the devotion which bands like BTS inspire and see it compared to Duran Duran mania or New Kids on the Block at their peak, for example, even though those may be reasonable comparisons. Books on the James Bond phenomenon often point out that Bondmania in the mid-sixties was akin to Beatlemania. This is undoubtedly true, but it is noticeable that no Beatles books feel the need to make a similar claim about how the reaction to the Beatles was like Bondmania. Beatlemania is the unchallenged archetype of hysteria.

One of the side effects of the scream, at least according to disgruntled theatre owners, was that fans had a tendency to wet themselves during the concerts. Here we gain a glimpse of the difference in the energy of 1950s rock 'n' roll compared to that of Beatlemania. Rock 'n' roll was empowering. It made people feel taller. It had a vital, masculine energy that did not always find a healthy outlet. Rock 'n' roll films of the 1950s were accused of creating 'teenage delinquents', as male fans became so worked up by the energy of the music that they famously took out knives and slashed the cinema seats. The unfocused energy that the music created was directed outwards, at whoever or whatever happened to be in the way. Violence was common to the lifestyle of the sharply dressed 'Teddy boy' rockers in the 1950s.

The energy created by the Beatles, in contrast, led to surrender. It was more about ecstatic transcendence than it was about feeling powerful. For a teenage girl at a Beatles concert, screaming hysterically with their peers for hours on end, their regular respectable identity would dissolve in the emotion and the excitement. The loss of control in the face of this higher force could be terrible, but it would also be blissful. Theatre owners were far from happy about their audience members wetting the seats, but it was probably better than slashing them.

For teenage boys, it was all very confusing. They thought they had a clear sense of what being a man was all about. They had masculine role models to learn from, and they understood what behaviour was expected of them. They knew they were expected to be brave, and good at fighting, in order to protect girls or their family. Having long hair and singing about love had no part of it.

The problem was, this no longer seemed to be what girls were attracted to. Here, in the different versions of male identity that the Beatles and Bond audiences were encountering, a crisis of masculinity was being born.

1964: IAN FLEMING (1908–1964)

In the last year of his life, Ann Fleming coined a new nickname for her husband. In her letters she had previously referred to him as Thunderbird, in mocking reference to the large American car that he drove. Now, he became Thunderbeatle. He was, in her opinion, the fifth Beatle – as rich and famous as the original four. As she wrote, 'In both cases something undefinable appealed to public fancy, and was immediately fastened on to by those who batten on exploiting original talent.'

Apart from their levels of success, however, the differences between the Beatles and Ian Fleming were more striking than the similarities. The Beatles were young, enthusiastic and at the start of their story. Fleming already suspected that he would not live much longer. The Fab Four were an outpouring of energy, but Fleming's energy was spent. The Beatles were an expression of joy. Fleming was deeply unhappy.

Ian Fleming's fame had taken a long time to arrive. He stuck rigidly to a yearly routine after completing his first novel *Dr. No*, which saw him write a new Bond novel at Goldeneye in the first months of every year. He would then return home to prepare for the publication of the previous title. Sometimes these novels were rushed and not as good as they could be, as we've noted, but Fleming never failed to produce a book a year, even if it was on occasions a few short stories rather than a novel. The rushed nature of his books meant that they had a great energy to them, which all page-turners and thrillers need. It also meant that opinions he might have thought twice about and edited out remained in the books. As a result, that elusive quality of Flemingness was always present.

When his first book *Casino Royale* was released, the reviews in the *Sunday Times*, *Daily Telegraph* and *Times Literary Supplement* were all written by friends of Fleming's, and hence were all extremely positive. It also helped that the bookselling chain W.H. Smith was owned by family friends. Reviews not written by his friends were less kind, however, as were American reviews. Sales of the US hardback were disappointing. This led to the paperback edition being retitled *You Asked for It*, complete with a pulpy cover painting of a hard-drinking American working-class man leering at a sassy, barely dressed woman, in front of an orange background. The back-cover blurb began, 'If he hadn't been a tough operator, Jimmy Bond would never have risked a weekend with a woman who used her magnificent body as a weapon to destroy him.' This was not how Fleming wanted his work to be marketed.

Fleming soon began to talk disparagingly about his creation, and his inability to generate the ideas or the enthusiasm needed to keep going. It did not help that his wife and her friends were so openly dismissive of his books. As he wrote to Raymond Chandler in 1956:

Probably the fault about my books is that I don't take them seriously enough and meekly accept having my head ragged off about them in the family circle. If one has a grain of intelligence

*it is difficult to go on being serious about a character like James
Bond. You after all write 'novels of suspense' – if not sociological
studies – whereas my books are straight pillow fantasies of the
bang-bang, kiss-kiss variety.*

At the time, Fleming had just returned from Goldeneye where he
had written *From Russia with Love*, the fifth Bond novel. Seriously
considering killing off James Bond, he ended that book on a cliff-
hanger, in which Bond collapsed lifelessly to the floor after being
stabbed by the poisoned shoe-knife of Russian spymaster Rosa
Klebb. Fleming would ultimately go on to write fourteen Bond
books in total, but he never stopped musing on whether it was
time to kill his troubling creation.

Fleming's regular schedule of a book a year meant that his
audience gradually grew, however. His second novel *Live and
Let Die* was banned in Ireland, which helped its reputation and
sales elsewhere. One incident in particular helped to cement the
popularity of Bond in America. Fleming had met John F. Kennedy
through a mutual friend in Washington and always made a point
of sending him copies of each new Bond book. After Kennedy
was inaugurated as US President in 1961, *Life* magazine ran an
article about his reading habits, which included a list of his top
ten books. These included *From Russia with Love* and, following the
approval of JFK, the sales of Fleming's books exploded. According
to Fleming's biographer Andrew Lycett, it was said that JFK was
reading a Bond novel on the night before he was assassinated, and
so too was Lee Harvey Oswald. The publishing sensation that Bond
became after the *Life* magazine article could only continue when
the Sean Connery movie series hit screens the following year. By
the time Fleming died in 1964, he had sold over 30 million books.

In the late 1930s, Fleming had told his friend Lady Mary Clive
that he wanted to be famous. She lived long enough to see his

name in big letters on cinema hoardings. His dream, clearly, had come true. So why was he so unhappy? In Lady Mary's view, it was because he was lauded for making a huge financial success of his creation, not because he was a great writer or an admired thinker. He was world famous for creating James Bond, a character looked down upon by his wife, her social circle and the establishment in general. As his books had become more successful, a dissenting critical opinion had also grown. His 1958 novel *Dr. No* had been famously described in a *New Statesman* review by Paul Johnson as 'Sex, sadism and snobbery', and even those loyal to Fleming had to concede that Johnson had a point. For all that the everyday readers of his books loved to live vicariously through this shameless escapism, the society that Fleming moved in, riddled as it was with envy and insecurity, was never going to admire him for the success of Bond.

Another factor in his unhappiness was that the success came too late for him to enjoy it. He had always dreamed of becoming hugely wealthy, for both the status and freedom it would grant. Before the war, he had told the intelligence agent Conrad O'Brien-ffrench that financial security was all that mattered in life. But his new Bond wealth did not impress his peers, and he no longer had the physical capacity to make the most of freedom. His mother died two weeks before he did, which meant that in his final days he finally inherited his share of the Fleming family fortune. 'What use is it to me now?' he complained to Ann.

The great irony of Fleming's acquisition of this immense wealth at the very end of his life was that he had always been wealthy, as most people would define it. He had multiple houses and servants, and spent months each year holidaying abroad. If he wanted a bespoke gold-plated typewriter, he could go and buy one. It is hard to think of any material possessions that he lacked or was unable to obtain. He had been rich all his life – he just hadn't realised it.

Despite his large number of friends, Fleming wasn't universally popular. He believed he was charming, and in the eyes of some he was, but many found him intensely dislikeable. When Sean Connery was asked about him in a TV interview, he just shrugged and said, 'Well, he was a terrible snob.' Others commented on his cruelty and immaturity. The opinion of the novelist Sarah Gainham, who knew Fleming for many years, was typical: 'highly intelligent and accomplished, but his emotional age was pre-puberty'.

His marriage was, as Noël Coward predicted, a deeply unhappy one. Inflicting physical pain in the bedroom had drawn Ann and Ian together initially, but neither had enjoyed the emotional cruelty that came to define their marriage. Ann maintained an affair with the Labour Party leader Hugh Gaitskell during most of their marriage. The woman Ann called Ian's 'Jamaican wife' was Blanche Blackwell, the mother of Chris Blackwell, founder of Island Records. Ian and Ann were different people who wanted different things from life, and neither were prepared to change in order to accommodate the other.

According to Fleming's friend Lady Mary Clive, 'You simply never could anticipate how Ian would behave. In a wreck I simply don't know whether he would go off in the first lifeboat, or go down with the ship. In the war, if the Germans had invaded and Ian had turned out to be a great Quisling, I would never have been surprised. He was totally unpredictable.' Fleming, of course, served loyally during the war, but it is probably fair to say that he was motivated to fight for England rather than against fascism. Though he was never sufficiently politically motivated to endorse fascism, he was strikingly tolerant of it. During his time at Eton he edited a magazine called *The Wyvern*, which included an article arguing that it was of the 'utmost importance' that fascism centres were established in British public schools and universities. In the 1930s he bought Mussolini's passport, which he proudly displayed in his London flat before the war. That flat had previously been used for meetings of the British Union of Fascists before Fleming bought the lease from Oswald Mosely. Mosely was then moving into a larger home ahead of his marriage to Diana Mitford, a family friend of Ian's. That wedding took place in Germany at the family home of Joseph Goebbels, with Adolf Hitler as guest of honour.

The friends that Fleming welcomed to this flat included Oswald's best man, Robert Gordon-Canning, a notorious anti-Semite and fascist who was imprisoned during the war for his views, and John Fox-Strangways, the second son of the Earl of Ilchester. According to Andrew Lycett, Strangways 'is best remembered for kicking the socialist politician Aneurin Bevan on the steps of White's in 1951'. Aneurin Bevan, of course, was the architect of the National Health Service, which was established in time to save the life of young Ringo Starr. Fleming was against the National Health Service and the Welfare State and was disappointed that Churchill didn't dismantle it when he returned to power in 1951.

The level of support for fascism among the British upper classes in the 1930s is a subject that few aristocratic families want to dwell upon. When examples emerge, they seem shocking – such as the photograph published by the *Sun* in 2015 of Queen Elizabeth II performing a Nazi salute at the age of seven, having been taught to do so by her mother. The logic of British aristocracy insists that certain bloodlines are 'superior' to others, and fascism can be attractive to those who believe this. Fleming's politics were less ideological than this, however. He was simply opposed to communism, socialism or anything that threatened the hierarchical privileged world he had been born into. One of the rare political acts in his life was manning the signals at Leighton Buzzard railway station to help support the government during the General Strike of 1926.

Although he wrote the children's story *Chitty-Chitty-Bang-Bang* for his son Caspar, who he affectionately called 003-and-a-half, Fleming was not a good parent. Largely absent, he relied on nannies and boarding schools to raise his son. Even when they were living under the same roof, Caspar was expected to stay with his nanny in the servant quarters. He believed that his son was spoilt, a view also shared by many who knew the family. Fleming was far from happy when, at the age of four, Caspar took to wearing a hibiscus flower behind his ear and referring to himself as Mary. For Fleming, carefree childhood play and explorations of identity like this were not to be encouraged.

When Caspar was eleven, Fleming gave him an air rifle. The boy developed an unhealthy obsession with guns and was eventually expelled from Eton after a loaded handgun was found in his room. Badly affected by his father's death on his twelfth birthday, Caspar grew up rich but with profound mental health problems, which were exacerbated by his excessive use of recreational drugs. As his mother wrote to Evelyn Waugh, 'Caspar hates me and talks of little but matricide. What shall I do?' Following a failed suicide attempt at Goldeneye, in which he took an overdose and swam out to sea to drown, Caspar finally succeeded in killing himself in London when he was still only twenty-three years old. His suicide note simply read, 'If it is not this time it will be the next.'

Fleming lived his life as an individual, committed to his own wants and desires and unwilling to accommodate the needs of others. He was true to his beliefs and worldview, but it left him miserable. Even success on his own terms through novels that were a creative expression of his beliefs, rather than something inherited or gifted by family connections, seemed hollow. When his success was seen alongside his idyllic life at Goldeneye and his young family, you could be forgiven for thinking his life must have been paradise. But there was no transcendence in Fleming's life, and no compassion. He could not give himself to others. Instead, he looked down on people, especially women, and made little attempt to hide it. Emotionally, he never matured beyond his schoolboy years, so life naturally proved to be as cold and indifferent as he was. Snobbery always leaves people unhappy.

Fleming did, however, have a sense of adventure, a desire to travel and the belief that something better was attainable. These qualities alone were not enough to lighten his soul. But distilled into pacey, entertaining fiction, they did take on a life of their own and resonated with a global audience. In some sense Ann's nickname of Thunderbeatle was valid – after all, who else but Ian Fleming and the Beatles hit such a deep nerve with the public, both at home in England and globally?

In 1964, at the height of his success, Fleming's heart gave out and he died. James Bond, as dispassionate as his creator, carried on regardless, unaffected by the death. Fleming's personality had already been condensed into the fantasy of secret agent 007, and so it seemed set to outlive him. But this super-spy was now no longer bound by his creator's views. As a result, Bond would evolve over the following decades with the changing culture in ways that Ian Fleming would have been horrified by.

1964: A FILM WITH FOUR LONG-HAIRED SCHNOOKS

The character of a particular nation, we might think, is readily identifiable. Certain attitudes and cultural styles come to mind when we think of the USA, or Spain, or Japan. These national characteristics are like a rainbow, however. They are only visible from a distance. When you get too close, or try to nail down specifics, they vanish like the illusions they are. In actuality, nations are patchworks of wildly different people, attitudes and experiences. Few things illustrate this as neatly as the contrasting depictions of Britain in the 1964 films *Goldfinger* and *A Hard Day's Night*.

Both these United Artists films were incredibly successful. Both are in the US top ten list of the highest grossing films of the year. *Goldfinger* cost $3m to make and took $125m at the global box office, which is more than a billion in today's money. '*Goldfinger* isn't just big,' *Variety* explained. 'It is, to use the word advisedly, incomparable.' *A Hard Day's Night* was much cheaper to make but, by taking $11m on a budget of around $250,000, it had a slightly higher return on investment. Both films remain critically lauded to this day and appear in the BFI's list of the hundred best British films of the twentieth century.

Both films were nominated for Oscars and both had hugely successful soundtracks – John Barry's *Goldfinger* soundtrack album knocked the Beatles off the top of the charts when it reached number one in the US. Both films also had trouble with the censors. The US censor Geoffrey Shurlock threatened to ban *Goldfinger* completely, due to the fact that Honor Blackman's character was named Pussy Galore. The producers managed to change Shurlock's mind by showing him pictures of Honor Blackman at the UK premiere with Prince Philip. If the name was acceptable to the royal family, their argument went, then it was clearly acceptable for everyone else. Amazingly, this strategy worked. *A Hard Day's Night*, meanwhile, had the phrase 'get knotted' cut by the British Board of Film Censors to achieve its U certificate, for reasons that no doubt made sense to someone at the time. In the absence of royal support, the censors won this argument.

Beyond these similarities, however, the two films couldn't be more different. *A Hard Day's Night* was a black-and-white semi-documentary film which told a story of fame, pressure and northern humour. *Goldfinger* was a colourful globe-trotting fantasy about gold, expensive sports cars and the fate of the world's economy. *A Hard Day's Night* depicted a now-lost post-war Britain of milk vending machines, smoking on trains and bombed-out churches. *Goldfinger* depicted a never-was fantasy of a Britain that was still saving the world, with America assisting as a junior partner. In the world of *Goldfinger*, a bowler hat was a lethal weapon to be feared. In *A Hard Day's Night*, a bowler hat was a sign of pompous authority that needed to be mocked.

The Beatles' first movie is a look at a day in the life of the band. In the opening shot John, George and Ringo are being chased down the street by a mob of screaming fans, accompanied by that extraordinary opening chord from the title song. George falls as he runs, and Ringo trips over him, much to the amusement of John. Neither are seriously hurt, and they pick themselves up and continue running, laughing as they go. This was not scripted or planned, but one of the many happy accidents that give the film its *cinema verité* style. It perfectly sets the mood for the rest of the film – full of energy, a hint of danger and a lot of laughter. The characters in *Goldfinger* do not smile in the way that people in *A Hard Day's Night* smile.

The two films differ in their attitude to wealth. *Goldfinger* is the story of one man's lust for gold, and the lengths he goes to for riches. The central villain is Auric Goldfinger, played by Gert Fröbe, a psychopathic businessman who ties Bond to a metal table and runs an industrial laser between his legs. 'This is gold, Mr Bond,' he explains, indicating the table. 'All my life I've been in love with its colour, its brilliance, its divine heaviness. I welcome any enterprise that will increase my stock.' This is a fetish that the film's designers and photographers shared, with gold costuming and an enormous gold-filled set for the inside of Fort Knox.

The colour of gold is used vividly throughout the film, and the metal is used to seduce, intrigue and kill. Bond gets the attention of Goldfinger during a round of golf when he drops a bar of Nazi gold onto the green just as Goldfinger is about to attempt a putt. Given the real-life history of Fröbe, this scene is loaded with meaning. Fröbe had joined the Nazi Party in 1929 at the age of sixteen, and fought as a German soldier during the war, but he left the party in 1937 and saved the lives of a pair of German Jews by hiding them from the Gestapo.

The audience's lust for gold was used by the film's marketing people to seduce them into the cinema. The film's poster, for example, showed a beautiful near-naked woman whose whole body was painted gold. As marketing went, it was highly successful. *A*

Hard Day's Night, in contrast, specifically rejects greed. The key sequence here is McCartney's 'Can't Buy Me Love', a song which dismisses wealth as being less important than emotional riches. 'Can't Buy Me Love' was released as a single and hit number one around the world. It sold 2 million singles in its first week of release in the USA, clocking up a million pre-orders in the UK alone.

In the song, McCartney claims that he doesn't care too much for money because it can't buy the things that truly matter. Money is a secondary concern in his worldview because it can only be used to obtain material objects. 'The premise stands, I think,' McCartney wrote in 2021 when he looked back at the song. 'Money can't buy you a happy family or friends you can trust.' The wealthy are not noted for their happiness, joy or love. It's an obvious point, of course, but in a culture then beginning to embrace conspicuous consumerism after the grim austerity post-war years, it was still one worth making. It took Ian Fleming until the last days of his life to understand it.

In the film, the 'Can't Buy Me Love' sequence is presented as liberation and freedom, as if realising what was more important than money was a transcendent moment. The Beatles had spent the day avoiding screaming fans, which meant they were cooped up on trains, in rehearsal halls or hotel rooms. All their attempts to have a drink, a dance or a bite to eat were thwarted by their manager. Suddenly, the band find a fire exit in a theatre and are able to escape into the outside world. 'We're out!' calls Ringo, as the song kicks in and the four friends run gleefully down the fire escape and play in the adjacent sports field. The sequence, with its jump cuts, handheld camerawork, helicopter shots and rapid edits to the beat of the music, is widely credited with inventing the modern music video. When the director Richard Lester was labelled as the father of MTV, however, he responded by asking for a paternity test.

For all that *A Hard Day's Night* portrays a very different face of British society to that depicted in the Bond films, there's a case to be made that both movies are set in the same cinematic universe. When we first encounter Bond at the start of his first film, *Dr. No*, he is playing the card game chemin de fer in the Le Cercle gaming rooms of the exclusive Les Ambassadeurs members club. It is here that a beautiful brunette in a red dress asks him his name and he pauses to snap his cigarette lighter closed as he answers. In *A Hard Day's Night*, Ringo also receives an invitation to Le Cercle, which attempts to entice him to visit by promising games of chemin de fer, baccarat and a champagne buffet.

Ringo's invite is confiscated by Paul's fictitious Irish grandfather, played by Wilfrid Brambell. Brambell was best known for playing the lead in the popular sitcom *Steptoe and Son*, where he was often described as a 'dirty old man'. In *A Hard Day's Night* he plays against type, and throughout the film characters remark on how clean he is. Being clean, he is able to pass himself off as an Irish lord when he visits Le Cercle, where he is able to spoof the Bond world by failing to read the social cues around him and calling out 'Bingo!' and 'Soufflé!' at inappropriate moments.

While playing chemin de fer in the club, Brambell attracts the attention of a beautiful society girl played by Margaret Nolan. This is the same actor who also played Dink, Bond's masseuse, in *Goldfinger*, and who was painted gold for the film's posters and opening titles. When she leans across the gambling table in her low-cut dress, Brambell's line 'I bet you're a great swimmer' seemed like it was mocking Bond's character. The joke is less apparent now, however, because that is exactly the sort of line Pierce Brosnan's Bond would say.

As *A Hard Day's Night* is partly set in Bond's world, it makes sense that the Beatles also exist in his universe. In *Goldfinger*, Bond declares himself to be anti-Beatles. The last thing he says to his latest sexual conquest – shortly before she is found dead, naked and covered in gold – is, 'My dear girl, there are some things that just aren't done, such as drinking Dom Perignon '53 above the temperature of thirty-eight degrees Fahrenheit. That's just as bad as listening to the Beatles without earmuffs.'

This now seems like a shocking lapse of taste by Bond. The character was supposed to know quality – he knew exactly which restaurant, tailor or brand of vermouth was the finest, and always insisted on having the very best for himself. But his mastery only extends to the material world, and music, along with the emotions it generates, are immaterial. Bond no more has good taste in music than he has an understanding of empathy or intimacy.

Outside of the world of fiction, Bond's anti-Beatles stance reflected the feelings of Fleming and the film producers. Cubby Broccoli and Harry Saltzman were not fans. They had originally been offered the chance to produce *A Hard Day's Night*, but chose to make a now-forgotten Bob Hope movie instead. As Saltzman asked Broccoli, 'Would you rather make a film with four long-haired schnooks from Liverpool who nobody's ever heard of, when we've got Bob Hope?' Fleming moved in circles where the Beatles were considered vulgar and working class. His friend Noël Coward had been quoted in the press as saying that they were 'totally devoid of talent', but this did not prevent him from feeling entitled to meet them after a concert in Rome. Coward caused a fuss when he was not initially granted an audience. McCartney eventually came out to smooth things over, but Coward still took the view that the Beatles were 'bad-mannered little shits'.

If we say that *A Hard Day's Night* and *Goldfinger* are set in the same world, then we can also imagine that the actor Richard Vernon, who also appears in both films, is playing the same person in both. In *Goldfinger*, he plays Colonel Smithers, an executive at the Bank of England, who briefs Bond on gold smuggling while complaining about his 'indifferent brandy'. In *A Hard Day's Night*, he is credited only as 'Man on Train' and so we can't say for certain that he is also Smithers, but he certainly looks and acts as if he is the same character. Sharing a cabin with the four young Beatles, he insists on having the window closed when they want it open, and is not persuaded by the democratic argument that there are four of them and only one of him. 'I fought a war for your sort,' he tells them, to which Ringo replies, 'I bet you're sorry you won.'

This is an exchange that perfectly captures the cultural divide that was then opening. The contrasting depictions of Vernon's character in these two films highlights the opposing arguments about how modern Britain should regard the old establishment. In 1964 the question as to whether the bowler-hatted Colonel Smithers was a person to respect, as in *Goldfinger*, or a person to mock, as in *A Hard Day's Night*, was one that the country was struggling to answer.

1965: IT WOULD TAKE TOO MUCH ELSE AWAY

In 1968, the novelist and screenwriter Hanif Kureishi was a thirteen-year-old student at an all-male comprehensive school on the border between London and Kent. It was here that he was told by his music teacher Mr Hogg that John Lennon and Paul McCartney did not write the Beatles' songs. The whole set-up, apparently, was a con. All that wonderful music had to have been written by others, most likely the more cultured Brian Epstein and George Martin. As to the question of whether the four Beatles were allowed to play on their records, Hogg thought it more likely that 'real' musicians were used instead.

It is easy now to scoff at Hogg's snobbery, but for many people with a privileged upbringing this was a logical position to take. People like Hogg had been taught from childhood that those who went to the right schools and came from better families were superior to those who didn't. This fact was so central to their worldview, and so wedded to the rest of their thinking, that any challenge to it was dangerous. If it was the case that talent, imagination, commitment and even genius were evenly spread throughout the population, and that the only thing which was localised in the children of the wealthy was opportunity, then the implications were too shocking to contemplate. It would imply that rather than being run by the brightest and the best, as many in positions of power claimed, the country was run by a small gang who were statistically likely to be mediocre. Great Britain would in fact be Lesser Britain if this were true, a country that failed to live up to its potential by some margin. To entertain this idea, therefore, put an entire worldview at risk – and there is nothing we unconsciously try to protect as much as our worldview. In circumstances like these it can be safer to cling to a conspiracy theory, because a small delusion is often the best way to protect a large one. As Kureishi later wrote, he 'began to see that to admit to the Beatles' genius would devastate Hogg. It would take too much else away with it.'

The arrival of the Beatles was a profound challenge to the British status quo. The Beatles hadn't gone to the right schools, and they were certainly not from the right families. They were northern, and they were not deferential. How was it possible that they were more talented songwriters than their social betters? It may seem like a trivial point, but the legitimacy of the British establishment hinged on the answer.

At first, it was easy enough to deny that they were talented. This was the approach that James Bond took in *Goldfinger*, when he mocked 'listening to the Beatles without earmuffs'. Given the energy of their early singles, it was possible to dismiss it as just noise, which only impacted on hormonal teenage girls. But this position became increasingly difficult to maintain as their song-writing matured, and by the time they were writing songs like 'Eleanor Rigby' or 'Yesterday' a different tactic was needed. It was at this point that Mr Hogg retreated into conspiracy theory – after all, if you deny that they wrote those songs, the problem simply goes away.

For all that their Liverpudlian cheek convinced the establishment that the Beatles were working class, such pigeon-holing wasn't quite accurate. Ringo was the most working class of the four and had little education, but the other three benefited hugely from the 1944 Education Act. A key part of the post-war progressive roadmap, the Act paved the way for bright children from less wealthy areas to attend more aspirational schools. It meant Paul and George were able to attend the Liverpool Institute, a highly respected grammar school. Lennon was the most middle class of the four, having been raised by his Aunt Mimi who lived in a detached home, Mendips, on Menlove Avenue, an area popular with doctors, accountants and other professionals. They still had to take in lodgers to make ends meet, so they were hardly wealthy, but Mimi certainly had social aspirations and in many ways was as much of a snob as Fleming.

For the southern establishment, however, the fact that one of the Beatles edged into the Liverpudlian lower middle class was irrelevant. Their accents alone were reason enough to patronise them. Lennon knew what it was like to be looked down upon. Attending an ambassador's reception and signing an autograph, Lennon was incensed when one upper-class aristocrat said loudly, 'Look, he can actually write!'

'There's always the guy in the bowler hat who hates what you're doing,' McCartney told the journalist John Harris in 2021. 'We always knew that there's the establishment, then there's the working people. And we were the working people. Working people tended to get us, and understand what we were doing. And occasionally, you would get the kind of snob who would get angry. In a way, that was part of the fun.'

The existence of the Beatles became a wild card in British

society which could be weaponised by a canny politician against the political establishment. This was the approach taken by the Labour leader Harold Wilson, who firmly and astutely positioned himself as pro-Beatle. The boys were an example of the more equal Britain he wanted to build, where talent could shine regardless of where it came from, and the country would no longer be limited by promoting well-bred mediocrities. According to the later Labour Prime Minister Gordon Brown, it was Wilson's adoption of the Beatles that led to his 1964 election victory.

Ahead of their performance in front of the Queen Mother at the 1963 Royal Variety Performance, the band were asked about comments by Ted Heath, who would shortly become leader of the Conservative Party. Heath had complained he couldn't understand a word the Beatles said. At first, Lennon played this for laughs, adopting an upper-class accent and replying, 'I can't understand Teddy saying that at all really.' He then looked down and muttered, in an almost threatening tone, 'We're not going to vote for Ted,' before turning and staring straight down the camera. It is one of those moments when you can see the political history of the country turn. This was also the Royal Variety Performance where Lennon had joked, 'Would the people in the cheaper seats clap your hands, and the rest of you if you'd just rattle your jewellery.' This was a relief for Brian Epstein, because earlier Lennon had told him he planned to say '... if you'd just rattle your fucking jewellery'.

When the Beatles were filming *Help!* in Twickenham Studios, Brian Epstein ushered them into a dressing room to give them some secret news. 'I've got some news for you – the Prime Minister and the Queen have awarded you an MBE.' McCartney's response – 'What's that?' – illustrates how little the British honours system meant to most British people at the time. It was a method of policing the establishment, and of little interest to most of the country.

People with backgrounds like the Beatles had not been given awards like MBEs before.

The Second World War veteran Richard Pape, who had been shot down close to the German/Dutch border and who was captured and escaped twice, returned his MBE in protest. He was quoted in *The Times* as saying that 'The Beatles' MBE reeks of mawkish, bizarre effrontery to our wartime endeavours.' Colonel Frederick Wagg, a veteran of both world wars, returned twelve military medals and declared, 'Decorating the Beatles makes a mockery of everything this country stands for. I've heard them sing and play and I think they're terrible.' Many others who had been honoured kept their medals but felt that the Beatles had devalued them. In his diary, Fleming's friend Noël Coward wrote that the decision to honour the Beatles, 'is, of course, a tactless and major blunder on the part of the Prime Minister. And also I don't think the Queen should have agreed. Some other decoration should have been selected to reward them for their talentless but considerable contributions to the Exchequer.'

The decision to honour the band was officially in recognition of their impact on British exports and the balance of trade. But it was also a profoundly political act by Harold Wilson. The Beatles represented Wilson's alternative vision of Britain, one which recognised talent and creativity wherever it arose, and which was not held back by old-school-tie patronage. This was why the establishment reacted so angrily to the honouring of the Beatles – whether they recognised it consciously or subconsciously, it was an attack on a status quo which suited them well.

Ian Fleming felt that he should have been honoured in some way. 'My contribution to the export drive is simply staggering,' he told an interviewer shortly before he died. 'They ought to give me some sort of medal. I suppose it's the equivalent of the earning power of a small boot factory.' But, unlike the Beatles, there was no political advantage to be gained from honouring Fleming. As if to show that he was unbothered by his lack of honours, Fleming wrote in his final novel, *The Man with the Golden Gun*, that Bond was offered a knighthood but turned it down.

The idea that popular public figures like pop musicians and sports stars receive medals in the British honours system is now considered uncontroversial. Indeed, the inclusion of a few famous faces is used to raise the profile of the system. Arguments against celebrity recipients of honours now claim that they are being used to lend legitimacy to an otherwise corrupt system, in which political donors are rewarded for financial gifts and politicians reward mediocre civil servants for their support. That the system awards medals in the name of the 'British Empire' is also an anachronism that has caused many people to refuse theirs, including the writer Benjamin Zephaniah. In 1965, however, such implications for accepting honours were not yet in focus. As Ringo saw it, 'We're going to meet the Queen and she's going to give us a badge – I thought, "This is cool!" '

At the time, the idea of a trip to the palace delighted the Beatles, including Lennon, although he would later have a change of heart and return his MBE. Having experience of extreme fame and adulation, he wondered whether the Queen and the rest of the royal family genuinely believed that they were in some way special and different from other people. 'Imagine being brought up like that for 2,000 years! It must be pretty freaky. They must have a hard time trying to be human beings. I don't know if any of them ever make it, because I don't know much about them, but you feel sorry for people like that, because it's like us – only worse. If they believe they are royal, that's the joke.'

Lennon saw that the class system was basically absurd and therefore easy to dismiss outright. His Aunt Mimi had tried to impart her essential snobbery to him as a child, but he had reacted against it. His attitude was different to that of the ambitious McCartney – the Beatle most likely to mix with wealthy people. In his pre-fame days, McCartney had had little contact with higher social groups, but thanks to Beatlemania he now had access to these strange areas of society. As he would later explain, the McCartney family 'always thought of ourselves as posh working class. It's a mental attitude. Our attitude was posh. We aspire to do better in every department.' Paul was always curious and looking to learn something new.

McCartney's interest in privilege may also have been a subconscious desire to please his late mother. Mary McCartney had always worked hard and wanted the family to better themselves. Her attitude, coupled with her early death, led to a regret that Paul carried for decades. 'There's one moment that I've regretted all my life which is a strange little awkwardness for me,' he has said. 'There was one time when she said "ask" and she pronounced it posh. And I made fun of her and it slightly embarrassed her. Years later I've never forgiven myself. It's a terrible little thing. I wish I could go back and say, "I was only kidding, Mum."'

For all that McCartney was open to people from the establishment, he was not blind to their faults. It is telling that when he was raising his children in the 1970s, he did not send them to private schools, even though he could easily have afforded to. He had seen how such people turn out, and he didn't want his children to grow up limited by the particular view of the world common to those given a British non-state school education.

Prior to the Beatles, adopting the voice, attitudes and social signals of the upper classes was seen as a necessary way to advance in British society. Some of those who adopted these affectations were some of the class system's most strident defenders, such as our friend the anti-Beatle Noël Coward, who came from a much poorer background than he let on. Hereditary status rather than hard work was seen as the source of quality and worth. Newly rich industrialists and merchants would go to great lengths acquiring coats of arms and exploring family trees, in the hope that they could discover ancient links to the aristocracy. It is an irony that Mr Hogg believed that George Martin must have written the Beatles' material, because Martin also came from a relatively working-class north London background, and consciously adopted the accent and manners of his social 'betters' in order to get on. It is possible that his real background was why he was able to connect with the Beatles and decided to work with them, while staff at rival record companies turned them down.

Since the Beatles, all this has changed. Even the aristocracy themselves now insist that they got to where they are in life through hard work. In a 2021 study in the journal *Sociology*, it was reported that people are now more likely to downplay inherited privileges and overstress the extent to which they are self-made. '47 per cent of those in "middle-class" professional and managerial occupations identify as working class,' the report claims; 24 per cent of people doing middle-class jobs, and who also had middle-class parents, also claimed to be working class, thanks to family stories of less-privileged grandparents. Social legitimacy now stems from earning your place in society, and the privileges that come from being born into the right families are seen as detracting from this. This is clearly a very different world to the Britain in which the Beatles arrived, but it is exactly what Harold Wilson hoped to achieve when he gave John, Paul, George and Ringo their MBEs.

In 1969, the band played their final gig on the roof of their office building in Savile Row, London. This was in the heart of the exclusive Mayfair area of central London – the most expensive property on a UK Monopoly board, and a location that symbolised wealth and privilege. The well-heeled City gents in the streets craned their necks up to the sky to try and work out what this music was, and where it was coming from. Something strange and uninvited had appeared above them. This was not a situation they were used to. Despite complaints to the police, they proved unable to get it to stop. It was a scenario that neatly symbolised the impact of the Beatles on the British establishment.

1965: NOT AS GOOD AS JAMES BOND

In the wake of the success of *A Hard Day's Night*, the Beatles were interviewed during a trip to Liverpool in November 1964 about their ambitions.

> INTERVIEWER: Have you got any future in mind now? Any other ambitions?
>
> JOHN: Don't know . . . like to make more films, I think. We'd all like to do that because it's good fun, you know. It's hard work, but you can have a good laugh in films.
>
> INTERVIEWER: What about you, Ringo?
>
> RINGO: Same. I enjoy films.
>
> PAUL: Well, I think, you know, all of us want to do, sort of . . . a good film. One that we all think is good. And make more good records.
>
> GEORGE: Don't you think this one's any good, then?
>
> PAUL: Well, it's okay, you know what I mean.
>
> JOHN: It's not as good as James Bond though, is it?
>
> PAUL: Oh, not as good as James Bond.

Such was the spell that James Bond had cast over the world – not even the Beatles were immune. By 1965, it seemed as if they were living the perfect life. They had money, adulation and global fame, which they earned themselves doing what they loved, rather than having it handed to them through family connections. Every door was open to them, and everyone wanted to know them. They had come from nothing, and so they truly appreciated the fast cars and other luxuries that those raised in privilege took for granted. Perhaps best of all, they also had each other – the most fun gang going. What could be better than being a Beatle in the mid-1960s? But everyone needs a dream to aspire to. Everyone needs a fantasy about a better life to orient themselves by and to push them forward. The one seductive fantasy that the Beatles had not already made reality was being James Bond. It is perhaps unsurprising, given this context, that for their second film the Beatles put themselves into what was essentially a Bond movie, but with songs. That these four young men living such a desirable life still dreamed of being James Bond reveals the extent to which Bond was seen as the pinnacle of masculine wish-fulfilment in the Western world.

A Hard Day's Night had been a black-and-white documentary-style account of a day in the life of the band in a recognisable post-war England. In contrast, *Help!* was a full-colour globe-trotting adventure that aped the world and the logic of the Bond movies. It featured ski chases in the Alps, tanks, an airship, and scenes set in the Bahamas for tax rather than plot reasons. It included gadgets such as a flamethrower umbrella and an exploding baseball, along with realistic facial-mask disguises which the TV series *Mission: Impossible* would copy extensively when it appeared the following year. At one point the band play the game curling, in a scene that prefigures an almost identical one in *On Her Majesty's Secret Service*, released four years later. The Beatles' version is arguably the more

Bondian of the two, however, because the polished granite stone that George slides across the ice contains a bomb.

The most Bond-like scene takes place in the Bahamas, and features a captured Ringo being driven away in the boot of a bright-pink Hillman Super Minx car. George runs after the car and jumps onto the back, clinging to the roof and boot of the vehicle as it makes its escape. George visibly did this dangerous stunt for real, with no safety harness or stuntman training, and his extreme calm and cocky confidence is incredibly Bond-like. In particular, the casual way he climbs up into the branches of the tree that the car eventually crashes into suggests that, had he not been a guitarist, he would have been a natural in the circus.

The US soundtrack album doesn't start with the song 'Help!' as the UK version did. It begins instead with a short uncredited instrumental clearly based on the Bond theme. This even featured Vic Flick on guitar, the musician who had played the distinctive riff in the original version of the Bond theme. It was uncredited on the sleeve notes and ran straight into the first credited song 'Help!' American fans who knew the song from the album thought that the Bond theme was part of it.

A longer version of this Bond theme appeared about ten minutes into *Help!*, when the villains are about to chase the departing Beatles in a van. This vehicle had a few modifications of its own, just like Bond's Aston Martin, including a headlamp that, on the press of a switch, scattered nails over the road. The joke here was that this was on the front of the van, rather than the back, so that the villains then drove over the nails themselves.

It wasn't just onscreen that the band enjoyed playing at Bond. When Paul bought a London townhouse in Cavendish Avenue near Abbey Road studios, he had it kitted out with lots of James Bond-style gadgets such as a concealed movie screen that descended from the top of a fitted bookcase. These, unfortunately, didn't tend to work as well as he had hoped. 'I had electric curtains upstairs in the bedroom, but they were like a Hornby double-O train set, not at all like James Bond which it was supposed to be,' McCartney has said.

Five days after the premiere of *Goldfinger*, McCartney became the proud owner of an Aston Martin, just like Bond's famous DB5. 'I'd seen the first James Bond film and was quite impressed by the car,' he recalled. For someone who grew up in a family that couldn't afford a car, this was quite an entry into motoring. McCartney's Aston Martin also had a unique gadget of its own – a Philips Auto-Mignon in-car record player. This was the car McCartney was driving when he started composing the song 'Hey Jude', when he went to visit Julian Lennon after Cynthia and John's divorce. There is a photograph, taken by Linda McCartney, of Paul sat in this parked car with his guitar as he was writing 'Two of Us'. In 2017, McCartney's Aston Martin was sold at auction for £1,345,500.

For a holiday in November 1966, McCartney decided to escape from the pressures of Beatlemania by the very Bondian means of driving his Aston Martin around France while wearing a disguise. McCartney was so famous in France that, in 1967, he didn't bother taking his passport when he went there, confident that they would let him in anyway. To avoid being recognised on his 1966 trip, he slicked his hair back with Vaseline and wore a long blue overcoat, glasses, and a fake moustache. This was made by Wig Creations, the film cosmetics company who worked on *A Hard Day's Night*, and it perfectly matched his own hair. He soon got bored of being a mysterious stranger, however. After being refused entry into a nightclub he realised that he liked being recognised and the opportunities this offered. He went back to his hotel, removed the disguise, and returned to the club as Paul McCartney. Still, the experience of being a Beatle in disguise inspired the Beatles to pretend to be *Sgt. Pepper's Lonely Hearts Club Band* the following year.

The film *Help!*, it is probably fair to say, is not quite as loved by Beatles aficionados as their other films. On paper, it seems like it should be. The drastic change from the black-and-white *cinema verité* of their first film to the globetrotting glamour of their second is a quintessentially Beatle-ish leap to make – they were never for repeating themselves and were always trying to do something new. The pop-art colourful comedy that resulted was hugely influential and provided the blueprints for *The Monkees* television series that followed. The problem was, however, that it just wasn't quite as funny as it should have been.

While *A Hard Day's Night* was set in the real world and the *Yellow Submarine* and *Magical Mystery Tour* films were set in a world of the Beatles' imagination, *Help!* was set in a parody of the cinematic world of Bond movies. The band didn't really belong in that world, or even a comedy spoof of it. Here the Beatles could only be light entertainers, rather than epoch-shaking agents of cultural change. This is not to say that the world of light entertainment or surreal comedy were not important parts of the Beatles' DNA, of course. Lennon had published two volumes of surreal jokes and nonsense stories, *In His Own Write* (1964) and *A Spaniard in the Works* (1965), with Ian Fleming's publisher Jonathan Cape. These were inspired by his love of the Goons and Edward Lear. Even their gritty realist film *A Hard Day's Night* is remembered for how funny it was. It's telling that there are more memorable lines in *A Hard Day's Night* – 'He's very clean', 'She looks more like him than I do', 'Turn left at Greenland' – than there are in *Help!* The latter film managed to be daft, but it never quite reached the Beatle-esque heights of being genuinely silly. The Beatles had wanted to be in a Bond film because that was the ultimate male fantasy our culture offered up, but when they did this it proved to be limiting and less thrilling than they had hoped. Britain's pinnacle of wish-fulfilment was okay, but surely they should be coming up with something better?

The Beatles were on the verge of an unpredictable metamorphosis. They had, by this point, achieved all that they had ever dreamed of. In a few short years they had gone from what McCartney called a 'good little rock 'n' roll group' to being the most famous band on the planet. They were on their way to becoming the best-selling group in history, as every record they released shot to number one around the world. They had grown too big for the British music industry and its tours of regional theatre. They had conquered America in a way no foreign band have ever done – at one point, Beatles records occupied every spot in the top five of the US singles chart. Three months after *Help!* was released they were awarded honours by the Queen at Buckingham Palace. Where could a 'good little rock 'n' roll band' go from there? They had reached the peak, and there was no known career path from this point on. Surely all they could hope to do was sustain their success for as long as possible, before the inevitable decline began.

Of course, that is not what happened. In 1965, the idea that there was more that they could achieve seemed ludicrous. With hindsight, we know they were only just beginning. The artistic triumphs that would follow would dwarf their earlier work. No one could predict what they would be, of course, because there was no precedent for their journey from this point on. They had left the edge of the map. The Beatles would now have to invent the territory they travelled over.

1965: GREATER THAN THE SUM OF THEIR PARTS

When the playwright Joe Orton was asked to write a screenplay for a Beatles film, he treated the band as essentially one person. They stood at the altar together as all four of them married the same woman, and they were all shown lying in bed together with their new wife on their honeymoon. Orton's screenplay may have been deeply misogynistic and rejected by Brian Epstein, but his choice to depict the Fab Four as one person was insightful. As George Martin noted, 'The significant thing about them is they are unified. The four of them are really one person, almost.' The early, touring Beatles, according to Mick Jagger, were a 'four-headed monster'. They were friends who chose to hang out with each other after hours, to an extent that other musicians found unusual. They spent so much time together that they would finish each other's sentences, having an almost telepathic rapport. The hundreds of hours spent slogging away on the Hamburg stage had blended John, Paul and George's voices into an extraordinary harmony, and the arrival of Ringo had grounded them into a solid, unarguable unit. For all their distinct personalities, the four Beatles were effectively a gestalt entity. This was one of the reasons why they so perfectly represented *Eros*, or the Freudian drive to lose your limited self and become part of something larger.

In the decades after the band split, much debate occurred about why they were so special, with the assumption being that the answer must lie with one of the four. In the seventies and eighties, many rock critics took the view that John Lennon was the special ingredient which explained the extraordinary impact of the Beatles. Thinking like this was entirely in keeping with the individualism of the second half of the twentieth century. But as a framework, individualism was always too limited a perspective to understand something as interesting as the Beatles. It was the combination of those four personalities which made the Beatles greater than the sum of their parts. They were, in occult terms, a combination of the four alchemical elements. Ringo was earth, John was fire, Paul was air and George was water. Combined, they produced the fifth, transcendent element: spirit. Or alternatively, Ringo had a big nose, George had big ears, Paul had big eyes and John was always a big mouth. As individuals these attributes may be unfortunate, but when they are combined you get the face of a giant.

And then Paul McCartney wrote 'Yesterday'.

This is, of course, one of the most covered songs in history. The melody famously came to McCartney fully formed during a dream, a gift from his subconscious that would change his life forever. It elevated him from being part of his 'good little rock 'n' roll band' to becoming the author of the front page of the twentieth century's songbook. Even half a century after it was written, it's impossible to grow up in the West and not know this song. It hinted at the scale of the new territory that the Beatles would now occupy. But it also hinted at the cost.

Before 'Yesterday', the Beatles were a unit. Lennon and

McCartney had previously written songs alone, without the insights and finishing touches of their partner. But this was the first solo song that didn't need the other three Beatles. Instead, it was recorded in two takes with Paul alone, playing acoustic guitar and singing, and George Martin added a string quartet three days later. On the same day that McCartney recorded 'Yesterday', the full band also recorded two more of Paul's songs, the larynx-shredding rocker 'I'm Down' and the acoustic folk rock 'I've Just Seen a Face' – an example not just of the phenomenal work rate that the band operated at, but the variety of styles of both singing and songwriting that McCartney was capable of.

The solo nature of the song clearly troubled the band; here was a situation that they had never had to deal with before. It is striking that, uncomfortable with such a solo effort being credited to the Beatles, they didn't release the song as a single in the UK. It's hard to imagine any other band writing a song as strong and commercial as 'Yesterday', then only using it as filler on the second side of a film soundtrack album.

What 'Yesterday' showed was that new horizons for the band's music were imaginable. It was not that they had plateaued and were on the way down, it was more that they had barely started. If they were to reach those new artistic peaks it would require the four Beatles to grow and evolve as individuals. They could not remain loveable mop-tops forever. But if the four of them were to change in unexpected and unpredictable ways, then how could they be expected to fit together so neatly into the perfect unit that won the hearts of the world? The future was unparalleled creative growth, yet as the melancholic mood of 'Yesterday' realised, it would come at a cost.

'Yesterday' is a song about realising that something special has changed and wishing to go back in time to how things used to be. The Beatles were going to mature into four extraordinary individuals who would offer the world so much more than the pre-'Yesterday' Fab Four. For all four musicians, their greatest work was ahead of them. But there is a reason why many children fear growing up. The arrival of the future, after all, must mean the death of the past. To evolve and fulfil their potential would mean allowing fractures to grow in the best gang imaginable.

1965: THE THINGS I DO FOR ENGLAND

For all that James Bond and the Beatles are both English and, in theory, products of the same culture, they often appear to be quite alien to each other. One area in which this difference is evident is that great British pastime, drinking cups of tea. This was something that Bond was adamantly against. When a woman working in a British Intelligence canteen brings him a cup of tea in the novel *Goldfinger*, Bond 'looked at her severely' and declared, 'I don't drink tea. I hate it. It's mud. Moreover, it's one of the main reasons for the downfall of the British Empire. Be a good girl and make me some coffee.' In *Thunderball*, Fleming reiterates the point when he writes, 'Bond loathed and despised tea, that flat, soft, time-wasting opium of the masses.' The extent to which Bond felt threatened by a cup of tea is quite startling.

The Beatles, in contrast, drank endless cups of tea, especially when they were working in the studio. They drank so much of the stuff that there is now a popular Twitter account and fanzine called the Teatles, which is dedicated to photos of the band in which cups of tea are visible. When the docuseries *The Beatles: Get Back* was streamed on Disney+, it was promoted on Instagram with a montage of clips of the band drinking tea, which was entitled 'Let It Tea'. Following the series, a pair of brown, white and black striped period mugs like the ones the Beatles drank from sold for £305.50 on eBay, plus £3.20 postage.

Another area of cultural difference which divides Bond and the Beatles is the subject of football. While the Beatles were not overly interested in the game, they clearly belonged to a world where it was accepted as important. Lennon namechecks Sir Matt Busby on 'Dig It', for example, while Liverpool's Albert Stubbins appears on the cover of *Sgt. Pepper's Lonely Hearts Club Band*. The band sent a telegram to Liverpool manager Bill Shankly, ahead of the 1965 FA Cup final, which read, 'Best of luck, lads, we'll be watching on the telly. John, Paul, George and Ringo.' The designs of the 'red' and 'blue' greatest hits compilations are believed to reference the colours of the two main Merseyside clubs, Liverpool and Everton. When the Beatles act like cheeky kids in *A Hard Day's Night* and knock on the train window shouting, 'Hey, mister, can we have our ball back?' it feels entirely in character.

Football, in contrast, is absent from the world of James Bond. It's not that Bond has no interest in sport – golf, horse racing and skiing all feature in Fleming's novels and the subsequent films. But these are all, notably, single-player sports. Bond seeks glory for himself, not as something to be shared with a team. They are also all sports that are expensive to play. It helps the elite maintain their belief in their own superiority if they play sports where they don't have to compete with the working class.

For all that the Beatles and James Bond are both British, and specifically English, subjects like tea and football emphasise how they seem to come from two entirely different places. This is confusing, especially as England is such an integral part of both Bond and the Beatles that they have both shaped how the country is seen in the eyes of the world. It forces us to take seriously the idea that the country of England, and what the establishment calls 'England', are two different things. As the novelist and historian James Hawes explains, 'When [the rulers of England] said *England* they didn't actually mean the whole country at all. They meant Imperial HQ, a network of exclusive southern spaces: the great public schools, Oxbridge, country houses, the right parts of London and the Home Counties, Lords, Henley, Cowes, the Inns of Court, Parliament, the Guards, St James's, and so on. Their England was a South of the mind, a vision, as unconnected to any real place as the RP accent in which they all spoke.' This is very much the 'England' of James Bond.

From this perspective, places like the Kop at Anfield, Newcastle's Bigg Market or the Blackpool Illuminations are something other than 'England' as the establishment used the word – they were parts of a 'non-England' that was usually all but invisible to much of the ruling class. But the arrival of the Beatles from this non-England complicated matters, because they made it harder to ignore. As the *Herald-Tribune* dismissed the band, they were 'a magic act that owed less to Britain than to Barnum'. How could it be that these four lads from northern England were not considered to be sufficiently English, or even British? If they weren't from 'England', then where were they from?

It would seem crazy not to call the football-loving, tea-drinking land that the Beatles came from 'England'. It is, after all, the society which the great majority of people who live in geographical England recognise. But if that is the 'real' England, then what is the strange place that the establishment also call 'England', the society that gave birth to James Bond? This is a network of great wealth which was established nearly a thousand years ago, when William the Bastard of Normandy defeated King Harold at Hastings and claimed this newly conquered land for himself. He then distributed that land among the Norman barons who assisted him. This pattern of ownership of the country has remained amazingly consistent over the centuries. Even today a third of the UK is still owned by just 1,200 aristocrats and their families. Gerald Grosvenor was the sixth Duke of Westminster and one of the richest people, and largest landowners, in the country. When asked to give advice to young entrepreneurs, he replied, 'Make sure they have an ancestor who was a very close friend of William the Conqueror.'

An accurate term to describe this particular 'England', then, would be to call it the Norman Continuity Empire. This is not bound by geography in the way that the Beatles' England is. The reason that its base is in southern England is a quirk of history – it lost its preferred lands in Aquitaine and southern France during the medieval period.

The Norman Continuity Empire speaks with an invented accent which its members can use to identify each other, and which its children are taught at special schools. This is called Received Pronunciation, or RP. When the BBC was established in 1922, it promoted the RP accent as the one 'true' standard British accent, the 'Queen's English'. This encouraged many, including George Martin, to drop their natural English accents and adopt the voice of the establishment. *Doctor Who* in the 1970s, for example, starred Tom Baker and Elizabeth Sladen. They were both from Liverpool, but you would never have known it from listening to them. In order to find work as actors, they had had to drop their natural Scouse accents and speak with an RP accent.

RP is pointedly not one of the many and varied geographic English accents, such as Cornish, Scouse or Geordie. Although it is most common in the wealthier parts of southern England, it is not a natural geographic southern accent, like the Sussex or Cockney accents. At the height of the British Empire, it was as likely to be heard and taught in colonial outposts around the globe as it was in England. Indeed, the disconnect from physical England that it emphasised was an important part of the psychology of the British Empire. To the English establishment of the early 1960s, Ian Fleming's home Goldeneye on the north shore of Jamaica was seen as 'England', as were many imperial outposts around the globe. This is why Anthony Eden chose to recover there, rather than in any Jamaican-owned villa or hotel.

Concentrations of wealth are not automatically bad things. They are necessary for humanity to create its greatest achievements, such as the construction of cathedrals like Notre-Dame, landing a man on the moon, or the great medical breakthroughs achieved in treating a disease like AIDS. Great wealth can fund orchestras and support the artists whose work now hangs in the Louvre, just as it can build the Louvre itself. Often, however, great wealth is held by people who lack the imagination or empathy to know how to use it. Some of these people are so uninspired that all they can think to do, when they possess more money than they could ever use, is to try and make more. Typically, it does not occur to them to be embarrassed by this. Then there are the situations in which concentrations of wealth are actively harmful to a country. When a system designed to protect concentrations of wealth actively prevents talented, hard-working and creative people across the land from working for the good of the country, and places privileged but clearly mediocre people in important positions instead, the result is a dysfunctional dark comedy.

Immense concentrations of wealth are not natural. In time, you would expect them to dissipate, allowing the country's wealth to flow around the economy. To maintain concentrations of wealth for a thousand years or more requires laws and a system designed to do exactly that. As we will see later, this is a situation that Russian oligarchs, who obtained the bulk of their nation's wealth following the collapse of the Soviet Union, are now having to grapple with.

Early attempts to maintain concentrations of wealth are

usually unsophisticated, and focus on fear, threats and violence. The Harrying of the North – King William's campaign of looting, widespread slaughter and the burning of crops and villages in northern England around the year 1070 – is one example. In time, however, subtler methods of control appear, not least the control of government, law and the media. Our newspapers are extremely skilled at identifying and neutralising any politician who looks like a threat to established concentrations of wealth.

An important part of this process is the construction of a story which justifies those fortunes as in some way good or necessary. In the maintenance of this story, James Bond quickly became a most important foot soldier. In the film *You Only Live Twice*, Sean Connery mutters, 'The things I do for England,' after he is interrogated, and then seduced, by the SPECTRE agent Helga Brandt. It is clear which England he is referring to here. In this context, the fact that he says that line in a Scottish accent no longer seems odd. The 'England' that employs him is not the geographic country but the establishment, and like a good foot soldier he risks his life to maintain the status quo. It can be helpful to think of the Norman Continuity Empire as a cuckoo placed in the nest of physical England, claiming an outsized share of resources compared to the smaller chicks who hatched there. A metaphor like this is interesting in the light of the Bond films *Spectre* and *No Time to Die*, in which Bond is directly identified as a 'cuckoo' by Blofeld.

It is here that we see why the Norman Continuity Empire calls itself 'England'. As Guy Debord argued in *The Society of the Spectacle*, 'The more powerful the class, the more it claims not to exist.' Nothing neutralises a threat more than claiming it and the opposing force are one and the same. In this confusion we find much of the reason for the crisis of English identity. There is evidence of this in George Orwell's classic 1941 essay 'England Your England', where he wrote, 'England is perhaps the only great country whose intellectuals are ashamed of their own nationality.' Here the intellectuals are confused by who it is they are against, because they all share the same name. This linguistic sleight of hand has been of great benefit to the establishment.

When we cheer on Bond, and fantasise about living his life, we too unconsciously find ourselves supporting the powers that be. Bond casts a glamour over us, in the archaic sense of the word. The spell was massively weakened, however, by the arrival of the Beatles, whose very existence was a reminder that the 'England' that Bond fought for was something very different to the place where we lived and raised our families. This other England of the Beatles was far more relatable, and fun. Once you grasped that 'England' had two meanings, it was not difficult to decide where your allegiance lay.

When people sent back their honours in protest at Harold Wilson's promotion of the Beatles, they were probably right to do so. The Beatles were indeed a threat to the system. But as McCartney described the situation, 'It didn't worry me that the Empire was crumbling. I thought it was a good thing. I was very pleased to see that old regime get out.'

1967: WHAT DID HE WANT TO COMMUNICATE?

In October 1957, the earth gained its first man-made satellite. Sputnik 1 was a strangely elegant creation. It consisted of a round, shiny, silver ball trailing four long wires, like a metal jellyfish drifting in an expanse far larger and emptier than any earthbound ocean. For all its huge technological and political importance, however, it didn't actually do much. The ball contained a small radio transmitter that rhythmically pulsed on two separate frequencies, and not much else. This was enough, however, to announce the Russian achievement to the world. It caused fear in ordinary Americans, who could tune their home radios and hear evidence of the Soviet presence in the heavens above. Fear of the threat posed by this unnatural new technology was enough to inspire many James Bond adventures. There have been six Bond films with plots based around the danger of satellites.

Technology moved quickly, and ten years later the Earth was ringed with satellites that could do far more than just go 'bip'. A string of communication satellites orbited the planet, capable of sending and receiving television signals. This meant that people around the world could, for the first time, watch the same thing simultaneously. To prove it, the first global television broadcast was produced in 1967, a 2½-hour programme called *Our World*. It featured contributions from fourteen countries and was witnessed by an estimated audience of up to 700 million people.

A great deal of effort was spent keeping politics out of the programme. Each country was told that their segments could not be political or include politicians or heads of state. Russia pulled out four days before broadcast. But although politics were out, most countries would still use their segments to promote themselves to the world in ways that were traditional and nationalistic. Numerous sequences were included about national and sporting achievements, and lots of traditional costumes and culture were on display. The programme certainly had its moments – Spain's segment showed Pablo Picasso at work – but most of it was serious and dry, or at least it appears that way to modern eyes. It is remembered now mainly because of what happened when it cut to London.

By this point the Beatles had stopped touring the world due to the grinding pressures involved and the realisation that, in an era before modern PA systems had been developed, no one in the immense screaming crowds could hear what they were playing. Brian Epstein needed to find new ways to keep promoting his band on the global stage, so he had been delighted when the BBC asked if the Beatles would feature in the British segment of this historic broadcast. *Our World*, he realised, offered a cutting-edge opportunity to play to people in every country at the same time, without ever leaving London.

John and Paul both tried to write a song especially for the broadcast, but John came up with the goods first. He wanted to write something simple and immediate enough to connect with all cultures and nationalities, most of whom did not use English as their first language. In this, his experience writing those early Beatles singles which went straight into the hearts of their teenage audience was invaluable. The question was, however, what did he want to communicate? If you had one chance to express one idea to the whole of the planet, what would *you* say?

When the Beatles had stopped gigging in 1966, John and Paul reacted to their newfound freedom in opposite but complementary ways. McCartney lived in central London, and he was always attending events, art exhibitions and counterculture happenings. Constantly on the hunt for new ideas, he discovered *avant garde* experiments like tape loops, minimalism and the cut-up techniques of William Burroughs and Brion Gysin. He brought these new ideas back to the Beatles, so they could play with them in the studio. But while McCartney was always going out, Lennon, in contrast, stayed in his big house in the Surrey countryside, and he turned inwards. His productivity dropped, and a certain lethargy became noticeable in his songs, such as 'I'm Only Sleeping'.

After Lennon discovered the psychedelic drug LSD his intake quickly became excessive and unwise, especially for a person with considerable childhood trauma, and it led to him becoming distant from his wife Cynthia. As she recalled, 'When John was tripping I felt as if I was living with a stranger. He would be distant, so spaced-out that he couldn't talk to me coherently. I hated that, and I hated the fact that LSD was pulling him away from me. I wouldn't take it with him so he found others who would.' It was clear, however, that Lennon was finding something of value in the state of mind that the drug gave him. This caused him to continue his internal explorations despite the divide this opened up with his wife and child.

From the evidence of his work, it seems that this something was a state of mind that religious and spiritual writers have been attempting to describe for centuries. This state is the moment when all your cares and worries fall away, and the world is revealed to be exactly right and correct. Everything is what it is supposed to be, and there is nothing that you need to do, except witness it. It is the realisation that – as Lennon wrote in his lyrics – there is nowhere you can be that isn't where you're meant to be. In this state there is no guilt or shame or anxiety – all that has been transcended. Everything is right, everything is blessed, and nothing hurts. This state has been given many different names over the centuries. William Blake called it 'Beulah' and Timothy Leary called it the 'neurosomatic' level. In Hinduism, it is the state of mind experienced after a kundalini awakening. In the Christian West, it is more usually referred to as grace. For those who have experience of it, there is no question that if there was only one thing you could communicate to the world, it would be confirmation that this state is real and available to all.

In those different traditions there has been much debate about the extent to which this state arrives unbidden, like an obligation-free gift from the cosmos, or whether it needs to be earned. William Blake believed that it could be earned by creative work and by engaging with the imagination, and this appears to be the case for Paul McCartney as well. 'The creative moment when you come up with the idea is the greatest, it's the best. It's like sex. You're filled with the knowledge that you're right,' he has said. His description of what inspiration feels like is strikingly similar to that of a classic kundalini experience: 'It's a very warm feeling that comes all over you, and for some reason it comes from the spine, through the cranium and out of the mouth.' Regardless of how this state of mind is achieved, there is agreement on what it is like to experience. As Lennon wrote, it's easy – there is no struggle or difficulty involved. All you need to do is to be open enough to allow it to happen.

In his song, Lennon described what experiencing this state

was like as simply and immediately as he could: 'All You Need Is Love'. Here Lennon is using the word 'Love' to refer to something more than the romantic love of one person for their partner. He is referring to what Christians call *agape*, a Greek word for the highest form of love – a universal, unconditional love for all, such as that felt by God for man and by man for God. That was the message that Lennon, when put on the spot, offered to the world – an assurance that he knew first-hand that grace was real. And indeed, what other message was more important? What else did the world need to hear?

Eighteen months later, during the *Get Back* sessions in January 1969, Lennon would think back to this moment of global communication as a reason for both him and the band to continue. 'I've decided, all the things that we do ... the whole point of it is communication. And to be on TV is communication because we've got a chance to smile at people, like "All You Need Is Love". So that's my incentive for doing it,' he said. 'If we need to think of any incentive, the incentive is to communicate.' The ability to communicate an idea like this, then, was the reason John continued to be a Beatle. The Beatles had found the dream of being James Bond unsatisfying, but they had found a far worthier goal. They were exploring emotional territory far beyond anything Fleming or Bond was familiar with.

Lennon was astute enough to know that, by communicating so simply and directly, he would be misunderstood by overly rational and intelligent people. The Cambridge-educated author Ian Macdonald, for example, described this era-defining number-one single as 'wilfully substandard work' and thought that Lennon's lyric 'shows the rot setting in'. In his mind, the refrain 'it's easy' was 'half-ingenuous, half-sarcastic'. Macdonald did not entertain the idea that it might be true.

Lennon knew that the song would go over the heads of

intellectuals who had a worldview which denied the possibility of transcendence. To counter this, he made a point of explaining how the song's title had a double meaning. On the one hand, the phrase 'All You Need Is Love' suggests that love is the only important thing. This was an interpretation that he knew overly literal critics would take issue with, claiming that you need other things as well such as food, shelter and money. For those critics, the second meaning kicked in. These were people who are smart, sophisticated and proud of their intellect. They almost have it all, but they are missing something important – all they need is love.

Lennon explained this double meaning to the highly respected Beatles biographer Hunter Davies. He was listed on Abbey Road paperwork as being present at the recording and singing in the chorus, but has no memory of this – perhaps the most perfectly sixties anecdote there is. Davies dutifully recorded Lennon's explanation of the title's double meaning, but it's not clear he really understood what John was trying to tell him. His attempts to apply a rational analysis to a description of transcendence resulted in him struggling to grasp the meaning of the lyrics. 'Is it true there's nothing you can make that can't be made?' he wrote. 'Science is continually discovering things we didn't know – though I suppose you could say that God knew about them all the time, being awfully clever.' Beyond the cleverness of journalists, however, the song's message was readily understood, as Lennon knew it would be. The single reached number one in eleven countries and sold over a million copies in the USA alone. The time of its release is now widely known as the 'Summer of Love'.

As we've noted, the love that the 1967 Beatles sang about to the world was something more than the love of their earlier boy-meets-girl songs. That love was an expansion of a person's sense of identity to include one other person. In romantic love like this, that other person is considered to have become an aspect of their partner, so that separation or loss can be almost physically painful. The lover discards their identity as an isolated individual and starts to think of themselves as part of a couple. The type of love Lennon was singing about took this idea further. This love goes from no longer seeing a division between the self and a partner to no longer seeing a division between the self and the wider universe. At a moment like that, when the heart is open, it is possible to experience love without measure. When the surviving Beatles look back at their work with hindsight, they single this idea out as the core message of what they did.

From a Bondian perspective, however, to allow yourself to be open like this is to lower your guard and risk being hurt. It makes you vulnerable. It requires you to see the world as overwhelmingly accepting, rather than malevolent. In the Daniel Craig Bond films, and several Fleming novels, Bond makes the mistake of opening himself to another, only to be betrayed. At this point, his psychological armour returns and Bond closes himself off, afraid of ever making the same mistake again. To the rational mind this is logical and sensible, but it condemns you to live in a smaller, colder world. And what, exactly, is worth fighting for in a world like that?

This aspect of the Beatles was a counterweight to the prevailing trend of the late twentieth century, which was concerned with growing individualism. The primacy of the individual was preached by 1960s hippies, 1970s punks, 1980s Thatcherites and 1990s Blairite Britpoppers. The message of bands like the Rolling Stones, for example, was in harmony with all these decades. Songs like '(I Can't Get No) Satisfaction' or 'You Can't Always Get What You Want' were about the personal gratification of the isolated individual. The way in which the Beatles stood behind individualism-eroding universal love was far more radical than they are usually given credit for, because it was in direct opposition to the way society was changing. For all that Beatles albums were burned in the American Bible Belt, their stance was remarkably Christian. St Augustine would have agreed with Lennon that 'All You Need Is Love'.

This, then, was the sentiment expressed when the *Our World* programme cut to London, and found the Beatles recording in Studio 3 of Abbey Road, surrounded by flowers, balloons and a small audience of Swinging London's key faces. We saw George Martin in his white shirt controlling the proceedings, and the professional violinists and brass musicians he assembled dressed in black tie among the wild colours of the hippy clothes of the Beatles and their friends.

All *Our World* segments had to be live, so the Beatles were seen in the process of recording, rather than miming to a finished piece of material. The work-in-progress nature of 'All You Need Is Love' is a large part of its appeal. The recording was not tidied up and finished off when it was released as a single. As a result, it has a slightly tinny sound, compared to the rest of Martin's productions, and some quite blatant mistakes. Harrison's guitar solo is of particular note, and it sometimes finds itself on lists of the worst guitar solos ever. It's not so much that the solo is bad, just that it sounds like George forgets what he is supposed to be doing and gives up and stops playing halfway through. Considering that he was playing to hundreds of millions of people around the planet, it's a remarkably relaxed approach. It would have been easy to fix later with an overdub, but they were confident enough to leave it as it was. What mattered, they knew, was the focused simplicity of the songwriting, the sentiment they were communicating and, as always, the glorious vocal harmonies that made the whole thing work.

Such a universal message was entirely at odds with the nationalistic tone of many of the other countries' segments. With hindsight, the Beatles' approach to the prevailing nationalism of *Our World* was perfect. Their message to the rest of the world would start with a national anthem, they decided. To be specific, it would start with the French national anthem. So the 'Marseillaise' rang out at the start of the song, and the Beatles sent their message of love to the rest of the world.

1967: LARGER THAN REALITY

The volcano was visible from three miles away. It was 125ft high, about 400ft in diameter and cost $1m to build – the same price as the budget for the entirety of *Dr. No*. In later years the largest soundstage in the world, the Albert R. Broccoli 007 Stage, would be built on the same site at Pinewood Studios, just west of London. But this legendary stage would still only be half the height and footprint of the set that Ken Adam built for the climax of *You Only Live Twice*.

In the book, the villain Blofeld used a castle on the Japanese coast, surrounded by gardens of poisonous plants, as his base. But after many lengthy location-scouting helicopter trips over Japan, it became clear to the filmmakers that the Japanese did not build castles by the sea. The location scouts had, however, been impressed by the number of extinct volcanos they had flown over. Instead of a castle, could SPECTRE's leader Blofeld be operating from an extinct volcano instead? It was the sort of brief that production designer Ken Adam was born for.

Nobody knew if building a set of this scale was possible, because nobody had ever attempted anything like it before. There are no go-to experts familiar with the engineering problems involved with building volcano interiors. As Adam recalled, 'You wake up at night wondering if the whole thing will work. You surround yourself with the best possible construction engineers and they can't help. They may be qualified to build the Empire State Building or the Eiffel Tower – buildings that follow normal construction techniques – but we have built a structure for which there is no previous terms of reference.' Even if it could be built, lighting a set that size was going to be a whole other matter.

Adam's volcano contained a working monorail. Mini Mokes and Land Rovers drove around its interior. One hundred and twenty stuntmen were involved in the climactic battle, which included forty ninjas abseiling down from the volcano's crater. No one would dream of attempting anything like this now. Today, the sequence would be shot largely against green screen and the volcano would be created in a computer. But at the time, it was an expression of the confidence of both Hollywood and British culture during the 1960s. The press was invited *en masse* to visit the set, and Adam was delighted when a photograph of the volcano appeared in nearly every newspaper in the world. It became an icon of both spy films and the 1960s in general. In the 1999 spy spoof *Austin Powers: The Spy Who Shagged Me*, Powers travels to Dr Evil's secret volcano island base in a yellow submarine.

The whole thing was, of course, wonderfully ridiculous. For all Ian Fleming's experience in Naval Intelligence during the war, his Bond novels were powered more by his personal fantasies than by the type of accurate espionage accounts that you'd find in the books of John le Carré. Fleming's 1950s novels had placed Bond in opposition to the Russian Secret Service in general and SMERSH in particular, but after the Cold War escalated he dropped realistic world politics. Instead, he pitched Bond against the fictitious and inherently ludicrous multinational criminal organisation SPECTRE.

By the time the world was reacting to events like the Cuban Missile Crisis in 1962, Bond's adventures took place in a fantasy world of his own devising. Bond was escapism. That's what his audience wanted. The less it had to do with reality the better.

When Broccoli and Saltzman began developing the novels for screen there was uncertainty about exactly what tone they should aim for, and what level of realism or fantasy they should depict. The original screenplay for *Dr. No*, for example, was a wild affair that reimagined the title villain as an evil marmoset monkey. This was an adaptation of a book that ended with the hero fighting a giant squid and then drowning the villain in bird shit, so the monkey was perhaps not so great a leap as you might think. The script was rejected, however, and the finished film took a more grounded and reality-based approach to the story. In the novel the character of Dr Julius No is six foot six, has his heart on the wrong side of his body, and metal pincers for hands. In the film he is a more human antagonist, played with an understated sinister aloofness by Joseph Wiseman. He does still have bionic hands, but these are hidden under black leather gloves so that he doesn't look too silly.

The second Bond movie *From Russia with Love* also attempted an adaptation that was reasonably faithful to the novel's plot. Tonally, it is now seen as one of the most realistic and grounded Bond movies, but it did replace the story's antagonists, which in the novel were the Russian espionage agency SMERSH, with the fictional Blofeld and SPECTRE. The gritty realism that has made *From Russia with Love* a favourite among Bond-movie aficionados has to therefore rub up against some accidentally comedic sequences in a secret location known only as SPECTRE Island. Here characters deliver serious dialogue in the foreground while behind them assorted henchmen undergo flamethrower training.

By the third film, the lure of fantasy was becoming too strong to ignore. *Goldfinger* offered naked dead women painted gold, cars with ejector seats and a henchman who killed people by throwing a razor-sharp bowler hat at them. To top it all off, there was also Pussy Galore's flying circus. At the end of the movie, when a nuclear bomb inside Fort Knox is finally defused, the countdown clock on the bomb stops at '007' – a detail that got a big laugh from cinema audiences. This little wink at the audience indicated that the world of the film was not intended to be real, but a fun escape into the fantasy universe of James Bond.

Given the huge commercial success of *Goldfinger*, it was clear that leaning into fantasy was an important ingredient in the franchise. It was, therefore, not something to be resisted too strongly and, before you knew it, a $1m volcano lair was rising up over the fields of Buckinghamshire. It is true that in the world of Bond fandom, the more grounded films such as *From Russia with Love*, *For Your Eyes Only* or *The Living Daylights* are typically highly rated, and the more outlandish films such as *You Only Live Twice*, *Moonraker* and *Die Another Day* are heavily criticised. But for the movie-going public, the opposite appears to be true – if the box-office receipts for these films is any guide. James Bond movies are thought of as places where we can escape from the real world. The audience expects to enter a fantasy that exists to entertain and divert.

Three weeks before people thrilled to the sight of ninjas abseiling into a rocket base inside a hollowed-out volcano, the Beatles also introduced us to a world of fantasy. The release of their psychedelic album *Sgt. Pepper's Lonely Hearts Club Band* provided the default soundtrack to the Summer of Love. The album has come to symbolise the moment when the world went from black and white into colour. The record is typically no longer considered by critics to be the Beatles' best, but there is no doubt that those who experienced it at the time feel it was the pinnacle of their work.

Only those present can truly grasp the extent to which one record seemed to change the world.

The album, and the Beatles' psychedelic period in general, is strongly influenced by the band's use of LSD. The drug led to Lennon writing surreal songs like 'I Am the Walrus', 'Strawberry Fields Forever' and 'Lucy in the Sky With Diamonds'. Lennon would later insist that the initial letters of that latter song title were not an intentional reference to LSD, and that the phrase came instead from a drawing by his son Julian. The finished song was still very much a product of his psychedelic use, however. The coincidence of the title was just one of those strange synchronicities that plague people experimenting with expanded consciousness.

Prior to 1967, the band's drug use had not caused a disconnect between them and the mainstream family audience. They had started out on speed, a drug they would not have made it through the gruelling Hamburg days without. When you listen to the sheer energy of the almost proto-punk 'She Loves You', it is hard not to see their use of speed as an integral part of their breakthrough. Their use of this drug was not particularly hidden. In 1964, when Harold Wilson presented them with Variety Club Silver Hearts for show-business personalities of the year, Lennon thanked the soon-to-be prime minister with the words, 'Thanks for the purple hearts.' The laughter that followed illustrated how familiar people were with slang terms for speed. Its use wasn't seen as overly shocking by the establishment at the time. In the novel *Moonraker*, for example, Bond calls his secretary at the Secret Service and arranges for an envelope of Benzedrine to be delivered to his casino. He mixes this with his champagne because he wants the novel's villain to think he is overconfident.

In 1964 the Beatles discovered Bob Dylan and marijuana, which quickly replaced speed as their drug of choice. This was a change that James Bond never made, for his drug use remained fixed at the level of speed, alcohol and nicotine. The result of the Beatles' discovery of marijuana was that the energy in their music subsided, but their creative ambition rose. Their use of the drug was not exactly hidden, but it was easy to miss the references that started to appear in their work – from the line 'turn me on when I get lonely' in 1964's 'She's a Woman', to the cloud of smoke in footage of the band at the end of *Help!* But thanks to the quality of songs like 'Eleanor Rigby' or 'Yesterday', the Beatles' audience had no problem following them through this change. The move to LSD in 1966 was harder to overlook.

Outside of Lennon, the rest of the band's interest in LSD was fairly short-lived. The *Sgt. Pepper* album was mainly led by McCartney, who had already drifted more towards cocaine as his preferred drug in 1967. Harrison gave up on LSD in August of that year, following a disturbing visit to Haight-Ashbury in San Francisco that shattered many of his illusions about the drug culture. That trip 'certainly showed me what was really happening in the drug cult,' he recalled. 'It wasn't what I thought with all these groovy people having spiritual awakenings and being artis-tic. It was like any addiction. So at that point, I stopped taking it actually, the dreadful lysergic. That's where I really went for the meditation.'

The Beatles had released psychedelic music in 1966, the most notable example being the extraordinary 'Tomorrow Never Knows'. This was, as Harrison claimed, 'easily the most amazing new thing we've ever come up with'. Featuring reversed guitars, tape loops, Ringo's syncopated drumming, sitars, lyrics adapted from Timothy Leary's book *The Psychedelic Experience* and the sound of McCartney's laughter sped up to sound like bird calls, it was music far beyond the mop-top's Merseybeat that had con-quered America a couple of years earlier. It was also hidden away at the end of the *Revolver* album, so it did not receive the full glare of attention that their more mainstream hits received.

That changed with their first double-A-sided single of 1967, 'Strawberry Fields Forever' b/w 'Penny Lane'. Here was the new psychedelic Beatles at their finest. It was also the first Beatles single since 'Please Please Me' not to reach number one – it peaked at number two in the UK, and number eight in the US. It was, for many, too strange and alien. In his diaries, the playwright Joe Orton recalled a meeting with Paul McCartney during which McCartney played him both sides of their forthcoming single. Orton admired 'Penny Lane' but, 'Then he played the other side – Strawberry something. I didn't like this as much.' Orton was not alone. As the Queen is said to have remarked to Sir Joseph Lockwood, chairman of EMI, 'The Beatles are turning awfully funny, aren't they?'

Of course, the song does not sound as alien and unsettling to contemporary listeners. 'Strawberry Fields Forever' is now routinely spoken of as a high point in the Beatles' career, and arguably John Lennon's finest moment. Having grown up in a world where music like this exists, we can never fully appreciate how bewildering it was when it first appeared. That the Beatles were always going to explore mental landscapes seems, with hindsight, inevitable. The first song they recorded when they went into Abbey Road Studios in February 1963 to make their first album was 'There's a Place'. This song talks about a place that the singer can escape to in times of trouble – and that place is his mind.

The unprecedented success of the *Sgt. Pepper* album later that year suggested that many record buyers were prepared to follow them on this journey. For the cross-generational family audience that had watched their rise with approval, however, full-on psychedelic weirdness was to prove a bridge too far. Pop music was about to give birth to its more youthful subgenre rock, and a divide was about to emerge between popular entertainment and countercultural revolution. This became apparent with the Beatles' next film, *Magical Mystery Tour*.

Magical Mystery Tour was inspired by the American psychedelic pioneers Ken Kesey and the Merry Pranksters, who drove a wild multicoloured bus across America in 1964. The destination on the front of the bus was 'Furthur'. McCartney had the idea of crossing this historic acid test with something closer to home – a working-class coach trip. This was another fond look back at their Liverpool years, when coach trips to Blackpool or the North Wales coast would be much anticipated events, complete with singalongs and plenty of alcohol.

Rather than write a script, or put the project in the hands of a capable director, the psychedelically confident band decided to busk the whole thing. They would direct it themselves, making it up as they went along, with no one really in charge. They gathered up a raggle-taggle bunch of admired actors and musicians – including Ivor Cutler, Victor Spinetti and the Bonzo Dog Doo-Dah Band – climbed on the bus and waited to see what would happen. They were open to chance, surprise and moments of unexpected profundity. They were also open to accusations of self-indulgence, amateurism and failure.

The film was sold to the BBC, who knew only that it was the next Beatles film and would include performances of new songs. This was sufficient to persuade them to broadcast it on a prime slot on Boxing Day, when families would be looking for comfortable entertainment. Had *Magical Mystery Tour* been tonally similar to *Help!* it would have gone down extremely well. It was, however, an experimental surreal art film with a strong dreamlike atmosphere, and as such it lacked a strong narrative drive. Strange, aimless and at times nightmarish, it was some distance from what the Boxing Day family audience expected from the BBC. It didn't help matters that it was broadcast in black-and-white, when it was clearly intended to be viewed in colour. It achieved high ratings, and the accompanying soundtrack EP sold well, but the film itself was seen as the Beatles' first failure.

The press were not kind. Paul McCartney felt duty-bound to appear on *The David Frost Programme* the following day to try and defend his film or, failing that, to apologise. 'At first people thought we were mad and just thought it was completely indulgent,' McCartney summarised on his director's commentary for the film, 'and I must say I kind of took that on board and thought, well, yeah, it's certainly not untrue, it was pretty indulgent. But I enjoyed what we had done and thought it had worked out in a quirky way. So I was surprised years later to hear – I think it was Stephen Spielberg – say that they had shown this and taught him about it in film school.'

Time and context have been far kinder than the initial critics, not least because the film includes the only Beatles performances of 'I Am the Walrus' and 'Your Mother Should Know'. We have become more familiar with British surrealism, and now have a context for its madness that the original Boxing Day audience lacked. The scene in which Paul is dressed as an army officer sat at a desk in the middle of a field next to a hatstand and a cow, for example, was an image that would later be shamelessly borrowed by the likes of *Monty Python's Flying Circus*.

The film also records a side of post-war Britain that was otherwise invisible in the films, books and TV programmes of the period. It depicts a working-class day out in a way that is neither condescending nor sentimentalised. 'I enjoyed the fish-and-chip quality of *Magical Mystery*,' Paul has said. 'Sequences were just suggested, often by memories from our childhood. A lot of these things found their way in as ideas – I suppose the whole film has a village fete atmosphere to it.' The film does not sugar-coat the world the band grew up in, and the scene in which all the men separate to watch a stripper now feels awkward, but it is a genuine reflection of the period. The unscripted, experimental, instinctual process of filmmaking captured something honest, which makes it a lasting testament to its time.

The fantasy world of the Beatles returned the following year with the animated movie *Yellow Submarine*. This was received rather better, perhaps partly because people were then more familiar with psychedelia, and partly because it was undeniably a visual triumph. This was a film that the four Beatles themselves had very little to do with, besides popping up at the end for a cameo. They did not even voice their cartoon selves. Rather than the Beatles presenting themselves to the world, it was an expression of how people now saw them, and the strange mind-expanding world they were creating.

The song 'Yellow Submarine' is, of course, a children's song. It is also an indicator of how different the Beatles were from any other band, then or now. It was recorded in the same period they were recording songs like 'Taxman' and 'Tomorrow Never Knows'. At that moment, still with the global adulation of the mop-top years in their sails but their eyes on a new psychedelic horizon, they were about as cool as any band has ever been. Oasis, for example, took their sound from the Beatles' 1966 B-side 'Rain', and their haircuts from that era, because as far as they could see this was the absolute pinnacle of style. This was the point when the Beatles decided to record a children's song and gave it to Ringo to sing.

No other band could have got away with doing this with their credibility intact. It's impossible to imagine the Rolling Stones or the Who, for example, either wanting to do this or doing it and not becoming a joke afterwards. Paul McCartney alone could not get away with it in the 1980s. He is to this day still mocked for his *Rupert the Bear and the Frog Chorus* song 'We All Stand Together'.

But the four Beatles together were working in a bigger world than any of their contemporaries. They were inclusive and saw everyone as their audience, and that included the young as well as the old. It helped that George Martin was exactly the right man to produce such a crazy soundscape, along with the extraordinary affection people felt for Ringo. But ultimately it worked because the Beatles wanted to see if they could do it. Restless ambition and a lack of interest in repeating themselves was at the heart of their work.

Although *Magical Mystery Tour* was seen as a stumble and a sign that the Beatles had gone too far and become too strange, *Yellow Submarine* is a reminder that people did eventually catch up with and assimilate their psychedelic phase. 'Strawberry Fields Forever' may not have got to number one at the time, but its critical and cultural standing in the decades that followed have drowned out any initial uncertainty. It seems funny to us now that Joe Orton did not like it.

In their psychedelic phase, the Beatles ran ahead of their audience. They lost some of their older listeners at the time, but the audiences that followed soon caught up. The Beatles fantasy world was a place that was larger than reality, which expanded our culture in new and initially frightening ways, but which ultimately left us artistically richer. Its humour and its influence on Monty Python are now seen as a fundamental aspect of Britishness. The United Kingdom pavilion at Epcot in Florida, for example, contains country pubs, red phone boxes and fish-and-chip shops – and a shop that sells mainly Beatles and Monty Python merchandise.

This sense of fantasy as a force that can expand our world is the opposite of the fantasy world of James Bond. That was a temporary escape from the real world – not a way to enlarge it. Once again, the Beatles and Bond were forces that worked in opposition with each other. Imagination is something we can hide in and also something that will allow us to grow – depending on whether it is wielded by the opposing forces of love or death.

1967: 007 (SHANTY TOWN)

In 1967, the Jamaican musician Desmond Dekker released a song about the riots which followed protests over the industrial development of Jamaica's shoreline. The song was post-ska and pre-reggae, and its lyrics served as reportage to contemporary events occurring in the streets of Kingston in a way that prefigures the later emergence of hip-hop. It was an authentic expression of the voice of Kingston youth, and as such it might have seemed to have nothing in common with the illusionary Jamaica that existed in Ian Fleming's mind.

Jamaica, as Fleming saw it, was one of the last bastions of the British Empire as it existed in his romanticised imperial imagination. It was a place where a well-bred Englishman could settle in comfort, where the weather was glorious, the landscape bewitching, and the servants were not too uppity. Fleming often stressed how much he liked Black Jamaicans, but he did so in a way that highlighted his racism, rather than denied it. For all that he approved of their values and temperament, it was quite clear that he did not see them as equals. His relationship with Black Jamaicans was not unlike that of the relationship between Bond and Quarrel, a fisherman from the Cayman Islands who appears in the books *Live and Let Die* and *Dr. No*. Bond admired the competent, no-nonsense way in which Quarrel obeyed his instructions. Their relationship was, Fleming wrote, 'that of a Scots laird with his head stalker; authority was unspoken and there was no room for servility'. Quarrel respectfully referred to Bond as 'Cap'n', in a similar way to how Fleming's Black servants always called him 'Commander'. It wasn't quite 'Master', but there was a similar power dynamic at play.

Quarrel was a wish-fulfilment character for Fleming, a loyal assistant who was an expression of his belief that Black Jamaicans were happy working for colonial overlords. The reality of Jamaican politics and culture was very different, of course, and in 1962 the country achieved independence from the United Kingdom. Princess Margaret flew to Jamaica for the handover ceremony, in which the Union flag was lowered, and the Jamaican flag raised. The anti-colonial campaigner Alexander Bustamante of the Jamaican Labour Party became prime minister, two decades after he had been imprisoned for 'subversive activities'.

The music of Desmond Dekker was an expression of this new Jamaica. It was an original cultural portrait of the realities of an island which was, for all its inequalities and troubles, looking forward with optimism, free to be itself for good or ill. It seemed as if all the outdated colonial perspectives that Fleming had poured into the James Bond books had been swept away. Yet Dekker's song was called '007 (Shanty Town)'. It was a strange mix of topical political reportage and Bond fandom.

The Kingston youth movement that Dekker was addressing were known as rude boys. The name 'rudies' – meaning rude boys or girls – was street slang for the discontented young. Surrounded by poverty and violence, they lived in the shanty towns and poorer parts of Kingston. In their visual appearance, however, they were clearly intent on rising above their lot. Rude boys favoured sharp suits paired with thin ties and trilby hats. Life may have been hard, but they still had standards. Connery's James Bond was someone they admired, both in his style and his willingness to do what was necessary to live his life on his own terms. Bond was not someone who was subservient or who allowed himself to be bossed around. He was also unapologetic about his desire to have a good time, be that through alcohol, women or fast cars. He understood that regardless of how life was treating you, there was no excuse for not dressing well.

The James Bond films had been taken to heart by the same Kingston youth cultures which had no place in Fleming's worldview. Bond's mastery of the physical world connected with people on a universal level, separate from the frustrated imperialism that caused the character to manifest in the first place. He had transcended his origins. Many have argued that Fleming's post-imperial fantasies of British exceptionalism were a vital part of the success of James Bond. This may have been true for British readers in the 1950s, but by the time the character had mutated to the screen it was clearly no longer the case – as his extraordinary global fan base shows. It was James Bond that mattered. The British imperialism was incidental.

By this point, the Bond film formula was already well established and, critics felt, in danger of repeating itself. Sean Connery was already talking about leaving the role, because he thought there was nothing new that could be done with it. The franchise was almost already fully formed when it arrived in 1962 with *Dr. No*, with its crazed SPECTRE supervillain in his impressive Ken Adam-designed exotic lair plotting to destroy American rockets. It began with the scrolling white circle and the trademark 'gun barrel' scene, before blaring straight into John Barry's brass-and-twangy guitar arrangement of Monty Norman's 'James Bond

Theme'. When James Bond passes into the public domain – which in the UK should be by 2035, seventy years after Fleming's death – anyone will be able to make films with Bond, M, Q, Moneypenny, Leiter, shaken-not-stirred martinis and the '007' licence to kill. The only two key parts of the franchise that EON productions, the film company founded by Broccoli and Saltzman in 1962, will still have sole rights to are the theme and the gun-barrel sequence – both of which were established in the first twenty seconds of the first film. Because these elements have been used constantly for the following sixty years, they may be enough to mark EON's Bond films as the only 'real' ones, at least in the public's eyes. As a start to a franchise goes, this was a strong one.

In terms of pacing, editing, action, dancing, music and style, *Dr. No* felt incredibly modern when it arrived on screen. In the days before mass tourism and affordable international flights, the untouched paradise of the Jamaican beach it portrayed – together with Ursula Andress walking out of the clear blue sea – appeared impossibly glamorous, especially in post-austerity Britain. So exotic was international travel in those years that Fleming once spent an entire chapter of a Bond novel describing an unremarkable flight to America.

Dr. No was followed by *From Russia with Love* the following year. It had twice the budget, introduced Desmond Llewelyn, better known as Q, in the first of his seventeen appearances, and included elements that Austin Powers would later spoof, such as villains with knife-shoes. It was also the film that established that women in Bond films were to be treated like objects. This was apparent from the titles onwards, which featured a shot of the 007 logo projected onto a pair of jiggling breasts. *Goldfinger* appeared one year later, which introduced a pre-title action sequence un-related to the rest of the plot, and a theme song over the opening titles. The Bond franchise, by this point, was complete. You knew a

Bond film would include a wealthy, cultured villain protected by a unique henchman and assorted expendable goons, along with cars, women, gadgets and death. By 1965's *Thunderball*, the commercial peak of Connery's Bond, there was nothing more that needed to be added to the template. Plot elements such as stolen satellites, ski chases or underwater shark fights were now going to be reused again and again. But ultimately, it did not matter. The character of James Bond himself had connected with the global audience in a way that no one had predicted, and the template was what allowed this to happen.

There were many spies and cops having exciting adventures in films. At times they would be played by someone as charismatic as Connery, such as the British spy Harry Palmer, who was portrayed by Michael Caine. Harry Palmer's 1965 debut *The Ipcress File* was produced by Bond's Harry Saltzman and, like Bond, also boasted music by John Barry and art direction by Ken Adam. The result is considered a classic of the genre. But Harry Palmer has not sustained like James Bond, even with the similar level of talent involved before and behind the camera. No other screen hero has lasted like Bond, or been able to survive being recast.

Outside the spy genre, there are other film and TV characters who work as masculine wish-fulfilments. These heroes are often physically powerful, unencumbered by family or responsibilities, and wander the world as they please fighting evil wherever they find it. Modern examples of this archetype include Jack Reacher and the Witcher. Characters like this are successful enough, but they don't resonate in the culture in the way that Bond has. There is an aspirational quality to Bond that all these other characters lack. He had style, charm, mastery of the physical world and the ability to pass through all echelons of society, including upper ones. He was not a decent man making his way in the world as best he can, like many male fantasy figures. He was flawed, and troubled. But he was also the king of men, and everyone knew it.

Bond was not just another spy, and he was not just another action hero. He was an icon, global cultural shorthand for the desire to live a materially better life. Jamaican rude boys took the character to heart, as did countless young people in less wealthy areas of the world. The crime writer Ian Rankin, for example, who grew up in Cardenden in Fife, has vividly recalled going to see Sean Connery as James Bond on the big screen as a child. 'I was a kid in a grey-hued town in 1960s Scotland, but when I entered my local fleapit the world suddenly turned Technicolor. Eye-popping adventures were played out in impossibly glamorous locations.' Across the globe countless young people, and particularly young boys, looked up at Bond on the screen and thought, 'I could be better than I am.'

These films connected to their audience on a very different level to a song such as 'All You Need Is Love', the Beatles' global expression of grace which was released in the same year as '007 (Shanty Town)'. That's not to say that the shanty towns around Kingston could not connect with that message, for it was from here that the original version of 'One Love' by Bob Marley and the Wailers emerged in 1965. Marley's expression of his Rastafarian beliefs had much in common with the Beatles' worldview, and indeed the video for its posthumous 1997 re-release included a cameo appearance from Paul McCartney. It was just that, for those in poverty, the idea of improving material conditions took precedent. By singing about 007, Dekker was speaking to his audience about their immediate aspirations. The song also included a reference to *Ocean's 11*, the 1960 'rat pack' heist movie starring Frank Sinatra, Dean Martin and Sammy Davis Jr, which was also admired for its winning combination of criminal audacity and sharp suits.

Dekker's song resonated around the world in a manner that

was new for Jamaican music. It reached number fourteen in the UK singles chart, and the following year his single 'Israelites' entered the US top ten, becoming the first purely Jamaican music to become an American hit. It also reached number one in the UK singles chart, in a moment that seemed to crystallise the new relationship between the UK and Jamaica – the dreams of which fuelled the long campaign for independence. At this moment, the two countries were interacting not from the geopolitics of power and control, but from mutual appreciation of their home-grown cultures. In this arena, the two countries gave to each other as equals. True, Dekker's single was knocked off the number-one spot by 'Get Back' from the Beatles and Billy Preston, but then in 1968 getting knocked off the top by the Beatles was pretty much inevitable.

It is apt, then, that when a new agent took the codename 007 after James Bond had retired in the 2021 film *No Time to Die*, they were played by Lashana Lynch, an actor of Jamaican descent. Lynch's character Nomi interacts with Bond in a way that is entirely different to the relationship between Bond and Quarrel. Nomi and Bond are competitive, but they come to respect each other's abilities and see themselves as equals. Ian Fleming would probably have been horrified if he had lived to see this.

1967: WELLES WAS TRYING TO PUT A VOODOO MIND-GRIP ON HIM

The deal that Broccoli and Saltzman's EON Productions signed for the film rights to Fleming's books did not include his first novel, *Casino Royale*. Rights to this had previously been sold back in 1955, although attempts to put the story on screen then had stalled due to a lack of studio interest. Once Bond had become the biggest cinematic hit of the 1960s, however, those neglected rights suddenly became very attractive. As a result, a big-budget film version of *Casino Royale* arrived in cinemas in 1967.

On paper, it looks amazing. It starred Orson Welles as Le Chiffre, John Huston as M and Ursula Andress as Vesper Lynd. Music was by Burt Bacharach and included Dusty Springfield singing 'The Look of Love'. It starred David Niven, Fleming's preferred version of Bond, as the retired Sir James Bond returning to service following the death of M, in order to get his revenge on SMERSH. It also starred Peter Sellers as the card shark Evelyn Tremble, who is recruited into the service and given the code name James Bond 007. The supporting cast was full of terrific British comedy actors like Bernard Cribbins, Ronnie Corbett, Burt Kwouk, Derek Nimmo and John Le Mesurier, and the movie had a budget millions of dollars higher than any of the 1960s Bond films. Despite having so much in its favour, the film is almost universally regarded as a disaster, the peak of 1960s hubris or, at best, just an embarrassing hot mess.

In the wake of the huge commercial success of Bond, film and TV soon became riddled with spies. Audiences were treated to *The Man From U.N.C.L.E.*, *Get Smart*, *I Spy*, *The Saint*, *The Avengers*, *Danger Man* and *Mission: Impossible*, as well as the adventures of Derek Flint in *Our Man Flint* and Dean Martin as the American government counter-agent Matt Helm. There was a boom in 'Eurospy' films, as well as less fantastical and more grounded Cold War thrillers such as *The Ipcress File* or John le Carré's *The Spy Who Came in from the Cold*. The craze peaked in 1966, when American cinema goers had thirty secret-agent films to choose from. This coincided with a collapse in the popularity of the Western genre, which had been a staple of Hollywood cinema since the birth of film. Spy films offered similar opportunities for action, gunplay and the triumph of the good guys over the bad guys, but crucially they looked forward rather than back. Spy films often seemed to be set in a slightly more futuristic version of the present day, where technology was excitingly just a little bit more advanced than reality. The decline of the Western indicated that, despite all the Cold War fears of nuclear war, people in the sixties preferred the romance of the future to nostalgia about the past.

Perhaps the most shameless of the Eurospy cash-in films was 1967's *O.K. Connery*, which was released in the US as *Operation Kid Brother*. This starred Sean Connery's younger brother Neil, a plasterer in Edinburgh with no previous acting experience. He was paid $5,000 to play an action hero helpfully named Dr Neil Connery, alongside a cast familiar to viewers of the official

Bond films. This included Bernard Lee, who is better known as M, Daniela Bianchi, who starred as Tatiana Romanova in *From Russia with Love*, and Adolfo Celi, who was the villain Largo in *Thunderball*. Appropriately for an action film, the evil organisation Celi ran was called THANATOS, the same name as Freud's death drive. Lois Maxwell, who played Moneypenny in the first fourteen official Bond films, also appeared in the film. She has spoken about how this annoyed Sean Connery, who felt that the movie was exploiting his family. 'I told him I was making more money in that one film than I had made in all of the official Bond films put together,' Maxwell recalled. This was an explanation that Sean Connery begrudgingly appreciated.

The *Casino Royale* film, then, faced a lot of competition when it was released in 1967. Although it could legally use the character of James Bond 007 and was based on an Ian Fleming novel, it was going to emerge into a crowded marketplace stuffed with wannabe Bond movies, at a time when people were starting to think that the Bond craze had peaked. These factors led to the decision to turn the film into a comedy, rather than a straight adaptation. Bond films are often spoofed, most successfully by the Austin Powers and Johnny English franchises. This is a hard thing to do successfully, however, not least because the official Bond films frequently mock themselves. They wink at the audience to reassure them that the film itself is aware of just how ridiculous things are. It takes some skill to spoof something that is self-aware enough to spoof itself.

Bond aficionados are often unhappy about some of the sillier humour in Bond films. A shot of a pigeon in *Moonraker*, which performs a double-take when it spots Bond driving a hovercraft-gondola around St Mark's Square in Venice, is a frequent source of complaint. So is the addition of a Swanee whistle sound effect on the 360-degree rotating-car jump in *The Man with the Golden Gun*. These may be excesses, but humour remains a vital part of the Bond alchemy, as Sean Connery immediately recognised. If it comes down to a choice between pleasing critics and serious Fleming buffs, or giving a laugh to the people who turn up every few years to spend a few dollars to be entertained, then it's clear where the franchise's loyalties lie.

For all that James Bond and the Beatles can seem like opposing sides in the fight to define the nature of post-Empire Britain, they are both equally self-mocking. This is one aspect of the new national character that nobody argues with. The Beatles were quick to laugh at themselves and, based on the evidence of their interviews, films and in-studio banter, they were all extremely funny. As the comedian Kevin Eldon has noted, they had distinct comedic personas, from the 'benign cheerfulness of Paul, the child-like drollery of Ringo, the bone-dry irony of George or John's keen sense of the absurd [. . .] it's a major part of the Scouse make-up to go for the laugh whenever possible.' Given how chin-strokingly serious rock music became in the 1970s, their willingness to undercut a profound song such as 'The End' by following it with 'Her Majesty', a funny ditty about seducing the Queen, now seems remarkable. So is their decision to place the Goons-like tomfoolery of 'You Know My Name (Look Up the Number)' on the B-side of the sincere, spiritual 'Let It Be'. Humour is a powerful shield. It can protect you from mean-spirited attacks as well as from excess praise. But it also takes confidence to refuse to take yourselves seriously.

Like the Bond franchise, the Beatles were followed by a seemingly endless number of imitators – with the Monkees perhaps the most shameless. There were also attempts to mock and spoof them but, like with Bond, spoofing something that already mocks itself is far from easy. The most successful attempt was Eric Idle's band and comedy documentary the Rutles, which is as much a love letter to the band as it is an attack. The spoof songs, written by the late Neil Innes, show a fan-like obsession with their subject that is in equal parts respectful and silly. They are much loved by Beatles fans for that reason.

The production of the 1967 Bond spoof *Casino Royale* was, famously, utter chaos. It went many months over schedule and eventually cost $12m, twice the original budget. The finished film included material shot by five different directors, and the uncountable number of screenwriters included Peter Sellers, Woody Allen, Billy Wilder, Terry Southern and Joseph Heller, the author of *Catch-22*. Heller was approached by the producer Charles K. Feldman at the start of 1965 and offered $150,000 for two weeks' work rewriting an existing draft of the script. This was complicated by Feldman's paranoia about industry spies stealing ideas. He initially refused to allow Heller to read the script he was supposed to be rewriting, then hired Bulgarian bodyguards to follow Heller around to make sure that he wasn't talking to anyone about what he was doing. Heller later wrote an account of the experience called 'How I Found James Bond, Lost My Self-Respect and Almost Made $150,000 in My Spare Time'. It includes all the absurdity and paranoia you'd expect from his best work.

Heller's script was a straightforward fantasy Bond adventure rather than a spoof, even if he did name his SPECTRE-like criminal organisation SCHMECK – the Society for the Collection and Harnessing of Mundane, Elemental and Cosmic Knowledge. In Yiddish, 'schmeckel' is slang for a small penis. Curiously, Heller put the SCHMECK base in a dormant volcano, which naturally erupts at the end. This idea never made it to the final script of *Casino Royale*, but it is identical to the end of *You Only Live Twice*, the official EON Bond movie that was released in the same year. Quite what Feldman's paranoia would have made of this synchronicity is an interesting question.

Heller's relationship with Feldman broke down after he

discovered that several other authors had been hired to work separately on the script, which he found disrespectful. According to his account, Heller sarcastically suggested to Feldman that he throw the scripts away, hire a bunch of different directors to shoot different parts of the film, and make everyone in the cast James Bond. As it turned out, this is basically what happened. In the film, David Niven's Sir James Bond decides that, because he is universally recognised as the greatest spy in the world, MI6 will rename all their agents James Bond 007 in order to confuse the enemy. This was the given reason why the character of the card shark Evelyn Tremble, played by Peter Sellers, became the new James Bond. Behind the scenes, however, the real reason was the chaos caused by Peter Sellers himself.

Back in 1962, before his breakthrough role as Inspector Clouseau in *The Pink Panther*, Sellers was dismissive of the character of James Bond. If he ever played Bond, he mused, he would satirise his machismo. 'Ian Fleming... he's hysterically funny. I would like to make a comic film from one of the Fleming books [...] Bond ought to be not one of those mammoth characters, like Mr Universe, but some flabby type.' Five years later he was given the chance, but by this point Sellers was a very different man. He was now a wealthy and globally famous movie star who had married a future Bond Girl – *The Man with the Golden Gun*'s Britt Ekland. He found that he now rather liked the idea of being James Bond. He pushed to make a straight adaptation of the novel. As a result, his scenes in the casino are the closest the film comes to a faithful adaption of Fleming's work, even if Orson Welles's Le Chiffre does keep bizarrely performing conjuring tricks at the card table. Welles was very keen on magic tricks at the time, and no one was prepared to tell him he couldn't add them to the film.

By this point, Sellers had become what the film world calls 'difficult'. During the filming of the casino scenes, Orson Welles and the rest of the cast and crew were at Shepperton Studios and ready to work at 8:45 a.m., as per their contracts. Sellers would not appear until around 11 a.m. He stayed in his car circling the studios, in a deliberate attempt to aggravate his colleagues. Sellers had a phone in his car, and kept calling the set to get reports on how his absence was affecting people. He then disappeared without explanation for two days, while the cast and crew dutifully clocked in at the studio and spent their days waiting. When he reappeared, he said that he'd only come if he didn't have to speak to Orson Welles – on or off screen – ever again. According to Sellers's biographer Roger Lewis, 'He claimed that Welles was trying to put a voodoo mind-grip on him.' As the screenwriter Wolf Mankowitz has explained, 'by *Casino Royale* he was pretty much round the bend and couldn't function properly'.

Except for a couple of wide shots, all Sellers's and Welles's scenes in the climactic card game were filmed separately. As the director Ken Hughes recalls, 'I myself never met him. Indeed, I shot a scene with Orson Welles in which I used a double for Sellers. Welles himself told me that Sellers wouldn't come anywhere near him [...] The two never came face to face. This is evident in the cutting.'

Sellers's issues with Welles were provoked by a set visit from Princess Margaret, whom Sellers believed was a friend. He also believed that he was in love with her, and that one day they would be married. He spent the morning boasting that she was coming to see him, but she snubbed and ignored Sellers when she arrived. Orson Welles has recalled, with much amusement, how she 'walked on to the set and passed [Sellers] by and said, "Hello, Orson, I haven't seen you for days!" That was the real end. That's when we couldn't speak lines across to each other – "Orson, I haven't seen you for days!" absolutely killed him.' Sellers ultimately abandoned the film with many of his scenes still to be shot. This resulted in rewrites, restructuring and the general sense of incoherent mess that reviews of the film remark upon.

For all that few would defend the film as a whole, the final half-hour or so does deserve to be seen – by fans of wild excess and chaos, at least. The film picks up markedly around the time when Sellers's Bond is captured and tortured. Unlike the genital torture Bond endures in the book and the 2006 Daniel Craig film, here Bond is subjected to 'psychedelic mind torture'. This was 1967, after all. Shortly afterwards, a UFO lands in Trafalgar Square, and the film briefly becomes more like *Thunderbirds* than *Thunderball*. It is around this point that Sellers's character mysteriously vanishes from the narrative. Instead, we discover that the supervillain behind everything is a character called Dr Noah, played by Woody Allen.

Although the film has great comedic actors and broad comic music courtesy of Herb Alpert & the Tijuana Brass, it had until this point been remarkably devoid of any actual jokes. It is a relief when Woody Allen turns up, therefore, as he has clearly written some of his own. Dr Noah is also Jimmy Bond, the nephew of David Niven's original James Bond, and his ultimate scheme is to release a chemical weapon that will turn all women beautiful and all men short. Events after this are not easy to summarise, although they include the arrival of many cowboys and the screen debut of Darth Vader actor David Prowse, here playing Frankenstein's monster. Something about the wild ambition and stoned shambolic execution of these final sequences, which misused so much talent and wasted so much time and money, can tell you more about 1967 than perhaps any other cultural artefact.

The Beatles had grown up as huge fans of Peter Sellers, who they used to listen to on the radio in *The Goon Show*. They were initially impressed by both George Martin and *A Hard Day's Night* director Richard Lester because they had previously worked with

Sellers and the Goons. Sellers himself recorded a version of *A Hard Day's Night*, which he recited in the style of Laurence Olivier. This was released as a single, backed by his cover of *Help!*, which he performed in the style of a sermon. He starred in the film *The Magic Christian* with Ringo Starr in 1969, and can be seen visiting the band, somewhat awkwardly, in Peter Jackson's docuseries *Get Back*. For all his new wealth and snobbery, and his film-star wife, Peter Sellers was ultimately more a part of the Beatles' world than he was a part of Fleming's.

Indeed, perhaps the thing that doomed the 1967 *Casino Royale* and Sellers's desire to be James Bond is the very thing that it acknowledges in its opening shot. The first frame of the film is focused on some French graffiti which reads 'Les Beatles'. As the film academic Robert Dassanowsky has argued, starting with this shot reveals 'the intended manifesto for the film – the band's non-sequiturs, visionary tableaux, dry humour, outrageous spectacle, in-jokes, the mod, the now'. The *Casino Royale* movie clearly has more in common with the Beatles' Bond spoof *Help!* than with Ian Fleming's novel.

Any hope of a respectful adaptation of Fleming's 1953 thriller in 1967 was futile. As that initial shot of graffiti proclaimed, Fleming's elegant, sophisticated, upper-class world was no more. We were in the Beatles' world now.

1968: ON THE BANKS OF
THE RIVER GANGES

In February 1968 the Beatles travelled to Rishikesh in northern India. George Harrison had, for the first time, stepped up and taken the reins of the band. His idea was that the four of them would study the practice of transcendental meditation, which they had been introduced to the previous summer. They would do this at the ashram of Maharishi Mahesh Yogi on the banks of the River Ganges. It would be the last time that all four Beatles would travel anywhere together. During this trip, something would happen that would create a block in the relationship between Lennon and McCartney. After they returned home, they were never as close again.

For some, like the Canadian filmmaker Paul Saltzman, the trip was 'a turning point in twentieth-century consciousness'. Others portray it as the point at which the band lost touch with their mainstream audience and became perceived as chasers of ill-judged fads. These differing perspectives are, of course, not contradictory.

At the time, Harrison seemed to have everything; he was still only twenty-five years old, and he was rich, globally famous, successful beyond his wildest dreams and had recently married the beautiful model Pattie Boyd, who he seemed to love very much. Despite all this – or, perhaps, because of it – he was acutely aware that there was a spiritual hole in his life which his Catholic upbringing seemed peculiarly incapable of fulfilling. For all that the use of LSD had helped him clarify the problem, he was perceptive enough to have realised that he would not find what he was looking for in the 1960s drug culture. The only thing that seemed to speak to that hole in himself was Eastern religion and Indian music in general. He became a vocal, lifelong advocate for these traditions, and it became immediately apparent in his contributions to the Beatles. The B-side to the March 1968 Beatles single 'Lady Madonna', for example, was George's song 'The Inner Light', which was recorded in Bombay (modern-day Mumbai) with Indian musicians and lyrics inspired by the Chinese *Tao Te Ching*.

That the most famous Western group in the world began talking and singing about non-Christian religion came as something of a shock to many. In October 1967, Lennon and Harrison gave an hour-long interview with David Frost on *The Frost Programme*, during which they offered an enthusiastic explanation of what meditation is and why they had taken up the practice. For most of the watching British public, this would have been the first time they had been exposed to ideas like these – remarkable given the long history of British colonialism in India. The imperial British romanticised and perhaps even fetishised India, but ultimately they looked down upon it. The idea that Asia had religious ideas which were of value and which we could learn from was rare indeed, in mainstream British culture at least.

Even if Eastern ideas didn't appeal to the audience of *The Frost Programme*, the very fact that they were being shown an alternative way of thinking, compared to that of the church they were taken to in early childhood, proved to have a profound impact on the post-war generation. Lennon and Harrison celebrating meditation unintentionally revealed the unspoken failing of British Christianity. They were saying, essentially, that Indian religious practices were more insightful and valuable than those they were brought up with. As an editorial in the *Guardian* noted, after the 2021 census showed that for the first time fewer than 50 per cent of Britons identified as Christian, 'Just as Christian belief was once passed down through the generations, the Baby Boomers' great rejection of organised religion has gained unstoppable momentum among their millennial children and Generation Z. Post-Christian Britain is now a fait accompli.'

In 1967, the press and many of the watching TV audience did not know what to make of John and George's interview. With hindsight, we recognise that by planting those ideas in mainstream popular media, they were seeding a profound change in British culture and identity. Yoga studios are now an accepted and un-remarkable sight in many towns, which was certainly not the case then, and practices like vegetarianism and meditation have become common. Saltzman's description of the Beatles' promotion of transcendental meditation as 'a turning point in twentieth-century consciousness' is easy to dismiss as hyperbole, but there is a solid argument behind it.

Transcendental meditation, or TM, is a practice, developed by Maharishi Mahesh Yogi, whose origins are rooted in Hindu thought but which is not religious itself. As a form of meditation it is both easy to do and effective, which helps explain its appeal. Regular practice is like wiping the anxieties from your mind twice a day, in much the same way as you brush the plaque off your teeth twice a day to help prevent serious build-up and problems later. Many studies have shown regular practice to be beneficial for both mental and physical health, for example by helping to reduce hypertension and anxiety. TM is a silent meditation that is practised for twenty minutes twice a day. Each student is given a personalised mantra, a meaningless word of a few syllables which they are encouraged to keep secret, so that the mantra has no connection with anything in the exterior world. This mantra is then mentally repeated during practice. As with most forms of meditation, the intention is to quieten the mind and stop the brain's endless monkey chatter. This can be a struggle using other techniques, but the mantra side-steps this problem by giving our monkey brains something to do, and as a result quieting the mind is not such a struggle.

McCartney later described one meditation he experienced in Rishikesh to his friend Barry Miles, giving a good impression of what the practice was like. 'It was a pleasant afternoon, in the shade of these big tropical trees on the flat roof of this bungalow,' he said. He began meditating and 'It appeared to me that I was like a feather over a hot-air pipe, a warm air-pipe. I was just suspended by this hot air, which was something to do with the meditation. And it was a very very blissful feeling. It took you back to child-hood when you were a baby, some of the secure moments when you've just been fed or you were having your nap. It reminded me of those nice, secure feelings. And I thought, Well, hell, that's great, I couldn't buy that anywhere. That was the most pleasant, the most relaxed I ever got, for a few minutes I really felt so light, so floating, so complete.'

All this appears, at first glance, to be a long way from the surface-only world of James Bond. There are moments in Fleming's writing, however, when he almost approaches something similar. These are the sequences when he writes about the underwater world. Fleming used to dive and snorkel around the coral reefs of the Caribbean, back when they were unpolluted, plastic-free, and teaming with aquatic life. Bond would frequently find himself doing the same. There is a real change to Fleming's writing in these sequences, as if he loses himself in something larger, endlessly fascinated by the alien beauty of this hidden other world. The spell breaks as soon as Bond resurfaces, unchanged by his experience, but it is a reminder that something larger can impinge on even the most worldly and physical of fictions.

A common side effect of taking up transcendental meditation is to experience an initial surge in productivity and creativity. The Beatles are a good example of this. When they returned from Rishikesh, they went into the studio and recorded a double album containing thirty new songs. This is just one of the ways in which an understanding of TM helps make sense of their strange and enigmatic self-titled album, better known as the *White Album*. The cover of that album, if it wanted to represent this state of transcendence that the band were experiencing, could only be entirely white. It is especially striking when compared with the wild psychedelic colours and intricate detail of their previous album, *Sgt. Pepper's Lonely Hearts Club Band*. The white cover suggests the source from which all the forms of their earlier works springs, just as white light is the source of all the colours of the rainbow. This sense of the void being the source of everything is also represented by the variety and quantity of the songs that pour out when the blank white sleeve is opened. These range from acoustic ballads to Jamaican ska, music hall, proto-punk, children's songs, AOR, lullabies, country, blues, *musique concrète* and straight rock. Out of nothing, everything flows.

The experience of practising meditation is illustrated by listening to John Lennon, Yoko Ono and George Martin's *avant garde* sound collage 'Revolution 9', one of the best known – or perhaps most notorious – tracks on the *White Album*. The constant mix of voices, music and disconnected sounds reflects the stream of consciousness of the busy mind's usual state, jumping from one idea to the next in a seemingly unstoppable chaotic train. This is like the thoughts and mental chatter that inevitably bubble up during meditation, but the practitioner is trained to accept this and simply return their focus to the mantra. In 'Revolution 9', the mantra is represented by the repeated phrase 'number nine', which fades in and out like a mind returning to the mantra during meditation. This continues until an experience of transcendence suddenly sweeps over the meditator; a feeling of light, sweet release, not unlike the moment when the harsh inharmonious 'Revolution 9' ends and is replaced by 'Good Night', the gentle lullaby at the end of side four of the *White Album*.

'Revolution 9' is the least popular track on the *White Album*, if the number of streams on Spotify is any guide. Many have questioned whether it should have been included on the record at all. But its presence has a profound effect on the impact of the album as a whole. It turns it into the sort of record that is prepared to go to such extreme territory. The *White Album* is a larger, more impactful and slightly scarier record as a result, even for those who regularly skip the track. A 1968 list of the *White Album* songs exists on which Paul and John scribbled visual images for each song – 'I'm So Tired' was John in bed, for example, while 'Mother Nature's Son' suggested the image of Paul by a stream. For 'Revolution 9', the image could only be a white space, which ultimately became the album cover.

While the form and content of the *White Album* make perfect sense to those familiar with transcendental meditation, many others found it overwhelming. It was, by anyone's standards, a lot of songs to get to know. Even George Martin thought it was too much. 'I thought we should probably have made a very, very good single album rather than a double,' he said. 'But [the band] insisted. I think it could have been made fantastically good if it had been compressed a bit and condensed.' Many Beatles fans have thought along similar lines and compiled their own cut-down versions of the album by omitting their least favourite songs. It's striking, however, how little consensus there is about which should be included – everyone, it seems, has different favourites and comes up with their own unique track listing. It's also noticeable that these shortened versions always feel lesser than the original *White Album*. Judicious critical editing always seems to somehow lose the strange innate magic that record had, which no other album has ever recreated. The Beatles included everything, and somehow managed to create a record that was more than the sum of its parts. Despite his desire to cut it down, George Martin acknowledges that 'A lot of people I know think it's still the best album they made.'

The trip to Rishikesh marked the beginning of the highest period of creativity for each of the individual Beatles. This period lasted for around three years or so, from about 1968 to 1971. For George Harrison, those years elevated him into a songwriter on a par with Lennon and McCartney. It was during these years that he wrote 'Something' and 'Here Comes the Sun', arguably his best-loved songs, as well as the huge stockpile of tracks that made up his first, greatest solo album *All Things Must Pass*. Lennon had been writing only a few songs a year before Rishikesh, but the years that followed would see songs like 'Imagine', 'Give Peace a Chance' and 'Come Together' pouring out of him, as well as his most critically successful solo albums *Plastic Ono Band* and *Imagine*. In a similar way, Paul McCartney wrote songs like 'Let It Be', 'Blackbird' and 'Hey Jude', as well as being the principal architect of the Abbey Road medley, writing solo albums like *McCartney* and *Ram*, and forming the band Wings. He had so much music flowing out of him at this point that he was constantly writing top-ten hits just to give to other artists, such as 'Goodbye' by Mary Hopkin and 'Come and Get It' by Badfinger. Ringo may have experienced a period of doubt about the quality of his playing during the *White*

Album sessions, but he quickly rallied and produced what many consider his finest performances on albums like *Abbey Road* and Lennon's *Plastic Ono Band*. For many drummers, the fact that he stopped focusing on his drumming after this and instead put his energies into becoming an actor and entertainer is a great disappointment, akin to Elvis's post-army career choices. As Lennon noted, referring to 'Don't Pass Me By', a song Starr wrote for the *White Album*, 'Look what meditation did for Ringo – after all this time he wrote his first song.'

In recent years transcendental meditation has been rebranded as TM in an effort to reassure those who find the suspiciously spiritual-sounding nature of its original name off-putting. It has become popular among those who aren't sixties-style spiritual seekers, in worlds such as business, politics, sports and entertainment. A brief list of well-known practitioners of TM includes such diverse names as Clint Eastwood, Nick Cave, Ellen DeGeneres, ex-England football manager Sam Allardyce, president of Marvel Studios Kevin Feige, Jennifer Aniston, Hugh Jackman, Leonard Bernstein, Madonna, Harry Styles, Ivanka Trump and Smokey Robinson. Meanwhile, the David Lynch Foundation raises money to train people who might not otherwise have access to classes, ranging from school children with ADHD to African war refugees, prisoners and military veterans. The filmmaker David Lynch, who is perhaps the most prominent advocate of TM, is a Beatles fan who attended their very first concert in America. In the years since the Beatles left Rishikesh, the practice of TM has come far from its roots in Indian spirituality; a large part of public awareness is a result of its role in the Beatles story.

Individual Beatles have continued to promote TM in the half-century since they left Rishikesh. George, of course, was deeply committed to the spiritual path and Eastern religion for the rest of his life, and he always promoted the practice of this form of meditation. Ringo may have left the ashram first, after only eleven days, but he often talks about how much he values what he had learned there. On his eightieth birthday in 2020, for example, he held a virtual concert to raise money for the David Lynch Foundation, as well as the Black Lives Matter Global Network and other charities. As he said at the time, 'One of the best gifts I ever got was from the Maharishi, who gave me my mantra and taught me to meditate.' McCartney has likewise continued to support and promote both TM and the David Lynch Foundation. 'I still use the mantra,' he said in the mid-1990s, 'When I was in jail in Japan [for marijuana possession in 1980] it came in very handy.' On the song 'Happy With You' on his 2018 solo album *Egypt Station*, he sings about the pleasure he still gets from rolling the mantra around his mind in the early morning. McCartney was very proud of the fact that he received his mantra personally from the Maharishi, just as he was proud of being introduced to pot by Bob Dylan.

The idea that the Beatles rejected transcendental meditation, however, is common in many Beatles histories. This comes from John Lennon's later reaction to the Maharishi. At the beginning of his stay, Lennon seems to have been in a remarkably positive mood. Visitors to the ashram who met him at that time, such as the filmmaker Paul Saltzman, remember him as being open, friendly, very funny and clearly close to McCartney and his fellow Beatles. He was also extremely enthusiastic about meditation. In a filmed interview at Rishikesh, Lennon was asked, 'Do you propose to play any extra part in the propagation of TM?' He replied, 'We'll do everything we can. Anything that's possible. Everything we can – and we might be able to do a lot.' By the time he had left, however, he had decisively turned against the Maharishi. As he said in an interview in May, 'I think the Maharishi was a mistake. His teachings have some truth in them, but I think that we made a mistake.'

One factor in this souring of relations was the Maharishi's unhappiness about drug use by the Beatles and their party in his ashram. Another important factor seems to have been the presence of Lennon's then current guru, the television repair man 'Magic' Alex Mardas. Magic Alex is best known in the Beatles story for convincing Lennon that he could create all sorts of wonderful-sounding inventions, including a flying saucer, a force field which could make a building invisible by surrounding it with 'coloured air', and wallpaper that worked as a loudspeaker called 'loud-paper'. He was made head of Apple Electronics, spent a great deal of the Beatles' money, and failed to produce anything that actually worked. In 2009, Mardas sued the *New York Times* for describing him as a charlatan. He agreed to drop the case if the newspaper printed a clarification that, by labelling him as a charlatan, it did not mean to imply he was a con man.

Mardas displayed great antipathy towards the Maharishi in Rishikesh, and the reasons behind this have been the subject of much speculation. As the author Craig Brown notes, 'Mardas seems to have taken against the Maharishi. Perhaps he was jealous of the way his own shamanic place in the Beatles' hearts had been usurped by this leathery old guru.' It also seems possible that Mardas feared that the Maharishi, who happened to have a degree in physics from Allahabad University, had become suspicious that Magic Alex did not possess the scientific knowledge he claimed. According to Tony Bramwell, a childhood friend of Paul, John and George, the Maharishi 'asked many searching [scientific] questions that Alex was unable to answer, and [Mardas] panicked'.

Whatever the reason for his antipathy, Mardas convinced Lennon that the Maharishi was a fraud. He told him that he had been acting inappropriately with young women. Rumours spread, stories quickly escalated, and Lennon became convinced that the Maharishi was not all that he had thought he was. Lennon, Harrison and their families and hangers-on called a cab and announced they were leaving. The Maharishi, who had seen the support of the Beatles as hugely important in his mission to popularise TM around the world, was confused about why they were going. As Lennon later recalled, 'I said, "Well if you're so cosmic, you'll know why" [...] He said, "I don't know why, you must tell me."'

The taxis took a while to arrive, and Lennon's reaction to this is revealing of the paranoid mindset he was in. 'We thought: "They're deliberately keeping the taxi back so as we can't escape from this madman's camp." And we had the mad Greek [Mardas] with us who was paranoid as hell. He kept saying, "It's black magic, black magic. They're gonna keep you here forever."'

Harrison later apologised to the Maharishi for the abrupt exit. As he said with the benefit of hindsight, the 'whole piece of bullshit was invented'. His sister-in-law, Jenny Boyd, later wrote of their exit, 'Poor Maharishi. I remember him standing at the gate of the ashram, under an aide's umbrella, as the Beatles filed by, out of his life. "Wait," he cried. "Talk to me." But no one listened.' Lennon's wife Cynthia wrote, 'I hated leaving on a note of discord and mistrust, when we had enjoyed so much kindness and goodwill from the Maharishi and his followers. I felt ashamed that we had turned our backs on him without giving him a chance. Once again John was running away, and I had little choice but to run with him.'

TM, of course, does not imply that its teachers should have cosmic knowledge about Lennon's motives, and neither does it promote celibacy among practitioners. Lennon's issues were not with the technique he had been taught, but about who he had wanted the Maharishi to be. During a 1970 interview, Yoko Ono remarked that Lennon had been expecting too much from the Maharishi, to which Lennon perceptively replied, 'I always do. I always expect too much. I'm always expecting my mother, and I don't get her, that's what it is.' Lennon's search for people who could fill the mother-sized hole in his life is something that we'll return to. On another occasion he said, 'We thought that [the Maharishi] was something other than he was. But we were looking for it and probably superimposed it on him. We were waiting for a guru, and along he came.' As McCartney later pointed out, 'He never said he was a god. In fact very much the opposite, he said, "Don't treat me like a god, I'm just a meditation teacher."'

Lennon's confusion here has its roots in a culture clash between the East and the West. In Western thought – in the centuries since the Age of Enlightenment at least – the West has been guided by the notion of progress. With progress, things are refined and improved, until they are better in the future than they were in the past. The change in the music of the Beatles over the course of the 1960s is a good example of this. They could have repeated themselves after the success of their early Merseybeat singles, but they constantly strove to improve, and this led to entirely new creative achievements like 'Tomorrow Never Knows', 'A Day in the Life' or 'Strawberry Fields Forever'. Western progress implies that the student will eventually supersede their teacher.

In Indian philosophy, however, perfection was in the past, so the aim is to recover an awareness of what has been lost. Ancient texts like the Vedas are considered to be among the purest trans-mission of the spirit that survive, and as such they are treated with the utmost reverence. Elder teachers who are believed to have achieved the direct experience of ultimate reality are similarly re-vered, to the extent that they are frequently seen as being above reproach. The experienced teacher, it is assumed, will always understand the way of things more clearly than their pupils do, and so will always be worthy of their respect. The ancient Hindu *Laws of Manu* includes a passage about the perils of criticising a teacher: 'By censuring his teacher, though justly, he will become in his next birth an ass'. As the philosopher Julian Baggini has noted, the 'though justly' in this sentence reveals a lot about Indian reverence for the wisdom of their elders and ancestors. It is wrong, this passage states, to criticise something that is wrong, because being right or wrong is less important than respecting the wisdom of the past. As Baggini points out, 'This is deference in the extreme.'

When Western countercultural seekers started to explore Eastern ideas in the 1960s, then, there was a tendency to misinterpret the nature of swamis or gurus. Lennon, for example, wanted a guru who could solve his problems, give him answers and make him a better person in the future. He wanted a guru, in other words, for reasons of progress. Indian teachers, however, aimed to point people back towards the direct experience of reality that was once achieved by the authors of the Vedas. The Maharishi was there to teach a meditation technique that could help do this, and to share his long experience of exploring consciousness. He was not there to offer a handy solution that would fix all of Lennon's personal problems. His failure to do so, therefore, was a problem with Lennon's expectations rather than the Maharishi's techniques. It is why Ono told Lennon that he had expected too much of the Maharishi. In the mid-1990s Harrison said to the director Geoff Wonfor, 'I know John would have a different view [about the Maharishi] now. There was no substance to those rumours, John was just pissed off.'

Behind all this lies the change in Lennon's state of mind between February 1968, when he arrived in the ashram, and April 1968 when he left. This is evident from the songs that he wrote in India. At the beginning, he was writing positive, beautiful songs like 'Child of Nature', in which he sings about how little he needs and how the dream he had was true. Here the word 'dream' is interesting, as he would often use this word to refer to the whole Beatles project. It was a word his mother used to use whenever she was happy. When John called round to see her, for example, she

185

would delightedly cry, 'Oh! My dream's out!' On his solo album *Plastic Ono Band*, after the Beatles had split, he declared that 'the dream was over'. By the time he was writing '#9 Dream' in 1974, however, he had once again come to believe in that dream.

At some point during his stay at Rishikesh, Lennon's songwriting took a dark turn. It was here that he wrote the song 'Yer Blues', a howl of wounded anger in which he sings about being so lonely that he wants to die. For years Lennon had been masking his personal problems, and the pressures created by Beatlemania and global celebrity, through the use of drugs. In Rishikesh, there was minimal access to drugs and an excess of meditation, which would have brought his psychological issues into stark focus.

Lennon proceeded to write songs like 'I'm So Tired' and 'Look at Me', which show him obsessing about a relationship in which he and his needs are not being properly recognised. Curiously, these songs do not seem to be about his own marriage or relationship with Cynthia, for all that he would abandon his wife and child after returning from Rishikesh. Many Beatles aficionados suspect that he is depicting his relationship with McCartney.

In the years leading up to India, John and Paul had become incredibly close. McCartney has talked about experiences they had on acid, in which they looked into each other's eyes, lost their personal sense of identity and became one with each other. 'Me and John, we'd known each other for a long time,' McCartney has said. 'We were best mates. And we looked into each other's eyes, the eye contact thing we used to do, which is fairly mind-boggling. You dissolve into each other [...] It was amazing. You're looking into each other's eyes and you would want to look away, but you wouldn't, and you could see yourself in the other person. It was a very freaky experience and I was totally blown away.' Lennon has said that he believed he and Paul were able to communicate telepathically.

Before their trip to India, Lennon's dream had been for the four Beatles to buy a Greek island where they could all live together in interconnected houses, not too dissimilar to how they all lived together in Rishikesh. Given the abandonment issues that marked his childhood and the intense global celebrity that followed, it is perhaps unsurprising that he would seek security in his bandmates like this. In an interview with Hunter Davies shortly before Rishikesh, Cynthia Lennon remarked to her husband that he needed the other three Beatles more than they needed him, and he agreed. Lennon was always the neediest of the four.

Yet after Rishikesh, Lennon's relationship with McCartney was never the same. A block had appeared in how they communicated, and what was once effortless suddenly became difficult. McCartney left the ashram after a month, in order to see more of India with his partner Jane Asher. Asher had not been interested in meditation and needed to return by a certain date for work reasons. To McCartney, this seemed reasonable. A full month was, by anyone's standards, a long time for a meditation retreat. To Lennon, confronted by his long-standing abandonment issues, his friend's decision to leave him, just when a lack of drugs and excessive meditation were bringing up his childhood abandonment issues, could not have come at a worse time.

McCartney was always the most ambitious, dedicated and naturally talented of the four musicians. He had grown in stature during the life of the band. Following the death of Brian Epstein in 1967, it was inevitable that he would take a greater role in managing the band and developing future projects, if only because no one else was going to do it. It is also natural that his bandmates would to some degree resent this, especially George.

The four musicians would return from India and embark on what was probably the most creative three-year period in all their lives. They would return to the studio and create the thirty songs which make up that most inscrutable and enigmatic of things, the Beatles' *White Album*. But they did not do this as the gestalt entity they had been before, the 'four-headed monster' that was greater than the sum of its parts. They did this as four older, wiser individuals, together through habit and history. The point at which the band would split was getting ever closer.

1968: YOKO AND BILLY

And suddenly, there was Yoko. She was by John's side in business meetings and in the studio. Without Paul, George or Ringo being consulted, there was now a fifth Beatle. There she was, singing a lead vocal line on 'The Continuing Story of Bungalow Bill', the only person other than the Fab Four themselves to sing lead on a Beatles song. That her singing was not to the taste of all listeners, many of whom thought that Lennon had temporarily adopted a Goons-style comedy voice, made it all the more unexpected. And there she was, bringing her tape loops of experimental cut-up sounds into the studio and playing them during the sessions for 'Revolution', in what eventually became 'Revolution 9'. Lennon took no arguments about her presence. He loved her, he said, and he wanted to always be with her. John and Yoko were one entity. If he was to be a Beatle, then to all intents and purposes so was she.

John and Yoko did at first seem an unlikely couple. Yoko was a highly educated conceptual artist who had been classically trained in music and composition at elite schools. She had previously said that she didn't like rock 'n' roll music, which she considered culturally crude. Lennon, in turn, had said that only 'Rock and

Roll was real. Everything else was unreal,' and thought that *'avant garde* is French for bullshit'. Yoko was also some distance from Lennon's usual 'type', which was blonde, curvy and seductive – the Brigitte Bardot archetype. Perhaps Lennon's meeting with Bardot shortly after his relationship with Ono began was a factor here. Invited to meet her at her hotel, he was so nervous that he took acid beforehand and was unable to speak. Bardot talked to her friends in French instead and John returned home early, calling the meeting a 'terrible night'.

Despite their differences, John quickly fell deeply in love with Yoko. She soon became someone who meant more to him than the Beatles. His sense of his own identity shifted from 'Beatle John' to 'John and Yoko', a change he found liberating and thrilling. Klaus Voormann, the bass player the Beatles befriended in Hamburg who went on to draw the cover of *Revolver*, said of John, 'He had definitely been very lost. I had several experiences with him where he had been very down, and didn't want to live. He didn't have much joy in his life and he didn't know where he was going to, or what he was doing [...] Yoko really was the start of him getting better and better.' As he told his old childhood friend Pete Shotton, he had 'finally found someone as barmy as I am'.

The way John ended his marriage to Cynthia was cruel. Knowing that Cynthia was returning home, he arranged it so that she would discover him and Yoko together in their home. Yoko was wearing Cynthia's dressing gown when Cynthia found them. 'I was in shock, operating on auto-pilot. I had no idea how to react,' Cynthia later wrote. 'It was clear that they had arranged for me to find them like that and the cruelty of John's betrayal was hard to absorb [...] It's bad enough to be tossed aside by your husband, but to be tossed aside so publicly was humiliating as well as painful.' As she later told the writer Ray Connolly, 'You had to be in the situation to realise the horror of it. It was vicious. He knew

I'd be coming.' As Yoko later described the situation, 'We didn't stop to think about anyone else's feelings. We just went ahead, gung ho. What we had was more precious than anything else.'

Of the four Beatles, it was George who was the most unhappy about Yoko's arrival. A major change to the band had occurred, and he had not been consulted. 'George insulted her right to her face in the Apple office at the beginning,' Lennon recalled in a 1970 interview, claiming that George said, 'Well, I'm going to be upfront because this is what I've heard and Dylan and a few people said you've got a lousy name in New York and you give off bad vibes.' John then added, 'we both sat through it. And I didn't hit him, I don't know why.' To accuse someone of giving off bad vibes was, in the culture at that time, a serious and damning allegation.

After John and Yoko had been in a car accident in Scotland, George was far from happy to find that a bed had been installed in Studio 2 of Abbey Road, so that Yoko could convalesce in the room where the band was working. Nor was he happy that she ate his digestive biscuits without asking. One of the legs from Yoko's Abbey Road bed was subsequently stolen. The thief was never identified, but many suspect that Harrison was behind the deed.

'Yoko just moved in,' Harrison said later. 'At first it was a novelty, but after a while it became apparent that she was always going to be there and it was very uncomfortable because this was us at work and we were used to doing it a certain way [...] It was very odd, her sitting there all the time. It wasn't just that it was Yoko or that we were opposed to the idea of having a stranger sitting there; there was a definite vibe, and that's what bothered me. It was a weird vibe.'

Ringo also found the situation strange. Yoko being in the studio 'created tension because most of the time the four of us were very close, and very possessive of each other in a way; we didn't like strangers coming in too much. And that's what Yoko was (not to

John, but to the three of us). That was where *we* were together, and that's why we worked so well. We were all trying to be cool and not mention it, but inside we were all feeling it and talking in corners.'

McCartney reported a similar reaction. 'It was fairly off-putting having her sitting on one of the amps. You want to say, "Excuse me, love – can I turn the volume up?" We were always wondering how to say: "Could you get off my amp?" without interfering in their relationship. It was a very difficult time [...] We were The Beatles, after all, and here was this girl ... It was like we were her courtiers, and it was very embarrassing. The *White Album* was a very tense one to make.' Many observers wondered if Lennon was insisting on Ono's presence as an act of deliberate provocation towards the rest of the band – and Paul in particular.

It is tempting to see the influence of Ono's privileged upbringing as part of the reason for these tensions. Ono was from an extremely wealthy family and was educated at Gakushuin, the most elite and prestigious private school in Japan, where the Crown Prince Akihito was among her contemporaries. As a child the family's servants had to approach her on their knees and then shuffle backwards, still on their knees, when they left, forbidden to turn their backs on her. It is perhaps unsurprising with this background that she would feel entitled to sit on whatever amp she pleased, or not worry about the social dynamics of the situation in the same way that others would.

The situation during the *Get Back* sessions in early 1969, when the African American singer and keyboardist Billy Preston arrived in the studio, was very different. The Beatles had first met Preston back in 1962, when he was only sixteen years old and part of Little Richard's touring band. They reconnected again after Harrison saw him playing organ at a Ray Charles concert. Harrison invited Preston to the studio, conscious that his presence might ease the tension between the four Beatles, in a similar way to how Eric Clapton's presence during the recording of 'While My Guitar Gently Weeps' had put the band on their best behaviour.

The Beatles had used guest musicians many times in the past, be that Clapton, David Mason (the piccolo trumpet player on 'Penny Lane'), or the Indian musicians that Harrison had recorded in Bombay for 'The Inner Light'. These musicians, however, had always seemed like garnish; they were brought in to do a specific job, but they were not there to organically grow the music. The musical bond between Lennon, McCartney, Harrison and Starr was almost supernatural at this point, forged in long hours on Hamburg stages and from the intense shared pressure of living in the eye of Beatlemania. It is remarkable, then, to listen back to the 1969 sessions and hear how smoothly Preston fitted into the band. Somehow, he played as if he had always been there, humble enough to support the song when he needed to and confident enough to add his own touches when it felt right. The Beatles appreciated Preston's contributions in a way that the Rolling Stones, who he played with in the 1970s, did not. 'He was used to being a star in his own right,' Keith Richards has written. 'There was one time in Glasgow when he was playing so loud he was drowning out the rest of the band. I took him backstage and showed him the blade. "You know what this is, Bill? Dear William. If you don't turn that fucking thing down right now, you're going to feel it." ' In Richards's eyes, he was a backing musician who needed to know his place. This was not how the Beatles saw him.

Preston played on seven songs on the album that became *Let It Be*, as well as on a couple of tracks on *Abbey Road*. Their single 'Get Back' b/w 'Don't Let Me Down' was credited to 'The Beatles with Billy Preston' and when the band played what proved to be their final gig, on the roof of the Apple building in Savile Row, they played as a five-piece band with Preston on keyboards. So striking was the way that Preston gelled with the four Liverpudlian musicians that Lennon suggested he be made a full member of the band, the fifth Beatle, an idea Harrison enthusiastically endorsed. Studio out-takes, such as the Trident Studios version of 'I Want You (She's So Heavy)' released in 2018, show the extent to which his involvement could have impacted their music going forward. McCartney dismissed the idea, unfortunately, saying that it was 'bad enough with four' of them.

It is tempting to speculate on how different their future may have been, if McCartney had agreed with Lennon and Harrison. The strength of the Beatles, after all, was their unwillingness to repeat themselves. They were constantly experimenting, playing and changing. The only thing that remained fixed was their line-up – the Beatles were always John, Paul, George and Ringo. This made sense when the alchemy of their extraordinary chemistry was flourishing, but as the band chemistry had become increasingly dysfunctional after Rishikesh, the argument for not touching it made less and less sense. Preston brought in soul, R&B and gospel influences that the Beatles loved but had not mastered themselves. It is easy to imagine how his presence as an equal working on a new album could have rejuvenated the four jaded Beatles' interest in their own music once more, especially if he was also used as a songwriter and vocalist. This was a time when John and George were becoming increasingly resentful of the Beatles being seen as Paul and his three sidemen. Perhaps the extent to which this dynamic suited McCartney was a factor in his vetoing of Preston's becoming a permanent member.

For those who know Preston mainly through Peter Jackson's docuseries *Get Back*, where he arrives like a dazzling spirit of humour and good cheer, discovering the dark side of his life can be a shock. Like Lennon, his father was absent as a child, and he came to adore his mother. Preston's best-known song 'You Are So

Beautiful', which was a big hit for Joe Cocker, was written about her. His mother, however, did not believe him when, at the age of nine, he told her he had been sexually abused. As a result, the abuse he suffered continued for some time, and he was also later abused by a pastor from his local church. As he grew into adulthood Preston wrestled with his homosexuality, which clashed with his Christian upbringing, and he increasingly struggled with drug addiction. According to Keith Richards, 'sometimes he would get on the rag. I had to stop him beating up his boyfriend in an elevator once.' In 1991, he was arrested at his home in Malibu on suspicion of sexually assaulting a sixteen-year-old boy, who Preston had picked up at a gathering place for day labourers. According to the *Los Angeles Times*, Preston 'was arrested for investigation of sexual battery, showing pornographic material to a minor, possessing cocaine and being under the influence of a controlled substance'. He was later jailed twice for drug offences and insurance fraud.

The influence of Ono and Preston, then, couldn't have been more different. Ono brought influences from the world of conceptual art, which unexpectedly fascinated Lennon at the expense of his interest in making Beatle music. John took on a new seriousness, in contrast to the humour and silliness that used to define him, and the playfulness that used to mark his best work vanished. When the couple invited the press to their honeymoon 'bed-in' and were photographed under a sign that read 'HAIR PEACE', for example, this was understood to be Yoko's naming conventions for conceptual art. It was not seen, as it would have been a few years earlier, as John making a pun about wigs. The band's press officer Tony Barrow said that from the moment John got together with Yoko he barely recognised him as the man he'd known for five years. All this highlighted and exaggerated the fault lines between the four Beatles.

Preston, in contrast, brought new musical influences which

attracted and reinvigorated the four bandmates and renewed their interest in playing music together. That was, always, what they needed. In the end, it wasn't quite enough, and the forces pulling them apart were just too strong. But it was not inevitable that the band would split after Rishikesh. Despite their problems, there was an alternate future possible.

The arrival of Preston and Ono in the Beatles' inner circle is a reminder that the band had a very inclusive attitude to race. In 1964, they discovered that the audience for their concert at the Gator Bowl in Jacksonville, Florida, was to be segregated, with Black and white audience members kept apart. The band refused to play until the audience was integrated. 'We never play to segregated audiences and we aren't going to start now,' Lennon said, 'I'd sooner lose our appearance money.' The city officials relented and a minor victory in the civil rights movement was achieved. Epstein then had a clause stating that the Beatles would 'not be required to perform in front of a segregated audience' added to all their American contracts. In the video for 'Hey Jude', the Beatles are surrounded by an audience who, the band insisted, had to be representative of all the different ethnicities then living in Britain. This seems like an obvious thing to do now, but at the time it was quietly radical. An extremely dapper Sikh gent in the crowd standing behind Paul McCartney has gone on to become a cult favourite in certain areas of Beatle fandom. In the post-war years there was still a great deal of British resentment towards Germany and Japan, so the importance of Hamburg and Yoko Ono in the Beatles story proved to be significant and ultimately healing.

If there is one element of the Beatles story that hasn't aged well with respect to race, it is the portrayal of Indian people in the film Help! The Beatles' understanding of India quickly deepened after this film, however, and became genuinely respectful. George Harrison, for example, would sit at the feet of his lifelong friend

Ravi Shankar, and acknowledge him as the master musician. Harrison would go on to raise a lot of money for the people of Bangladesh, and greatly increased Western awareness of the conditions in that new country.

The portrayals of Indian people in *Help!* were comedy stereotypes which would not be accepted now. Of course, everyone in the film was a comedy stereotype, from the evil mad scientists to the crazed army officers and even the Beatles themselves. This point is especially notable when the film is compared to the 1983 Bond movie *Octopussy*, in which Bond visits India. Here the Indian people are depicted as the same broad comedy stereotypes found in *Help!*, but the Western characters are portrayed as sophisticated and stylish. The result is considerably more awkward to watch than *Help!* It highlights how long the ingrained racism that Fleming added to the character of Bond lingered in the films.

Ian Fleming's racism makes several of his books uncomfortable to read. His second novel *Live and Let Die* is often singled out here, not least because it used the N-word in a chapter title. The most profoundly racist of Fleming's books, however, is probably *Goldfinger*. While it includes one of Fleming's rare non-mixed-race villains, it does depict Korean people as not fully human. Koreans, Fleming tells us, like to eat cats and have no 'respect for human life [...] They are the cruellest, most ruthless people in the world.' He refers to them as apes with 'ten-minutes-to-two' eyes. Bond is determined to put Goldfinger's servant Oddjob 'and any other Korean firmly in his place, which, in Bond's estimation, was rather lower than apes in the mammalian hierarchy'. Fleming may have felt comfortable writing things like this because the British establishment he came from was, at the time, quite openly racist. In 1968, for example, when the Beatles were insisting on a diverse audience for the 'Hey Jude' video, the Queen's chief financial manager thought nothing of informing civil servants that 'it was not, in fact, the practice to appoint coloured immigrants or foreigners to clerical roles in the royal household'. Non-white people were, however, permitted to work as cleaners or domestic servants.

The establishment, unfortunately, still has a problem with race. In 2021, following the Duchess of Sussex's comments about racism in the royal household, a Buckingham Palace spokesperson admitted they 'must do more' in terms of diversity and that the Palace was 'not where we would like to be'. A 2021 court case which highlighted the extent to which open racism was still tolerated in moneyed circles concerned one of Ian Fleming's favourite casinos, Aspinalls, dubbed 'The Real Casino Royale' in a 2009 Channel Four documentary. The case against Aspinalls was brought by Semhar Tesfagiorgis, who worked as a dealer there between 2007 and 2020. According to the *Guardian*, Tesfagiorgis claims 'millionaire members aimed racial slurs at her and black colleagues, including use of the N-word, comparing black people to gorillas and calling them "stupid fucking black girls". She alleges the casino not only failed to bar offending patrons but acceded to their requests to not have black dealers at their tables.' The court found in her favour.

When we look at the Beatles with 21st-century eyes, it can be a relief that they are not more problematic than they were, considering the society that raised them. A year after they recorded the 'Hey Jude' video, for example, the Rolling Stones recorded 'Brown Sugar', a song that sexually fetishised underage African enslaved girls. Perhaps fortunately for the Stones, most people didn't look too closely at the lyrics and simply assumed that it was an ode to heroin. In 2021, however, the band announced that they would no longer play the song.

In this context, the Beatles attitude to race – and especially German, Japanese, Indian and African American people – was significant. The British establishment is based on the idea that some people are superior to others. While wealth can be more important than skin colour in this calculation, blatant racism can flourish in this culture, as it has for centuries. Racism is also common in working-class communities, of course, but it is not ideologically necessary in this context, and it can be fought and rejected. Ultimately the establishment benefited from racism in a way that a bunch of mostly working-class Liverpudlians did not. Perhaps it is unsurprising that a vision of a better way would come from a band like the Beatles – and not from a writer like Fleming.

1969: JOHN, PAUL AND JAMES GET MARRIED

1969 was a year of wedding bells for Paul McCartney, John Lennon and James Bond. The nuptials began on 12 March 1969, when Linda Eastman married Paul McCartney, the last bachelor Beatle, at Marylebone registry office.

Eastman was not entirely sure she wanted to be a Beatle wife. She feared the fame and the hatred from Beatle fans that was bound to follow, and she had her young daughter Heather from a previous marriage to think of. Her relationship with Paul was only a matter of months old, and it was still less than nine months since McCartney's long-term relationship with the actor Jane Asher had ended, following his many infidelities. Among fans, there was the common suspicion that Linda wasn't good enough for him. As she described herself, 'I was an unfashionable woman who married a Beatle,' and that wasn't the ticket to an easy life. The wedding was nearly called off in the heat of an argument the night before. Fortunately, it went ahead regardless, perhaps because Eastman was four months pregnant. McCartney had bought a £12 wedding ring. When it went on Eastman's finger, one of the strongest and most successful rock weddings began.

At the time, there would have been few who would have predicted this. All four Beatles had been womanisers in the 1960s. None of them had been particularly faithful to their partners, but McCartney had a reputation for being the worst offender. As he saw it, cheating on Jane Asher was fine, because they weren't married. Although all four Beatles had their admirers, he was generally regarded as the prettiest and most prestigious catch. The last Beatle to marry was the most eligible bachelor in the country, and there was no shortage of women who wanted to claim him. Ringo's birthday present to his wife Maureen in 1968 was a recording of her hero Frank Sinatra singing a specially rewritten version of 'The Lady Is a Tramp', now retitled 'Maureen Is a Champ'. The new lyrics included, 'She married Ringo / When she could have had Paul / That's why the lady is a champ'.

Against expectation, Paul threw himself into family life. He adopted Heather and the pair soon added three more children to the family, along with several dogs and other pets. Despite McCartney's extraordinary fame, the couple managed to bring up their children in a grounded, relatively normal way, sending them to state schools rather than private ones. Paul and Linda remained together until her death from breast cancer in 1998. She became his main musical partner for the rest of her life, sharing songwriting credits, vocals and keyboard duties as part of the band Wings and on his solo albums. They shared many interests, most notably animal welfare and vegetarianism. For all their rush to the aisle, they soon became seen as an ideal match.

Lennon's marriage to Yoko Ono shared many similarities. Like McCartney, he was marrying an older woman with a young daughter – Ono was seven years his senior. It may be significant that both John and Paul, who lost their mothers during adolescence, chose to marry older women who had married previously and were already mothers. Yoko, like Linda, became the primary musical and creative collaborator of her husband for the rest of his life.

That these two weddings gave both Lennon and McCartney a new musical partner seems to be a significant factor in the breakup of their songwriting partnership. It was as if they could only separate when they had both found someone else to inspire them, and that they saw songwriting as an activity they could only do with someone they deeply loved. To create music together required openness and a deep emotional connection. It is noticeable that neither Lennon nor McCartney made a habit of writing with anyone other than each other or these two women.

John and Yoko's wedding took place eight days after Paul and Linda's, on 20 March 1969. This does not seem to be coincidental. The primary driving force that pushed John back into matrimony was the news that Paul had got married. Students of the Lennon–McCartney relationship ruminate about this a lot. Ono, it seems, was not as eager to marry as Lennon was. She had recently come out of her second failed marriage and, as she told writer Philip Norman, 'I didn't particularly like the idea of limiting myself to one man again.'

Lennon's sudden desire to get married immediately after Paul was hindered by bureaucracy and Ono's American citizenship. He initially wanted to marry on the cross-channel ferry between Southampton and France, but Yoko was unable to get the day visa required, and cross-channel ferry captains do not, they discovered, have the legal power to marry passengers anyway. Instead, they flew to Paris, only to find that the French had length-of-residency rules for those wishing to marry. After a round of phone calls, it was established that they could marry at Gibraltar, because it was a British Crown dependency. They immediately flew there in a private jet. 'We liked it in the symbolic sense, and the Rock foundation of our relationship,' Lennon said. This symbolism of a solid marriage based on this great rock has made Gibraltar a popular wedding location. Sean Connery married both of his wives there.

Lennon was increasingly interested in Ono's understanding of conceptual art, not least the idea that the true art is the artist's life. Their creative focus, according to this theory, should be presenting the minutiae of their life to the world. This is not every artist's understanding of the purpose of art, of course – the idea would have made William Blake, to give one example, turn in his grave. But it made a powerful impression on John, who had struggled with finding suitable subjects for songs, and who was aware that he had probably exhausted the creative potential of surreal nonsense lyrics. Following a honeymoon that was co-opted into a global advert for peace and a huge amount of press and interviews, Lennon returned home and turned the story of his wedding into a song. He scooped up Paul to help him record it at Abbey Road. 'The Ballad of John and Yoko' was released as a Beatles single in May, despite the absence of George and Ringo on the recording. It is not perhaps one of the more highly regarded Beatles singles, but it has a special place in the Beatles story as a late example of John and Paul working closely together, so close to their split. Their positive experience helped convince them to return to the studio and record *Abbey Road*. It also defined the essence of Lennon's emerging solo career, in which he wrote an awful lot of songs about himself.

Lennon and McCartney's marriages both lasted until 'death us do part' – the tragic early deaths of John and Linda. The Beatles represent love, so it is fitting that they forged long loving relationships. James Bond, in contrast, also got married that year, in the film *On Her Majesty's Secret Service*. Even if you have not seen that film, you can probably guess how the marriage ended. James Bond is death. Marrying him is deeply unwise.

On Her Majesty's Secret Service featured a new actor portraying Bond, after Connery refused to return to the role. The departure of Connery was a huge worry for the studio and producers, who were aware of the extent to which he was identified with the role among the movie-going population. There was hope that Bond could be played by different actors, in a similar way to Sherlock Holmes or Tarzan, but they did not know for sure whether the audience would agree. When discussing how to recast, the director Peter Hunt raised the question, 'Do we want to become modern and have a long-haired one?' The world had changed radically between the early sixties and the late sixties, and there was uncertainty about the extent to which they should reflect this. The decision was made to go for 'another Sean Connery type'.

The role eventually went to the Australian model George Lazenby. Lazenby was not an actor and he had little experience in front of the camera, but he looked the part and he broke the nose of a stuntman during a screen test, which particularly impressed producer Harry Saltzman. When he heard that the role was being recast Lazenby went to Connery's barber, Kurt's, in the basement of the Dorchester hotel, and asked for his hair to be cut like Bond's. He then went to Connery's tailor, Anthony Sinclair, and requested a new suit. There was not time to have one specially made, but the tailor had one that Connery had rejected. This, in a moment loaded with symbolism and serendipity, proved to fit perfectly. Lazenby went to his audition and the producers were struck by his striking self-assurance. He may not have been an actor, but he could have been a star. A male employee of the producers brought sex workers to Lazenby's hotel room and stayed to watch, to make sure that he wasn't gay. With this test passed, the world had a new James Bond. It seems unlikely that current Bond actors are tested in this way. If nothing else, it is a reminder of how much society has changed since the 1960s.

Although the intention was to keep Bond traditional, the changing world could not be entirely kept at bay. Bond is noticeably dandier in his Lazenby incarnation than he was when portrayed by Connery. Shirts became flouncier, and dialogue became groovier. In a number of scenes Bond wears a neck frill, which the comedian Mike Myers would later adopt as a key element of the wardrobe of his spoof Bond spy Austin Powers. It is probably fortunate that Fleming was no longer around to see how his avatar was changing. It is unlikely that he would have been pleased.

In 1964 Bond was insulting the Beatles and making it clear that they were the opposite of what he stood for. Five years later, he was trying to catch up, desperately trying to fit into the world they had shaped. The influence of the changing times was such that Lazenby's Bond attempted to reject the mantle of death in favour of a Beatlesesque position of love. This is the only pre-Daniel Craig film in which Bond looked at a woman and said the words 'I love you', and meant it.

The woman in question was the Contessa Teresa di Vicenzo, also known as Tracy, played by Diana Rigg. Bond had been selected as a suitable suitor for Tracy by her father, the head of a large crime syndicate, who was concerned about his daughter's mental health following a suicide attempt. 'What she needs is a man to dominate her, to make love to her!' he tells Bond, 'A man like you!' He then promises to give Bond a million dollars on the day he marries her. Tracy's father is a poor parent who, at one point, believing he does not have time to argue with her, punches his daughter in the face. Perhaps such an upbringing explains why Tracy takes it so well when Bond also slaps her across the face.

It is rare for crime bosses to pay secret agents a million dollars to seduce and marry their daughter, especially when their daughter looks like Diana Rigg. We are deep in fantasy now. This is very much the kind of scenario that Fleming's mind arrives at, when it is allowed its freedom. It is noticeable that, in Fleming's book, the character of Tracy was considerably more two-dimensional and undefined, in comparison to female leads in his other books. It is the dream scenario that Fleming is interested in, not the woman herself.

Bond saying 'I love you' and marrying his beloved was a bold change in the portrayal of the character. That it occurred with a new actor instead of Connery may have helped perceptions that this new guy wasn't really Bond as the audience knew him. It was a mistake, the box-office receipts suggested, to move Bond so far into the world of love. The film *On His Majesty's Secret Service* is now rated highly by Bond fans and it took $64.6m at the box office, which was very profitable for a film that cost $7m to make. But this was considerably less than the previous couple of films, which took $141m and $111m, or Connery's return to the role two years later, which made $116m.

The wedding of James Bond could only end one way. As the happy couple drove away from the ceremony, they were ambushed by Blofeld and his SPECTRE henchwoman Irma Bunt. Tracy was murdered in a drive-by shooting, leaving Bond alive to cradle her body. Lazenby thought that he was getting the hang of acting by this stage of the production, but the director softened his initial emotional performance in subsequent takes. 'Get rid of the tears,' he was told. 'James Bond doesn't cry.'

As deaths go, it felt inevitable. Fleming seemed aware, when he wrote the initial story, that love fundamentally changed the character. He described Bond's realisation that 'he would no longer be alone. He would be half of two people.' When he put himself in danger from this point on, he had other people to think about: 'Now, if he got himself killed, there would be Tracy who would at any rate partially die with him.' The character of James Bond being happy and in love was a paradox. Clearly, it had to be curtains for Tracy.

But if Bond can never be motivated by love, what was the point of his life? Why did he choose to live the type of life that he did? He certainly wasn't driven by a moral crusade against crime or immorality. Tracy's father was the leader of the Corsican mafia, an organisation older and, Bond thought, perhaps more deadly than the Sicilian mafia. It was known for its control of protection rackets, smuggling and prostitution, and there was a great deal of blood on Tracy's father's hands. Bond took a shine to him regardless – as Fleming wrote, Bond 'had developed much love, and total respect, for this man. He couldn't say why. It was partly animal magnetism.' Perhaps being an assassin limits your capacity for moral righteousness.

Nor does Bond seem to be particularly driven by a loyalty to Queen and country, regardless of the extent to which he uses that excuse. Bond is constantly 'going rogue' and acting outside the chain of command. He is only on Her Majesty's service when it suits him.

Bond, it seems, is in it for the kicks. He is driven by the urge to compete and the desire to best the other man. This is competition for competition's sake, in the best public-school tradition. As a child he was told he was superior to others, and then expected to prove it. Lennon and McCartney were also driven by competition, but theirs was competition with a purpose. Each used the other to up their game, becoming far greater songwriters in the process than they could ever have been by themselves. Inter-Beatle competition, as we shall see, was soon going to push George Harrison to create his greatest achievement. Competition for no other purpose than beating others was fundamentally isolating and could become borderline sociopathic. But competition, when used as a tool and applied wisely, was also an aspect of the male personality that could be profoundly beneficial. There's a thin line between being driven by a desire to see others fail and being driven to see your team succeed, but it is a significant one.

Just as the Beatles tried and failed to be like Bond in the film *Help!*, 007 also tried to be more in tune with the Beatles by allowing himself to love Tracy. In doing so, however, he confused audiences, who felt that he wasn't really James Bond anymore. This was something that the producers would learn from, and which later films would correct. Bond is death and must always be so. The women he touches, therefore, must die. The Contessa Teresa di Vicenzo, who was briefly Tracy Bond, learned this lesson the hard way.

1969: GEORGE LAZENBY'S HAIR

George Lazenby was instructed not to attend the Odeon Leicester Square royal premiere of 1969's *On Her Majesty's Secret Service*, his debut Bond movie. He had grown a black beard and long hair after filming had finished, and looked not unlike the Northern Irish footballer George Best. In the eyes of producer Cubby Broccoli, he looked like a hippy and failed to represent the classy wish-fulfilment that the Bond brand stood for. He would rather premiere his film with no star than one who looked like that.

Lazenby was not the type of man to meekly do as he was told, and he turned up at the premiere regardless. This act of insubordination angered Broccoli, who cancelled Lazenby's forthcoming promotional tour of America in retaliation. He sent Lazenby's glamorous and sophisticated co-star Diana Rigg to the States instead, believing that she would be a better advert for the film. This was a blow for Lazenby, who had long dreamed of visiting America as he grew up in rural Australia. He went to America anyway, at his own expense. Numerous American TV and radio stations were surprised to receive a call from James Bond, asking if they wanted to interview him.

To modern eyes, Broccoli's attitude looks like a major over-reaction. The idea that actors may have different hairstyles to their characters during promotional duties is not a confusing one, and Lazenby's 1969 appearance does not strike us as particularly wild or remarkable. But the issue of men's hair in the late 1960s was a loaded one. It was the frontline of a culture war. Cutting to the heart of people's sense of identity, hair could generate strong emotions.

The beginnings of this clash were evident when the Beatles first landed in America in February 1964, where they were due to play *The Ed Sullivan Show* and would be watched by what was then the largest ever American TV audience. Beatlemania exploded in the United States and the band were greeted at the airport by thousands of screaming girls and a huge mob of press. Much has been said about how sharp, confident and funny the Beatles were in these interviews, but less is said about the press and how patronising they were. Their condescending attitude was most evident when they asked the Beatles about their mop-top hair, which they did repeatedly. The press conference at the airport immediately after they had landed in New York is a good example.

Reporter #1: How many of you are bald if you have to wear those wigs?

Ringo: It's all of us.

Paul: I'm bald.

John: Oh, we're all bald.

Paul: Don't tell anyone please.

John: And deaf and dumb too.

Reporter #2: Are you for real?

John: Come on and have a feel.

Reporter #3: I have a question – won't you get a haircut at all?

Ringo: No.
Paul: No thanks.
George: I had one yesterday.

The American press pack were almost entirely male and typically wore their hair short, either swept back or with a side parting, and with a liberal application of pomade, Brylcreem or some other shiny hair product. No hair was out of place, even if each strand was plastered to the scalp in a manner that now looks dirty or greasy. This style had been common since the Victorian era, when men applied macassar oil to their hair. This necessitated squares of white material – called antimacassars – being placed over the back of armchairs to protect the fabric from oily male heads. One of the issues that led to Ian Fleming being removed from Eton in 1927 was his use of hair oil against school orders.

It was the same look that James Bond had worn when he arrived on screen in 1962's *Dr. No*. It was, simply, the socially accepted way in which men in Western Europe and North America were supposed to wear their hair. In the novel of *From Russia with Love*, the Russian spy Tatiana watches Bond wash and shave in their cabin on the Orient Express and is surprised but pleased when he doesn't apply hair oil. 'It is a dirty habit,' she tells him. 'I was told that many Europeans have it. We would not think of doing it in Russia. It dirties the pillows. But it is odd that you in the West do not use perfume. All our men do.' Bond replies simply, 'We wash.'

The Teddy Boys and rockers of the 1950s had made a point of growing their hair longer than would have been allowed in the armed forces. They knew how much collar-length hair and large quiffs annoyed those who had fought in the Second World War and spent their youth with army regulation haircuts. But they too used plenty of product to keep their hair in place, and they too had hair which was shiny and unmoving. They did not want to have their masculinity questioned. The Beatles had initially worn their hair in this style during the long hours they spent playing the clubs of Hamburg in the early 1960s. Inspired by their German friends Klaus Voormann and Astrid Kirchherr, however, they started to wear their hair clean and swept forward in 1962; the famous 'mop-top' that first marked out men's hair as a symbol of the coming cultural clashes. It was an act of individualism – a desire to be visibly different from the crowd. It was also a rejection of the status quo and the aesthetics of the older generation. It is easy to detect a hint of disgust when Lennon recalled that his mother's partner Bobby Dykins had 'thinning margarine-coated hair'. This may have been truer than he realised. Dykins's daughter Julia recalled that he would occasionally use butter on his hair when he was out of Brylcreem.

Four days after the Beatles' arrival in New York they were invited to a reception at the British Embassy in Washington. Here they had their first encounter with Fleming's class. One reception guest standing behind Ringo produced a pair of scissors and cut off a piece of his hair. Recollections of the culprit and the Beatles' reactions vary, and multiple people have claimed to possess this lock of hair, so the exact reasons behind the incident have been lost in the fog of time. It's clear, however, that the attack was loaded with significance. This was not the act of a hormone-crazed teenage fan desperate for a keepsake, it was an adult member of the establishment who must have believed they had the right to cut the hair of this working-class northerner without permission, and that their social standing meant they could get away with doing so. Perhaps subconsciously, they may have recognised that the hair represented a dangerous attack on the deferential attitudes which maintained their hierarchical world. If that was the case, it might explain why they felt the urge to lash out in such a childish and petty way.

The idea that men should have short hair and women long was a concept that was supported by the Bible. As the Book of Corinthians states, 'Doth not even nature itself teach you, that, if a man have long hair, it is a shame unto him? But if a woman have long hair, it is a glory to her: for her hair is given her for a covering.' As McCartney remarked in 1966, 'There they were in America, all getting house-trained for adulthood with their indisputable principle of life: short hair equals men, long hair equals women. Well, we got rid of that small convention for them.'

Such was the social taboo about feminine-appearing men that Fleming gave Blofeld, his most evil of villains, a feminine aspect. 'Blofeld's own eyes were deep black pools, surrounded – totally surrounded, as Mussolini's were – by very clear whites,' he wrote. 'The doll-like effect of this unusual symmetry was enhanced by the long silken black eyelashes, that should have belonged to a woman.' It's striking how much this description of Fleming's ultimate villain sounds like Paul McCartney.

As the 1960s progressed, long hair on men became the clearest indicator that they had moved past old ways of thinking and instead favoured 'hippy' ideals that rejected greed, materialism and competition. In this way, hair became the most immediate and visible indication of the fault line between the Silent Generation and the Baby Boomers. The older generation railed against this change in attitudes like King Canute ordering back the tide, and with about the same results. What argument did they have to support their belief that men should have short hair, other than that's just how it is? How could they claim the vital importance of short hair without looking absurd, uptight and foolish? The increasing visibility of longer male hair was an ever-present indication to older conservatives that their views were on the way out.

There were countless examples of the significance of male hair length. The Broadway musical about the hippy generation, for example, was called *Hair: The American Tribal Love-Rock Musical*. When the counterculture writer Hunter S. Thompson ran for sheriff of Pitkin County, Colorado, as a 'Freak Power' candidate, he shaved his head specifically so he could dismiss his crew-cut sporting Republican opponent as a 'long hair'. On BBC TV, *Doctor Who* was happy to borrow heavily from the Bond films, not least in a 1967 episode in which the Doctor was tied to the floor while a slow-moving laser beam inched its way towards him. But although the Doctor had originally been a stern patriarch figure, he was then played by Patrick Troughton in a Beatles mop-top haircut, and was tied down next to a teenage girl with a strong Liverpool accent. You were unlikely to have found such a haircut, or indeed the Liverpudlian accent, on the BBC just a few years earlier.

These changes were also evident in the Bond films. Sean Connery's receding hairline meant that he wore a toupee when he played James Bond, but his wigs began to get gradually longer as the films went on. Lazenby's Bond may have had the same neat side parting as Connery, but his hair was notably fuller, cleaner and longer than Connery's was when the films began. When Connery returned to the role for 1971's *Diamonds Are Forever*, his wig was longer still. Roger Moore also had a problem with his hair when he took over the role in 1972. As the director Guy Hamilton recalled, 'Roger had enough hair to stuff a mattress and we had to get his hair cut, which was quite dramatic. He kept popping in at Tilbury Street and saying, "How's this, Guy?" I said, "No, Roger, it's got to be short back and sides. Proper." And he'd go off again.'

Although Lazenby's one Bond movie is now highly rated by Bond fans, his performance was not held in such high esteem at the time. As far as the public was concerned, Connery was Bond. He had created the role and gained their respect over the previous years. This new guy couldn't just turn up, step into Connery's shoes and expect the same reaction. He hadn't yet earned the right to be treated with the same love from the audience. It didn't help that Lazenby was a model, and not an actor. As charming as he may have been, he couldn't bring quite the same level of seriousness to the role. He sometimes came across as a man who had wandered onto the set and couldn't quite believe his own luck. The performance of a non-actor who is just happy to be there can be utterly charming, as it was when the comedian Bob Mortimer starred in the 2000 TV series *Randall and Hopkirk (Deceased)*, but this was not what audiences wanted from Bond.

Lazenby attempted to act how he imagined a movie star who played James Bond would act, but this did not help him make friends with the cast and crew. Nor did it help that Lazenby, as he later told the authors Matthew Field and Ajay Chowdhury, illegally bought guns when on location in the small Swiss Alpine village of Mürren and fired them near the worried crew. This may have been an attempt to embody James Bond, but deep down Lazenby knew it wasn't him.

Actor Joanna Lumley, who played one of Blofeld's 'Angels of Death', remembers that Lazenby kept himself to himself on the set, and spent a long time alone trying to play the Beatles' 'Hey Jude' on the guitar. As Lazenby described the situation, 'People weren't into James Bond. Out of vogue, it wasn't current. Make love not war [...] Even Wall Street had taken their ties off. I'd go into a restaurant and they'd say, "Waiter!" ' The idea that Bond films were no longer relevant and should be retired was a common theme in the reviews Lazenby's film received, as indeed it has been for every Bond film in the fifty years that have followed. The tradition continued ahead of the release of the 2021 Bond film, in articles such as the *Guardian*'s 'It's No Time to Die: But is it time to revoke James Bond's licence to kill?'

'I look around and everyone else has got long hair, bell-bottoms, and flowered shirts,' Lazenby said. 'I also found that it was very hard to get laid in the suit. I thought, "What's the point of doing James Bond? What's life all about?" This comment makes Lazenby the only actor to claim that being cast as James Bond was an impediment to their sex lives. In an attempt to stay relevant in the post-pill sexually liberated 1960s, *On Her Majesty's Secret Service* tried to highlight Bond's libido and love of sex, but by doing so it damaged the perceived classiness of the character. The film includes a scene in which Lazenby's Bond looks at a pornographic magazine while cracking a safe, and then walks out of the building openly carrying the magazine. It is a scene that fails to recognise that the appeal of the sexual side of Bond's character is that he is desired, not that he is a masturbator.

For Lazenby, it seemed evident that an establishment assassin was so against the spirit of the times that there could be no future in the role. 'Bond is a brute [...] I've already put him behind me. I will never play him again. Peace – that's the message now,' he said at the end of 1969. He had been offered a seven-film contract with a million-dollar signing fee, but chose instead to walk away. With hindsight, and with children to raise and little income in the 1970s, he came to recognise that he had made a bad choice. But no one can make decisions with hindsight, and by the logic of 1969 the counterculture had won – Bond's establishment was over.

The key factor here was deference. During the 1950s, it was still expected that working people would be deferential to members of the establishment. This was an aspect of England that other countries mocked, as if English people had some form of forelock-tugging gene. To the upper classes, it all seemed right and proper – a mark of deserved respect, rather than an act of fear or self-preservation. The scene on the train in *A Hard Day's Night* where the Beatles were not deferential to Richard Vernon's establishment gentleman captured the moment that, after many centuries, this practice ended. To the post-war young, aristocrats weren't impressive or 'better'. They were ridiculous, because they believed in the delusion of their superiority. Once you got the joke, you could never take them seriously again. This end of deference in the 1960s paved the way for comedy troupes in the 1970s like Monty Python to endlessly mock the 'upper-class twits'.

Deference towards the upper classes had long been a significant social tool for maintaining and policing the status quo. Once that ended, the establishment were in trouble – or so it seemed at the time. In this context, it made sense that Lazenby would walk away from Bond in the belief that the establishment was over. The Beatles, it seemed, had won.

Or had they? By 1969, the tide was starting to turn. Long hair had begun as an ideological statement, but it had evolved into little more than fashion. As the character Danny laments in *Withnail and I*, Bruce Robinson's film about the fag-end of the 1960s dream, 'They're selling hippy wigs in Woolworth's, man.' More ominously, after filming had wrapped on Lazenby's one and only Bond film, the Beatles held a photo session in the grounds of Tittenhurst Park, Lennon's Berkshire mansion, on 22 August that year. And in those photographs, Lennon had objectively bad hair. When a Beatle was photographed with bad hair, we were suddenly in uncharted waters.

There had never been a photo of the Beatles with truly terrible hair before. Usually, they had great hair. Sometimes their hair was just okay, and there had been questionable moustache choices along the way, but never before had their hair made you wince. Lennon's problem was partly the size of his beard, which now overwhelmed his face and made his eyes look as if they were struggling to escape from a strangely mousey hedge. He was growing his hair down to his shoulders, but it frizzed out at the ends, giving his head a triangular shape. It was not dissimilar to Yoko Ono's hair at the time, which may have been intentional, but Ono could carry it off in a way that Lennon couldn't. His decision to top the look off with a wide-brimmed hat and what looks like Batman's utility belt didn't help. Given how long male hair symbolised the culture of the 1960s, this was a deeply troubling omen. Lennon was in a bad way emotionally, psychologically and narcotically at the time. With hindsight his appearance looks like a cry for help.

They did not realise it on the day, but these would prove to be the last photographs taken of all the Beatles together. It was the last time the four of them were together for the good of the band. From then on in, they would only ever all meet for legal reasons. As unthinkable as it would have been to George Lazenby when he grew his wild, wavy locks and turned down wealth and fame, it was not James Bond that was about to die. It was the Beatles.

1969: PAUL IS DEAD

Bond was dead – or at least, he was according to the opening sequence of 1967's *You Only Live Twice*. James Bond was gunned down in Hong Kong, his body was buried at sea and his obituary published in *The Times*. All this, however, was a cunning hoax to fool Blofeld – Bond was really alive, and free to go about his mission while the world thought he was dead.

In the same year, a rumour started circling that Paul McCartney had died. This was also a hoax. McCartney, like Bond, was free to go about his work while people believed him to be dead.

The rumour bubbled along harmlessly enough for a couple of years. In late 1969, however, it hit the mainstream after the story was discussed in depth on American college radio. This led to it being picked up first by college newspapers, and then by other newspapers across America. According to the theory, Paul had died in a car crash in late 1966, having driven angrily away from a recording session following an argument with his bandmates. It was a particularly horrific accident, and Paul had been decapitated. In response, the Beatles decided to replace him with a lookalike, either to spare the world the grief that news of his death would cause, or perhaps because the Beatles were strange and inscrutable and this was the sort of thing they would do. Regardless of the reason, they quickly found a replacement. This person was sometimes said to be the 'Billy Shears' introduced on *Sgt. Pepper's Lonely Hearts Club Band*, and sometimes William Campbell, an orphan from Edinburgh. Not only did this replacement look, sing, speak and play bass like the original McCartney, he was also capable of writing songs like 'Let It Be' and 'Hey Jude'. He was, by anyone's standards, a spectacularly successful piece of casting.

The Beatles would have got away with their deception and successfully duped the world, the story went, except that they had made the fatal mistake of leaving a string of clues throughout their work admitting to what they had done. For example, it was said that Lennon could be heard saying 'I buried Paul' during the fade-out on 'Strawberry Fields Forever'. Lennon himself insisted that this was just him saying 'cranberry sauce', for no real reason – but then he would say that, wouldn't he? Sometimes the clues were more cunningly hidden. If you played the repeated refrain of 'number nine' in the track 'Revolution 9' backwards it sounded a little like 'turn me on, dead man'. Lennon's confession in 'Glass Onion' that 'the walrus was Paul' also led to great leaps of interpretation.

A lot of the supposed clues were found on album sleeves and in videos. On the back cover of *Sgt. Pepper's Lonely Hearts Club Band*, there is a photo of John, George and Ringo facing the camera, while Paul has his back turned to it. In the performance of 'Your Mother Should Know' that closes *Magical Mystery Tour*, Paul is wearing a black carnation while his bandmates are wearing red. This was clearly meaningful, people insisted, although McCartney later explained they only had a black one left. The cover of *Abbey Road* also offered up further evidence. It was said that the four Beatles walking across the pedestrian crossing represented a funeral. Lennon was at the front in a white suit like an angel, followed by Ringo in black like an undertaker. Then came Paul, who was barefoot and out of step with the other three, which clearly indicated he was a dead body. Last came George who was dressed in double denim, making him the gravedigger. The registration plate of a white Mini parked on the pavement outside Abbey Road studios – LMW 28IF – was also a giveaway. The LMW stood for either Linda McCartney Weeps or Linda McCartney, Widow, and the 28IF was a reference to Paul's age – twenty-eight, if he had lived. That Paul had supposedly died before he met Linda, and that his age was twenty-seven when the album was released, did not trouble people unduly.

Quite how seriously people took all this can be difficult to assess. It's hard to grasp now, but the Beatles albums from 1966 onwards were unprecedented alien things that people had little context for. People studied their records to a degree that earlier albums had not been subjected to, simply because albums had not been as rich or as interesting before. They were put under the same sort of scrutiny as religious texts, in the hope that they would reveal profound hidden truths. Given the amount of marijuana smoked by student Beatles fans in the late 1960s, it is perhaps not surprising that people found the patterns and coincidences they were hoping to uncover. Still, it was odd that people had fixated on Paul being replaced. You could imagine someone thinking that the arty, serious and relatively humourless post-Rishikesh John Lennon was a different person to the earlier version, but Paul was clearly still the same old Paul.

Finding and solving clues like this was a great deal of fun – regardless of whether there was any truth behind them. To join in the game, you only had to entertain the idea that there might be something there, rather than wholeheartedly believe it. Like many conspiracy theories, such as Flat Earth or QAnon, it seems probable that there were a core of true believers at the heart of the conspiracy who were being led further down the rabbit hole by assorted tricksters and trolls.

All this may have been harmless enough, but the extent to which it spread was strange because it was so obviously crazy. Even after Paul gave an interview to *Life* magazine to prove he was still alive, the conspiracy continued to circulate. The theory is still widely known now, over half a century later.

What is interesting here is the timing of when the theory took off and went global. The Irish Beatles experts and podcasters Jason Carty and Steven Cockcroft refer to the period between Lennon quitting the band on 20 September 1969, and the news of the band's split becoming public on 10 April 1970, as 'Schrödinger's Beatles'. In the Schrödinger's Cat thought experiment, a poor cat is both dead and alive at the same time, just as during this period it was impossible to say whether the band was still a going concern or beyond hope. It could have been, as Lennon had told his band, the end of the Beatles. But his bandmates and the staff at Apple knew how changeable Lennon's moods were. It could easily have been just another row that passed. The Beatles industry continued on as normal after Lennon informed the others of his decision to quit. A new deal with EMI was signed, and work on the *Let It Be* album continued. Had McCartney given Lennon more attention and listened to his concerns, without the pressure of business differences, it is conceivable that they could have repaired their relationship. Had Lennon regained enthusiasm for something other than Yoko and the heroin that the pair were by then taking, and become creatively engaged with his bandmates again, it is conceivable that he would have returned.

Out of the four bandmates, the death of the Beatles was hardest for Paul. John was more interested in Yoko and George was more interested in God. Both spoke disparagingly about being Beatles.

Ringo loved being in the Beatles and being with the Beatles. It was only Paul who truly loved them as a band. This period of the breakup, then, was hardest on McCartney. He was drinking heavily, and he changed from one of the most social Beatles to a virtual recluse – the 'Hermit of St John's Wood', as the *NME* dubbed him in February 1970. He entered a period of depression. Without the support of his new wife, he could easily have succumbed to a breakdown.

McCartney was always the most ambitious, practical and hardworking of the four. After Brian Epstein died, he naturally took on more of a leadership role, instigating projects such as *Sgt. Pepper*, *Magical Mystery Tour*, *Get Back* and *Abbey Road*. As we've noted, his work ethic started to cause resentment among the lazier Beatles, especially as the impression grew that he had usurped the role of band leader which had originally been Lennon's. As Lennon said in 1970, 'We got fed up with being sidemen for Paul. After Brian died, that's what began to happen to us.'

It was strange timing, then, that the world became obsessed with the idea that Paul was dead at the very point when the Beatles started to see themselves as Paul McCartney's band and broke up in response. Even though the 'Paul is Dead' story was absurd, people couldn't stop obsessing over it. As with all revelations brought to light by the study of holy texts, it is a mistake to take them too literally. Yet for all the absurdity of the conspiracies, had people stumbled upon a fundamental truth without truly grasping what it meant? At that exact point in time when the world fixated on the idea that Paul was dead, in the eyes of John Lennon, Paul was the Beatles and the Beatles were dead.

PART 3: AFTERMATH

1970: ANSWER: NO

PAUL IS QUITTING THE BEATLES ran the front-page headline of the Friday 10 April 1970 edition of the *Daily Mirror*. Above that shocking statement were the words, 'Lennon-McCartney song team splits up'. With this, a narrative was established that would survive for decades: it was all Paul's fault.

Ironically, Paul was the only Beatle who never left the group. Ringo had been the first to quit, in 1968, when post-Rishikesh tensions between the Beatles first became undeniable, Yoko arrived in the studio, and he felt unloved and an outsider. He flew to the Mediterranean and spent two weeks on Peter Sellers' yacht. During this holiday, he learned that cave-dwelling octopuses arranged shiny stones, bits of tin cans or whatever they found on the ocean floor outside their caves, like a garden, and a song was born. As he later recalled, he then 'got a telegram saying, "You're the best rock'n'roll drummer in the world. Come on home, we love you." And so I came back. We all needed that little shake-up. When I got back to the studio I found George had had it decked out with flowers – there were flowers everywhere. I felt good about myself again.'

George was the next to leave, on Friday 10 January 1969, during the recording sessions for what became the *Let It Be* movie at Twickenham Film Studios. He announced his departure by approaching his bandmates at lunchtime, uttering the phrase 'See you "round the clubs",' and heading home. Lennon's reaction was, 'I think if George doesn't come back by Monday or Tuesday we ask Eric Clapton to play. Eric would be pleased to join us.' Harrison's diary entry for the day reads, 'Got up went to Twickenham rehearsed until lunchtime – left the Beatles – went home and in the evening did "King of Fuh" at Trident studio – had chips later at Klaus and Christines went home.' 'King of Fuh' referred to adding strings to a song of that name by Brute Force, which both EMI and Capitol refused to distribute. This was perhaps unsurprising, given the song's lyrics: 'All hail the Fuh King, the mighty, mighty, Fuh King.' George rejoined the band five days later, after they had agreed to a number of changes to their filming plans. During Ringo and George's departures from the band, the press and public remained blissfully unaware of the drama.

Lennon made the decision to quit in September that year but was persuaded by his new manager Allen Klein to keep quiet until a lucrative new contract had been signed. He informed the rest of the band of his decision on the day of the signing, telling Paul that he wanted 'a divorce'. As we've seen, how seriously the rest of the band were supposed to take this is an open question. They knew John well, and knew how flighty his personality was. He had a history of making bold statements about issues that struck him as being of the utmost importance, before losing interest and moving on. In his acid phase, for example, he had called all the members of the band together for an emergency meeting in the Apple boardroom. 'I've got something very important to tell you,' he announced. 'I am Jesus Christ. I have come back again. This is my thing.' The band nodded and nobody spoke until Ringo suggested they go and get lunch. That night Lennon began his relationship with Yoko Ono and never mentioned being Jesus again.

The band continued with their plans for the next six months or so, with nobody entirely sure whether Lennon would return or not – least of all John himself. Lennon could easily have declared that he had quit when he was promoting his solo single 'Cold Turkey', or used the announcement to generate more publicity for his peace crusade. The longer he stayed silent in public, the easier it was to believe that maybe there was still hope and that the band would get over this difficult patch. He did tell the journalist Ray Connolly that he had left the band at Christmas 1969, but then said, 'But don't write it yet. I'll tell you when you can.' Connolly, impressively, kept his word.

The matter came to a head when Paul released his first solo album *McCartney* in April 1970. He sent out copies of an interview as a press release to help publicise the album, because he had stopped talking to the press. This included the following questions and answers:

Question: Are you planning a new album or single with the Beatles?
Answer: No.

Question: Is this album a rest away from the Beatles, or the start of a solo career?
Answer: Time will tell. Being a solo album means it's 'the start of a solo career' . . . and not being done with the Beatles means it's a rest. So, it's both.

Question: Is your break with the Beatles temporary or permanent, due to personal differences, or musical ones?

Answer: Personal differences, business differences, musical differences, but most of all because I have a better time with my family. Temporary or permanent? I don't know.

Question: Do you foresee a time when Lennon–McCartney becomes an active songwriting partnership again?
Answer: No.

Apple's new manager Allen Klein lived in fear that Lennon would open his mouth and jeopardise the Beatles' business deals, but no one had expected McCartney to make such a declaration. It was not, however, a straightforward statement that the band had split. He talked of 'not being done with the Beatles' and admitted that he didn't know if the current pause in group activities was temporary or permanent. This was arguably vaguer than an interview with *Life* magazine he did six months earlier, during which he stated that 'the Beatles thing is over'. Amazingly, neither the press nor the public paid much attention at the time. Perhaps his phrasing felt too casual to be real; such a major announcement, surely, would be delivered in a more dramatic way. The killer detail in the press release for the *McCartney* album, however, was the statement that he didn't foresee writing with John in the future. It was this that people reacted to.

The Lennon–McCartney relationship was the heart of the Beatles. If that was over, then how could the Beatles continue? It was a telling detail that he had named his solo album *McCartney* rather than *Paul McCartney*. He was known to the world as Paul or Beatle Paul, and one of the few places that the name 'McCartney' was used without his Christian name attached was in the phrase 'Lennon and McCartney'. Suddenly, here was the word 'McCartney' by itself. Symbolically, it confirmed that John had got his divorce, regardless of whether that was what he really wanted.

This was why Paul's uncertain interview answers were turned into the definitive headline 'PAUL IS QUITTING THE BEATLES'.

In his question-and-answer interview McCartney had said that the themes of his solo album were 'home, family, love'. This was the opposite of the zeitgeist. It certainly wasn't rock 'n' roll. Where was the narcissism and self-indulgence? Where was the determination to put your own desires ahead of the wider concerns of others? Lennon, who was heavily influenced by Yoko Ono's belief that the only subject for an artist should be the artist themselves, increasingly wrote songs about himself. In light of the growing individualism of the era, as the 1960s turned into the 'Me Decade' of the 1970s, this was an approach that received heavyweight critical approval. Paul, in contrast, was talking about being a father and about the happiness he found with his new family on his rundown Scottish farm. He was committing the cardinal sin of the age: he not only appeared old-fashioned, he also appeared old.

Although his solo album sold well, it soon became much mocked in the court of public opinion. It was a gentle, low-key affair, full of little instrumentals and half-formed song ideas, and had been largely recorded at home without a mixing desk. It is now lauded as the first lo-fi alt-rock album, but this framing was not available in the early 1970s. Then, it was seen as indulgent and simply not good enough, especially as it came from an artist who had just been writing songs as strong as 'Let It Be', 'Hey Jude' and 'The Long and Winding Road'.

When the Beatles were still a going concern, John Lennon and George Harrison released solo albums that charitable critics admired for being uncommercial and experimental, and uncharitable ones considered to be unlistenable. When the Beatles were still delivering the goods, the quality of these solo projects didn't really matter. But *McCartney* was released as the shock news of the Beatles' end was still being processed. Perhaps if he had delivered an album of fully formed songs as strong as George Harrison's *All Things Must Pass,* or his own later *Band on the Run,* things would have been very different. But as it stood, it appeared that Paul had killed off the Beatles and replaced them with little more than half-baked noodling. Public opinion, in response, was not kind.

1970: MOTHER/LOVE

In 1970, John Lennon gave a lengthy interview to Jann Wenner, the co-founder and publisher of *Rolling Stone* magazine. He talked about how he was trying to decide which song should be the single from *Plastic Ono Band*, his forthcoming post-Beatles solo album. Should he choose 'Mother', a harrowing song about childhood abandonment, or the song 'Love', a romantic piano ballad?

This was the most notorious interview Lennon ever gave, recorded in the aftermath of the Beatles' breakup, at a time when Lennon was deeply involved with primal scream therapy. This was a challenging form of trauma therapy, devised by the American psychotherapist Arthur Janov. It was based on the idea that neuroses were formed by childhood trauma and that a patient needed to relive those incidents in order to heal. The way to fully express and embrace the pain a patient felt, Janov believed, was by screaming. As he explained, 'A lot of people go to psychoanalysis because they want to get their defences strengthened. We try to take those defences apart, so they can get back to their feelings and recapture some part of themselves.' Janov was dismissive of the idea that talking therapy could get to the roots of deeply buried trauma, as

Freudian analysts believed. He thought that screaming was a far more direct, powerful and effective treatment.

In treating Lennon, Janov used primal scream therapy to regress him to early childhood by detaching him from all the attachments he had made throughout his life. This process led to the song 'God' on his *Plastic Ono Band* album. Here Lennon begins by denying a series of belief systems, starting with magic and the Bible. He then denies belief in influential figures like Jesus and Kennedy, and even his own personal heroes like Elvis and Dylan. The song builds to the shocking denouement, in which Lennon declares, 'I don't believe in Beatles!' – a profoundly profane and shocking declaration both then and now. Here was Lennon dismissing all that he had ever achieved.

The problem with separating Lennon from all his attachments like this was that he was being psychologically separated from friends, family and his network of support, at a time when he most needed them. Janov's primal scream therapy sees a person as an isolated individual – a largely unquestioned concept in the late twentieth century but a framing that is not easy to support now. For this reason, Janov wanted to treat Lennon separately from Ono, and to psychologically separate him from her influence. This led to disputes between Ono and Janov. Ono had used screaming as part of her creative work for years and hence was less excited by it than John was. Lennon talked enthusiastically about how the therapy taught him to cry. As Ono saw it, women were perfectly able to cry and had little need for a male authority figure like Janov to teach them how.

Lennon abandoned the therapy after a few months, which, Janov believed, was a mistake. The early work taking Lennon apart had been done, but they had not yet done the work needed to rebuild him again and reintegrate the various aspects of his life. As Janov later said about Lennon and Ono, 'They cut the therapy off just as it started, really. We were just getting going. We had opened him up, and we didn't have time to put him back together again.'

Plastic Ono Band, the album that resulted from the therapy, is an emotionally harrowing listen. It begins with the potential single 'Mother' and ends with a short, nursery-rhyme-style song called 'My Mummy's Dead'. There are many critics who consider *Plastic Ono Band* to be Lennon's best solo album, but even its supporters will admit that it's not an album they choose to play often. Lennon had always written songs about how he was feeling, from 'Help!' to 'In My Life' or 'Strawberry Fields Forever', but he had usually found a way to make these very personal experiences universal. This was not the case with his new set of songs. Like 'The Ballad of John and Yoko', these were about him and nobody else. They rely on the listener being as fascinated with John Lennon as he was himself.

The interview with Wenner, then, was a portrait of Lennon at a very specific time, when he was in a frail and troubled psychological state. After the interview was serialised in *Rolling Stone*, Wenner republished it as a book called *Lennon Remembers*, without Lennon's consent. It played a large role in framing how Lennon was perceived by rock critics in the 1970s and beyond, as a troubled but brilliant emotionally honest artist dedicated to bravely expressing his truth. To 21st-century eyes, in contrast, it appears far less flattering.

In *Lennon Remembers*, the story of the Beatles is not viewed as the consequences of a rare bunch of extraordinary people coming together and creating a perfect storm of artistic and commercial success. Instead, Lennon is insistent that he was an artistic genius, and that everyone else in the story was a chancer or phony who profited from his talent. When Wenner asked him outright, 'Do you think you're a genius?' he replied 'Yes. If there's such a thing as one, I am one.' Being the sole genius in the Beatles story, it angered him when anyone who had helped him build his career received credit or praise. 'I just hate this illusion about George Martin, Brian Epstein, Dick Lester and all these people making something out of us. We're the ones that are still creating.' This anger extended to the people who had worked behind the scenes with the Beatles. 'A lot of people – Dick James and the Derek Taylors and Peter Brown, all of them, you know, they think they're the Beatles and Neil [Aspinall] and all of them. Well I say fuck 'em. After working with genius for ten, fifteen years, they begin to think they're it. They're not.' Business people like 'Dick James and all of them,' he believed, 'think I'm some kind of guy who struck lucky, a pal of Paul's or something. They're so fuckin' stupid, they don't know.'

He was no kinder to his fellow bandmates. 'I decided I'm sick of reading things about Paul is the musician and George is the philosopher and I wonder where I fit in.' Speaking about Harrison, Lennon said, 'I couldn't be bothered with him when he first came round. He used to follow me around like a bloody kid, hanging around all the time. It took me years to come round to him, to start considering him as an equal or anything [...] He's not the kind of person I would buy the records of.' Harrison, he makes clear, is less talented than he is. Ono also attacks Harrison, comparing his religious faith to telling children that Santa Claus exists, as if the intellectualised nihilism the couple were then espousing was some ultimate truth. Paul is endlessly criticised as a straight and a phony whose album was 'rubbish', as is Mick Jagger, who was endlessly ripping Lennon off. Only Ringo escaped unscathed.

In Lennon's view, only Ono was equal to his talent. She was the future of music, he believed, and her song 'Don't Worry Kyoko' was 'as important as anything [The Beatles] ever did'. He was equally laudatory of her art films. 'Yoko's *Bottoms* thing is [...] as important as *Sgt. Pepper*,' he insisted. Ono's 80-minute documentary *Film No. 4 (Bottoms)*, as described by IMDB.com, 'consists entirely of close ups of famous persons' bottoms. Ono meant it to encourage a dialogue for world peace.' It is possible that this film was ahead of its time. In Mike Judge's satire *Idiocracy* (2006), in which the population of the world in five hundred years' time have devolved into morons, a film of people's bottoms that looks suspiciously like Ono's is a smash hit.

To modern eyes, the Wenner interviews cast Lennon not as the brave truthful genius that he appeared as to 1970s rock journalists, but a delusional, cruel narcissist. Although Lennon claimed to have stopped using heroin at the time, his comments and reasoning sound remarkably like those of a junkie, not least when he says that he and Ono 'took H because of what the Beatles and their pals were doing to us'. What is most upsetting is the almost total lack of love he displays for anyone, except Yoko; this was the same person who wrote 'All You Need Is Love' only three years earlier. Of course, if the Beatles were love, then this was a fitting stance for Lennon to take once the band had died.

The intensity of the love that John displayed for Yoko always seemed odd. On the face of it, his insistence that they should never be apart and that the pair could be considered as one person, much to the annoyance of the other Beatles in the studio, can be framed as highly romantic. But it's hard to avoid the suspicion that there was something obsessional and unhealthy underpinning it. May Pang, who was the couple's assistant in the early 1970s before becoming Lennon's partner, wrote, 'I believe they did love each other, but their love was unlike any concept of love that I have known or read about. They spent enormous amounts of time in bed together, but they rarely kissed or touched. As far as I could see there was nothing sensual about their relationship.' This was not the case at the very start of their relationship, when they were constantly giggling and touching. Publicly they would promote themselves as always being that much in love, but privately after their marriage they did seem to settle into a different dynamic.

This is a relationship that needs to be seen in the context of Lennon's issues with abandonment, and his mother Julia. In the words of Beatles biographer Mark Lewisohn, 'Julia was very much the girl of John's dreams.' Julia was naturally flirtatious, and John's childhood friend Pete Shotton remembered how when he first met her, she didn't shake his hand, but stroked his hips and giggled girlishly. That she re-entered John's life when he was approaching puberty seems to have made her a confusing figure in his develop-ing psyche. In a private tape he recorded in 1979, Lennon said, 'I was just remembering the time when I had my hand on my mother's tit. It was when I was about fourteen. Took a day off school. I was always doing that, and hanging out in her house. And we were lying on the bed and I was thinking, "I wonder if I should do anything else?" And it was a strange moment [. . .] I always think I should have done it, presuming she would allow it.'

Lennon always called Yoko Ono 'Mother'. Should he refer to making love with his wife, for example, he would sometimes call it 'jumping Mother's bones'. There was a tradition among middle-class English married couples in the mid-twentieth century of referring to each other as 'Mother' and 'Father' in front of their children. It's possible that Lennon was riffing on this idea, but quite what the Japanese Ono made of it is unclear. Lennon started calling Ono 'Mother' from very early in their relationship, long before their son Sean was born. In the 1968 song 'Happiness Is a Warm Gun', for example, the 'Mother Superior' character is a reference to Yoko. She was nearly eight years older than him, and already the mother of a five-year-old child when they married.

Lennon's acoustic ballad 'Julia' is intended as a song for his mother, although it sounds more like a romantic love song than a maternal one, not least when he sings of Julia's floating, shimmering hair and asks that she touch him. Yet at the same time as being a song about his mother, it also morphs into a song for Yoko, with the word 'Oceanchild' in the lyrics a reference to a literal translation of Yoko's Japanese name. Ono was not the only partner who Lennon wanted to mother him. May Pang, a younger woman who Lennon had a significant affair with during the mid-1970s, has described their relationship by saying, 'He wanted me to be Mother, but I wouldn't do it.'

During his conversation with Wenner, Ono interjected to tell Lennon that he had expected too much of the Maharishi. As we noted earlier, he replied, 'I always do. I always expect too much. I'm always expecting my mother and don't get her, that's what it is.' This was an astute insight on Lennon's part. His abandonment issues caused him to endlessly seek his missing mother. He could never find her in the people and causes he latched on to and then angrily rejected, from people like the Maharishi and Janov to the Beatles themselves. Only Yoko could come close to filling that Julia-shaped hole in his life. Once he found her, he clung to her with the desperation of someone who expects to be betrayed or rejected. 'Don't Let Me Down' may seem a strange song to write for your new wife, especially as it was Lennon who had just abandoned his own wife and child, but it does express Lennon's deepest fears. Of course, emotions are complex and, for Lennon's Liverpool family who met Ono, the idea that she was a replacement for his mother didn't quite ring true. As they saw it, given her strong will and the control she had over John, she was more like a replacement for Aunt Mimi.

All this was the background to Lennon's decision to select either 'Mother' or 'Love' as the lead single to promote his first proper solo album. He was aware that 'Love' would be the more commercial choice. 'I mean to sell as many albums as I can, as many records as I possibly can because I'm an artist who wants everybody to love me and everybody to buy my stuff,' he said. 'The thing is, "Love" will attract more people because of the message, man. Many, many people will not like "Mother"; it hurts them.' The obvious solution was to release both tracks as a double-A-sided single, but he had already decided to give the second side to Yoko for one of her songs. Ultimately, 'Love' was a simple piano ballad with a pretty melody, and he knew it would sell better than the harrowing 'Mother'. 'I think "Love" will do me more good,' he admitted. But the Beatles were love and the Beatles were dead, and he had no love at that time for anyone other than himself and his wife.

When Wenner questioned him about his anti-war activism he perceptively asked, 'You chose the word "peace" and not "love", or another word that means the same thing. What did you like about the word "peace"?' For Lennon, the move from love to peace was a move away from the Beatles. In these circumstances, releasing 'Love' as a single for commercial reasons would be dishonest. Instead, he released 'Mother'. It was not a hit, and stalled at number 43 in the US charts. No single from the album was released in the UK.

In the years that followed, Lennon did a lot of apologising to the people he insulted and criticised in this interview. Many accepted his apologies, knowing that this was just what Lennon was like. Others were less forgiving. George Martin, for example, challenged Lennon about what he said in 1974. According to Martin, Lennon 'said, "Oh Christ, I was stoned out of my fucking mind. You didn't take any notice of that, did you?" I said, "Well, I did, and it hurt." '

The central message of the interview, however – that John Lennon was emotionally honest, brave, and the sole genius in the Beatles – was one that the emerging serious rock press was happy to accept at face value. This, as we shall see, would frame how the Beatles were remembered for decades.

1970: THE BEST

The 1970s began in a spirit of optimism and curiosity about what the future had in store. Given how much society, technology and culture had changed in the 1960s, the possibilities for the years ahead seemed endless. Man had just walked on the moon, and extraordinary new thinking machines called computers promised to change the world radically. The future seemed wonderfully exciting. Alongside this looking forward, however, began the long, ongoing process of trying to grasp what had happened in the 1960s. You can see the beginnings of this endeavour in a documentary screened on 30 December 1969, which attempted to define the 'Man of the Decade' – the one person whose actions had had the greatest impact on the world. John Lennon was one of three men nominated for the accolade. Lennon had been chosen by the anthropologist Desmond Morris, while Alistair Cooke selected John F. Kennedy and Mary McCarthy argued for Hồ Chí Minh. There was no talk of a 'Woman of the Decade', of course, because this was still the 1960s.

That Lennon should be 'Man of the Decade' was not a universally accepted idea – the *Daily Mirror*, for example, had crowned him 'Clown of the Year' less than two weeks earlier. But with the benefits of fifty years of hindsight, the nomination holds up quite well. If you were to select one person to define the extraordinary changes that took place in the 1960s, John Lennon has to be a strong choice.

Lennon and the Beatles did not make too much of a deal about this honour. To reference it would have been seen as arrogant, and evidence that Lennon had got 'up himself' – regardless of the fact that Lennon was indeed that significant. To say that the Beatles are the best band ever is generally uncontroversial, both in terms of sales and their music, yet the closest you will get to them boasting is McCartney's claim that they were 'a good little group'. Here is a striking difference between the world of the Beatles and the world of James Bond. Fleming and Bond were endlessly declaring that things in their lives were 'the best'. In the novel *Goldfinger*, for example, Bond has the best suite, the best table in the restaurant, the best caviar and, when playing golf, he hit the best drive of the day. There is talk of the best medical attention and the best man in Geneva, and at one point Bond considers writing a book that would contain the best of all that has been written about unarmed combat. It does not take long before the reader starts to wonder if all these things really are the best, or whether there is some psychological reason why he is compelled to endlessly insist they are. Enjoying some lamb cutlets in *Moonraker*, for example, Bond tells us that they are 'superb [...] The best English cooking is the best in the world.' They probably were very nice cutlets, but they would have tasted just as good without the hyperbole.

Bond's belief that he knows exactly what the best is appears early in the first novel *Casino Royale*, when he goes to the bar and orders a dry martini in a deep champagne goblet. Not trusting the barman to know how to make a martini, he gives him specific instructions. 'Three measures of Gordon's, one of vodka, half a measure of Kina Lillet. Shake it very well until it's ice cold, then add a large thin slice of lemon-peel.' When the drink arrives, he tells the barman that it is 'Excellent,' then adds, 'But if you can get a vodka made with grain instead of potatoes, you will find it still better.' Most people who have worked in the service industries will recognise a customer like this.

Bond's signature martini, one shaken and not stirred, had been born. It was a drink specially chosen to express Bond's modern sophistication – he does not drink whisky or brandy like the older establishment, neither does he drink anything common like beer. Bond's drink of choice became so iconic because of what it said about his character – that he recognised quality and the minutiae of the material world. This has kept Bond ordering martinis in the films long after the associations they had in the 1950s had gone. When Timothy Dalton's brooding Welsh Bond drinks one, for example, it makes him look almost camp. There is much debate among cocktail aficionados, however, as to the objective quality of this drink. Many feel that shaking rather than stirring 'bruises' the gin, giving a bitter taste that damages the overall effect. But it is not whether this is the best drink that matters here. It is that Bond needs to believe that he knows what is best.

The belief that superior people recognise the best in life was a core element of both Fleming and Bond's worldview. Wherever they went in the world, they would insist that they knew the best restaurant, or that the restaurant they were going to did the best version of a particular drink or dish, or that the sommelier was the best sommelier this side of the Alps. This was necessary to psychologically support an idea they had been taught as children, which was that they too were superior. It helped, of course, that what was considered best was also expensive, so only people like them could enjoy such quality. This is another aspect of Bond's character which comes directly from his creator. When Fleming invited Raymond Chandler to lunch, he insisted that the restaurant he chose had the best *pâté maison* in town, and when he introduced Chandler to his old friend Rupert Hart-Davis he described him as 'the best young publisher in town'.

This was a family trait. When Fleming's older brother Peter wanted to marry the actor Celia Johnson, who would go on to star in *Brief Encounter* (1945) and *The Prime of Miss Jean Brodie* (1969), their mother disapproved. She thought that the actor was beneath her son, so she threatened to cut Peter off from the family fortune – a common scenario in the Fleming family. Peter was the golden child, a talented travel writer and the author of popular books like *Brazilian Adventure* (1933) and *News From Tartary* (1936). Ian was always seen as a disappointment in comparison. Speaking in defence of his brother's wish to marry, Ian told his mother that Peter was 'without question one of the two or three most brilliant men of his generation [...] we, and ultimately the whole of England, have a lot to be grateful for in Peter's existence. He really is setting a standard of sanity and truthfulness for a whole generation – he alone, a lot of people think.' Peter Fleming, it hardly needs saying, was not one of the two or three most brilliant men of his generation, regardless of the upper-class need to make such claims. He was a good travel writer who had an impressive wartime career, and that's more than enough to be proud of. When he is remembered now, it is for being the brother of the man who invented James Bond or for being Celia Johnson's husband. To Peter's credit, he did marry Johnson despite his mother's protests.

Thanks to Bond, the link between privilege and spycraft is now firmly culturally established. The movie *Kingsman: The Secret Service* (2014) was an attempt to create a more fantastical version of the Bond franchise. It has many references to the films that inspired it, not least scenes in which the characters discuss Bond movies. The lead character, played by Taron Egerton, begins as a working-class apprentice, but before he can become a master spy at the end of the film he must first evolve into an expensively tailored Bond-like establishment figure.

The idea that privilege and breeding are the markers of a good spy can also be found outside the films, in the world of real espionage. After the Soviet spies responsible for the Salisbury poisoning were identified, for example, they were forced into a humiliating television interview. During this they claimed to be tourists who visited Britain to see Salisbury Cathedral's famous '123-metre spire'. After the interview, the former GRU agent and Soviet defector Viktor Suvorov complained about the quality of current Soviet espionage. The Salisbury poisoners 'were poorly educated and provincial', he thought, and he longed for the days when 'GRU officers were Moscow slicks with university degrees, unaccented foreign languages, and Soviet-posh manners'. A similar complaint was voiced by Andrei Soldatov, co-founder and editor of an investigative website that monitors Russian secret services. The FSB, the Russian Federal Security Services, he lamented, 'are narrow-minded people. They are not like MI6 officers who have been to Cambridge and are supposedly the cream of the crop.' The link between background and competence, however, is not borne out by reality.

The reality of intelligence work is more accurately depicted in the films featuring Michael Caine's working-class spy Harry Palmer, or in the work of John le Carré, than in the books of Ian Fleming. Even these fictions had to take certain liberties to keep the subject interesting. Le Carré had been a spy himself, and it was his experience that the world of spies was a world of incompetence. As he described it, 'For a while you wondered whether the fools were pretending to be fools as some kind of deception, or whether there was a real efficient service somewhere else. Later in my fiction, I invented one. But alas the reality was the mediocrity. Ex-colonial policemen mingling with failed academics, failed lawyers, failed missionaries and failed debutantes gave our canteen the amorphous quality of an Old School outing on the Orient Express. Everyone seemed to smell of failure.'

Le Carré's opinion matched that of journalists who have investigated the secret services. Our initial assumption about spies is that they are competent and know what they are doing. 'But the strange fact is that often when you look into the history of spies what you discover is something very different,' concluded the BBC's Adam Curtis. 'It is not the story of men and women who have a better and deeper understanding of the world than we do. In fact in many cases it is the story of weirdos who have created a completely mad version of the world that they then impose on the rest of us.' The journalist Phillip Knightley quotes an intelligence officer who describes British Intelligence as a dumping ground for the establishment's most mediocre. 'The whole organisation was riddled with nepotism – dim, dreary people of utter unmemorability [...] The entire service was decrepit and incompetent.' There is concern that the system remains an inept 'old boys club' to this day. A government-backed 2021 report concluded that senior civil servants are as privileged today as they were fifty years ago, with fewer than one in five coming from a working-class background.

The British writer Simon Winder has also commented on how an elite background 'seems or seemed to imply a close and valuable link with the world of espionage'. He suspected that something may be amiss with this picture while at Oxford, when it became known that a fellow student had been recruited – 'a tubby oddball who as a student had dressed in SS uniform. Photos showed him to be an almost Monty Python-like security risk, and the fact that someone somewhere [had recruited him] rather knocked the last of the bloom from the secret service rose.'

Most of these analyses are from people who went to Oxbridge, it should be noted. A distinctive belief common to people of this background is that the world is made up of people who are not very good, so whether these are fair assessments of the security services is hard to say. The level of secrecy surrounding intelligence work prevents us from seeing the true picture. This secrecy, however, is useful because it allows writers like Fleming to offer an alternative view – that British spies are the best in the world.

In *From Russia with Love*, Lieutenant-General Vozdvishensky of the Ministry of Foreign Affairs reminds a meeting of top Soviet espionage agencies how much they all respect the British. 'Their Security Service is excellent,' he says. 'England, being an island, has great security advantages and their so-called MI5 employs men with good education and good brains. Their Secret Service is still better.' Fearful of praising the enemy too much, he then adds, 'Of course, most of their strength lies in myth – in the myth of Scotland Yard, of Sherlock Holmes, of the Secret Service. We certainly have nothing to fear from these gentlemen. But this myth is a hindrance which it would be good to set aside.' The best way to destroy the British myth of intelligence competence, they decide, is to kill James Bond. Fleming wrote this in 1956, before the series really took off, at a time when he had lost interest in Bond and was thinking of killing him off. He did not know then that his fiction would turn into truth, and that James Bond would indeed become the myth of competence and quality in British Intelligence.

Of course, it is not reality that matters here. The world of the establishment is itself like a spell or a glamour, which bewitches and seduces, and can easily distract us away from boring old reality. The Bond films are that spell at its strongest, still convincing the rest of the world that Britain is more like *Downton Abbey* than *Monty Python*. For all that Harold Wilson recognised the importance of the Beatles in presenting a new, fairer, more vibrant story of Britain, there was nothing he could do about the seductive appeal of the establishment's champion. As the 1970s began, Bond, despite everything that had changed in the 1960s, continued to insist that he and the British establishment were the best in the world. And now that the Beatles had broken up there was nothing of equal stature to contradict him. As the establishment knows well, if you keep up a story for long enough it will eventually begin to seem almost plausible.

1970: PHIL AND ALLEN

The ultimate enemy of James Bond was the cruel, murderous criminal organisation SPECTRE – the Special Executive for Counter-intelligence, Terrorism, Revenge and Extortion. It's a name that is nothing if not honest, but it does highlight just how ludicrous the idea of such an organisation is. When SPECTRE returned for the 2015 Daniel Craig movie *Spectre*, they wisely dropped the idea that the name was an acronym.

While Bond had SPECTRE, the 1970 Beatles had Phil Spector, a cruel, murderous record producer. Spector was a horror. He kept his second wife, Ronnie Spector of the Ronettes, as a virtual prisoner in a home surrounded by guard dogs and barbed wire. On the occasions she was allowed out on her own, it was on the condition that she drove with a life-sized mannequin of Spector in the passenger seat of her car. He had a glass-topped, gold-plated coffin installed in the basement of their home and told her that this was where her body would be displayed, after he had her killed, if she attempted to leave him. He had a great love for guns and the feeling of power they gave him. While working on a John Lennon solo album in 1973, he arrived at the LA studio dressed

as a surgeon and fired a gun next to Lennon's ear. When producing Leonard Cohen's 1977 album *Death of a Ladies Man*, he held a
gun to Cohen's throat and said, 'Leonard, I love you.' Cohen later
described Spector as 'the worst human being I've ever met'.

When Spector eventually murdered someone, then, it was not
completely unexpected. In 2003, he killed the actor Lana Clarkson
by shooting her in the mouth in his Californian home. In 2009 he
was found guilty of murder and sentenced to nineteen years-to-life,
eventually dying of Covid-19 related complications in prison in
2021.

That Spector was dangerous was readily apparent for years, but
the music industry was more than ready to overlook such details as
long as he kept delivering hits. Violent tendencies were one thing,
but the ability to record the drum sound on the Ronettes' 'Be My
Baby' was quite another. The Beatles had all loved his production
work for girl groups like the Crystals and the Ronettes. Lennon,
in particular, would stick with Spector long after others decided
to keep their distance.

The Beatles' recordings of the 1960s had benefited from the pro-
fessionalism and talent of their original producer George Martin.
Even at their wildest and most experimental, the production of
Beatles recordings had always showed exceptional good taste. Or at
least they did, until Lennon handed recordings of the aborted early
1969 *Get Back* project to Phil Spector. This was originally intended
as a 'warts and all' depiction of the Beatles as four musicians in
a room, with no overdubs, retakes or studio polish, writing and
recording an album from scratch over the course of a month. It
was, as Lennon liked to say, the Beatles with their trousers down.
When the producer Glyn Johns delivered the finished album,
painstakingly assembled from many hours of rehearsal recordings, he had fulfilled his brief perfectly. In the cold light of day,
however, the band were less keen on appearing in public with

their trousers down than they had first thought. Glyn Johns' *Get Back* album was quietly shelved, and the band went back to the safety of George Martin to record *Abbey Road*, a 'proper' album they could be proud of.

On 23 March 1970 Lennon gave the *Get Back* tapes to Spector, with the brief to make something of them. Lennon and his new manager Allen Klein did this with Harrison's approval, but without telling McCartney. Spector spent less than six weeks on the project, and he does not appear to have sifted through all the hours of tapes to find the best takes of each song. He smothered a few of the songs with an avalanche of syrupy, sentimental strings and overdubs, and put together the posthumous album *Let It Be*, which was released in 1970 after the band's split had become public knowledge. McCartney's song 'The Long and Winding Road', in particular, went from an open-hearted piano ballad to a saccharine slog which ruined the song for a generation.

Spector's attempts to tart up the recordings were in opposition to the original aim of the project. The result was roughly recorded rehearsals smothered with orchestras and overdubs, an awkward mashup that failed to find a clear identity. Klein was delighted, because he now had a 'new' Beatles album to sell, but the band would never have dropped their quality controls like this in the 1960s. As Lennon described the situation, '[Spector] always wanted to work with the Beatles and he was given the shittiest load of badly recorded shit – and with a lousy feeling to it – ever. And he made something out of it. It wasn't fantastic, but I heard it, I didn't puke.'

George Martin was not happy about Spector's involvement. 'That made me very angry,' he later said. 'And it made Paul even angrier, because neither he nor I knew about it till it had been done. It happened behind our backs because it was done when Allen Klein was running John. He'd organised Phil Spector and I think George and Ringo had gone along with it.' When McCartney heard the finished product, he wrote Klein a formal letter asking for it to be changed, but this was ignored. As Derek Taylor recalled, 'I know that Paul was very cross about "The Long and Winding Road" being interfered with. I took the view that nobody should have ever interfered with their music. That was for me – I don't want to say shocking – but wrong, certainly. And if you were a McCartney seeing your work being altered ... I can imagine the outrage!'

Over thirty years later, in 2003, McCartney attempted to fix the situation by stripping the album of Spector's overdubs and re-releasing it under the name *Let It Be ... Naked*. Spector responded by saying, 'Paul had no problem picking up the Academy Award for the *Let It Be* movie soundtrack, nor did he have any problem in using my arrangement of the string and horn and choir parts when he performed it during twenty-five years of touring on his own. If Paul wants to get into a pissing contest about it, he's got me mixed up with someone who gives a shit.' Phil Spector was, as you can probably tell, very different to George Martin.

In their early years, the Beatles had a strange knack of finding thoroughly decent human beings to help them, who would turn up just when they were needed. Brian Epstein and George Martin are widely seen as diamonds, who worked hard for the band and used their unique talents to further the Beatles' career. It is hard to imagine how the Beatles story could ever have occurred had the band not met, and trusted, these two special individuals. It's true that, with hindsight, some of Epstein's business deals could be criticised, especially those related to the licensing of American merchandise. But nobody had ever managed anything like the Beatles before, and Epstein was essentially inventing the role of a modern rock manager as he went along. Anyone in the same position would have been equally inexperienced.

Both Epstein and Martin met the Beatles before the band was rich and famous, so their decisions to work with them were not swayed by ulterior motives. After Beatlemania, they would never be able to meet anyone on this level again. Their wealth and global celebrity was an ever-present factor in their relationships with every new person they met for the rest of their lives. In the years after Rishikesh, after Lennon had replaced Cynthia and acid with Yoko and heroin, he began attracting people who were not just unlike Epstein and Martin, but almost their complete opposites.

Allen Klein was the New Jersey-born manager of the Rolling Stones. On his desk in New York was a plinth carved with an amended version of Psalm 23, which gives a clear account of how he saw himself: 'Yea, though I walk through the valley of the shadow of death, I will fear no evil, 'cause I'm the biggest bastard in the valley . . .' In a 1971 *Playboy* interview he was asked if he would lie to get what he wanted. 'Oh sure,' he replied. And would he steal? 'Probably'. As he described his worldview, 'The music business is about 99 per cent no-talent losers who can't stand a winner in their midst. I'm a winner, and if they want to sour grape my success by calling me names, let them. I don't give a shit [. . .] It's a game, for Chrissakes, and winning is everything.'

Klein's great dream was to be the manager of the Beatles. That was how you won the rock manager game. When he heard that the band had business problems following the death of Brian Epstein and the establishing of their company Apple, he saw his opportunity. He calculated that the way to get the Beatles was to target John, in the belief that the rest of the band would follow his lead. His strategy here was to not only flatter John, but to also praise the artistic talent of Yoko. It worked perfectly. Lennon enthused about Klein to Harrison after he and Yoko first met him in January 1969, saying, 'He knows me as much as you do. *Incredible* guy. We were both stunned.' In later years, after it was clear to even John that Klein was a crook who couldn't be trusted, he side-stepped his decision to hire him by saying, 'He was the only one that Yoko liked.'

Once Klein had Lennon, it looked like he would soon have control of all the Beatles. George and Ringo were never going to argue with John, and both agreed to accept Klein. McCartney, however, refused. As he later put it, 'I didn't trust him and I certainly didn't want him as my manager.' McCartney's reasons were clear to anyone who read the two-page *Sunday Times* investigation into Klein that was published on 13 April 1969, entitled 'The Toughest Wheeler-Dealer in the Pop Jungle'. It was a tale of dubious share dealings, multiple court cases and investigations by the US tax authorities. It also claimed that Klein negotiated a $1.25m advance from Decca records for the Rolling Stones in 1965 and kept it for himself. Klein had incorporated a US company called Nanker Phelge – the same name as the Stones' own company. The band had not realised that this version of Nanker Phelge was different, and wholly owned by Klein. Jagger warned McCartney to have nothing to do with Klein, or he would be making 'the biggest mistake you can make'.

McCartney's resolve to not be managed by Klein proved to be a further wedge that separated him from his three bandmates. As McCartney saw it, working with people like Klein was just not the sort of thing that the Beatles did. The whole point of being in the Beatles, in a sense, was to show that you did not need to compromise, and you did not need to put up with villains. The resulting division was a large factor in McCartney's subsequent depression. 'I was going through a bad time, what I suspect was almost a nervous breakdown,' he said. 'I remember lying awake at nights shaking, which has not happened to me since.' When McCartney did sleep, he had terrifying dreams in which Klein was his dentist. 'I can't be with this guy any longer,' he told people, 'he's in my dreams and he's a baddie.' Lennon, Starr and Harrison would eventually agree that McCartney had been right about Klein, especially after Klein was jailed for tax fraud in 1980.

One thing Klein did achieve which hugely benefited the Beatles – and himself – was to negotiate a far better royalty rate on their records with EMI, once the existing contract had expired. Given the extraordinary sales of the *White Album* and *Abbey Road*, however, it would have been surprising if he had not been able to do this, seeing as he held all the cards in the negotiations. In many other areas he failed the band badly. These included his attempts to acquire the publishing company Northern Songs and the share in the Beatles owned by Epstein's family company NEMS, advising Lennon when he was sued for plagiarism for 'Come Together', and failing to arrange charity tax status for Harrison's *Concert for Bangladesh*. More importantly, his use of a 'divide and conquer' strategy to acquire control of the Beatles by focusing on John, at a time when Lennon and McCartney needed to mend their relation-ship, was a large factor in preventing it from healing. For those who want to blame someone for the end of the Beatles – someone other than John – then Allen Klein is a strong choice. Indeed, the depictions of Klein in many Beatles biographies paint him as such a cartoon villain that you wonder whether a more nuanced re-evaluation is long overdue. At the time of writing, however, there is no sign of this happening.

Allen Klein and Phil Spector, then, were like evil versions of Epstein and Martin from a parallel dimension. It is tempting to speculate whether Lennon's decision to work with them indicated that there was some unconscious self-sabotage at play. He was not noted for his skill at judging people, but usually the dubious characters he befriended were harmless. With Klein and Spector, however, his poor character choices were anything but. He was recasting the Beatles story and replacing decent people with terrible ones. No band could have survived that.

The end of the Beatles was always going to be sad, but they didn't deserve Phil Spector and Allen Klein. It would have been better to face Bond's SPECTRE than foes like these.

1971: TO DENY THAT LOVE
WAS DESIRABLE

After the long-haired George Lazenby walked away from fame, fortune and Bond, the search was on for a new actor to play the role. The next film was *Diamonds Are Forever*, a predominantly Las Vegas-based story that would, it was hoped, appeal to an American market that had been unconvinced by Lazenby. To this end producers Broccoli and Saltzman considered a number of American actors for the role, including Clint Eastwood, Adam West and Burt Reynolds, before they eventually cast the Los Angeles-born John Gavin. The studio, however, were nervous. They wanted the winning formula of mid-sixties Bond back. This meant a return for *Goldfinger*'s director Guy Hamilton, a Shirley Bassey-sung theme tune – and Sean Connery, no matter how much it cost to get him. It turned out that it would cost an unprecedented $1.25m plus the funding of two unrelated films of Connery's choice. John Gavin's contract also had to be honoured, so there was the added expense of paying him in full.

This course correction for the Bond franchise was clearly an expensive operation, but such was the unease at United Artists that it was seen as a cost that had to be paid. Lazenby had left Bond in a position that broke the character – he had fallen in love. Obviously, his love was heading straight to the grave, but that still didn't change the fact that Bond's spell had been broken. It was as if Robin Hood had robbed from the poor, or King Arthur had cowardly run from battle. There was no point spending millions on bringing the old team back together if this problem was not addressed. The response was perhaps the bleakest sequence in any of the Bond films, a strident, unashamed declaration that they would choose death over love, and be proud of it. We are talking, or course, about the *Diamonds Are Forever* theme tune.

Such was the verve and confidence of the *Diamonds Are Forever* title sequence that audiences largely failed to recognise just how dark it was. For most people, the overwhelming message was that diamonds are absolutely brilliant, which didn't sound too problematic. Perhaps the way the title sequence lingered on huge glittering gems being worn by otherwise naked women was a factor here. John Barry's gorgeous arrangement of his theme and Shirley Bassey in full effect were also a masterpiece of misdirection. But the Don Black lyrics that Bassey made her own were a full-fronted embrace of a loveless future.

The song was about a woman who had been rejected or had her heart broken, and who vowed never to allow herself to be hurt again. Instead of risking a new relationship, her future would be focused on the owning of diamonds. These would never leave her, being inanimate lumps of carbon. They were also transparent, so she could see inside them and know that nothing hides in there that would hurt her. Possessing glittering stones with a hefty resale value, Bassey proclaimed, was a better future goal than risking the experience of love. To reach this conclusion, she had to deny that love was desirable. 'I don't need love, for what good will love do me?' the character in the song declared, tragically, as her heart closed and her isolation from others became complete. In the works of William Blake, Hell was something that existed in this world, not the next. It was the state that followed when people closed themselves off from others – a 'Hell of our own making'.

Here, then, was the opposite philosophy to McCartney's song 'Can't Buy Me Love', which claimed that material possessions were ultimately unimportant compared to genuine relationships and their pivotal role in a life worth living. You can only admire how skilfully the film sold it. John Barry, Don Black and Shirley Bassey were able to make Blakean eternal death incredibly appealing. When this horrific song opened the film, audiences marvelled at it and aspired to the glamorous world it painted. The Lazenby misstep was forgotten. Bond was death once again. It would be a very long time before anyone in the Bond world would dare to bring back love.

For the following Bond film *Live and Let Die*, Roger Moore's debut as 007, John Barry was for the first time unavailable to write the score. Producers Saltzman and Broccoli realised that this was an opportunity to try something new, because the arrival of a new lead actor was the perfect time for a fresh, contemporary approach. They asked George Martin to score the film and Paul McCartney to write the theme tune. McCartney has recalled how he responded to the initial approach by casually saying, ' "Yeah, I'd probably be interested" – you know, not trying to seem too enthusiastic. Writing a Bond song is a bit of an accolade, and I always had a sneaking ambition to do it.' *Rolling Stone* magazine responded to the news with the catty comment, 'So, it's come to that.'

The offer of the Bond theme came at a time when Paul's critical standing was at rock bottom. His first solo album *McCartney* had been seen as lightweight and throwaway. He had attempted to address those criticisms by working harder on his next solo album, the more polished *Ram* (1971). This is now considered by McCartney aficionados to be one of his best records, but the reviews were vicious. *Rolling Stone*, for example, called it 'incredibly inconsequential' and 'monumentally irrelevant'. By this point the narrative of brilliant Lennon and old-fashioned McCartney was set. He responded by dropping his solo career and forming a new band, Wings, although the reviews for the debut Wings album *Wild Life* were no better. Meanwhile, Ringo proved to be the solo Beatle most able to achieve hit singles, and the critical and commercial success of Harrison's *All Things Must Pass* saw the two minor Beatles, freed from the shackles of the band, overtaking the famed Lennon–McCartney partnership as successful recording artists.

It seemed that whatever he tried, McCartney just made himself more and more unhip. Seeing as he'd been about the hippest person on the planet in the mid-1960s, this must have been a serious shock to his sense of self-worth. In 1972, Paul tried to write a Lennon-style bold, political song in the vein of John's critically approved 'Power to the People' or 'Give Peace a Chance'. Reacting to the horror of the 'Bloody Sunday' Bogside Massacre in Derry, the first Wings single was a Slade-like singalong called 'Give Ireland Back to the Irish' that was generally seen as naive and a little embarrassing, even by Irish nationalists. Wings' guitarist was then Henry McCullough, a Protestant from Portstewart in Northern Ireland, and McCartney did not seem to grasp how this song would affect him or his family. The reaction may explain why, since the single's release, McCartney has never gigged in Northern Ireland.

In what is surely one of the most abrupt and unsuccessful course-corrections in music history, Wings followed 'Give Ireland Back to the Irish' with their second single, a cover of the nursery rhyme 'Mary Had a Little Lamb'. By this point, it seemed hard to imagine how Paul could ever recover his commercial and critical appeal. The answer, it turned out, was to do the unthinkable. The Beatles had been a celebration of love, but the love had died and Paul's career also seemed close to death. And so McCartney crossed the Rubicon, and entered the world of Bond.

To survive, McCartney put his values and sense of identity to one side. He wrote a song of death rather than love. 'Live and Let Die' is surely the most unMcCartney-ish sentiment you can imagine, but then McCartney was nothing if not versatile, ambitious and unnaturally talented. The crowd-pleasing classy bombast of the Bond films was a world away from the music he had recorded before, but he was bold enough to take on the challenge regardless. Lyrically, the song talks of someone who used to believe in 'live and let live', but who was broken by the world, and instead goes on the attack. Given the context, it's tempting to see this as autobiographical.

It was a huge hit. 'Live and Let Die' became the first Bond theme to be nominated for an Oscar, and also the first to top a number of US charts. It transformed the career of Wings, who went on to become one of the biggest bands of the 1970s, particularly in America. McCartney's dangerous gamble proved to be a great success, and the song was so bombastic and full on that Guns N' Roses covered it in the 1990s. When the Guns N' Roses version was a big hit, McCartney's children told their school friends that their dad had written it, but their friends didn't believe them. The song is also one of the few aspects of the Bond franchise that is generally recognised by Generation Z. They don't associate it with Bond, admittedly. They know it from the Frog King's funeral in *Shrek the Third*.

All this happened when the likelihood of a Beatles reunion was as high as it would ever be. By 1973, relations between the four were improving. John and Paul had stopped lashing out at each other in songs and interviews, and the growing rift between

George and John still seemed mendable. When Ringo recorded his self-titled solo album that year, John, Paul and George all wrote and played on it. The big sticking point in the inter-band politics had been the presence of Allen Klein, who Paul still refused to have anything to do with. Klein's contract with John, George and Ringo expired in 1973, however, and was not renewed. John, George and Ringo were talking about playing together again.

Had Paul not then finally found success outside the band, it is possible that he may have agreed to a reunion. The success of 'Live and Let Die', followed by the album *Band on the Run*, made Paul McCartney and Wings a going concern at exactly the point when a Beatles reunion looked most plausible. Bond didn't kill the Beatles, but it is a strange irony that once they had split, he kept them dead.

1973: CHRISTOPHER LEE (1922–2015)

On 28 October 1973 the actor Christopher Lee joined a strange and unlikely group of entertainers outside a sixteenth-century Tudor mansion in Hounslow, west London, for a night shoot. Here Lee and several others posed with Paul and Linda McCartney as they shot the cover of the Wings album *Band on the Run*.

Just over a week later, filming began on the Bond movie *The Man with the Golden Gun,* in which Lee starred as the title character, the triple-nippled upper-class assassin Scaramanga. Lee played an evil mirror of Bond – an English killer every bit as suave and charming as 007, but who is deemed a villain because he kills for money instead of Queen and country. The character was named after a pupil at Eton that Ian Fleming had particularly disliked.

Alongside Lee on the cover were the three members of Wings – Paul, Linda and Denny Laine – plus the boxer John Conteh, the talk-show host Michael Parkinson, the actor James Coburn, and the singer Kenny Lynch, who shared the bill with the Beatles on a number of their early theatre shows and was the first person to cover a Lennon–McCartney song. To contemporary eyes, the cover image now seems far darker than it did in the 1970s, because the final member of the cast was the celebrity chef, Liberal Member of Parliament and – if multiple credible posthumous allegations are to be believed – serial child abuser Clement Freud.

It seemed then, as it does now, to be an unlikely group of 1970s celebrities. Whatever the logic Paul used when he chose those particular people, it was noticeably different from that which selected the collection of heroes and icons on the sleeve of *Sgt. Pepper*. He clearly wasn't using this image to appeal to youth culture or to bring him cultural hipness. If he was hoping to bypass the critics and appeal directly to a mainstream, slightly older record-buying audience, then the choice of faces on the cover proved to be very successful. This was the album that put McCartney back on track towards the extraordinary commercial success he achieved in the late 1970s and early 1980s.

Dressed in black suits, the group posed as escaping prisoners caught in the glare of a security spotlight. The shoot required darkness, so McCartney threw a party for his models beforehand, to kill the time until night had fallen. Only the photographer Clive Arrowsmith remained sober. As he later recalled, 'I was the only one there who wasn't wasted, I was too scared. This was my first really big job.'

Perhaps because of McCartney's then-toxic critical reputation, it was a while before people recognised the record's quality. The album took eight months to reach number one in the UK, during which time Lee completed his portrayal of his iconic Bond villain. The film took him around the world, with shoots in England, Bangkok, Thailand and the then remote island of Ko Khao Phing Kan. This has since become a popular tourist attraction and is now called James Bond Island.

One indication of the extent to which *Band on the Run* became a commercial breakthrough for McCartney came in 1977, when the album was officially released in Russia on the government-run label *Melodiya*. It was a significant milestone: the first Beatle-related album to become officially available in the USSR, where the actual music of the Beatles was still considered too subversive to receive an official release. This remained the case until the album *A Hard Day's Night* was finally released in 1986, following the arrival of President Gorbachev and his programme of *Perestroika*.

The Russian release of *Band on the Run* was indicative of McCartney's career in the late 1970s. He had built his new band up until it became an extraordinary commercial success, as documented in the *Wings Over America* tour film. On some measures his success was over and above that of the Beatles. His 'Mull of Kintyre' single, for example, outsold the Beatles' 'She Loves You' and became the biggest-selling UK single at that time. But McCartney's huge commercial success came without the culture-shifting, transcendent quality that made Moscow fear the music of the Beatles. The success of Wings was enormous in all the ways that can be measured, but that extra, ineffable quality which the Beatles possessed was absent. When Steve Coogan's comedy character Alan Partridge described Wings as 'Only the band the Beatles could have been!' it is the audience's recognition of this unmeasurable missing quality that makes the joke work.

That's not to say that McCartney had lost all his previous sub-versiveness, or that Wings were wholly acceptable to the Soviet state. The title track to *Band on the Run* was removed from its Russian release; its references to jailbreaks, prisoners and freedom were considered unacceptable to the Russian censors. It was re-placed with the more palatable 'Silly Love Songs', which became the new album opener. Changes like this were common on the few Western albums allowed a release during the brief period of cultural relaxation that followed the 1975 Helsinki Accords. Disco proved to be popular with the Russian censors, with the notable exception of Boney M's description of Rasputin as 'Russia's greatest love machine'. That was never going to be allowed.

The loss of the song 'Band on the Run' meant that the jailbreak cover with Christopher Lee was also changed, to an inoffensive portrait of McCartney. This was not the only indignity that Lee had to suffer from the Russian state. Cubby Broccoli organised a private screening of *The Man with the Golden Gun* for Soviet officials. This gave the film the honour of being the first Bond film to be screened in Moscow – although not, of course, for the Russian public. Quite why Broccoli did this was unclear, but perhaps he hoped that one day James Bond would be permitted in Russian cinemas, or that he would be granted permission to film there. As Lee later told the story, one of the officials approached Broccoli after the screening and said, ' "That man Scaramanga – interesting!" Cubby waited, while the Russian's eyes bored into him. Then the Russian added sternly, "Inadequate training." ' To the eyes of Soviet officials, what mattered was the failure of the villain's mission.

In many ways, Lee is ideally suited to cross between the worlds of both Bond and Beatledom. The Beatles had originally met him at the film studios when they were making *A Hard Day's Night*, and Lee also starred with Ringo in the 1969 movie *The Magic Christian*. McCartney got in touch again ten years after they first met to ask him to appear on the album cover. Lee also always seemed likely to enter the Bond film universe. He was a member of the same elevated and incestuous social world as Ian Fleming, and indeed the brother of Ian's mother Evelyn was Lee's stepfather. As Lee noted about their slightly complicated family connection, 'It pleased [Fleming] to call me his cousin, and it pleases me to return the compliment.' When the first Bond film was about to enter production, Fleming offered Lee the title role of *Dr. No* during a round of golf. Lee was delighted, but Fleming was unaware that the director and producers had already settled on Joseph Wiseman for the part.

Like Fleming, Lee's relationship with his parents appears cold and dysfunctional to us now, with his mother frequently telling him he was a mistake and his father leaving when he was four. His memory of his first private school was that 'I felt I had only to breathe nervously to be beaten.' Another similarity with Fleming was that Lee could rely on family connections to find employment. Although he had been a disappointing student and left education with no real qualifications or apparent skills, he was given a job at a shipping company as a favour to his banker stepfather. After serving in the Second World War he lunched in London with the Italian Ambassador, his cousin Nicolò, and talk turned to what Lee should do next. Nicolò suddenly suggested, 'Why don't you become an actor, Christopher?' After Lee considered this and found it appealed, Nicolò arranged for him to meet a friend at the Rank Organisation. Despite his lack of acting experience, Lee was promptly given a seven-year contract.

His first part was opposite Lois Maxwell, better known to the public as Miss Moneypenny, in a film directed by Terence Young, who directed *Dr. No, From Russia with Love* and *Thunderball*. This casual employment-via-family-friends arrangement was in stark contrast to the career of the Beatles, who played over 600 gigs in Hamburg, Liverpool and the northwest before they attracted the interest of EMI. As McCartney often noted, the Beatles had to work for it.

For all the nepotism that launched his career, however, there is no doubt that Lee proved himself to be an actor of some distinction. He went on to appear in over 200 films over seven decades. As well as playing the Bond villain Scaramanga, Lee was perhaps the definitive Dracula as well as Frankenstein's monster, Fu Manchu and the Mummy. He was Count Dooku in *Star Wars*, the wizard

Saruman in *Lord of the Rings* and *The Hobbit*, Lord Summerisle in *The Wicker Man*, and he played both Sherlock and Mycroft Holmes. He was knighted by Prince Charles in 2009 for services to drama and charity, received a BAFTA fellowship in 2011, and a BFI fellowship in 2013.

For all their connections, friendship and similarities, Lee and Fleming were men with very different characters. Fleming dreamed of being a brave action hero and had to invent a fictional avatar to compensate for his cushy desk job during the war. In contrast, Lee's life was genuinely one of heroic adventure. He had a strange knack of meeting historically significant people or finding himself in glamorous and dangerous situations.

As a child, Lee remembered being woken from his bed and brought downstairs so that he could meet the killers of Rasputin. This incident seems to have set the tone of melodrama that was such a recurring theme in his life. He would later meet the man who executed Mussolini, and at the age of seventeen he witnessed the last public execution by guillotine in France. After the execution he travelled south and crossed into Italy in drag, with two large peaches in his shirt to help sell the illusion, seemingly just for the fun of it. His little finger was misshapen because it was damaged in a sword fight with Errol Flynn, following what he described as 'a long lunch'. He caught malaria seven times, climbed the Pyramids of Giza, captained England in golf, and was stabbed in the neck in the Egyptian city of Ismailia. He was once attempting to escape from a troop of around forty baboons who were chasing his truck in Zimbabwe, when a leopard jumped on its roof. He was also very proud of his ability to forge signatures. Mae West once invited him up to see her in her suite at the Savoy, and his friends included the oil magnate Paul Getty, the English hangman Albert Pierrepoint and Johnny Depp. When Bond Girls Britt Ekland and Maud Adams gossiped about the cast and crew in their native Swedish on the set of *The Man with the Golden Gun*, they were horrified to discover that Lee was fluent in Swedish and understood everything they were saying. He also spoke German, Spanish, French, Italian, English, Greek, Russian and Mandarin. Just ahead of his ninetieth birthday, he recorded a pair of heavy-metal concept albums about Charlemagne with Judas Priest's Richie Faulkner. He was, if his family history is to be believed, related to Charlemagne himself.

Lee was delighted to star in *The Lord of the Rings* trilogy for director Peter Jackson, who would go on to make the acclaimed docuseries *The Beatles: Get Back*. The fantasy books were favourites of Lee's, who had once known Tolkien. While filming a scene in which Lee's character Saruman was killed by being stabbed in the back and pushed off the Tower of Orthanc, Jackson directed Lee to let out a scream. Lee questioned Jackson's choice. 'Have you any idea what kind of noise happens when somebody is stabbed in the back,' he asked Jackson, 'because I do.' According to Lee, the sound is more of a gasp than a scream, because the breath is driven out of your body.

The most likely period when Lee would have learned this information was directly after the war, when he served with the Central Registry of War Crimes and Security Suspects, or CROWCASS. This was, in effect, a crack international team of Nazi hunters. Lee had served in the RAF during the war, but he experienced a sudden, crippling headache and temporary loss of vision in his left eye while piloting a plane at 5,000ft over what is now Zimbabwe. It was the end of his flying career, but resulted in a move into intelligence work. His time tracking down war criminals in the immediate aftermath of the war is the one part of his life he couldn't bring himself to talk about in his autobiography, saying only that it 'has left me with a residue of tension [...] It possibly had more effect on me than I realised at the time.' He does mention, however, that the work took him to a number of concentration camps, some 'which had only just been cleaned up, and some that hadn't'.

Christopher Lee, then, was a real-life version of Fleming's Bondian fantasy. His politics were similar to Fleming's, as Lee was a staunch conservative who was saddened by the end of the British Empire and expressed concern about immigration. And yet, in significant ways, Lee was more like Paul McCartney than Ian Fleming. Like McCartney, Lee's long and happy marriage was often remarked upon, and considered unusual in his profession. Lee married the Danish actor Birgit 'Gitte' Krøncke in 1961, with whom he had a daughter, and the pair remained together until the end of Lee's long life. Lee's personal life was a long way from the unhappy affairs and womanising of Ian Fleming.

Perhaps more importantly, Lee possessed little of the snobbery so common in his social circles. Part of Fleming was embarrassed to be a writer of populist thrillers. He was aware that he was mocked by his wife and her friends, who looked down on his work. Lee, in contrast, felt nothing but gratitude for the horror films that made his name, and he would often speak out in favour of melodrama and genre movies in particular. Lee always fully committed to even the ropiest of roles and, unlike Fleming, never showed any sign that he was ashamed of his work or that it was beneath someone of his social background. He acts as a reminder that people are not completely shaped by their backgrounds, and that it is rash to judge people by the world they came from.

The example of Lee's life story offers up the possibility that there exists a fantasy of masculinity that is not as damaged or as toxic as Bond. It also offers the tantalising suggestion that Bond and the Beatles are not just rigid opposites, but positions that can be bridged. It makes sense, then, that if anyone in 1973 belonged in both a Bond film and on a Wings album, it was Christopher Lee.

1973: THE PROBLEM IS BOND

When the film series started in the 1960s, the concept of 'Bond Girls' was often viewed as something progressive. They were seen as a new type of woman. The Hollywood portrayal of women in the 1950s tended towards the curvaceous, bubbly and extremely feminine, like Marilyn Monroe. As the *Young Bond* author Charlie Higson has noted, Fleming 'kicked against the old-fashioned, 1950s view that women should be simpering housewives, put on a pedestal and wooed. Many in his books were athletic and independent.' When Ursula Andress stepped out of the Caribbean Sea in *Dr. No* in her bikini and knife, this was something new. Andress was strong, powerful and athletic, and a very different image of female beauty compared to Monroe. The scene as directed had Bond watching her arrival and as such has been criticised as an example of the male gaze. Yet it was both the male and female gaze that looked on Andress as she emerged from the blue waters. As the actor Britt Ekland, the lead Bond Girl in *The Man with the Golden Gun*, recalled, 'I'd seen Ursula Andress in *Dr. No* and I thought that was the most incredible-looking person I'd ever seen, not as much a role model but as a truly fun and exciting kind of woman and I thought that's what I want to do.'

The women in that first Bond film often had a sense of agency about them, possibly because it was one of the rare Bond movies to have a female co-writer, Johanna Harwood. It included details such as female receptionists checking out Bond's body when his back was turned, which suggests a level of female liberation largely missing in the rest of the franchise. Of course, for all the power and impact of Andress's arrival, she then proceeded to establish the Bond Girl template by spending the rest of the film barely dressed and in dire need of rescuing.

The toned, athletic image of Andress was taken from the depiction of women found in Fleming's books. The rushed and barely edited nature of some of his novels could reveal things about the author that a more careful writer might have covered up, and one such revealing quirk was his interest in women who had backsides that looked like young boys. As he describes Andress's character in the novel of *Dr. No*, 'the behind was almost as firm and rounded as a boy's'. Watching two gypsy women fight in *From Russia with Love*, he notes their 'hard, boyish flanks', while in the same book the bum of the Russian agent Corporal Tatiana Romanov is described as being 'flat and hard at the sides, it jutted like a man's'.

For all that this strong, confident image of women was admired at the time, there is much about the portrayal of women in 1960s Bond films that can now be difficult to watch. Even allowing for the violent world that the films are set in, the violence towards women is striking, such as the scene in which Connery approaches a sunbathing woman, rips her bikini top off and starts to strangle her with it. In *On Her Majesty's Secret Service*, as we've noted, Diana Rigg's character manages to get slapped across the face by both Bond and her own father. As her father explains to Bond when he offers him a million-dollar dowry to marry her, what she really needs is to be dominated. It is an exchange entirely in keeping with Fleming's view of women. The context of this violence towards women – in which Bond was seen as a hero and an aspirational figure – and Sean Connery saying publicly that hitting women was sometimes necessary, casts a dark shadow over these films.

The Beatles had also been brought up in a misogynistic culture, and John Lennon in particular treated women badly. His first wife Cynthia recalls that, when they first became a couple, 'John's temper could be frightening and at times I felt torn to pieces by him. All sense of reason disappeared and his tantrums were awesome: he would batter away at me verbally until I gave in, overwhelmed by the force of his determination. Then he was back to his usual self, apologetic and loving.' In December 1959, shortly after their relationship began, Lennon suspected she had danced with another man. He reacted by slapping her across the face. As she later described the assault, 'Before I could speak he raised his arm and hit me across the face, knocking my head into the pipes that ran down the wall behind me.' Cynthia responded by leaving him. Three months later he called to apologise, and she took him back.

This violent and controlling side of Lennon's nature occasionally surfaced in his work. It is most notable on the 1965 song 'Run for Your Life', in which Lennon threatens to kill his girl if he finds her with another man. In *In His Own Write*, his 1964 book of surrealist nonsense stories, Lennon includes a story called 'No Flies on Frank' in which he writes, 'not even his wife's battered face could raise a smile on poor Frank's head'. Frank then beats his wife to death, before taking her body back to her parents in a sack because the flies she attracted bothered him. From his LSD-period onwards, however, Lennon came to recognise his violent impulses and to take responsibility for them, a process he details in the lyrics to the song 'Getting Better'. As he said in 1967, talking about the time

273

he slapped Cynthia, 'I was just hysterical. That was the trouble. I was jealous of anyone she had anything to do with. I demanded absolute trust from her, just because I wasn't trustworthy myself. I was neurotic, taking out all of my frustrations on her.' When he apologised to Cynthia he had promised that it would never happen again and, as she wrote, 'John was true to his word. He was deeply ashamed of what he had done: I think he had been so shocked to discover he had it in him to hit me.'

Lennon came to understand that even though he was the product of a violent and sexist culture, he did not have to accept those values. Change was possible. In response, he became an advocate for non-violence, even if he did relapse during his heavy drinking period in the early 1970s. Yoko, tellingly, limited the amount of alcohol that was kept in their New York apartment. Lennon's desire to change does not excuse what happened, of course, but it does recognise that when a toxic situation exists it is then necessary to begin the journey to a healthier place, regardless of when that journey should ideally have begun. If Lennon could start this transition, it raises the question of whether James Bond could as well. For many, this does not seem like something that the character could ever do. Is it possible for Bond to change, or is misogyny too central to his character?

Even more so than violence towards women, the issue that makes Connery-era Bond so contentious is consent. In both *Thunderball* and *Goldfinger*, Bond forces himself on women who clearly and verbally do not consent, in scenes that show a situation which we now understand as rape. As the lyrics to the theme song 'Thunderball' warn us, 'Any woman he wants, he'll get [...] His days of asking are all gone'. This issue was publicly raised by the director of *No Time to Die* in 2021. 'Is it *Thunderball* or *Goldfinger* where basically Sean Connery's character rapes a woman?' said Cary Fukunaga. 'She's like "No, no, no," and he's like, "Yes, yes,

yes." ' It's noticeable that this contemporary focus on Connery's disregard of consent has not yet stopped people naming Connery as their favourite James Bond. It will be interesting to see whether this changes in the coming years.

The scenes in question shed a revealing light on mid-twentieth-century attitudes. They were not intended to show Bond as a rapist; instead, they played to the then commonly held male belief that women needed to say 'no' at first even when they were willing, in order not to be thought of as easy. You can no doubt see the problem with this scenario. It is a stark illustration of how far attitudes to female sexuality have progressed over the last half-century. In both these films, the scenes that start with a clear lack of consent are followed by scenes in which Bond's post-coital partner is shown as being deeply satisfied. The masseuse who tries in vain to fight him off in *Thunderball* is shown almost purring like a kitten afterwards.

In *Goldfinger*, Honor Blackman's Pussy Galore verbally warns Bond away and then uses all her strength to attempt to push him off her, but afterwards she is so affected by the experience that she betrays her employer and sabotages his plot in order to help Bond. The scenes with Pussy Galore are among the most troubling to contemporary eyes, due to the character being written as a lesbian in the novel. In the film this is not made explicit, although it's hard to imagine that there would be many in the audience who would see a character called Pussy Galore who leads an all-female flying circus, and not have a few suspicions.

The scenes between Bond and Galore in the novel are brutally revealing of Fleming's sexual politics. When Bond notes that another female character, Tilly Masterton, is interested in Galore, Fleming tells us that 'Bond came to the conclusion that Tilly Masterton was one of those girls whose hormones had got mixed up. He knew the type well and thought they and their male

275

counterparts were a direct consequence of giving votes to women and "sex equality". As a result of fifty years of emancipation, feminine qualities were dying out or being transferred to the males. Pansies of both sexes were everywhere, not yet homosexual, but confused, not knowing what they were. The result was a herd of unhappy sexual misfits – barren and full of frustrations, the women wanting to dominate and the men to be nannied. He was sorry for them, but he had no time for them.'

Here Fleming's prose opens a window on how misunderstood sexuality was in the 1950s, when homosexuality was still illegal. It seems crazy now that Fleming would find female suffrage a plausible explanation for lesbianism, but at the time there were those who thought this reasonable. In *The Man with the Golden Gun*, Fleming wrote, 'Now it may only be a myth, and it is certainly not medical science, but there is a popular theory that a man who cannot whistle has homosexual tendencies [...] M hadn't whistled since he was a boy. Unconsciously his mouth pursed and a clear note was emitted.' Fleming's homophobia came, as it so often does, from a place of ignorance. When issues like this were not discussed in society, and the voices of gay and lesbian people were not heard, ignorance to this degree was inevitable.

Fleming's novels include a number of gay characters, but they are usually evil and deviant. The killers Mr Wint and Mr Kidd from *Diamonds are Forever*, for example, are described to Bond as a 'Coupla lavender boys. You know, pansies.' A 'pansy' was one of Fleming's favourite terms for gay or effeminate men, and he would happily write descriptions like 'Bill, a pansified Italian, hurried towards them.' When it came to lesbians, Fleming depicted them as victims, traumatised by a cruel and unjust world, who only needed to have sex with a real man in order to be 'cured'. Their desire for the feminine was a coping mechanism, as Fleming saw it, rather than genuine attraction. Pussy Galore, it is explained, became a lesbian because she was raped by her uncle at the age of twelve. When Bond and Galore meet, Fleming writes, 'Bond liked the look of her. He felt the sexual challenge all beautiful lesbians have for men.' Naturally enough he was able to rise to that challenge, and at the end of the book Pussy Galore throws herself into his arms. Bond says to her, 'They told me you only liked women,' to which she replies, 'I never met a man before.' You can imagine the look on Fleming's face as he was typing that.

Tiffany Case, the heroine of *Diamonds are Forever*, had a similar backstory. Case was gang raped by the mob after her mother failed to pay them protection money. As Felix Leiter tells Bond, 'She was only sixteen at the time. Not surprising she won't have anything to do with men since then.' As she tells Bond when they meet, and he offers to buy her dinner, 'I'm not going to sleep with you [...] It will take more than Crabmeat Ravigote to get me into bed with a man.' Once she has realised that Bond is a real man, however, she develops a hugely enthusiastic interest in heterosexual sex. Stepping out of her dress, she tells Bond, 'I want it all, James. Everything you've ever done to a girl. Now. Quickly.' Fleming's fantasy about victimised and sexually traumatised young girls being redeemed by the powerful masculinity of his avatar Bond is made more disturbing by his habit of referring to them as children. Pussy Galore climbs into his bed, for example, 'like an obedient child'.

When Roger Moore took over the role of James Bond in the early 1970s, he consciously made the character less dark and more comedic. He wanted to move away from the cold-blooded killer that Connery had portrayed. While spies had been seen as heroes during the 1960s, they were increasingly viewed as villains in the post-Watergate world, and Moore's use of humour helped to deflect this. When the producers attempted to return to a more Connery-esque Bond in the 1980 movie *For Your Eyes Only*, Moore was unhappy, especially about a scene in which Bond killed a man in cold blood by pushing the car he was in over a cliff. 'It was Bond, but it wasn't my Bond,' he explained. In Moore's preferred portrayal, Bond was a lover, not a fighter.

This was a change that fitted the cultural shift from the 1960s to the 1970s well. This was the 'Me decade'. The spiritual questing of the 1960s which the Beatles personified had been dialled down, and hedonism and self-gratification became the new focus. This was the period after the pill and before AIDS, and a certain level of sexual liberation had entered the mainstream. The Bond movies, conscious of their family audiences, never included explicit nudity, but the silhouetted naked women in 1970s Bond titles came as close as they dared. As producer Barbara Broccoli explained, 'When you look at the early films, the women were very extraordinary for the '60s. They were pilots, and tough and strong women who did extraordinary things; who were sexual and had an equal sort of sexual appetite. They weren't the wilting flowers. I think that what happened was that maybe in the '70s and '80s it became more window dressing. We had groups of girls in bikinis sitting around swimming pools.'

There were no more problems regarding consent when Roger Moore became James Bond in 1973, because all the women in his films threw themselves at him the moment they met him. This approach had its own problems. Moore was forty-four when he was cast in his first film and stayed in the role until he was fifty-eight – notably older than Fleming's Bond, who was in his thirties. In the books, '00' agents are forcibly retired when they turn forty-five. Moore's age, therefore, led to many awkward relationships, as the Bond Girls remained as young as ever. Moore could perhaps be described as a straight bloke's idea of an attractive man, and the way women threw themselves at him was often not entirely convincing.

In response, there were efforts made to make the role of the leading Bond Girl stronger. Resourceful and capable female characters were introduced. The films, however, couldn't seem to resist undermining these supposedly more independent characters. Problems of consent were left in the sixties, but they were replaced with very 1970s chauvinism. In *The Spy Who Loved Me*, for example, Bond's reaction to a female Russian spy attempting to escape when the villain lifts her vehicle off the ground is, 'Women drivers!' Lois Chiles played a brave, fiercely intelligent NASA scientist and CIA secret agent in *Moonraker*. When Bond meets this noted scientist and realises that she is female he says, in a shocked tone, 'A woman!' The role was further sabotaged by naming the character Dr Goodhead. Heavily sexualised female names like Pussy Galore and Plenty O'Toole are a much-mocked aspect of early Bond films, and it is often noted how male characters never have similar, *Carry On*-style suggestive names. Perhaps the producers thought it was not necessary. They had, after all, already cast an actor named Roger Moore.

Outside the lead roles, the women in 1970s Bond movies became increasingly subservient. In *The Spy Who Loved Me*, for example, Bond meets a British agent in Cairo and is surrounded by a harem, while the agent insists that Bond stays the night to enjoy their 'hospitality'. Being desired by attractive people is a common part of everyone's fantasy, so it should not be surprising to find it in Bond's archetypal heterosexual masculine fantasy world. But the very name 'Bond Girls' – as opposed to 'Bond Women' – highlights the sense that the female cast were expected to be secondary, subservient figures whose function was to be decorative and to keep quiet in the background while the men drove the mission.

As the seventies progressed and second-wave feminism grew, the producers attempted to address the issue of how the Bond movies portray women. It became common when announcing female cast members to insist that they were a 'new kind of Bond Girl'. The next film was modern and progressive and would not suffer from the flaws that earlier Bond films did, the producers would insist, as if they weren't the same people who had made those earlier films. Carole Bouquet, who played Melina Havelock in *For Your Eyes Only* (1981), explained that she was not 'just another Bond girl. I'm not simply a plastic doll like the rest of them!' Famke Janssen, who played Xenia Onatopp in *GoldenEye* (1995), explained that 'I've always wanted to *be* James Bond, not any of the women in the movies, and I thought Xenia came as close to *being* James Bond as you could come without being him.' Olga Kurylenko, who played Camille in *Quantum of Solace* (2008), said, 'I don't think Camille is a typical Bond girl.' Lea Seydoux, who played Dr Madeleine Swann in *Spectre* (2015), said, 'I don't mind the cliché of the Bond girl. But Madeleine, she is very different. And to choose me as a Bond girl, it's a choice. A statement. I'm not the typical James Bond girl.' *No Time to Die*'s (2021) Ana de Armas said, 'Bond women have always been, for me at least, unrelatable [...] My character feels like a real woman.'

The first major attempt at a female character who was depicted as being as capable as Bond occurred in 1977, when the American actor and model Barbara Bach was cast as the female lead in *The Spy Who Loved Me*. Bach played Anya Amasova, a female Russian version of Bond – a woman as cool, charismatic and ruthless as the English spy. She too was a killer with her own triple-digit codename, albeit a more unfortunate one. Known as Agent XXX, Amasova proved to be every bit Bond's equal – for the first two-thirds of the film at least. By the final reel she was barely dressed and in desperate need of rescuing, as tradition dictates.

Perhaps this is why Barbara Bach did not return to the franchise. She had been such a success in the role that the producers hoped to bring her back for a cameo in *A View to a Kill* (1985). For a Bond Girl, this was a rare honour indeed, but Bach turned down the offer. In 1980 she filmed a slapstick comedy called *Caveman*, in which all dialogue was in a 'caveman language' of grunts and invented words. If the film is remembered at all today, it is usually for the scene in which a Tyrannosaurus Rex gets stoned by eating a cannabis-like plant. It is a significant movie, however, because this is where Barbara Bach met her co-star Ringo Starr. The pair married a year later, and are still together to this day. Who can blame her that, when there was a chance to return to James Bond, she picked love over death and walked away, choosing to be a Beatle wife instead?

In the years that followed, there have been many attempts to solve the problem of female portrayals in Bond movies. In Timothy Dalton's first movie *The Living Daylights*, for example, Bond was not depicted as a womaniser. Although admired by aficionados now, the film had a lacklustre response from the general audience at the time. There was a suspicion that by making Bond more sexless something important had been lost. The most successful attempt at dealing with the problem was probably the casting of Monica Bellucci as an assassin's widow in *Spectre*. Bellucci was fifty-one when the film came out and Daniel Craig was forty-seven, so this was a much more age-appropriate seduction than most. Bond and a Bond Woman engaged in a relationship that had all the glamour and danger that Bond films required but, crucially, there was no power imbalance, and the film did not then kill Bellucci's character after sex.

Bellucci aside, however, all the other attempts to fix the Bond Girl problem seem to point to the same conclusion: it can't be done. It doesn't matter how much you change the characterisation of the women. The problem is not the women. The problem is Bond.

1974: IN THE MATERIAL WORLD

With the exception of a carefully curated short list of dates in Japan in 1992, George Harrison only toured once as a solo artist. That tour – the 1974 Dark Horse tour – is usually remembered as something of a disaster, which convinced Harrison he should never put himself through something like that again. Looking junkie-thin and with his voice shot to pieces, Harrison had booked forty-five shows around Canada and North America to promote his *Dark Horse* album. But the record was not ready in time for the shows, and only arrived in shops around the end of the tour. The tour's reputation as a disaster comes largely from the vitriolic press condemnation it received from *Rolling Stone*, who were vicious about anything related to the Beatles which might challenge their belief that Lennon was the only true genius in the band.

For Harrison, it marked the end of a brief but triumphant period in his solo career. He had been the Beatle to emerge with the most critical acclaim and commercial success. His *All Things Must Pass* triple album is still frequently spoken of as the greatest Beatle solo album. Its lead single 'My Sweet Lord' went to number one around the world and was the bestselling single in the UK in

1971. He then organised a pair of concerts in New York to raise money and awareness for those displaced by war and floods in Bangladesh. These concerts effectively invented the idea of large-scale all-star rock benefit gigs and were the direct inspiration for Bob Geldof's Live Aid concerts in the following decade. The shows were recorded and released as another triple album, called *Concert for Bangladesh*, which followed *All Things Must Pass* to number one around the world and generated millions in relief aid. His next album, *Living in the Material World*, was less adventurous and a more laid-back affair, but it also went to number one and still has its supporters.

None of the other Beatles were then enjoying anything like this level of commercial and critical success in their solo careers. For the Beatle long seen as the 'quiet one' who was largely depicted as a lesser talent to the Lennon and McCartney songwriting partnership, this was a terrific vindication. Harrison was revealed as a unique talent, which the other Beatles had failed to value or appreciate during his time in the band. That, at least, was the story until around 1974 and the *Dark Horse* album and tour. This was the point when the record-buying public and music journalists alike largely lost interest in Harrison's solo career.

The problem was best symbolised by his cover version of Lennon's 'In My Life', one of the rare Beatles songs to be performed on the tour. The other Beatles songs included were all written by George: 'Something', 'While My Guitar Gently Weeps' and 'For You Blue'. At times, it felt like he didn't even want the tour to be a 'George Harrison' show. It was billed as a Harrison and Ravi Shankar co-tour, and Shankar and Billy Preston performed a number of tracks during the concert. The blending of Eastern and Western music was years ahead of its time and laid the ground for the world-music boom of the 1980s, and Harrison's desire to put his friends in the spotlight showed an admirable lack of ego, but the people buying tickets wanted to hear songs like 'Taxman' or 'Here Comes the Sun', and were disappointed that Harrison had no interest in playing them.

'In My Life' should have been a highlight, but Harrison made a crucial lyrical change to the song which served to entirely undercut its meaning. It was an unusual Lennon song, in that its lyrics were passive and reflective. Lennon was looking back at his past – he was only twenty-five when he recorded it, but he had lived quite a life by that age – and declaring that, for all he values and treasures the people and events in his earlier life, it is his current love who is the most important. But where Lennon had sung, 'In my life I love you more', Harrison sang, 'In my life I love God more'. At a stroke he had declared that all the people he had known over the years were less important to him than an abstract spiritual concept.

There are plenty of songs where it appears that George was singing a song of love for a person, but in actuality he was singing about his love of God. His great standard 'Something' is usually assumed to be a love song for his then wife Pattie Boyd, not least because of the footage of the pair looking into each other's eyes in the video. But as he later explained to friends, 'Actually, it's about Krishna, but I couldn't say *he*, could I? I had to say *she*, or they'd think I'm a poof.'

George's spiritual beliefs were front and centre in his hugely successful early-1970s albums. They meant that while at times he could be preachy and judgemental, he was undoubtedly sincere and devout. And yet, for all his spiritual devotion, the evidence of his songs leaves us with the sneaking suspicion that George just didn't like people very much. As his biographer Graeme Thomson writes, 'At times listening to Harrison's music, it's a struggle to find much evidence at all of his faith in the redeeming qualities of humanity.' This made it very easy for rock journalists to portray him as isolated, hypocritical and out of touch, especially after he bought Friar Park, a large late-Victorian mansion in Henley-On-Thames, complete with 32 acres of land.

Friar Park was a gothic fairy tale of turrets, gargoyles, stained-glass windows, secret passages and underground caverns. The oak-panelled main hall was double height, with a minstrel's gallery, and the house packed with eccentric and humorous details. The light switches were carved monk's faces, for example, and you turned the light on by pressing their nose. The gardens contained lakes, fountains and a replica of the Matterhorn made from 20,000 tons of granite. Its previous residents had been six nuns and one monk, a situation which clearly amused Harrison. Yet despite the extent to which Friar Park's odd history and comical quirks were a good match for Harrison's sense of humour, a rambling mansion is clearly a very large house for one man and his wife. The couple employed staff, of course, and friends, family and fellow musicians would often visit, but ultimately Friar Park could be seen as a huge world devoid of people, which was just how George liked it.

According to Harrison and Boyd's assistant Chris O'Dell, who lived for a time with them in Friar Park, there were three different George Harrisons, and you never really knew which one you would get each day. 'The first George was great fun and loved to gossip, drink, smoke a little pot, and even, on rare occasions, snort a line or two of cocaine,' she wrote. This was the George she hoped that she would meet when she heard him approaching. It was this George you can hear in songs like 'Here Comes the Sun' and 'Apple Scrubs'. It was this version of him that loved comedy and financed the film *Monty Python and the Life of Brian* (1979) when all other funders backed away, afraid.

'The second George was intense, sarcastic, and detached,' O'Dell reported. 'Little things would set him off at these times, and we'd all have to watch our step,' she continued. This was the George that film director Terry Gilliam was describing when he talked about his 'weird kind of angry bitterness about certain things in life'. It is this George that you hear on songs like 'Taxman', 'I Don't Care Anymore' or 'Only a Northern Song'. Those around him knew that, when George was acting prickly, cruel or entitled, they would have to adjust to his mood because he wasn't going to accommodate them.

One example involved the journalist David Dalton, who recalled repeatedly turning up the sound of a TV at Harrison's request. 'After several more requests to "turn the fucking thing up", I told him that that was as loud as it went. George looked at me ferociously and in high imperial mode demanded that I *turn the bloody volume up*.' As his biographer Graeme Thomson writes, Harrison 'was accustomed to his bidding being done at the first asking and could be arrogant and unreasonable when reality proved reluctant to bend immediately to his needs'. This is a description that also sounds remarkably like Ian Fleming. Indeed, of all the Beatles, George Harrison was the one whose personality was, in certain respects, the most Bond-like. He loved fast cars, for example. He bought many of them and counted several racing drivers among his closest friends.

Harrison once spent £540,000 on a McLaren Formula 1 'supercar', which could travel at 230mph. There is footage of Paul, Ringo and George arriving at Friar Park in this car in the 1990s. 'Nice motor!' McCartney exclaims to Harrison, in the insincere manner of a man who has zero interest in cars but who was making an effort to be friendly. George, like Paul, also bought one of Bond's Aston Martin DB5s in the 1960s, and he wore a T-shirt with the 007 logo. As well as loving speed, Harrison's womanising was also remarkably Bond-like, as we shall see. Harrison illustrates another way in which the world of Bond and the Beatles can be bridged, which is entirely different to the example of Christopher

Lee. Harrison's example suggests that enjoying the material world can complement, not contradict, a spiritual worldview.

This brings us to the third George Harrison, in which aspects of his character come to the fore that initially seem at odds with the Bond-like millionaire playboy. This is Harrison the spiritual seeker, who would spend days chanting or meditating, and contemplating the mystery of karma, reincarnation and the mind of God. This is the George who wrote songs like 'The Inner Light', 'Within You Without You', 'My Sweet Lord' and 'All Things Must Pass', among many others. When in this mode, he could be intense and inspiring, but he could also be judgemental, hypocritical and distant. As O'Dell summed up the struggle between the material and spiritual sides of George, 'Pattie and I used to joke that we didn't know if his hand was in the prayer bag or the coke bag.' Friends would sometimes call him 'His Lectureship' behind his back. Among the other three Beatles, his nickname was 'His Holiness'.

The arrival of spiritual George was a strain on his marriage with Pattie. He became distant and detached and, as she explained, 'I couldn't reach him.' O'Dell recalled George saying that, when he was in a period of intense chanting, 'I start beginning to relate less and less to the people I know. I suddenly find myself on such a different level where it's really hard to relate. It feels as though I'm at a point where I should slow down or pull back toward those people in order to take them with me [...] There's a point where I can't relate to anyone anymore.' According to Boyd, George's post-Rishikesh spiritual quest was the start of the long breakdown of their marriage, and this was not simply due to religion making him distant. After George returned from India, he was 'wanting to be some kind of spiritual being surrounded by concubines,' Boyd said, 'And no woman was out of bounds.'

George's Bond-like desire to flirt and seduce women was hampered by the small social circles of trusted insiders that such rich and famous people lived in. Like love affairs among the aristocracy, the sex lives of 1970s rock stars could be remarkably incestuous. These were the circumstances that led to George Harrison having an affair with Ringo Starr's wife Maureen.

Maureen had been with the band from the start. She first met Ringo outside the Cavern in Liverpool when she was a sixteen-year-old trainee hairdresser, in the same week that Ringo joined the Beatles and they were filmed by Leslie Woodhead in the Cavern for Granada TV. She became pregnant in January 1965. The pair married the following month, and another two children soon followed. O'Dell recalled seeing Maureen and Ringo together in 1968, when she worked in the Apple offices. 'They were always holding hands,' she wrote. 'Every time she picked up a cigarette, Ringo would suddenly appear next to her with his silver lighter. He'd look at her adoringly, she'd look at him lovingly, and when she exhaled, she'd lower her eyes as if the moment was too intimate even for a man and woman who had been married for four years. They were crazy about each other [...] their casual intimacy assured me that it is possible to keep a love story going even after several years of marriage.' Maureen had been by the side of the band from the excitement of the early Liverpool days to the madness of Beatlemania and the politics of their eventual end. She was the ultimate insider, and a constant, stabilising presence in the Beatles family. When Harrison temporarily quit the band in 1969, McCartney joked that if she could master the chords A7, D7 and G7 over the weekend, then the gig was hers. When Lennon heard about the affair, he referred to it as 'incest'.

The situation came to a head in January 1974, when George and Pattie, along with Chris O'Dell, paid a visit to Ringo and Maureen at their home in Tittenhurst Park. Ringo had bought the house from Lennon after John and Yoko moved to New York, and it is familiar to Beatles fans because it is featured in the video for

'Imagine'. Their visit was during the dark nights in the middle of winter, and the guests sat around the long wooden table in the kitchen. It was here that, in front of both Pattie and Maureen, George turned to Ringo and said, 'You know, Ringo, I'm in love with your wife.'

The room fell silent. Maureen stood frozen by the sink. As O'Dell tells the story, 'Ringo looked down at the table. He flicked his cigarette ash in the ashtray. His jaw clenched, and a muscle by his mouth twitched. We sat there. Waiting. Finally, he looked at George. "Better you than someone we don't know," he said in a steady voice.' Harrison's biographer Graeme Thomson wrote that, in the days after this incident, 'Starr was distraught, muttering, "nothing is real, nothing is real".'

It's not clear exactly what the relationship between George and Maureen consisted of. Maureen always insisted that it was purely emotional and not physical, although Pattie never saw it in those terms. She recalled the times that Maureen would come over to Friar Park, when George and Maureen would lock themselves in a distant room in the giant mansion, and refuse to answer the door or let Pattie in. Regardless of what actually happened, it was enough to ruin two marriages. A short while later, Ringo had an affair with Chris O'Dell, which began after the pair returned from a visit to the current James Bond, Roger Moore, at his LA home. Both George and Pattie and Ringo and Maureen would divorce in the years that followed. According to Cynthia Lennon, Maureen was so distraught about the end of her marriage to Ringo that 'she got on a motorbike and drove it straight into a brick wall, badly injuring herself'.

When George informed Ringo that he was in love with his wife, he was re-enacting a scene that had occurred a couple of years earlier with the guitarist Eric Clapton. George and Eric became friends during the late 1960s, which led to Clapton playing on 'While My

Guitar Gently Weeps'. Clapton then fell in love with Harrison's wife Pattie. She initially spurned his advances, but the situation came to a head when George found Eric and Pattie together in the garden at a party thrown by the Australian entertainment entrepreneur Robert Stigwood. 'I have to tell you, man,' said Clapton, 'that I'm in love with your wife.' Harrison, then, had first-hand knowledge of what it was like to hear a public confession like that, and the impact his later words would have had on Ringo.

The combination of infatuation and heroin use made the early seventies a difficult time for Clapton. It was during this period that he wrote 'Layla', a tale of unrequited love based on the twelfth-century Persian poem *Layla and Majnun*. It was readily apparent to all, however, that the song was really about his struggles with his feelings for Pattie Boyd. Harrison made little effort to fight for Pattie, viewing the situation from a detached, spiritual perspective. His attitude to Clapton was, 'If you want her, take her, she's yours'. His apathy towards the bonds of his marriage was a major factor in its failure.

Boyd eventually left Harrison in 1974, following his relationship with Maureen. After a brief affair with Ronnie Wood from the Faces, she started a relationship with Clapton, and they married in 1979. Yet throughout all this, Harrison remained friends with Clapton. He played at his and Pattie's wedding and referred to Eric as his 'husband-in-law'. 'I didn't get annoyed at [Clapton] and I think that has always annoyed him,' Harrison would later say, looking back at the situation over twenty years later, 'I think that deep down inside he wishes that it really pissed me off, but it didn't, because I was happy that she went off, because we were finished together, and it made things easier for me, you see, because otherwise we'd have had to go through all these big rows and divorces. And you know, she went off to live in the same style she had become accustomed to and it was really very convenient for me.'

Boyd divorced Clapton in 1989, after he had fathered two children with two different women. One of these women was the Italian television presenter Lory Del Santo, whose child Conor Clapton tragically fell from the fifty-third floor of a Manhattan apartment building at the age of four. Eric Clapton's song 'Tears in Heaven' was an expression of his grief about his son's death. Just to complicate matters, Del Santo later had a brief affair with Harrison, while he was on tour in Japan with Clapton in 1991. Del Santo believed Harrison's unresolved feelings about Clapton's pursuit of Boyd was a factor. 'It could have started as a payback day,' she said. 'It probably started because we both wanted revenge. We were hurting. We had this loneliness. But it turned out to be something special.'

The tangled, incestuous nature of these various relationships is of course striking, but it is not the thing that, to modern sensibilities, is the most surprising about the relationships between Clapton, Boyd and Harrison. Rather it is the way that both Harrison and Boyd stuck by Clapton and remained close to him after his infamous racist rants throughout a concert in Birmingham in 1976. Widely reported in the music press at the time, Clapton expressed his support for Enoch Powell and reiterated the National Front slogan 'Keep Britain white'. Considering the level of racism that would be sufficient to end a career in the contemporary world, it is worth reiterating the words he was reported to have said, and which he has never denied. They were: 'Do we have any foreigners in the audience tonight? If so, please put up your hands. So where are you? Well, wherever you all are, I think you should all just leave. Not just leave the hall, leave our country. I don't want you here, in the room or in my country. Listen to me, man! I think we should send them all back. Stop Britain from becoming a black colony. Get the foreigners out. Get the wogs out. Get the coons out. Keep Britain white.' Such were the views of a musician who made his name playing blues, and who had just had his first American number-one single with a cover of a Bob Marley song.

Clapton refused to apologise for these words until as late as 2017. In a 2007 *South Bank Show* interview with Melvyn Bragg, Clapton reiterated his belief that Powell was right and that this was not a racial stance. 'Obviously there's no way I could be a racist. But there was something about [Enoch Powell] that I thought was outrageously brave,' he told *The Times* in 2004. Outside of Clapton's rationalising, however, even the most charitable must conclude that there is very little room for interpretation in his words: Clapton was extremely, aggressively racist. He has continued to support right-wing causes, playing concerts to raise money for supporters of fox hunting and recording a song with Van Morrison during the global Covid-19 pandemic to promote the anti-mask and anti-lockdown argument.

Clapton's rant led directly to the formation of the campaigning organisation Rock Against Racism. This reflected the growing awareness that something about the coke-fuelled world of wealth and fame which the music industry created around its stars often led directly to isolation and fascism. 'I believe very strongly in fascism,' David Bowie said in 1976. 'People have always responded with greater efficiency under a regimental leadership. A liberal wastes time saying, "Well, now, what ideas have you got?" Show them what to do, for God's sake. If you don't, nothing will get done. I can't stand people just hanging about.' Bowie also claimed that 'Adolf Hitler was one of the first rock stars.' Unlike Clapton, however, he apologised for these 'two or three glib, theatrical observations' the following year, stressed that he was not a fascist, and regularly condemned racism throughout the rest of his life. A famous photograph from May 1976 appears to show Bowie greeting fans at Victoria Station in London with a Nazi salute. Film footage of the incident, however, reveals that the photograph was actually taken in the middle of a jolly, and slightly camp, wave to his fans at the back.

The most famous creative expression of this hardening of rock-star hearts was *The Wall*, a 1979 rock-opera concept album by Pink Floyd, which is still in the top thirty bestselling albums of all time. The incident which led to the album's creation occurred during a 1977 Pink Floyd concert in Montreal. The band's bassist and co-vocalist Roger Waters looked down from the stage at the adoring fans in front of him, and felt such contempt that he spat on them. The album he wrote explored the inner life of a rock star who, like him, had come to despise the people he was playing for – and indeed, people in general. His main character, Pink, responded by building an emotional 'wall' around himself. He came to realise, of course, that this left him utterly alone. The album was turned into the 1982 movie *Pink Floyd – The Wall*, which was directed by Alan Parker and included animated sequences directed by Gerald Scarfe. The film is not subtle, and the association between a rock star's isolation and fascism is repeatedly made explicit, not least by a scene where a rock concert is depicted as a Nazi rally and in the animated sequences depicting an army of marching hammers.

The Wall can be criticised as rock-star navel-gazing, in which a self-obsessed isolated individual blames his descent into fascism on other people and events, such as the death of his father during the Second World War. In its favour, it is a scathing, brutally honest insider's account of how a person can start out with the best intentions only to surrender their humanity before the glamour of success. As Waters details his mental descent, he shows what it is like when fame and wealth elevate a person above others, making them isolated and afraid. They become unable to meet others as equals because people always want things from them, be that money or the reflected glow of their celebrity. Drugs and alcohol appear to mask this disconnect, but in reality, they exaggerate it – cocaine in particular acts as fascism in powdered form. It erodes empathy and keeps the focus on the ever-hardening ego. Becoming a rock star offers money, luxuries and a lack of responsibility that all but the strongest cannot help but covet. The readily available drugs and casual sex keep the musician cocooned in an adolescent world they never want to leave. So what if this costs a person their ability to connect to other human beings? Rock stars, on the face of it, got a lot more for their soul than Faust did.

Harrison had been through a version of this scenario that was about as extreme as it was possible to get. The crushing pressures and unimaginable fame of the early years of Beatlemania left him permanently unable to have relationships with equals because who – apart from perhaps Bob Dylan or Elvis – was the equal of a Beatle? During Beatlemania the close brotherly relationships between the Fab Four offered him friends who understood, but as the band slowly pulled apart through drugs, outside interests and simple ageing, he was left isolated in his giant gothic mansion with no one who really understood what his life was like. He had become, as the *NME* noted, 'someone whose universe is confined to himself'. It is not surprising, then, that he clung to religion in order to stave off the isolation and bitterness that seduced Clapton into the dead-end of far-right politics.

George's religion, however, was very much a Western, twentieth-century take on ancient Eastern religions. For all his support of the Hare Krishna movement, he did not shave his hair, wear robes or renounce drink and drugs, as would have been required of other adherents. His understanding of a relationship with God was a direct, one-to-one connection which had no concern for other people or his wider community. This, it is possible, was a large part of why it appealed to him. His desire for the experience of closeness to God meant that Harrison was prepared to weaken his ties with other people, as Pattie Boyd and others were to discover. It gave him an unarguable fixed point to base his life around, but it also divorced him from the everyday relationships that give life value.

Harrison struggled with what appeared to be a deep contradiction at the heart of his personality. For all he longed for the world of pure spirit, he also loved the material world. He enjoyed wealth, sex and the benefits of extreme fame. This was a divide he particularly examined in his 1973 album *Living in the Material World*, the sleeve of which included a photograph of Harrison and his band staged like da Vinci's *The Last Supper*, but with a sports car in the background. The label on side one of the album shows a scene from Hindu mythology, while the label on side two shows his stretch limo and a chauffeur.

Perhaps, though, there is not really a contradiction here. Harrison craved an escape from the self, because this was the only way he could escape from the awareness that he was Beatle George. Drink, sex, drugs, rock 'n' roll, fast cars and comedy all offer moments that transcend the ego, where the story of a life is forgotten, and the present moment is everything. Meditation and spirituality offered the same, but with perhaps less of a price. This is what George craved. This is how he would escape the fate of Eric Clapton or Roger Waters. Both God and the pleasures of the material world offered him moments where he was free.

In 1978, George married Olivia Arias and in the same year they had a son, Dhani. Dhani only discovered his father's past when he was at school. 'I came home one day from school after being chased by kids singing "Yellow Submarine", and I didn't understand why,' he has said. 'It just seemed surreal: why are they singing that song to me? I came home and I freaked out on my dad: "Why didn't you tell me you were in the Beatles?" And he said, "Oh, sorry. Probably should have told you that." ' It's impossible to imagine John, Paul or Ringo neglecting to mention they were in the Beatles to their children.

Behind the walls of Friar Park, raising his son with his second wife, George attempted to forget who he was. He pursued all avenues that could lead to a loss of the sense of self which would remove the burden of being Beatle George from his shoulders. But, as his son discovered, the spell could never work outside Friar Park. God, women and motor racing may have helped him forget the world, but the world was never going to forget the Beatles.

1977: RISKING THEIR LIVES FOR THE AUDIENCE'S ENTERTAINMENT

Rick Sylvester was an unemployed American ski instructor when he received a call out of the blue from Cubby Broccoli, asking him to take part in the next Bond film.

A few years earlier, Sylvester had skied off El Capitan, an imposing 3,000ft-tall granite cliff face in Yosemite National Park, and parachuted safely to the ground. No one had ever done anything like this before. Sylvester named this new activity a skiBASE jump. A standard BASE jump is to parachute from a standing structure rather than out of a plane – the acronym stands for all the things that can be jumped off, namely Buildings, Antennae, Spans and Earth, which includes cliff faces. A skiBASE jump is similar, except that you go flying off the edge on skis at the start. 'I didn't see it as a stunt,' he later said, 'it was an outdoor mountain adventure. My intention was to only do it once.' Sylvester did a mocked-up photoshoot of a similar jump as an advert for Canadian Club whisky, however, and this was spotted in a copy of *Playboy* magazine by Cubby Broccoli's stepson, Michael G. Wilson. Wilson was then an international tax lawyer, a job that caused him to take an increasing interest in his stepfather's work. He thought the image was suitably Bondian and so suggested it as a sequence for the next film.

Sylvester agreed to perform another skiBASE jump. How could he turn down the chance to be James Bond, if only for one terrifying minute? He even suggested a suitable location, Mount Asgard at Baffin Island in Canada, which had an astonishing 5,800ft of vertical cliff face. He was, however, extremely nervous about what he had got himself into. He was unfamiliar with the location, which was within the Arctic Circle and subject to terrible weather conditions. 'I was really daring the devil. I was thinking: now I'm not just doing it for adventure, but I'm doing it for filthy lucre – to be paid. I was actually getting quite worried.' His nerves increased during the two weeks he spent with the film unit on location, testing camera locations and waiting for safe conditions. During a fall of that length, it would not have taken much wind to blow him into the cliff face, a collision that would result in certain death. The camera crew also needed weather with suitable visibility; there is little point doing something that heroic if it can't clearly be seen. 'I was becoming a drama queen awakening each morning hoping for rain with thoughts that I get to live for another day, that I'd been granted another stay of execution. I felt guilty that my fears were subversive to the entire operation. After all, I'd consented to do it. And now I didn't want to. I was secretly and privately rooting against it.' For all we may dream of becoming Bond, the subconscious suspicion that Bond is death is perhaps never far from the surface.

Eventually, the call came – conditions were okay, and there was a small window in which to perform the stunt. Cameramen and helicopter pilots moved into position. 'I got myself together and got my chute on,' Sylvester recalled. 'I was asked if I was ready.

With mixed feelings and unable to come up with any reason not to I answered "yes". Next it was communicated to me that the cameras were rolling. Film's expensive. That was it. I went.'

The shot was to follow a sequence in which Roger Moore, in his bright-yellow snow suit and yellow goggles paired with a bright-red woolly hat and red backpack, is chased on skis by four villains with machine guns, to a soundtrack of disco music. We then cut to Sylvester, wearing the same yellow and red outfit, as he skis towards the edge of the cliff. The disco music stops, leaving only the sound of the rushing wind. Sylvester goes flying off the edge of the cliff, a tiny, primary-coloured figure against epic Arctic mountains. He lets go of his ski poles and starts to tumble. His skis are ripped from his feet by the wind as the mountain rushes past behind him and he falls towards what looks like certain death. Eventually, Sylvester somehow manages to stop tumbling and get into the correct sky-diving posture, at which point he releases the chute. To get into this position had taken longer than intended, and he had fallen farther than planned. He had fallen out of frame in all but one of the four or five cameras trained on him. One camera, however, was all that was needed. After the silence of the heart-stopping fall, with only muted wind noise on the soundtrack, the full brass blare of the Bond fanfare rang out as a parachute opened, revealing its Union Jack design. The rush of relief meant that the cinema audience could breathe again.

The shot had all the timing of great comedy, as the tension of the silence was released at this one visual and audio cue. It was patriotism as punchline, and a moment of pure cinema guaranteed to bring the house down. The 30-second shot cost $250,000, but the results were priceless. The audience were so invested in the moment, and the rush of relief and amazement they felt, that no one paused to wonder why Bond had taken a parachute with him when he went skiing. Then a pair of silhouetted female hands reached up and caressed the parachute, and the title sequence began. The soft, beautiful voice of Carly Simon assured us that 'Nobody Does It Better', and few were prepared to argue.

The idea for the Union Jack parachute came from the co-screenwriter Christopher Wood. As he remarked, 'All over the world, whenever I saw the movie, instead of people howling and throwing stones at the Union Jack, they were bursting into spontaneous applause – which was kind of satisfactory.' Considering the extent to which parts of the world see the Union flag as 'the butcher's apron', this was quite an achievement. The Bond producers referenced this shot with another Union Jack parachute for the entrance of the villain in *Die Another Day*, but without Sylvester's terrifying fall and the incredible growing suspense of that shot, it came across as jingoistic and failed to have a similar impact.

Wood's idea was as good an example as you'll find of 'soft power', the political term for countries attracting others by showing their best qualities, rather than achieving their aims through force or domination. The shot captured an aspect of British identity that the British are especially proud of: unexpected triumph in the face of absolute disaster brought about by a particular mix of incredible bravery and utter stupidity. It is this love of the David-and-Goliath-like plucky escape which makes the British so fond of events such as the Dunkirk story, the Spanish Armada, the Battle of Britain or escapes from Colditz Castle. In contrast, the British do not tell stories of the victories at the Battle of El Alamein or the Battle of the Nive, for example, because they have little cultural interest in stories where the British win a regular battle between two reasonably well-matched armies. Sometimes, the unexpected triumph isn't even necessary, and a mix of absolute disaster, bravery and sheer stupidity is enough. The suicidal Charge of the Light Brigade, for example, is the sort of tragic disaster that most countries would prefer to forget, yet it has been immortalised by everyone from Lord Tennyson to Iron Maiden.

Michael G. Wilson's suggestion that the stunt should form part of the next Bond movie highlights a shift in the way the films were plotted in the 1970s compared to how they had been created in Sean Connery's time. Most of Connery's films were reasonably faithful adaptations of Fleming's novels. Certain details were changed, of course – perhaps to frame the villains as working for SPECTRE rather than Russian Intelligence, or to add more exciting and visually impressive elements. In general, the characters, locations and plots were taken from the books and changed only when it was thought that it would improve the film. After Fleming died, the producers became increasingly faithless to his work and took more radical departures, such as the volcano base lair in *You Only Live Twice*. The problem was that the 'better' novels, from a filmmaker's perspective, had been filmed first, so that the remaining books increasingly needed looser and more imaginative adaptations. The novel *The Spy Who Loved Me*, for example, is the story of a young Canadian woman who, after a couple of unhappy love affairs, ends up in a Canadian motel being attacked by the mafia. Bond himself only turns up at the motel about halfway through. The book did, however, have a terrific Bondian title. This was the only thing that was kept.

From *The Spy Who Loved Me* onwards – with the notable exception of *Casino Royale* in 2006 – the producers mined Fleming's life and work for a suitable title and the occasional character name, but then invented the rest of the film from scratch. By 1997, it was thought that all the good Fleming-related titles had been used – *Quantum of Solace* was not, at that point, considered a sensible title for a movie. The next Bond film, *Tomorrow Never Dies*, was the first to use a title that did not originate from Fleming. It came, instead, from Ringo Starr. *Tomorrow Never Dies* was based on Ringo's phrase 'Tomorrow Never Knows', which Lennon had borrowed for his ground-breaking psychedelic 1966 song.

After Fleming's death, several notable writers have continued the novels, including Kingsley Amis, Sebastian Faulks and Anthony Horowitz. It may have seemed logical, then, to use a similar writer to craft new Bond screenplays, but that is not how the filmmakers worked. Instead, they had an open-door policy for ideas. Producers, directors, actors and their friends and families could all pitch ideas for things they'd like Bond to do. The job of the screenwriter was to stitch all these disparate ideas into something resembling a coherent plot. Out of all these potential sources of ideas, perhaps the most important were those that came from the stunt crew.

It was no longer the case that a story would be written, and that story would include a number of exciting stunts and set pieces. Instead, original and thrilling stunts would be dreamed up, and the story would be written later to include them. One such example is the famous car jump from *The Man with the Golden Gun*, in which Bond's AMC Hornet hatchback jumped over the Mae Klong River in Thailand, using a broken bridge as a ramp. The twist was that the broken bridge was angled in such a way that the car rotated through 360 degrees along its forward axis as it flew through the air, before landing perfectly on four wheels at the other side. This was the first stunt which needed to be computer-simulated during development. It had been created by a demolition derby company called The American Thrill Show and first performed at Houston Astrodome. According to Christopher Lee, Cubby Broccoli agreed to buy their act for a year, at the price of around a quarter of a million dollars.

The stunt driver was Loren 'Bumps' Willert. To keep the balance correct during the spin, he had to lie down on his belly in the middle of the car, controlling the accelerator and brakes with his feet at the back. Bumps was dressed in black with his face painted black, so that he couldn't be seen. A dummy of Bond and another of his passenger were in the front seats either side of him. His job was to hit the ramp at exactly 48mph and, if the computer simulations were to be believed, physics would take care of the rest. The stunt went perfectly – perhaps too perfectly, some observers felt, in that it almost didn't look real. It was suggested that they try again for another take. Bumps exited the car with, Lee recalled, 'the stark face I've seen on men returning from a tough mission in the war'. When asked if he'd like to repeat the stunt, Bumps said, 'I would not. Because that is the first time I've ever done it, and I ain't going to do it again!'

In an age of CG-heavy blockbuster movies, it can be difficult to appreciate the impact of these stunt sequences in the 1970s. We are so used to people flying through the air now that we barely give it a thought. But the Bond audience knew that what they were looking at was real, and that when a man was seen falling or flying, it was dangerous and it really happened. If a skiBASE jump featured in a film now, instead of being shown as one continuous thirty-second shot, it is more likely it would be depicted as a rapidly edited sequence of many different shots from many different angles, in order to keep the film fast-paced and exciting. It would include multiple close-ups of the lead actors hanging on wires shot in front of a green screen, with wind machines blowing their hair. It would be expensive and polished, but you would never believe that the actor was in physical danger. The modern sequence would be exciting, of course, but it would not be heart-stopping in the way that Sylvester's fall still is. An example of this can be found in the Marvel superhero movie *Black Widow*, which includes a lengthy sequence of characters falling from the sky and fighting, where the hero has no parachute. This was such a clear reference to a similar scene in *Moonraker* that the film's heroine, played by Scarlett Johansson, was shown watching that Bond movie earlier in the film, in a respectful nod to their inspiration – another reminder of the extent to which Bond is in the DNA of modern action sequences.

In a scene from *The Living Daylights*, a cargo net is hanging out of the back of a plane in flight, while Bond and a villain are hanging on to the net and fighting. It was a dangerous scene to shoot, because the cargo net could whip upwards in the wind, crushing the stuntmen against the side of the plane – particularly after the point where the net broke and the cargo came spilling out. You can see the stuntman almost get hurt in this way at the very end of the sequence. The scene inspired a similar one in the PlayStation game *Uncharted 3: Drake's Deception*, in which the hero treasure hunter Nathan Drake is also hanging out of the back of a plane on cargo nets. The sequence returned to the screen in the 2022 movie adaptation *Uncharted*, which featured Tom Holland. This has none of the jeopardy of *The Living Daylights* original because you never believe that Holland is in danger.

When Roger Moore took over the role of Bond, he changed the character so that he was no longer portrayed as a cold-blooded killer. Such a move may have meant that the franchise was no longer an avatar of death, but that wasn't the case. Where Moore stepped down, the stunt team stepped up. Death was still part of every Bond movie – in fact, real death was potentially present in many scenes. The 23-year-old stuntman Paolo Rigoni, for example, was killed while filming a motorcycle and ski chase down a bobsleigh track in *For Your Eyes Only*.

The stunts that made 1970s Bond such a box-office success showed men and women risking their lives for the audience's entertainment. The audiences knew it, and they lapped it up. The appeal of these scenes is a good example of what Freudians call

Thanatos, which we discussed earlier – the seductive nature of the death drive. Roger Moore may have attempted to pass the buck, but the Bond films were, and always will be, about selling people death.

1980: THE NO-MARK

In Liverpudlian slang, a 'no-mark' is a nobody; someone inconsequential who has achieved nothing, who gained no marks in school exams, and who makes no mark on the wider world.

In 1980, an American no-mark made the decision to murder a celebrity. This particular no-mark had a narcissistic personality disorder and craved attention. Unable to achieve anything noteworthy himself, he decided that the way to be noticed was to murder a famous high achiever. This would forever link them in the eyes of the media. Paul McCartney was on his short list, but the fact that John Lennon lived in New York made him a more convenient target.

Fiction often portrays serial killers as extraordinary individuals, such as the cultured genius Hannibal Lecter. The reality is that most killers do not have special, desirable qualities; instead, they lack parts of the psyche that most others possess. They are not greater than us, like Nietzschean supermen, but lesser. And they are frequently incredibly dull people, a fact that many true crime writers cannot admit.

Around 10:50 p.m. on 8 December 1980 the no-mark was outside

John and Yoko's apartment building when the couple returned from a recording session. Pulling out a .38 revolver, the no-mark fired five shots at Lennon's back – BANG! BANG! BANG! BANG! BANG!

The first bullet – BANG! – took the life of a forty-year-old man. The second – BANG! – ripped apart the lives of his wife and children. The third – BANG! – shattered his friends and bandmates, and all who knew him over his too short life. The fourth bullet – BANG! – unleashed a tsunami of grief around the world, hitting all countries on earth, drowning millions in a wave of tears and loss. Four bullets hit Lennon in the back, but the fifth bullet missed. That bullet – BANG! – was aimed at the future. It would hit people not yet born who would discover the music of the Beatles but then be horrified to learn what happened to John. That bullet is still flying onwards.

The no-mark later gloated that 'all of my nobodyness and all of his somebodyness collided' when Lennon was killed. He believed he was being elevated by the act of murder. 'This was like, "Hey, I'm going to be a big king here, I'm really going to be somebody." It was much more than attention. It was like being the king.' By ending the life of the voice of his generation, he was claiming an aspect of Lennon's fame and reputation. In evolutionary biology, the technical term for a parasite that kills the host it has been feeding off is a parasitoid. In sociology, the committing of criminal acts in order to achieve infamy is called Herostratus syndrome. Herostratus was a Greek arsonist from the fourth century BC who burned down the Temple of Artemis, a building included on early lists of the seven wonders of the ancient world. He then proudly confessed to what he had done in order to immortalise his name. The Greek authorities responded by not only torturing and killing him, but by passing a law that prohibited mention of his name, either written or orally, to prevent him from being remembered.

The very name Herostratus syndrome shows how this law failed to achieve its aims.

After the murder, the no-mark pulled out a paperback copy of *The Catcher in the Rye* by J.D. Salinger. He stood at the scene of the crime pretending to read it, because he wanted newspaper reports to say that he was arrested while reading the book. *The Catcher in the Rye* is the story of Holden Caulfield, a rich, privileged, lonely schoolboy who views others with contempt and who believes this is a sign that he is deep, rather than a result of his emotional immaturity. It was considered by some people in the mid-twentieth century to be a profound and important book.

Twelve years earlier, Lennon had been shown the May 1968 edition of *American Rifleman* magazine and, like most non-Americans, found it shocking and surreal. In particular, he was struck by an article with the title 'Happiness Is a Warm Gun', which encouraged fathers to take children shooting at a young age. The article's title was a reference to a quote from the Peanuts cartoon strip, 'Happiness is a warm puppy'. The magazine used the headline with seemingly no understanding of how inappropriate their twist on it was. In Lennon's eyes, the magazine seemed to crystallise the insanity that ran through American culture, where love and sex were shunned as inappropriate or obscene, but murder was prime-time entertainment in television and films. As George Harrison saw the situation, 'If everyone who had a gun just shot themselves there wouldn't be a problem.'

The headline became the title of one of the most celebrated songs on the *White Album*. All four Beatles have singled out John's 'Happiness Is a Warm Gun' as a favourite from that record, in part because of how well they worked together when recording it, and in part for Lennon's vocal, which is one of his best from the period. In the song, he mocks the sexualised marketing of these killing tools, and combines the magazine's gun marketing with references to his sexual relationship with Yoko Ono, the 'Mother Superior' character in the lyrics. Mocking the magazine's attitudes, the band twist 1950s-style 'shoop shoop' backing vocals into a ridiculous harmonious 'shoot shoot, bang bang'. The Beatles response to American gun culture was to take the piss. It still seems the only reasonable reaction.

As a boy, the no-mark had obsessively played the American album *Meet the Beatles* over and over again, sitting on the floor of his room rocking back and forth as he did so. He made tiny cardboard guitars which he stuck onto his toy soldiers to replace their guns. The music inspired him to take the tiny plastic trained killers, ubiquitous in the playtime of twentieth-century boys, and imaginatively turn them into a band like the Beatles. He wanted to be just like his heroes. Unfortunately, his narcissism meant that he believed he automatically deserved to be just like them, without the tedious effort of spending thousands of hours learning his craft. When he grew up and found that he wasn't universally idealised, his dream was corrupted.

As we have seen, when the Beatles appeared they were balanced out by death, their shadow. In culture, that shadow was portrayed as stylish, confident and desirable – a man who could distract the audience from the moral horror of taking human life with a one-line quip. Here Hollywood recognises that their audience possess *Thanatos*, the Freudian death drive, and that this attracts them to exciting action movies. The make-believe of cinema is a safe way to indulge this dangerous part of our psyche. For this reason, the '007' logo is itself a gun, and you will have a hard job finding a Bond movie poster in which he is not holding a weapon. The problem is when this conscious marketing effort to turn something horrific into something glamorous starts to desensitise a culture to the reality of taking a life. This is the scenario that produces magazine articles entitled 'Happiness Is a Warm Gun', and allows the belief that killers are impressive to spread. In reality, a killer is more likely to be a dull no-mark, just like the one who shot John Lennon in the back when he was returning home with his wife.

The no-mark wanted attention, and to forever have his name linked with John Lennon's. In many ways, he got his wish. He has been the focus of many books, films and documentaries. He has been interviewed on American television by the likes of Larry King and Barbara Walters. But the more we analyse him in search of profound reasons to explain his actions, the more apparent it becomes that there is nothing interesting there. The inescapable conclusion is that the guy is just a no-mark. He has been in prison now for over forty years and is unlikely to ever be granted parole. If he had killed anyone else, he could have reasonably expected to be released after fifteen years; he could have worked through his issues and gone on to make something of his life. He may well have achieved something he would have been proud of. But he chose to pull the trigger, and that possible future will never happen now. As a result, his name will live on long after his death as the king of all no-marks.

1980: JOHN LENNON (1940–1980)

In the iconography that surrounds John Lennon, his round wire-framed NHS spectacles play a significant role. He started wearing these while filming Richard Lester's 1967 film *How I Won the War*. They were cheap, and helped position Lennon as a man of the people – an image further strengthened with songs like 1970's 'Working Class Hero'. This song was, Lennon said, 'for the people like me who are working class [...] I hope it's for workers and not for tarts and fags'. To those who knew him in Liverpool, however, the idea that Lennon was presenting himself as working class raised a few eyebrows. Doing so through NHS glasses was particularly ironic. As Cynthia Lennon recalled, when she met John in art school, he 'couldn't see a thing and hated wearing glasses, most of all, ironically, the little round lenses you got on the National Health. Instead he had horn-rimmed black ones, which cost quite a bit.'

Lennon's claim to be a working-class hero is not surprising in itself. In the UK, glorifying the working class is something usually done by lower-middle-class people like Lennon – especially those who attended art school, grammar school or university, and who don't work in the manufacturing, construction or service industries. The actual working class, in contrast, are typically less interested in praising themselves and more focused on trying to improve their lives. McCartney, Harrison and Starr were all genuine working-class heroes, but you couldn't imagine any of them ever writing a song like that.

'Working Class Hero' highlights the divide between the real John Lennon and his public persona. In the aftermath of his murder, it is perhaps unsurprising that he was seen in elevated, saint-like terms. His advocacy for peace and his involvement with 'new left' politics in the early 1970s, together with rallying anthems like 'Power to the People', gave him the image of a down-to-earth everyman fighting for a better world. As McCartney had commented, after his death people began talking about him 'as if he was Martin Luther Lennon'.

Lennon and Ono were, of course, incredibly rich. During the 1970s Yoko developed into a skilled businesswoman who made a lot of money investing John's Beatle wealth in real estate, antiquities and some more unexpected areas, such as farms and Holstein cows. In 1977, she bought 122 cows for $1.5m and ten bulls for $350,000. Lennon has boasted that she later sold a single cow for $250,000. If this is true, it shows an unusually astute business mind. Years later, Elton John asked her what became of the herd. She just shrugged and said, 'Oh, I got rid of them. All that *mooing*.'

Lennon and Ono had five or six apartments in the Dakota, an historic, imposing and strangely creepy building by Central Park in New York. The Lennons first moved into the Dakota after sub-letting an apartment owned by the actor Robert Ryan, who co-starred with Sean Connery in *The Longest Day* (1962). Most of John and Yoko's apartments were used to store the antiques, clothes and artworks they amassed. Elton John once sent them a card which riffed on the song 'Imagine'. 'Imagine six apartments,' he wrote, 'it isn't hard to do. One is full of fur coats, the other full of shoes.' There were indeed a lot of fur coats. When Lennon visited a posh Florida department store in January 1980, for example, he spent $25,000 on furs in ten minutes. Referring to a black fox-fur coat, Lennon told the shop assistant, 'I don't know what my wife is going to use it for, but it will be her breakfast fur.' It takes some doing to be such an excessive consumer that Elton John feels moved to comment on it.

Perhaps because of her privileged childhood in Japan, Ono was in the habit of referring to the people who worked for her as 'servants'. According to John Green, a tarot card reader on her payroll who also went by the name Charlie Swan, Yoko berated him if he expressed concern about the wellbeing of the other staff. 'Stop trying to be nice to the servants,' he claimed Yoko said to him, 'You're such a socialist, Charlie, always defending the working class. That kind of person needs orders. If you weren't so poor you'd understand that.' Green's account of Ono may be coloured by his animosity towards her, but other insider accounts do paint a very different picture of the couple than that suggested by songs like 'Power to the People'.

Although excessive consumption can be an accepted part of the image of many music superstars, from Elton John to Michael Jackson, Lennon is never seen in those terms. It is interesting that the general perception of Lennon and Ono in the decade before Lennon's death is still some distance from reality, given the extent to which Lennon's life has been so thoroughly explored by historians and writers. Indeed, there is a 'John Lennon Cinematic Universe' which tells his entire forty-year life story over a dozen films. It begins with Sam Taylor-Johnson's *Nowhere Boy* (2009), a film which deals with Lennon's childhood and ends with him and his band leaving for Hamburg. Those Hamburg days are explored in *Backbeat* (1994), while *Birth of the Beatles* (1979) covers the arrival of Ringo and the early days of Beatlemania – which becomes the focus of Richard Lester's *A Hard Day's Night* (1964). *The Hours and Times* (1991) examines Brian Epstein's relationship with Lennon, while *Help!* (1965) shows the Beatles as global icons at the moment they discover marijuana. Ron Howard's documentary *The Beatles: Eight Days a Week* (2016) looks at the end of their touring days, and this leads us to their exploration of psychedelia in *Magical Mystery Tour* (1967) and *Yellow Submarine* (1968). Their end is examined in Peter Jackson's *The Beatles: Get Back* (2021) and Michael Lindsay-Hogg's *Let It Be* (1970). John and Yoko's marriage is the focus of *Lennon Naked* (2010), and the rebuilding of the Lennon–McCartney relationship in the mid-1970s is the subject of *Two Of Us* (2000). The Lennon Cinematic Universe ends, for those who wish to include them, with the no-mark-focused *The Killing of John Lennon* (2006) and *Chapter 27* (2007). No other musician – and surely, no other twentieth-century figure – has had their life explored on film to such a degree. And yet, many questions remain about his last decade. It is probable that historians will not settle on an accepted version while Ono remains alive.

How Lennon described these years in interviews has been hugely influential, but it is clear that much of what he said was not true. For example, in many interviews he repeated an account of why he separated from Ono in 1973. He claimed he had been kicked out and embarked on a drunken 'lost weekend' which lasted eighteen months. He had wanted to go home, he said, but Yoko would not take him back until he was ready. This finally happened after the night he played at Madison Square Garden with Elton John in 1974. He had not known Yoko would attend the concert, but when they looked silently at each other afterwards it was obvious to everyone around them that they were still very much in love. It seems now that none of this was true, but it is end-lessly repeated, not least because there are so many direct quotes from the couple making those claims. As their friend the journalist Ray Connolly wrote, 'They decided upon a story and stuck to it, although they both knew that it wasn't true. The rewriting of history would always be a feature of their relationship.'

The real story is quite bizarre, and concerns Lennon's five-year relationship with May Pang, the couple's 22-year-old assistant. It began in 1973 and was initially arranged by Ono herself. She entered Pang's office in the Dakota wearing a long flannel nightgown and told her that she and Lennon were growing apart. This was not news to Pang, who was aware that the couple were having sexual problems. Ono had previously told her how Lennon had got drunk and slept with a girl at a party, while Ono was in the next room. Ono had always been tolerant of extramarital sex and had not been faithful to either of her previous husbands. Her guilt-free attitude to affairs may be because her parents had an open marriage when she was growing up, and she got to know their partners. The incident at the party was different, however. Everyone there knew what John was up to, and so she saw it as a public humiliation. This seems to have been a significant turning point in their marriage. John Green has said that Lennon told him in the aftermath of this that 'Yoko suggested a mistress, because she didn't want to deal with me in bed.'

Pang was not prepared for Ono's suggestion; Lennon liked Pang, Yoko said, and she should accept if he asked her to be with him. Pang's initial reaction was one of horror, as she knew she was being asked to sleep with her older, married employer. As she said, 'By then I knew that Yoko's suggestions were in fact orders.' According to Pang's account of the conversation, Yoko said, 'I know John will start going out with other people. I'd rather see him go out with someone who will be kind to him, wouldn't you?' It seemed that Ono had selected her young, relatively innocent employee to be Lennon's partner, rather than allow John to find someone new who Ono would have no control over. Pang suspected that Ono's desire to get John out of the way was because she wanted to start a new relationship herself with another musician. 'I think tonight when you go to the studio would be a good time for you to begin,' Pang recalls Ono saying as she stubbed out her cigarette and left. 'Don't worry about a thing. I'll take care of everything.'

There may also have been a cultural aspect to the arrangement. 'I knew that it was a tradition in Japan for wives of the upper class to understand the need of their husbands to have a mistress,' Pang has written. 'In Japan, often the wife and the mistress were friends. I was not a Japanese mistress, however, and the arrangement did make me uncomfortable and embarrassed.' Despite the unorthodox start to the relationship, Ono's instincts proved to be sound. Lennon and Pang's relationship seems to have quickly become a deep and loving one.

Pang and Lennon moved from New York to LA during much of their time together, but they did not leave Ono behind. She phoned them both multiple times a day and remained a significant presence in their relationship – much to Pang's frustration. While Ono may not have wanted John in her life at that point, she still wanted to retain control of him.

Where Ono's influence on John became negative was when she encouraged his distance from his old friends and family, and in particular from his son Julian. In 1970, when Lennon was recording the *Plastic Ono Band* album after undergoing primal scream therapy, he howled the phrase 'Daddy come home!' repeatedly in the song 'Mother'. In this song he addressed his feelings of abandonment caused by both parents, including how it felt not to be wanted by his father Alf. Shortly after recording this harrowing song he left the UK and never returned, and he did not bother to tell his son he was going. Julian and his mother Cynthia learned that he had left the country from news reports. 'There was no word from him between 1971 and 1974,' Cynthia has said, 'apart from birthday and Christmas presents for Julian each year, sent by his London office with no personal note or card.'

The pattern that marked the male line of the Lennon family had continued for another generation: John had walked out on Julian just as Alf had walked out on John and Alf's father had walked out on young Alf. As Julian would write, 'To me he wasn't a musician or peace icon, he was the father I loved and who let me down in so many ways. After the age of five, when my parents separated, I saw him only a handful of times, and when I did he was often remote and intimidating. I grew up longing for more contact with him but felt rejected and unimportant in his life.' For little Julian, who could watch his father's life playing out in the media, this was very hard. 'Dad's always telling people to love each other,' he once said to his mother, 'but how come he doesn't love me?'

In 1975, Ono fell pregnant with her son Sean. Given her history of miscarriages and her age, this was seen as something of an unexpected miracle child by both parents. John saw the birth of his second son as an opportunity to finally become a good father, and it is clear he was more present with Sean than he was with Julian. Because Sean would lose his father at the age of five, the memories he has of a playful, doting and loving dad are all the more precious. John's recognition of the need to be a good father for Sean, however, did not cause him to make amends with Julian. At no point after he acknowledged his failings as a father did John jump on a plane and visit his oldest son.

According to the 'official' narrative that Lennon would recite in interviews, he then became a house husband, preferring to bake bread and raise his son than make music. Political activism, conceptual art and making music were left behind. After five years of domestic bliss with Yoko, he then returned to music and recorded his final album *Double Fantasy*. That, at least, is the story as he usually told it. It suggests that, for all Lennon dismissed the 'Love, family, home' theme of McCartney's debut album as being 'about nothing', he eventually came to identify with those exact same values. Other accounts of the period are less idyllic, however, and instead tell a dysfunctional story of crippling depression, affairs, writer's block and relapses into heroin use, during which Sean was largely raised by nannies. Many of the accounts of those days are dismissed by Lennon's admirers as dubious or sensational because they come from disgruntled ex-employees. It is striking, however, that Ono and Lennon seem to have had an excessive number of disgruntled ex-employees – especially when compared to, say, Paul McCartney, George Harrison or Ringo Starr.

Tantalisingly, it is known that Lennon kept detailed diaries during the last five years of his life, which would clarify a great deal. But only small sections of these writings and audio recordings have surfaced, after they were stolen by yet another disgruntled ex-employee. Their extent and contents remain largely a mystery. A book by the respected Beatles expert Peter Doggett, who was thought to have access to some of the diaries, was due to be published in early 2021. The book was called *Prisoner of Love: Inside the Dakota With John Lennon*. But after its striking cover design appeared online the book was cancelled shortly before publication, with no explanation.

In all the official photographs and film of John and Yoko from this period, they present themselves as being deeply in love, always staring into each other's eyes and holding hands. In this respect, the iconography and branding of John and Yoko always remained resolutely on message. It could, however, at times feel like there was something performative about their expressions of love. No one doubts the depth of the love that Paul and Linda had, for example, although they were not continually pointing it out. It was such an integral part of their lives that there was no need to do so. The way Lennon kept insisting on the strength of his relationship, in contrast, does seem odd. A famous image of the couple graced the cover of *Rolling Stone* after John was murdered. It had been taken by Annie Leibovitz shortly before the shooting. In the image, Yoko is fully clothed while John is naked and clinging to her side in a foetal position. He is holding on to her tightly, kissing her cheek, while Yoko looks absent-mindedly away, seemingly uninterested. Lennon loved this photo. He told Leibovitz that she'd captured their relationship exactly.

This sense of John and Yoko's relationship being in some way a performance was present from the beginning. The film director Michael Lindsay-Hogg, for example, has said that when he had a meeting with all four Beatles ahead of making the film *Let It Be*, John played an audiocassette of him having sex with Yoko. 'At first, you couldn't be sure what it was, because you heard murmuring voices,' Lindsay-Hogg said. 'But then you knew because of the intimate way they were talking, because of pauses, because of silences, because of murmurs of pleasure that that's what was going on. I remember thinking it was an extraordinary salvo. And that it was him saying, "This is what's going on now. And it is her and me. It's not you, not the other three guys I have grown up with. It's her and me, and this is an aspect of my life that isn't going to change." ' The reaction of the other Beatles in the room at the time was described as 'awkward'.

In the official version of their story, Lennon's relationship with May Pang is described as something that just happened during his 'lost weekend'. In fact, it continued after they returned to New York, and after Yoko became pregnant and gave birth to Sean. It lasted until 1978, when John appears to have succumbed to a particularly severe period of depression. Based on an account of a call John made to May after he had been sent to Cape Town, their relationship could well have been rekindled and continued during the 1980s. The phrase 'lost weekend' implies a wasted period of hedonistic excess and loss of control, but this was a time when John was musically very productive. It is noticeable how the creativity and activity that marked John's time with May evaporated after he moved back in with Ono. Despite Lennon's problems with alcohol during their time in LA, it seems that Pang and Lennon had a loving and supportive relationship, and that May could have played a role in John's life similar to the one Linda played in Paul's. Ultimately, however, Lennon did not want a Linda. He wanted a strong-willed woman like his Aunt Mimi who would control him. That was never going to be Pang's role.

Shortly after Lennon's murder, Ono moved her new partner Sam Havadtoy into the Dakota to live with her. Havadtoy was a British-born gallery owner and interior designer from a Hungarian family who was almost twenty years her junior. He had previously worked as an interior designer for John and Yoko. Havadtoy would become the longest relationship of Ono's life. The couple remained together for a couple of decades, until around 2000 or 2001, but Ono was always cautious about mentioning her relationship status in interviews. During a 1990 *Los Angeles Times* interview, Havadtoy entered the room just before the interviewer asked Yoko directly about rumours the pair were secretly married. Ono denied this, and Havadtoy explained that 'We're happy. We're living together, boyfriend and girlfriend.' Generally, however, Yoko would portray herself as Lennon's widow rather than Havadtoy's partner. The author Peter Doggett once interviewed Yoko and wrote that, 'At the exact second when she talked about being forced to live alone since John's death, there was a loud cough from behind the closed door of her bathroom – a loud, distinctly male, cough. She looked at me, I looked at her, she glanced briefly towards the bathroom – and changed the subject.' Given the extent that Ono had previously used her life as her art, the relative secrecy surrounding her relationship with Havadtoy is curious.

Many fans believe that Ono and Havadtoy's relationship started in the late 1970s, during a period in which Lennon was severely depressed and rarely left his bedroom. This remains unproven, but if true it would shed light on a number of songs on their final album, 1980's *Double Fantasy*. The album marked a return to activity by Lennon after his five-year hiatus, and it largely alternated between Lennon songs and Ono songs. As Lennon later rationalised, the record was like a dialogue between man and wife. In this context, the fact that Ono's song 'I'm Moving On' follows Lennon's 'I'm Losing You' seems significant. Despite these tracks, *Double Fantasy* is otherwise 'on brand', with the album's cover of the couple kissing and love songs like 'Woman' as examples of their performative displays of the strength of their relationship. It is possible, however, that the album's title was a more accurate depiction of their marriage than the cover.

When Lennon was touring with the Beatles, one aspect of the circus he found particularly hard to accept was the sick, disabled or wheelchair-bound children who were brought to concerts in the hope that the Beatles could in some way cure them. John was uncomfortable with disabled people, and there are clips of the early Beatles in which he performs a mocking impersonation of people with cerebral palsy. To Lennon, the idea that he might be able to cure people was crazy. He was, as he insisted, just some guy from Liverpool. But by that point, this was no longer true. John Lennon had become much more than just some guy from Liverpool. Sick people would not flock to some random scouser in search of a cure. Whether he liked it or not, in the eyes of the world Lennon had become something more.

Of all the Beatles, John was the one it was easiest for most people to relate to. Paul was an ambitious, supernaturally gifted prodigy, a fascinating figure we can marvel at but not hope to relate to. George loved God just a bit too deeply for most. Charming Ringo was a hit in the LA celebrity world, but this doesn't resonate hugely for many. John, like the rest of us, was flawed. This made him the easiest to identify with. He was the archetypal wounded healer, the damaged soul who recognised his wounds and raised the possibility that things could be made better. It was his very flaws that caused people to elevate him. For these reasons, attempts to portray him as a saint or to sugar-coat his reputation only diminish his legacy.

Lennon was a mass of contradictions. His opinions would change from one interview to the next. He was the rich, privileged, working-class hero, the violent man of peace, a deadly serious comedian. He was Man of the Decade and Clown of the Year. He could be a patient, good friend and a bitter, fickle, terrible friend. He was, in other words, a profoundly human soul, and when he sang he connected directly to people on that level. His voice possessed a quality of honesty that few other rock or pop singers can touch. As the psychologist Arthur Janov has said, 'the feeling in John's voice – I don't think that it's matched by anybody today. He was loaded with feeling and that is why he moves you and that's why he was great.' His voice was proof that no matter how lost you may be, you are never alone, because there are people like John Lennon who can reach you.

His admirers viewed him as a seeker, a rare brave soul who was dedicated to embracing the truth, regardless of how ugly or difficult this was. As Jann Wenner said, 'Throughout his life, John was always enthusiastically searching for some kind of dream, answer or solution – something that would bring him peace.' An alternative perspective would be that he was always trying to get away from his current situation, and that the pain he felt caused him to sabotage his world in an effort to escape from it – from school, from Liverpool, from Cynthia, from drugs, from his family, from his friends, from Britain, and ultimately from the Beatles. Yoko was the only part of his life that he escaped from, but then chose to return to.

His legacy is the songs he left behind – 'Imagine', 'Help!', 'Strawberry Fields Forever', 'Come Together', 'Mind Games', 'She Loves You', 'Give Peace a Chance', 'A Day in the Life', 'Tomorrow Never Knows', 'Jealous Guy', 'In My Life', 'I Am the Walrus', 'Revolution' and dozens more. It is hard to imagine a stronger legacy than that.

1981: FOR A TRUE ARTIST
THEIR LIFE IS THEIR ART

Six months after John Lennon was shot dead, Yoko Ono released the Phil Spector-produced album *Season of Glass*. The cover was a photograph of the glasses Lennon had been wearing when he was shot, which Ono had recovered from the murder scene. The left lens was still splashed with John's blood. She photographed these blood-stained glasses next to a glass of water that was either half full or half empty, depending on your point of view.

Ono resisted pressure from the record company to change the cover. 'The record company called me and said the record shops would not stock the record unless I changed the cover,' she later wrote. 'I didn't understand it. Why? They said it was in bad taste. I felt like a person soaked in blood coming into a living room full of people and reporting that my husband was dead, his body was taken away, and the pair of glasses were the only thing I had managed to salvage.' Given Ono saw her life and her art as being essentially the same, it was not unexpected that she responded to her grief by presenting us with an image like this.

For many, however, the work confirmed their belief that there was something cold and distant about Yoko. For Lennon's old friends and family back in England, in particular, the cover was macabre. As Cynthia Lennon wrote, Yoko 'said that she wanted to bring home to people the reality of what had happened, but for Julian it was all too apparent without an unhappy reminder of his father's death in every record store.' That Ono would present a symbol of her husband's murder next to a 'glass half full' troubled many. But Ono's work is an exploration of her own thoughts. It is not concerned with other people, or her impact on them.

For many people, their image of Yoko Ono is shaped by her appearance in the video for 'Imagine', in which she is filmed opening the shutters in a large, empty, white room, before sitting down next to Lennon at a white grand piano. Many are struck by how blank and bored she looks when she sits down, and how uninterested she seems in the song or her husband's performance. This piece of film has surely had the largest audience of all the things that Yoko has ever done, and hence it has played an outsized role in defining her in the eyes of the public. It has led to her being perceived as cold, distant and self-absorbed. An impression of aloofness seemed to be confirmed by the way she made no effort to befriend anyone else in the Beatles' orbit, or the way she did not have many close female friends. One of the harshest judgements of her came from John's Aunt Mimi, after he took Yoko to meet her in 1968. 'I took one look at her and I thought, "My God, what's that?" ', Mimi said to a reporter later. She recalled that she took John outside and asked him, 'Who's the poisoned dwarf, John?'

When those upset by the end of the Beatles sought to understand what had happened or looked to find someone to blame, Yoko Ono proved to be an almost irresistible candidate. In this scenario, the fact that John had fallen so deeply in love was somehow her fault, as if she had bewitched him in order to intentionally split up the band. It did not help that she could come out with some hugely insensitive statements. 'I often wish my mother had died so that at least I could get some people's sympathy,' she once said, 'But there she was, a perfectly beautiful mother.' Although magazines like *Rolling Stone* stuck to the line that the breakup was McCartney's fault, many in the wider public preferred to point their finger at Yoko. These accusations were frequently expressed in racist and misogynistic terms. The level of abuse she received was horrendous.

Yoko's childhood began in wealth and comfort, but the fire-bombing of Tokyo during the Second World War led to her being sent into the country with her younger siblings and a maid, but without her parents. 'We were starving,' she has said. 'I was pushed into being an adult because I had to take care of the household, like getting food for my brother and sister, which meant that I had to go to different farmhouses and beg for it.' Ono recalled how she had to barter her possessions for a bag of rice. Incidents like this are bound to have a profound impact at that pivotal age.

The sense of being under attack in an uncaring and hostile world runs throughout Ono's life. Her history also explains why feminism was such an integral part of much of her work, given how she was initially treated by the male-dominated contemporary art world. Yoko spent her life being attacked, be that for her privilege, her gender, her work, her relationships or her ethnicity. Her constant campaigning for peace, given this background, is more heartfelt and genuine than is sometimes assumed. It can take first-hand experience of war to truly reveal the value of peace.

Yoko Ono was the great plot twist in the last chapter of the Beatles saga, somehow more prominent for her eighteen months in that story than Cynthia Lennon, despite Cynthia being present from before Hamburg until after Rishikesh. She went on to become a recording artist who has now released over a dozen solo albums, plus many collaborations. During her time with John her music was widely derided, but time has been kind to it, and her more *avant garde* albums are now often favourably reappraised. She had often been ahead of the curve, and her music makes more sense to us now than it did back in the 1970s. It helps, of course, that she was often surrounded by top-rank session musicians and recorded in the best studios. In many ways, her efforts to link her music with John's did her no favours. It gave the impression that she was using John's reputation to further her own ends. She wanted their tracks to alternate on *Double Fantasy*, for example, because she feared her songs would not be played if the record had Lennon on side A and Ono on side B. Yet being surrounded by John Lennon at his most sincere and straightforward was hardly the best showcase for her adventurous wailings. A song like 'Kiss Kiss Kiss', for example, which ends with Yoko simulating an orgasm, is perhaps not best encountered immediately after Lennon's bright optimistic '(Just Like) Starting Over'.

Control is a subject that comes up often in accounts of Ono, and it is usually expressed in strange ways. May Pang tells an interesting story about Yoko, during the production of her 1971 art film *Up Your Legs Forever*. This was a 70-minute film of people's legs. Pang looked up and found Ono next to her, staring into her face. 'I smiled at her, but even though she knew I was looking at her, she ignored me. She said nothing. Finally she murmured, almost to herself, "You know, I was famous before I met John." Then she walked away. It seemed as if Yoko had wanted me to eavesdrop on her own thoughts by creating the illusion that I wasn't there to hear. It was a very strange moment.'

One thing that Ono's supporters and detractors agree on is that she has an unusual ability to bend things to her will. It is almost as if reality is a little malleable around her, and respectful of her wishes. Ono was fascinated with fortune telling and other occult arts, particularly during the 1970s when she kept tarot readers, psychics, numerologists and astrologers on the payroll. No business decision was taken without occult advice. She bought a Persian mummy in a sarcophagus which she kept in the Dakota, believing she could profit from the mummy's magic. There are accounts of her using charms and protective magic. John Green, for example, says that when she had to attend a business meeting at Apple, Ono told him, 'I had a string tied around my waist to help seal my aura so that they couldn't send me any negative thoughts. That's how I kept centred.' She also had an interest in potions. When Lennon informed May that he was going to move back into the Dakota with his wife, he also told her that Yoko had given him two vials of liquid and instructed him that they use them to anoint each other. The vial for Lennon was flowery and attractive-smelling, while the vial intended to be rubbed on Pang was foul. An apothecary later told her that it was a mixture of sulphur, arrowroot and chili powder. Pang flushed it down the toilet.

Yoko would also occasionally instruct John to go on long journeys by himself, explaining that this would help him spiritually. She employed a 'directional man' called Takashi Yoshikawa who was an expert on feng shui and astrology. He would calculate the spiritually beneficial direction Lennon should travel. In 1980, for example, Yoko instructed John that, in order to reset his psychic alignment, he had to take a trip to the southeast. Lennon duly flew from New York to Cape Town, South Africa. Many people would like to be able to send their partner away for periods, but not many spouses would unquestioningly accept such instructions the way Lennon did. As Ringo described the situation, Yoko 'used to send [John] away on his own so he'd grow up. I don't know if he grew up, but he certainly went places without her.' On his *Plastic Ono Band* album in 1970, Lennon sang about how he didn't believe in magic. Anything that Ono believed in, however, he would accept without question.

Throughout the abuse Ono has received over the years, it was not unusual for her to be called a witch. This word is only a term of abuse if you accept gendered assumptions about the level of agency women should possess. A man can be called a wizard or a magician, for example, and it is not understood as an insult. As the musician and writer Barb Jungr has noted, Yoko 'always asserted herself as an artist. She behaved, effectively, like a man. She put her work first. She held her head up.' At the time, many people were shocked by this. If you accept that certain people have noticeable power over their world in a way that is unusual, and that this is not a negative thing unless they cause harm to others, then the notion that a woman is a witch should not be seen as an insult or an attack. Given the endless complexities of interpersonal power dynamics between people, it does not even need to be understood as something supernatural. In this context – when the word is stripped of its usual misogyny – the notion that Ono was a witch can become a useful way of understanding her. It may also be one that is respectful of how she wished to self-identify. She did, after all, release a 2007 album entitled *Yes, I'm a Witch*.

It will probably be some time after her death that a consensus forms about the strength of Yoko's work as a conceptual artist, and which elements of it were truly original. There is no doubt, however, that she made a huge impact on the British contemporary art world when she arrived in the 1960s. While the London art scene included some exciting work at the time, such as the op-art of Bridget Riley, in general London was then far behind places like New York. Ono's work was seen as a real shot in the arm that inspired many, not just John Lennon. It is still her work from the 1960s on which her reputation rests. She produced little of note in the late 1970s, in contrast, because she dedicated her energies for most of that decade into managing John and other business deals. This has led to claims that it was the Beatles who destroyed Yoko's career, and not the other way round.

For all the depression and writer's block that plagued Lennon's last five years, his time with Ono will always be remembered for his outpouring of creativity between 1969 and 1971. This would never have taken the form it did without Yoko's influence. The bond forged between them may not always have been harmonious, but it was deep and it was strong. While their later public declarations of romantic love may sometimes ring hollow, there was always a connection far stranger and more powerful underpinning it. 'I was a very lonely person before I met him,' she has said of John, 'I never met anybody else who could understand me.'

Yoko has been criticised for actively promoting the idea that she was the most significant artistic partner in John's life, more so than even Paul McCartney. In this framing, the John and Yoko years were John Lennon's true artistic expression. An example of this is how she, as controller of Lennon's estate, had the songwriting credit for 'Imagine' changed from just 'Lennon' to 'Lennon and Ono' in 2017. Lennon himself had spoken of how he had taken phrases from Ono's book *Grapefruit* to use as lyrics, so few objected to the change. But by the same logic the credits to a song like 'Tomorrow Never Knows' should be changed to include Timothy Leary, as the lyrics were taken from one of his books. No one expects this to happen. Yet even those who do not rate Yoko as an artist have to acknowledge that there is something remarkable about the 'John & Yoko' relationship between 1969 and 1971 – and that defining that relationship as a work of art may well be the most accurate way of describing it.

Yoko was deeply influenced by the idea that for a true artist their life is their art. Her espousal of this concept also made a huge impression on her husband. Could we then say that Ono's greatest art was her relationship with John Lennon? Can we credit the way she entered his life and offered him a way out of the Beatles as an expression of Ono's creativity? If this is the case, to take the most famous entertainer of his generation – the Man of the Decade – out of the mainstream and place him in the world of conceptual art and radical politics would be one of the most extraordinary works of art of her time. It is a situation that remains endlessly fascinating for countless different reasons, and it is still something we are discussing fifty years later. Such a framing would rob Lennon of his agency, of course, but he did surrender this to Yoko willingly. If it led to people admiring Ono's art, he would have been all for it.

If we were to see this idea as valid, then such an act would be an extraordinary artistic work. Yoko Ono, in this scenario, truly deserved her fame.

PART 4: GROW UP, 007

1983: A SYMBOL OF REAL VALUE TO THE FREE WORLD

The Royal World Charity Premiere of *Octopussy*, the thirteenth EON Bond film, was held at the Odeon Leicester Square cinema in London on 6 June 1983. The guests of honour were Prince Charles and Princess Diana. For the producers of the official Bond films, this show of establishment support was especially welcome. An 'unofficial' Bond movie would be released later that year, *Never Say Never Again*. This had taken advantage of legal issues surrounding the rights to *Thunderball* to tempt Sean Connery back to the role for one last time. The press loved this 'Battle of the Bonds', and there was much debate as to whether Connery or Moore would prove to be more popular with paying audiences. Prince Andrew had attended the *Never Say Never Again* premiere, so the presence of Charles and Diana at *Octopussy* was seen as a win for the Roger Moore movie. That said, the *Never Say Never Again* premiere also attracted Ringo Starr and his Bond Girl wife Barbara Bach. Ultimately both films were hugely successful, but

Moore's *Octopussy* won out by $23m. It took $183m to *Never Say Never Again*'s $160m.

By this point, it was not unusual for world leaders to lend their support to Bond. The same year saw a Roger Moore-hosted TV special called *James Bond: The First 21 Years*. This included a contribution from Ronald Reagan, then the President of the United States. 'As I see it, 007 is really a ten. He's a modern-day version of the great heroes that appeared from time to time throughout history,' Reagan said. 'James Bond is a man of honour. Maybe it sounds old-fashioned, but I believe he's a symbol of real value to the Free World.'

Octopussy was not Diana's first Bond premiere. She and Charles had been guests of honour at the premiere of *For Your Eyes Only* in June 1981. This was a month before their wedding, when she was still Lady Diana Spencer, and their public outing caused great excitement both in Britain and around the world. She and her husband then turned up for all the eighties Bond films. They saw out the Roger Moore era with the *A View to a Kill* premiere in 1985, and welcomed Timothy Dalton to the role at the June 1987 premiere of *The Living Daylights*, when Leicester Square had been renamed James Bond Square for the day to mark the series' silver jubilee. Charles and Diana had also visited Pinewood studios when the film was being made, where they saw the work of the stunt team in action. It was here that the Dutch actor Jeroen Krabbé suggested to Diana that she smash a wine bottle made from sugar glass over her husband's head. She proceeded to do so with considerable glee, and photos of the incident appeared on the front pages of newspapers around the world.

Diana's last Bond premiere was *Licence to Kill* in June 1989. The next Bond film was *GoldenEye* in 1995, and Charles attended that premiere by himself, having separated from Diana in 1992. Diana and her partner Dodi Fayed were due to visit the Pinewood set of

Tomorrow Never Dies in the first week of September 1997, but the pair were killed in a car crash less than a week before. The planned set visit was a result of a close friendship between Dodi Fayed and Bond producer Barbara Broccoli. 'I met him through friends at the American School in London. Dodi, who loved the cinema, used to visit my father's [Cubby Broccoli's] film sets. We became part of his family and he became part of ours.'

This connection between Dodi Fayed and Barbara Broccoli reveals much about how the British establishment works. Historically, many European aristocracies were structured around the primacy of bloodlines. For those not of the 'right families', there was simply no way they could be accepted as part of the ruling class. Strict aristocracies such as these were brittle, however, and fell from power when they were unable to adjust to changing times. In Britain, in contrast, the barrier between the ruling elite and everyone else was a little more permeable. Should a merchant or industrialist become sufficiently wealthy, they could afford to send their children to specific establishment schools. Here they would learn to speak with the right accent, perform the correct social cues that distinguish them from the 'common people' and build a network of relationships with other wealthy elites. Within a generation or two, the lowliest family could in this way become accepted by the establishment. This proved to be a far more durable system than many European aristocracies, because it was able to harness what was new or potentially threatening.

An example of the permeability of the establishment is the way that the British state awarded knighthoods to people like Mick Jagger and Elton John – and also Paul McCartney and Ringo Starr. This effectively brought them on board in a way that forced them to acknowledge the legitimacy of the existing system. An offer of acceptance and approval like this can be powerful and tempting. There are not many who, like David Bowie, are secure enough in their own identity to turn down an honour when it is offered to them, on the grounds that the whole system is absurd.

This system of gradual acceptance of the wealthy over a generation or two is seen clearly in the status of, and friendship between, Dodi Fayed and Barbara Broccoli. Dodi's father, the Egyptian-born businessman Mohamed Al-Fayed, was frequently vocal with his anger at not being truly accepted by the British establishment, despite his immense wealth. His son, in contrast, was not snubbed in this way. He had attended Sandhurst Royal Military Academy and a number of elite European schools, and he moved in circles where he was able to date the Princess of Wales and be invited as a VIP on set visits to Bond films. Dodi and Barbara moved in the same elevated circles even though Barbara's father, Albert R. 'Cubby' Broccoli, grew up in a working-class area of Queen's, New York City. After working a series of odd jobs, he got into the film business at the bottom, working as a gofer on a Howard Hughes movie. He rose to the top of the industry and, in his later years, was able to hand the Bond franchise to his daughter Barbara and stepson Michael G. Wilson. The Bond franchise has always been a family business.

By the time Barbara was producing Bond, it had become the establishment. It could count on the Prince and Princess of Wales turning up to help publicise each new film, in a way that other films couldn't. The Bond films achieved this by reliably making a lot of money, but also by keeping going for so long that they became, effectively, a tradition. Bond continued through the decades, through periods of being wildly popular and periods of being dismissed and mocked, always focused on delivering an ambitious and exciting movie to its audience. Bond could be relied on, and every couple of years or so it would return when expected. As President Reagan had recognised, the Bond franchise supported the existing order rather than opposed it, and hence became some-thing that was of 'real value to the Free World'.

As a marker of the extent to which the Bond franchise had merged with the establishment, it is noteworthy that the Prince and Princess of Wales attended the premiere of a movie titled *Octopussy*. The title was taken from one of Ian Fleming's posthumously published short stories. This was told from the perspective of a Second World War hero who murdered Bond's childhood skiing instructor in order to steal a cache of Nazi gold, and who then became a melancholy alcoholic living alone on a beach by a coral reef – a character not unlike Fleming himself. Octopussy was the name of his 'pet' octopus, who eventually drags him underwater and kills him.

By this point the Bond producers had used up all the suitable plots from Fleming's novels and had begun constructing new stories for each movie. But they still wanted to maintain links to Fleming's work, however minor they may be. By the mid-eighties, this often involved using the titles of otherwise unsuitable short stories for their films. 'The basic material begins to wear thin. We stuck closely to the books in the beginning, but we were finally forced to inject whole new ideas in later movies,' Cubby Broccoli explained. 'We're making "Octopussy" the name of a girl in our film. She's beautiful and powerful. A semi-villain, who gets redeemed in the end.'

The character of Octopussy was played by Maud Adams. In the film's poster, she is depicted with eight arms, like the Hindu mother goddess Durga, which she wraps around a typically confident-looking Roger Moore. One suggestion for a tagline for the movie was 'Eight arms to hold you', which was the original working title for the Beatles' Bond-spoof *Help!* Octopuses and octopus imagery figure heavily in Bond, not least in the logo for SPECTRE, so the producers felt that the title could be justified as being sufficiently

Bondian. None of this prevented there being some concern about the name 'Octopussy' from American distributers.

When the National Research Group asked women aged between twelve and forty-nine what they thought about a film called *Octopussy*, 37 per cent said they found it objectionable. When they were told that it was the name of a James Bond film, however, that number fell to just 4 per cent. When it comes to Bond, it seems, different rules apply – a clear indication that he was now the establishment. Many aspects of establishment culture – blood sports, sending away young children to be raised by others – would be roundly condemned if they were done by any other section of society. But when it comes to the establishment, such behaviour is often overlooked or accepted. Part of this, perhaps, is simply pragmatic. There is little point starting an argument with someone far more powerful and wealthy than you, because the outcome seems fairly certain. If the Bond movies want to call one instalment *Octopussy*, then there is really little you can do to stop them.

This was the second time the support of the British royal family gave the Bond franchise sufficient cover to use 'Pussy' as a name. Back in 1965, at the beginning of Bondmania, the US censor Geoffrey Shurlock threatened to ban *Goldfinger* because Honor Blackman's character was named Pussy Galore. This, he argued, was something that should have been cleared with the censors at script level, before the film was shot. As we noted earlier, Broccoli immediately flew over to America to meet with the censor, at which point he was able to show him photographs of the UK premiere, where the guest of honour had been Prince Philip. Connery had been unable to attend, which meant that Honor Blackman was the focus of attention. This was certainly the case for Prince Philip. As Blackman recalled, 'The Americans saw a picture on the front page of an English newspaper with me talking to Prince Philip and the headline read, "The Prince and The Pussy". They were taken aback but they took that as permission that it was a decent film and decent character otherwise Prince Philip wouldn't be talking to me.'

It is rare for a film franchise to become part of the establishment in this way, but of course the story of the Bond films is not like the story of other films. There are no other comparable examples of franchises based on a single character that lasts for sixty years, with each film being a major commercial success. This is not for a lack of film producers trying. All other contenders falter after a number of years, due to audience indifference. Uniquely, Bond has always delivered and the audience has always been there. The lesson of history, of course, is that even the longest of empires must eventually fall. That rule applies to wealthy elites as much as to film franchises. But despite the ever-present fear of eventual collapse, the establishment must keep on as it always has, building tradition one year at a time, hoping that it is flexible enough to survive the ever-changing society that supports it. There is nothing else it can do. In this paranoid scenario, change is always something to be feared. For all the Broccoli family is admired for its unique ability to maintain the Bond franchise, no one believes that they could create another, equally successful franchise of their own, unrelated to 007.

Here is what the idea that Bond is death ultimately means. He is not trying to build a better world. He kills to protect the status quo from external threats. He kills people that are a danger to the establishment, because they may in some way change it. That is the one thing that those with power can never allow. The establishment is therefore trapped by its need to endure. All it can do, as Winston Churchill so memorably phrased it, is to 'keep buggering on'.

1984: WACKY MACCA THUMBS ALOFT

The long, twisted history of the post-Beatles solo years includes many albums, projects and experiments that time, critics and the paying audience have not been kind to. While there are usually some people who have a fondness for those moments, and who are prepared to defend them, there is one major project which seems almost entirely lacking in supporters. At the time of writing, it is hard to find anyone prepared to defend Paul McCartney's 1984 movie *Give My Regards to Broad Street*.

When the film was released, movies starring musicians were going through a golden period. Prince's *Purple Rain* had been released three months earlier, and Madonna's *Desperately Seeking Susan* would be released five months later. Both films were commercial successes, with *Purple Rain* costing $7m to make and taking $70m at the box office. *Give My Regards to Broad Street*, in contrast, cost $9m but took only $1.4m. The audience stayed away, and critics were not kind. Writing in the *Chicago Sun-Times*, Roger Ebert said that it 'is about as close as you can get to a nonmovie, and the parts that do try something are the worst'. *Variety* called it 'characterless, bloodless and plotless', while the *Washington Post* said it was the 'worst movie of the year'. According to the *Sun*, it was 'overblown video rubbish', while *The Times* declared it was 'the worst film that ever cost $9million and two years' work'.

A flop like this is surprising, given how commercially successful McCartney was at that time. He had not been coasting on post-Beatles fame and his career had taken a very different path to his bandmates since the split. At the beginning of the seventies John, George and Ringo released albums like *All Things Must Pass*, *Ringo*, *Plastic Ono Band* and *Imagine*, when they were still in their post-Rishikesh creative peaks. These albums are generally seen as the high points of their solo careers. There were some gems in their later work, of course, but their later albums are typically not as well regarded. There is a sense that the law of diminishing returns kicked in.

McCartney's solo career was the reverse of this. He started in the doldrums with a solo album widely seen as lacklustre, at a time when he was being blamed for the breakup of the Beatles. While George and Ringo enjoyed great commercial success and John huge critical acclaim, Paul was dismissed as soppy and saccharine, and released work that was seen as half-baked. It did not help that John and Paul were exchanging barbs in the press and in songs at this point, and that John's insults were cleverer and funnier. His remark that Paul wrote 'granny music' was endlessly repeated by commentators and critics.

John, Ringo and George put music out under their own names, on the understanding they were huge stars in their own right. They were part of the decadent seventies music industry world of cocaine, alcohol and American celebrity. Paul, in contrast, attempted to vanish into another group, Wings. This returned him to his old life in a van on the motorways, touring the student unions of Britain. Inside the band, Paul would be able to collaborate and create with his new musicians, leaving his 'Beatle

Paul' days behind him – or at least, that was the plan. It was never going to work out that way, of course. No group of musicians in the seventies that included Paul McCartney could be a group of equals. The line-up of Wings rarely stayed stable for long, unlike the rock-solid unit he had shared with George, John and Ringo. But the fact that he tried to be part of something else was significant.

By the end of the seventies, McCartney had built Wings into a huge commercial success – albeit one almost entirely musically divorced from the emerging punk sensibility. As we've noted, their 1977 single 'Mull of Kintyre' became the bestselling single of all time, taking the crown from 'She Loves You' by the Beatles. This must have meant a lot to Paul – to be in a band that has the bestselling single ever is one thing, but to then form a second band a decade later which tops that is even more extraordinary. 'Mull of Kintyre' is still the bestselling non-charity UK single, and is unlikely to ever lose that title. To put it in some contemporary context, however, it was released two weeks after the Sex Pistols album *Never Mind the Bollocks, Here's the Sex Pistols*, when Johnny Rotten *et al* proclaimed that they were going to sweep away the old irrelevant dinosaurs. In 'London Calling' by the Clash, for example, Joe Strummer sang about how 'Phony Beatlemania has bitten the dust'. The unavoidable chart prominence of that acoustic folky strum-along 'Mull of Kintyre', complete with bagpipes and Aran jumpers, made it obvious that McCartney was one of those dinosaurs who still clogged up the charts with outdated crap, as the punks saw it, and who had to go.

'The big thought from me, and from everyone, was that it was 1977,' Paul has said. 'We couldn't release the song in those days of punk. I mean, it was madness, but I just thought, "Well sod it".' Punks, however, may not have been as uniform in their tastes as they are usually portrayed. Paul and Linda were once trapped in London traffic when an aggressive-looking gang of punks appeared. 'We were kind of crouching a little bit, trying not to get noticed, and thinking, "Jesus, what are they going to do?" ' he recalled. 'One of them comes to the car, so I wound down the window a little bit, and he goes, "Oy, Paul, that *Mull of Kintyre* is fucking great!" '

Even as early as 1972, when David Bowie wrote 'All the Young Dudes', it was evident that a generation was emerging who saw the Beatles as old people's music. In that song Bowie portrays 'the Beatles and the Stones' as the sort of music an older brother would play, and dismisses them with the line 'What a drag'. Paul McCartney and Mick Jagger were among the first of the post-war popstars to forge lengthy careers which made them noticeably older than the rest of youth culture. This was then such a new situation that they were endlessly mocked for their age. It probably didn't help that members of his generation had warned you should never trust anyone over thirty, or sang about how they wished they would die before they got old. When McCartney made *Give My Regards to Broad Street* he was, unforgivably, already in his forties. Following that first wave of older musicians, however, lengthy careers are no longer considered unusual. Bands that came in their wake like Metallica or U2 can now keep going through the decades without encountering anything like the ageist abuse received by McCartney or the Rolling Stones.

In the eighties, McCartney left Wings behind and embarked on his greatest period of solo success. Songs like 'Pipes of Peace' and 'Ebony and Ivory', a duet with Stevie Wonder, were huge number-one hits. When Michael Jackson released *Thriller* in 1982, the bestselling album of all time, it included 'The Girl is Mine', his duet with Paul McCartney. By this point, McCartney was once again hugely successful, and incredibly famous. This was not automatic recognition for being a Beatle, but success that he had built up slowly by working away over the previous decade. It must have seemed that a Paul McCartney movie would be a sure-fire hit.

Give My Regards to Broad Street occupies the middle ground between *A Hard Day's Night* and *Help!* It tells the story of a day in the life of hugely successful pop star Paul McCartney, as he goes from recording studios to meetings and radio interviews, weaving in a plot about the master tapes of a new album going missing. If this tape is not found by midnight, we are told, it will mean the collapse of Paul's entire music empire. This was a very different scenario to musician films such as Prince's *Purple Rain* or Eminem's *8 Mile*, where the superstar plays a young contender battling their demons and fighting for recognition, who the audience can identify with.

The film contains many sequences that make no attempt to move the plot forward. At one point Paul drives across London to visit a pub landlord to ask him about the guy who last had the tapes. The landlord doesn't know anything, so Paul drives back. Then there are several lengthy dream sequences, in which Paul imagines scenarios that might explain where the tapes are. None of this advances the narrative. When the tapes are eventually found, the mystery of their disappearance is revealed to be extremely mundane. They had been left at Broad Street Station, because the man carrying them became locked in a room he thought was a toilet. Broad Street Station was then a major transport hub in east London. It closed down two years after the film came out, possibly out of embarrassment. If this didn't undercut the drama sufficiently, it is revealed in the final moments that the whole thing was a dream anyway. It is as if the film was written by someone psychologically opposed to drama. The script is the primary culprit for the movie's failure, and it was written by McCartney himself.

The film's strength was, of course, the music. McCartney

revisited a number of Beatles songs and previous hit singles such as 'Silly Love Songs', to give as crowd-pleasing a soundtrack as he could. As a result, the soundtrack album sold well, despite the film flopping. That the script he wrote was so poor, and the music so successful, gives us an insight into McCartney as an artist, considering that he applied the same principles to creating both.

After sixty years of interviews, it's clear that McCartney does not understand why music comes so naturally to him, or flows out of him so easily, in a way that doesn't happen to other people. He seems at times afraid that it might stop – he has never learned how to read music, for example, in case it breaks the way he works. As the Irish poet Paul Muldoon has said when discussing McCartney's creativity, 'It's not a particularly fashionable idea right now but if you scratch any interesting artist you'll hear that one of the key components to how they do it is that they don't really know what they're doing. [...] If you don't know what to expect, there's a chance the listener and reader will find themselves in a place they wouldn't expect to end up, that's where interesting art resides.'

McCartney places great emphasis on starting and finishing work immediately, before you have had the chance to overanalyse or come up with an excuse not to do it. This is an attitude that he credits his father with instilling in him. Whenever Paul or his brother Mike would try to get out of a chore by saying they would do it tomorrow, their father would tell them 'D.I.N. – do it now'. As he explains, 'you get rid of the hesitation and the doubt, and you just steamroll through'. This approach paid dividends when he came to work with John Lennon. Every time they sat down to write a song they would finish it, and they never once came away from a writing session having failed to come up with something. 'I'm all for that way of working,' he has said. 'Once John and I or I alone started a song, there was nowhere else to go; we had to finish it, and it was a great discipline. There's something about doing it when you have the vision.'

Paul's method of songwriting was to not worry about it, and just let it happen. When extraordinary music of a quality others cannot achieve just pours out of you, there is little else you can do. The stories of Paul writing 'Yesterday' in a dream, or the footage of him conjuring up 'Get Back' out of nothing in a matter of minutes in Peter Jackson's docuseries *The Beatles: Get Back*, illustrate just how constant this process was. There was no writer's block or hoping for inspiration in McCartney's writing life. The music just came and all he had to do was get it down before it was lost.

When McCartney dabbled with tarot card readings in the 1960s, he found that he always drew the Fool card. This initially disturbed him, until the tarot reader explained what the card really meant. 'I used to say, "Oh Dear!"' he recalled, when he saw the Fool card, 'and she used to say, "No no no. The Fool's a very good card. On the surface it looks stupid, The Fool, but in fact it's one of the best cards, because it's the innocent, the child."' McCartney then began using the word 'fool' a lot in in his songwriting, starting with 'The Fool on the Hill', a song about the Maharishi. 'Some people think that my description of the Maharishi as a "fool" is disparaging. That's not the case at all,' he has said. 'I think "The Fool on the Hill" is a very complimentary portrait.' In the context of artistic creation, the Fool represents the first spark of an idea as it appears in the mind from nowhere. This unworldly innocent idea needs to be protected and allowed to grow and take the shape it wants, because initially it is too weak to withstand the criticism of the intellect. This is an idea that fits well with McCartney's creative process, which is based around recognising and nurturing these ideas when they come and seeing what they want to be.

McCartney tackles other creative work in the same way. When he sits down to paint, for example, he likes to start and finish a canvas during the same session. He is not as supernaturally talented in other artistic forms as he is with music, however, and for all that his paintings have their admirers, it is likely that he would struggle to ignite interest from the art world if he wasn't an ex-Beatle. It seems that he approached screenwriting with his usual 'get it done and let it happen' attitude. Screenwriting, however, is more about intricate focus on structure than it is inspiration. It is a world of rewriting and editing; McCartney's creative process is the opposite of what is needed.

The casual nature of his creative process was evident in his post-Beatles recording career, which critics felt often lacked the level of quality control found on the Beatles records. Here Paul probably did himself no favours by starting the first Wings album with the nonsense-song noodling of 'Mumbo' followed by 'Bip Bop'. To make uninhibited music like this was clearly liberating for McCartney after the polished songwriting that marked the late-Beatles era, but it left him open to accusations that, away from the searing eyes of John Lennon, his music was bland or half-baked. As he admitted recently, referring to the Wings years, 'I'm a bit more purposeful these days than I was then. I was probably smoking a little too much wacky baccy at the time.' In the punk years, when the drug of choice was cheap speed or sniffing glue, McCartney's preferred drug was seen as further proof that he was an out-of-date hippy. It seems suitably symbolic that Wings came to an end in 1980 after McCartney was put in jail in Japan for the crime of possessing a huge bag of 'dynamite weed'.

It says a lot about McCartney then that, despite the barrage of criticism he received, he didn't change his approach. When he was mocked by Lennon and others for the crime of writing silly love songs instead of making worthy, serious rock music, he wrote the single 'Silly Love Songs' as a defiant defence of such music. This then spent five weeks at number one in the US Billboard Hot 100 chart. For all the claims that he was soft, McCartney has never been weak or cowardly. As Michael Lindsay-Hogg, the director of *Let It Be*, has said, 'Liverpool is a tough town. I wouldn't particularly want to run into Paul McCartney in a dark alley, if he didn't like me.' McCartney's promotion of optimism and kindness took nerve. It was not an easy position to take. He stuck to it because he believed in it.

Lennon's barb that McCartney wrote 'granny music' reveals a fundamental difference between the pair. Lennon thought that music for that demographic was beneath him, while Paul saw nothing wrong with writing music older women would enjoy. The huge variety of styles used by McCartney over the years, ranging from pre-war music hall and children's songs to *avant garde* and cutting-edge experiments, illustrates how he loved all music and saw it all as valid. In the early 1970s, by contrast, Lennon was focused on only making music that hip and serious rock journalists would respect. McCartney couldn't have done this even if he had tried. The music that came through him was what it was, and it became what it wanted to be. He made no claims to be in control of it.

In 1984 the CBC journalist Barbara Frum sat down with him and told him, 'A lot of people say I used to love him, now he's insipid, now he's puerile. I suppose it's absurd like saying to Einstein, "Hey, what are you going to do after e=mc squared?", but they are really saying I don't like what you do now, I want something else.' McCartney calmly replied that those were the opinions of people who don't buy his records, but there were a huge amount of people who didn't think that way and who did go out and buy his records. Those people, he believed, were valid and should be respected. Although he remained calm during this particular interview, Paul could often be visibly annoyed by such insults, as he was during a 1984 CBS interview about *Give My Regards to Broad Street* with Gene Siskel, who said the film was terrible. McCartney turned to the camera and said to the watching viewers, 'You know, he's rubbished this film and I'm sitting here doing this bloody interview for him, isn't that terrific?' before debating whether to throw his orange juice over the interviewer. Ultimately, he decided not to.

The level of abuse that McCartney received in the 1980s is quite eye-opening. It was not always direct insults in interviews, and rumbled along as a low-level general tone of mockery. To readers of *Smash Hits* magazine, for example, he will always be known as Wacky Macca Thumbs Aloft. When the *Top of the Pops* host Steve Wright described McCartney as being 'almost as nice as Jason Donovan' in 1989, he did not mean this as a compliment. After Lennon's murder, the hipster joke was that they shot the wrong Beatle. The usual target was McCartney's amiable, chirpy, everyman persona, which struck many as either naff or just wrong for such a huge celebrity.

For McCartney, though, being ordinary was important. 'I'm actually quite a fan of "ordinary". I hope in many ways it defines me, and so also many of the songs I've written,' he has said. 'You can choose to be highly sophisticated but very uptight, or you can be not so sophisticated but at peace with yourself. I try and be a bit of a mixture, and I draw very strongly on that ordinariness.' This was, in part, an attempt to retain his links to his background and childhood, and not be changed by the money and success he had. As his daughter Mary McCartney has said, 'My own personal theory – I've not talked to Dad about this – is that he needs normality because that's what inspires him. Real life and real people. That's where all the music comes from.' For some, McCartney's regular everyman persona can be a source of irritation. He is clearly not ordinary, so his attempts to present himself that way appear insincere, or even calculated, and this makes him dislikeable. Despite all the abuse it earned him, however, it's possible that clinging to this mask of normality was ultimately a very wise move. It may have protected him from a far greater threat.

At times, McCartney acted as if he knew what the long-term reputation of the Beatles would be. Unlike George and John, who often seemed surprised that the world had not yet moved on from the Beatles, it can appear that Paul had glimpsed, if only partially, how historically significant they were. During the *Get Back* sessions in January 1969, he joked how comical it would be if in fifty years people were saying that the band split up 'because Yoko sat on an amp'. Fifty years later there were people saying just that, so this was indeed prescient. But it also reveals that he was aware people would be analysing their story to that degree in the distant future. Few bands today, in contrast, have reason to worry about how they will be talked about in the 2070s.

Did McCartney know, at this point, that he was more than a standard celebrity, someone destined to be forgotten when the next hot bands came along? Did he know that he was going to be an icon of British creativity whose stature would be similar to that of Shakespeare or Dickens? Did he know that, in the distant future, the twentieth century would be boiled down to the time of Einstein, Hitler, the moon landings and the Beatles? Or that it would be normal for people from around the world to know his name, centuries after he was dead? If so, how could anyone live with this knowledge? It is one thing to be famous, but quite another to be history. How does a legendary icon like that go about their daily lives among people that history will be quick to forget? That sort of knowledge could very easily turn someone into a monster.

In that context, McCartney's promotion of ordinariness appears to be a stroke of genius. Although the work he did in the Beatles was not going to be forgotten, he managed to undercut the reverence that surrounded him just enough that he could keep his feet on the ground and go about his daily business. McCartney's promotion of a down-to-earth unsophisticated everyman persona turned him into a joke in the eyes of critics in the 1980s, but it may also one day be seen as the most astute thing he ever did.

1995: TOO MUCH OF A GOOD TIME

In the twentieth century, new musical genres sprang up with wild abandon. From jazz and blues in the early decades of the century, to rock, reggae, metal, techno and rap in the later decades, huge undiscovered musical territories suddenly burst forth for musicians to explore. Often a new genre was a reaction to a new piece of technology or drug, such as the synthesiser, electric guitar or MDMA. The continual arrival of new and original genres kept pace with the huge social changes that characterised the century, serving as a reminder of how different life was for successive generations. If it was possible to play hip-hop or techno to the people of the 1930s, for example, their incomprehension of what they were hearing would illustrate starkly how much our daily lives had changed.

The genre of Britpop, however, was different. It was not a whole new musical language, in the way that earlier genres had been. Much of it was really not that different to music from twenty and even thirty years earlier. Instead, it was a genre defined by energy and competition. It was undoubtedly a creative, exciting time, but musically it looked back, rather than forward. Britpop superstars Oasis were often compared to the Beatles – usually by themselves. They had certainly copied the haircuts and the musical style of 'Rain', the B-side to 1966's 'Paperback Writer' single. But once they had mastered this sound, they stuck with it. If the Beatles were defined by their continual experimentation and an unwilling-ness to repeat themselves, Oasis were really very different to the Beatles.

The nostalgia of the Britpop years was good news for both the James Bond franchise and the legacy of the Beatles. Paul McCartney's reputation, in particular, finally began to undergo a favourable reassessment. Many contemporary artists were eager to express their admiration of him in a way that hadn't happened since the 1960s. McCartney recorded a version of Lennon's 'Come Together' with Noel Gallagher and Paul Weller, for example, under the name The Smokin' Mojo Filters. This was used as the final track and lead single for *The Help Album*, a 1995 charity CD. The record raised over a million pounds for War Child, a char-ity which provided aid to children in Bosnia and Herzegovina and other war-ravaged countries. It included contributions from Oasis, Portishead, the Stone Roses, Suede, Sinéad O'Connor, Blur, Radiohead and the KLF, making it an impressive snapshot of the British and Irish music scene at that point in time. Each contribu-tion was recorded in a single day, 4 September 1995, and the album was in stores five days later. The inspiration was Lennon's 'Instant Karma', which was driven by the Yoko-inspired idea that records should be like newspapers and be released as soon as they were recorded, in order to speak to the present moment. The Britpop movement found that the legacy of the Beatles was ripe with ideas worth borrowing.

The story of the Beatles was officially codified in the mid-1990s by the release of *Anthology*, a vast multimedia project that allowed the three surviving Beatles and Yoko Ono to correct what they saw as errors in the common understanding of the Beatles story. The project consisted of a six-part documentary series, three double albums of unreleased material, two new Beatles singles featuring Paul, George and Ringo finishing off rough John Lennon demos, and a huge, colourful and frustratingly difficult to read coffee-table book.

Anthology was a useful corrective to a widespread narrative, popularised in books like Philip Norman's *Shout!: The True Story of the Beatles*, that viewed Lennon as the one true genius in the band. Norman's hugely successful biography depicted McCartney as a scheming villain and Starr and Harrison as largely irrelevant. Lennon, in contrast, was a true artist who was 'three quarters of the Beatles'. Norman would later admit that making this claim 'was wrong of me – though it won me initial access to Yoko'. *Anthology* also established the story of the Beatles, separate to their music, as the great archetypal band story.

The 1990s backward-looking Britpop zeitgeist was also exactly what the James Bond movie franchise needed. Legal problems connected to the sale of MGM/UA to Pathé Communications had created an unprecedented six-year gap between 1989's *Licence to Kill* and 1995's *GoldenEye*. By the time these matters were finalised the Soviet Union had collapsed, the Cold War had ended, and it was unclear how relevant James Bond was. By the 1990s cinema goers still expected to see male British actors in big Hollywood films, but they expected them to be playing the villains while American actors would play the hero. The new MGM/UA Production Vice-President Jeff Kleeman was given the job of reviving the veteran franchise, but the audience research he conducted was not positive. 'The reasons were primarily that most teenage boys did not know who James Bond was, or if they did, they knew him as "that guy my father likes". From MGM/UA's perspective, Bond was a relic of its past that people loved but didn't know what to do with.'

A fresh relaunch was needed, which was bad news for the current Bond Timothy Dalton. Dalton is a firm favourite of Bond aficionados, who appreciate the way he moved the character away from the silliness of the Roger Moore era and made him closer to the troubled antihero of Fleming's books. What die-hard fans and the general public like, however, are often diametrically opposed. There was a reason, after all, that the character in the books was changed for the screen in the 1960s. As Kleeman explained, 'The Dalton Bonds had not performed significantly well at the box office. We were trying to grapple with the fact that the Dalton movies were not the most beloved of Bond films. We were trying to introduce Bond to a new audience. It seemed counterintuitive to what we were trying to accomplish, to continue on with Timothy at that point.'

Industry expectations for *GoldenEye* were low. Dalton's replacement was the Irish actor Pierce Brosnan, who was primarily known for his starring role in the American TV crime drama *Remington Steele* – a series that had ended eight years earlier. Brosnan, at that point in his career, was far from a box-office draw. The director Martin Campbell had not made a hit film and had worked mainly in British TV. The studio was worried about budget, and they were determined not to spend too much on what could well be the first Bond film to flop.

A lot depended on the audience's initial reaction to this new James Bond. The filmmakers were conscious that the opening pre-title sequence climaxed with a stunt that was, they feared, a bit silly. While escaping from a Soviet chemical weapons facility, Bond chases a pilot-less plane along a runway on a motorbike. The runway leads to the edge of the cliff, which the plane falls over. Bond drives his bike off the edge of the cliff and freefalls after the plane. Somehow, against the laws of physics, he catches up with the plane, gets in, and flies away. The director of photography Phil

Méheux watched this sequence for the first time with a paying audience at a 5,000-seat New York theatre. 'My heart was in my mouth,' he remembered. 'I thought, "If they laugh at this, then we've had it." But they didn't. There was a huge roar of approval and applause.' From that opening sequence on, the audience were immediately behind Brosnan's Bond. They had not only accepted, but they were actively hungry for, the absurd logic of the undefeatable hero.

The key was the sequence which led up to the stunt, which started with an astonishing 900ft bungee jump from the top of the Contra Dam in Switzerland. This was followed by a tense sabotage mission in which Bond sees his friend and colleague 006 killed. Director Martin Campbell introduced the new Bond so skilfully and confidently that the audience were won over before the title sequence kicked in.

After the titles, Bond is found driving his Aston Martin DB5 around the Monte Carlo coast, when he gets into a race with a mysterious and beautiful woman in a Ferrari. He then heads to the casino, plays baccarat, drinks a martini – shaken, not stirred – and talks in dialogue that is almost entirely innuendo. All this is shamelessly pure Bond. The mysterious woman is revealed to be Xenia Onatopp, a woman who is both a masochist and a sadist. She kills people by crushing them between her thighs and orgasms when they die. With the exception of Bond himself, she is arguably the most Fleming-esque character in all of the movies. Onatopp also has the first sexually suggestive comedic name in the Bond films since Dr Goodhead in *Moonraker*, sixteen years earlier. Needless to say, she is killed after her somewhat violent love scene with Bond.

The audience found themselves in a movie that was proud to be a Bond film. Brosnan grinned, chatted up women and revelled in being 007, a complete contrast to the scowling and unhappy Dalton. His performance is now sometimes seen as a bit smug, but that was not considered such a crime in the 1990s. There was no shame about the character and its place in the world, just an utterly confident sense of a movie that delighted in being what it was. Behind the scenes old hands such as director John Glen and writer Richard Maibaum, who had both worked on the series for over two decades, had been quietly let go. This made room for new filmmakers who were gleefully thrilled to be able to play in the Bond sandbox.

For all that United Artists had been worried by the results of their audience research, the young were quick to embrace *GoldenEye*. It helped that it was packaged in ways that seemed relevant to a new generation. The Nintendo 64 videogame *GoldenEye 007*, for example, was one of the defining games of the 1990s. *GoldenEye 007* was a first-person console shooter with a then ground-breaking multiplayer option which is still regularly included on lists of the greatest video games of all time. Crucially, it recognised that the fantasy of being Bond was the key to the franchise, so it allowed gamers to step into his shoes and undertake his missions. The game allowed players to compete against historic Bond villains such as Oddjob or Jaws, offering an introduction to the franchise's history. For gamers in the mid-1990s, the fantasy of being Bond was no longer embarrassing or dated – it was an immediate, visceral thrill. A consequence of this, as MGM/UA's Jeff Kleeman explained, was that 'those sixteen-year-old boys who went and saw *GoldenEye* and loved it also bought the video game. And when they played the video game at home, their younger siblings, who had not been allowed to see *GoldenEye*, became obsessed with the video game too. And so now you had six-year-olds, seven-year-olds, eight-year-olds who were suddenly *GoldenEye* and James Bond fans, even though they'd never seen the movie. And this just sent the studio into stratospheric joy.'

Outside of video game culture, the world of contemporary

music also helped to rejuvenate the Bond brand. Tina Turner's theme song, written by Bono and the Edge from U2, was a top-ten hit in the UK and many other countries. The musician David Arnold, meanwhile, released an album called *Shaken and Stirred: The David Arnold James Bond Project*, in which he updated classic Bond music with artists including Pulp, Leftfield, Propellerheads and Iggy Pop. Arnold, whose previous album was of course *Pop Go the Beatles*, went on to become the composer for the following Bond film.

The film itself was aware of how the character of James Bond had dated, particularly in his attitude to women. In a suitably post-modern way it made a point of explaining this itself. Moneypenny tells Bond for the first time that his behaviour towards her could be seen as sexual harassment, before proceeding to flirt outrageously with him herself. In 1990s Bond the female characters are as active and assertive as the men. The character of M had been recast with Judi Dench, after Stella Rimington became the real director general of MI5 in 1992. Dench's M tells Bond, 'I think you're a sexist, misogynist dinosaur. A relic of the Cold War.' With this acknowledged, Bond then continued with his sexist, misogynistic ways, confident that this is what the audience wanted from the character.

It was a very 1990s approach. In Britpop, the idea that bands could now contain women as well as men, or that all-female indie bands could compete on equal terms, was no longer controversial. It seemed that a victory had been won over the attitudes that shaped rock bands during the sixties and seventies. This was not equality, however, but a situation in which women were now allowed into male circles – especially the type of women then known as 'ladettes', or girls who embraced attitudes that were more typically male. That this was also the time of a boom in tits-and-lingerie-heavy 'lads mags' indicates how little had really changed.

The nineties were a time when the 1960s generation came to power. Tony Blair, who had been a teenager during the Beatles years, was elected prime minister. There was a belief that his generation's arguments had already been won. Issues like racism, homophobia and sexism were now universally acknowledged as bad things. This created the misguided belief that, because these things were known to be wrong, they were no longer problems. This attitude led to numerous white, university-educated British comedians of the late 1990s and early 2000s blacking up, including David Baddiel, David Walliams and Matt Lucas. Those comedians rationalised this as an inclusive act – everyone knew that racism was bad, the thinking went, so it wasn't intended as racist mockery. Instead, it was a way to make sure all British people were represented. This attitude shows the lack of awareness of structural racism in the wider culture at the time, particularly the extent to which white, university-educated males were given TV comedy shows while others were not. We now recognise that the belief that the problem was over because it was recognised was horribly naïve, as the apologies these comedians later gave show. But these attitudes were indicative of the culture of the time. In this context Bond could acknowledge his sexism, which was widely accepted as bad, and then simply continue with it.

In the 1990s everyone was having too much of a good time to realise that, although injustices and wrongs may have been identified and accepted, nothing had actually changed on a deeper, structural level. This was the background to Prime Minister Tony Blair's welcoming of the great and good of creative Britain to a 'Cool Britannia' party at Number 10. Guests included the future M Ralph Fiennes, Lenny Henry, Vivienne Westwood, Nick Hornby, Helen Mirren, Harry Enfield and the Beatles biographer Hunter

Davies. It was here that Noel Gallagher of Oasis was photographed having a drink with Tony Blair, saying afterwards that the party was 'top' and that he congratulated Blair 'on his success and he congratulated me on mine'. Gallagher would later regret attending, feeling that he had been used by politicians. He put his decision to attend down to taking too many drugs. 'I just thought, if the Prime Minister of England wanted to see me, then, fuck me, I must be a fucking geezer. I was convinced that I was going to get a knighthood that night. You live and learn, don't you?'

Behind all the energy and fun of the Cool Britannia Britpop years, inequality was widening in Britain. While the post-war decades had brought opportunity and growth to society as a whole, we were now entering a period in which it was mainly the rich who were once again getting richer and more powerful. The deregulation of the stock markets in the 1980s, commonly called the City of London's 'Big Bang', was a significant factor in an ongoing economic shift. This moved wealth away from those who worked and towards those who owned stuff. Even public and boarding schools, which had been in decline during the post-war years and had been seen as ridiculous outdated relics of the imperial era, were becoming increasingly popular; a trend helped by the success of the Harry Potter books. The culture-shaping class system may have crumbled in the 1960s, as the upper class became seen as ludicrous out-of-touch stereotypes, but that did not mean that concentrations of wealth, privilege and connections lost their power.

It was still possible, in the 1990s, to find somewhere to live in London for very little money. Those who didn't come from privileged backgrounds could still get a foot on the ladder in the creative industries, because there was not yet the expectation that they needed to work for free as interns or work-experience trainees. In the early twenty-first century, all this changed. For musicians, it meant that getting started became increasingly difficult without family money behind you. In 1990, 1 per cent of chart acts were privately educated. Twenty years later, that number had rocketed to 60 per cent. Bands with backgrounds like the Smiths, Oasis or the Happy Mondays had been replaced by musicians like Lily Allen, Mumford & Sons, Florence Welch and Laura Marling. The idea that the names of a musician's parents and school would be hyperlinked on Wikipedia slowly became normalised. At the same time, the idea that music was the vanguard of social change dropped away. Movements like punk and hip-hop – as well, as we have seen, as the Beatles – gave a voice to parts of society that were not otherwise heard, but who were making strong arguments for change. This drive was absent in the work of more privileged musicians because they were quite happy with the status quo.

The rise of working-class actors in the post-war period, which gave us the likes of Michael Caine, Julie Walters, Albert Finney, Richard Harris and of course Sean Connery, also proved to be a blip. Actors like Tom Hiddleston, Hugh Laurie, Eddie Redmayne and Damien Lewis are all old Etonians, like James Bond and Ian Fleming. A 2021 study by the London School of Economics reported that, out of all occupations, it is actors and television professionals from the middle classes who are most likely to pretend to be working class. A 2016 study showed that only 27 per cent of actors then came from a working-class background. In the same year a survey showed that 67 per cent of British Oscar winners went to private schools. In 2019, there were calls from the actors' union for bias against working-class performers to be made illegal. To close the 'privilege gap', they argued, required laws similar to those that dealt with race or sex discrimination.

Changes like this occur slowly and hence are rarely noticed at the time, especially when they are disguised. Around the Millennium, as the demographic makeup of media professionals changed, there was a shift in how working-class people were portrayed by the media. They went from decent, salt-of-the-earth types to either hopeless victims or idiotic thugs. The 'chav' stereotype became a common character on our television screens.

The youth culture in the sixties had once appeared to genuinely threaten the establishment. Noel Gallagher's glass of wine with Tony Blair, however, showed how that dangerous energy could be successfully neutralised. Threats to the system could always be defanged and absorbed. The playing field only has to be tilted a little for the long-term changes to be certain. The establishment plays the long game. This is the great power of tradition: like death itself, it carries on.

1999: DESMOND LLEWELYN
(1914–1999)

The actor Desmond Llewelyn died, at the age of eighty-five, twenty-three days after the UK release of *The World Is Not Enough*. Llewelyn had played Q, the head of the Secret Service's gadget division, in seventeen Bond films. He had acted alongside Sean Connery, George Lazenby, Roger Moore, Timothy Dalton and Pierce Brosnan. While many different Bonds, Ms, Blofelds and Moneypennys had come and gone, Q remained unchanged, making Llewelyn the longest-serving actor in the longest continuously running film franchise. The role did not make him rich, but it did make him loved.

The screenwriter Bruce Feirstein, who worked on all the 1990s Bond screenplays, recalled the reaction when Llewelyn shot his scenes for *The World Is Not Enough*. 'On the days that he shot, it was wild. All these grips who couldn't care less if there's a fireball going on, and all of the crew who were nonchalant about all this stuff – where driving a tank through a brick wall is a normal day's work – when Desmond showed up, they all brought their kids.

And Desmond sat on the set between takes, never went to his trailer, and just was the Bond Ambassador. He was incredibly gracious and kind and welcoming.' Llewelyn's Q had become a much-loved uncle or grandfather figure in the franchise, the Merlin to Bond's Lancelot. 'Yes, I know Q is beloved,' Llewelyn once said to Feirstein. 'But for God's sake, don't make him some kind of sentimental grandfather – that's what I am in real life.'

The affection people felt for him was remarkable when you remember that he played, essentially, an arms manufacturer – someone who developed and tested new weapons and ways to kill people. Such was his likeable, kindly charm that nobody, after any of his seventeen films, walked out of the cinema thinking that Q had blood on his hands. Instead, he was a vital part of the Bond film alchemy – the only character who was unimpressed and annoyed by Bond. This undercut the heroic nature of 007 just enough to prevent the films from taking their hero too seriously.

The name Q comes from 'quartermaster', a military title for the person in charge of equipment. Llewelyn was a member of the same generation as Fleming and had a dramatic and heroic Second World War. A second lieutenant with the Royal Welch Fusiliers, he was captured in France in the winter of 1940 after a failed attempt to hold back a German tank division. He was then held as a prisoner of war for five years at several camps, including Colditz, where he was active in numerous escape attempts. As the POWs calculated, the more they tried to escape, the more German guards would be needed to stop them. That would mean fighting German soldiers being removed from the front lines.

When the films began, there was no job called Q or quartermaster in the Secret Service, but such was the influence of Llewelyn's character on our culture that MI6 now employs its very own Q. Secrecy dictates that we know little about the real-life Qs, except that the last but one Q was female. In 2021, seeking her replacement, MI6 recruited for the role from outside the service for the first time. As the service chief Richard Moore – who is known as C – explained to the *Sunday Times*, 'In this one, life imitates art. We were reshaping our technical side and couldn't think of the right name for it. In the end we thought well, come on, let's go for it, and so we decided to call it Q.' He then added, 'Bond is a double-edged thing for us, but it is inescapable and I am very much looking forward to the next film. I love the films.'

As the job advert explained, 'As Q you are responsible for the teams who create and adopt technologies to enable our mission against the UK's hardest adversaries. You turn disruptive technologies from threats to our operations into opportunities, putting MI6 at the leading edge of digital innovation.' Llewelyn was famously hopeless with technology in real life, a trait shared by the actors John Cleese and Ben Whishaw who later took over the role. MI6 were looking, it seems, for someone very different to the on-screen Qs. The person they were seeking, the advert explained, 'will be a senior, entrepreneurial leader, with experience leading a cutting-edge digital, technology, or engineering business, and a track record of delivering digital transformation and cultural change'. When the advert first appeared, a pair of missing commas in the job description made it appear that MI6 worked to harm Britain. It originally read, 'We have the ability to disrupt activity to promote the UK's interests', which caused the *Daily Mail* to describe the Secret Service as 'More Mr Bean than Mr Bond'. The advert ended by saying, thrillingly, that 'The successful candidate will not be publicly avowed, so discretion is an essential factor in the recruitment process.'

It was Q's role to give Bond that most important part of the franchise's formula – his brand-new car, typically fitted 'with all the usual refinements'. The cars of James Bond are prominent in the promotion and legacy of the films and the Aston Martin DB5, in particular, has become an icon of the series. According to Paddy McGuinness on the BBC series *Top Gear*, the DB5 is 'not just the best car in Bond history, or even the best car in cinema history – this is the best car in history'. Q, clearly, had great taste in cars. This made him an apt role for Desmond Llewelyn, whose father bought the very first Bentley production car back in 1921.

Car chases and crashes have become an integral and expected part of the thrills and action of Bond films. The peak period for Bond car stunts was probably the early 1970s. *Diamonds Are Forever* included an almost uncountable number of police cars smashing into each other – often followed by a shot of their unharmed drivers exiting the cars and throwing their hats to the ground in frustration. This became something of a trope in 1970s and 1980s American television dramas. Of course, car accidents in Bond are sometimes fatal for the characters in the car – especially if the car explodes or goes flying over a cliff or when, as happened in *You Only Live Twice*, a large electromagnet hanging from a two-rotor helicopter picks up the car and drops it into the middle of Tokyo Bay. Generally speaking, however, people usually survive car accidents in the James Bond universe. Bond even survived his heart-stopping high-speed crash in *Casino Royale*, when his Aston Martin DBS rolled over a total of seven times, earning the stunt a Guinness World Record.

We are so normalised to watching car accidents in action films and video games that we don't tend to associate them with vehicle accidents in the real world. Despite the high number of fatalities they produce, and the amount of people who have lost loved ones to automobile accidents, no one feels it is necessary to include a trigger warning before filmed scenes of car crashes. Here is *Thanatos* – Freud's death drive – in action. There is a part of our psyche that thrills to see other people have car crashes, knowing that we are safe. The massively successful *Fast and Furious* franchise is designed to appeal to just this part of us. It can be jarring, then, to learn that Desmond Llewelyn's death was the result of a head-on crash in his blue Renault Megane.

Llewelyn was driving to a book signing at Drusillas Park, a small zoo in East Sussex, when the accident happened. An ambulance took him to Eastbourne hospital, but he died shortly afterwards. The couple in the other car in the accident were also taken to hospital, but thankfully survived.

Car crashes are an all-too-common aspect of life. All four Beatles have been in vehicle accidents. John Lennon, a notoriously poor driver, drove his Austin Maxi into a ditch near Durness in the Scottish Highlands in July 1969. Yoko Ono, her daughter Kyoko and Lennon's son Julian were also in the car. Lennon received seventeen stitches for a facial injury, and Ono had fourteen in her forehead. It was this accident that led to a bed being placed in EMI's Studio 2, so that Ono could recuperate during the recording of *Abbey Road* – much to the annoyance of the other Beatles. Lennon had previously written about a car crash in the song 'A Day in the Life'.

The 'Paul Is Dead' conspiracy claimed that Paul McCartney was killed in a car crash in November 1966. This was not true, although in December 1965 he did crash a moped on the Wirral. This left him with a cut lip and chipped tooth, which is visible in the 'Paperback Writer' and 'Rain' promotional films. This in part prompted him to grow a moustache, a fashion choice quickly adopted by his bandmates and which proved to be a strong sartorial influence on hip men in the late 1960s. George Harrison, meanwhile, wrote off his white Mercedes when he hit a lamppost on the central barrier of a roundabout near his home in Henley-on-Thames. He got away with just stitches, but his wife Patti suffered from concussion and several broken ribs. She spent two weeks recovering in hospital.

Ringo was also not good with roundabouts. His second wife

Barbara Bach had survived vehicle mayhem in *The Spy Who Loved Me*, most memorably when Roger Moore's Bond drove his Lotus Esprit off a pier and into the sea – only for it to turn into a submarine. This sudden shift from frantic car-chase action to the graceful, beautiful underwater world remains one of the most magical moments in the Bond franchise. Real car crashes are very different, however, and in 1980 Ringo lost control driving Barbara around the Robin Hood roundabout on the A3 near Kingston in Surrey. He swerved to avoid a lorry and rolled his Mercedes in a fifty-yard somersaulting skid. This was only half a mile from where Ringo's friend Marc Bolan had been killed in a car crash three years earlier. Despite his injured leg, Ringo pulled Barbara to safety, then returned to the wreck of his car to retrieve his cigarettes. The car was later crushed into a cube and turned into a coffee table for their home.

Llewelyn, sadly, wasn't as lucky as the Beatles. On the night of 19 December 1999, the excitement of fantasy cinema crashes gave way to the horror of real-world vehicle accidents. At the time of his death *The World Is Not Enough* was still playing in cinemas across the country, and audiences were watching Llewelyn being given a suitable ending for such an historic character. After introducing Bond to the 'young fellow' he was grooming to replace him, Q gives Bond some final advice. 'Don't let them see you bleed,' he says, and then, as he suddenly descends into a hole in the floor and out of shot, he adds, 'always have an escape plan'.

When that scene was shot, it was not certain that this would have been Llewelyn's last appearance. He intended to keep going as Q, as he explained during press for the film: 'As long as the producers want me – and the Almighty doesn't.'

2001: GEORGE HARRISON
(1943–2001)

From the evidence of George Harrison's songs, the fear that people would help themselves to his money was something of a personal obsession. This was apparent almost from the moment he started earning. It was George who created the scathing 'Taxman', for example – a song written by the spiritual Beatle at the birth of the hippy movement which complains about Prime Minister Harold Wilson's taxation policies. Harrison's 'Only a Northern Song' is one of those rare songs that becomes less interesting when you understand what it is about. On first listen it seems to be a beguilingly meta song which lyrically addresses and justifies its strangeness in composition and performance. Never before had a song directly addressed its own shape and style in this way, as if it was alive and aware, and it feels exciting and thrillingly unpredictable. To later discover that the song is about George's unhappiness with the financial structure of his publishing company can be a terrible disappointment.

It was a cruel quirk of fate that Harrison would become the

371

Beatle most bogged down by lawsuits about financial agreements. There were regular Apple lawsuits, the most notable of which being Paul suing the other three Beatles in order to bring about the formal dissolution of their partnership in 1975. Harrison and Starr would return the favour in 1985. They filed an $8.6m lawsuit against McCartney after he renegotiated his royalties on Beatles records with EMI. Harrison was also sued by Allen Klein in 1973, after George declined to renew his management contract. Harrison replaced Klein with a tall, bespectacled American accountant and lawyer called Denis O'Brien. The pair became close and set up the company Handmade Films together, but the relationship soured and in the mid-nineties Harrison sued O'Brien for fraud and negligence. Unknown to Harrison, O'Brien had been guaranteeing the finances of a string of films against George's personal wealth. The courts found in Harrison's favour, and he was awarded an $11m judgement, but O'Brien filed for bankruptcy. Harrison had trusted O'Brien and took the betrayal badly. According to Eric Idle, Harrison hated O'Brien 'with an intensity that was quite rare for George. It took him a long time to get over all that.'

Of all the court cases that dominated Harrison's life, the greatest was the plagiarism case brought against his hit single 'My Sweet Lord'. This was filed by the publishing company Bright Songs in February 1971, which argued that 'My Sweet Lord' infringed the copyright of 'He's So Fine', a song written by Ronnie Mack that had been a number-one hit for the Chiffons in 1963. For most listeners, it was a fairly clear-cut case; 'My Sweet Lord' does sound like a blatant copy of 'He's So Fine'. But the case became more complicated when Allen Klein attempted to buy Bright Songs in order to receive the benefits of the song himself, an action that generated further legal repercussions. The case was not settled until March 1998, making it one of the longest-running cases in

American legal history. The real winners in the case were, of course, lawyers.

Harrison had always tended to be a little light-fingered when it came to songwriting. The opening line to his great standard 'Something', for example, was a direct lift from James Taylor's 'Something in the Way She Moves'. The lyrics to 'All Things Must Pass' are largely taken from Timothy Leary's translation of the *Tao Te Ching*. Another example of Harrison's willingness to claim the work of others is found on his first experimental solo album. Intrigued by the new technology of the Moog synthesiser, which could mimic existing instruments as well as generating entirely new sounds, Harrison asked the American musician Bernie Krause to demonstrate the instrument for him in November 1968. 'What I didn't realise,' Krause later explained, 'was that he had asked the engineer to record the session that I was demonstrating. I didn't think anything of it at the time.' The following year, Harrison released the experimental solo album *Electronic Sound*, the first side of which consisted of Krause's secretly recorded demonstration, uncredited and released without his permission.

'My Sweet Lord' originated in 1969, when Harrison had joined a UK tour with the American blues-rock band Delaney and Bonnie. Harrison was impressed by the current gospel chart hit 'Oh Happy Day' by the Edwin Hawkins Singers, and the way it brought spirituality into the pop charts. He asked Delaney Bramlett for advice on writing a gospel song. As Bramlett later described the incident, he grabbed his guitar 'and started playing The Chiffons's melody from "He's So Fine" and then sang the words "My Sweet Lord / Oh my Lord / Oh my Lord / I just wanna be with you..." ' The song became something of a group singalong on the tour bus, evolving as it did so. After 'My Sweet Lord' was released as a single, Bramlett says he phoned George 'and told him that I didn't mean for him to use the melody of "He's So Fine". He said, "Well it's not *exactly* the same," and I guess it really wasn't.' Bramlett also claimed that Harrison promised him a writing credit for the song, which he never received. Given the importance that Harrison placed on Eastern religious ideas, it is hard not to see the iron law of karma playing out in the protracted legal dispute over 'My Sweet Lord', especially given George's long-standing fear of people coming for his money.

There was one other thing that, like karma, Harrison was never able to escape – being a Beatle. 'Well, that's it,' said George Harrison on the plane to LA after the Beatles played their final concert of their last tour, at Candlestick Park in San Francisco on 29 August 1966. 'I'm not a Beatle anymore.' He had not, at this point, realised that being a Beatle was a life sentence. He may have been the first of the band to mentally check out, but he would always be Beatle George in the eyes of the world. Over the following post-touring years, as Paul, John and George Martin revolutionised studio recording, Harrison played a relatively minor role. With the exception of his own song 'Within You Without You', for example, he made very few contributions to *Sgt. Pepper's Lonely Hearts Club Band*. It became common for Paul or John to play the lead guitar parts when they recorded their own songs.

Out of all the members of the band, it was Paul who was the biggest enthusiast for the Beatles. He had a genuine love of what they did and he always remained their number-one fan. His feelings here were well expressed in a 1997 interview with *Q* magazine when he was asked, 'What would you say if someone came up to you and said, "The Beatles were shit?"' McCartney's response was, 'I'd say, "Fuck off you twat"'. Paul never doubted how great the Beatles were. Ringo also loved the band, although for him the love was about being and playing with his fellow bandmates. John, meanwhile, loved the Beatles as a vehicle for his own creative expression, but he was quick to dismiss them after the split.

George, in comparison, was never really into the Beatles. Or at least, he wasn't after they left Hamburg and Liverpool, and the tsunami of Beatlemania began.

Harrison loved playing music and being part of a group, of course, but he wasn't impressed by the music John and Paul wrote in the same way that he was impressed by Bob Dylan or the Band. He could never work out why they mattered so much to other people. As he saw it, they were 'typical of a hundred groups in our area. We were lucky. We got away with it first.' In his opinion, 'the songs that Paul and John write, they're all right, but they are not the greatest.' He was never able to differentiate between the music as it was experienced by others and his own experience of being in a room with his old friends. Here he felt belittled and underappreciated by John, Paul and George Martin, and constantly viewed as a junior member. He also never really recovered from the intense pressures of Beatlemania at its height, which he described as 'a horror story ... awful ... manic ... crazy, a nightmare.' As his biographer Graeme Thomson writes, 'Being in the Beatles was the opportunity of anyone's lifetime, but the attendant mania was a trauma which Harrison spent his entire life alternately trying to blank out and comprehend. Right up until his death it could make him shiver just to recall it.'

Part of this trauma came from a deep sense of insecurity that accompanied his loss of privacy. Suddenly George had become one of the most famous people on the planet, and there was no way he could go back to how he was before. His fear and insecurity began with the death threats that the band received during their last touring years and was compounded by the murder of John Lennon by someone who had approached him as a fan. This fear of being attacked and of never being completely safe while out in public was one of the reasons he was so content to remain within the walls of Friar Park. When he was eventually attacked, it was by someone who broke into the sanctum of his own home, which made the aftereffects all the more distressing.

The attack happened sometime after 3 a.m. on 31 December 1999. His second wife Olivia Harrison woke when she heard the patio doors to the kitchen being smashed. She woke George, who left their room to investigate. From the top of the stairs he saw an intruder below, holding a kitchen knife in one hand and a spear – taken from a statue of St George killing a dragon – in the other. The intruder was a 34-year-old paranoid schizophrenic and recovering heroin addict from Liverpool. He had become obsessed with the idea that the Beatles were witches who flew around on broomsticks, and that George was a sorcerer and a devil. He had come to murder him.

The attacker and his intended victim faced each other at opposite ends of the staircase. George attempted to diffuse the situation by chanting 'Hare Krishna', but it really didn't help. George had loved copying James Bond's life of fast cars and loose women, but he had never had any desire to take part in the brutal fight scenes.

There followed a terrifying 20-minute attack on the gallery above the great hall, in which George was repeatedly stabbed with the kitchen knife before his wife attacked the intruder with a brass fireplace poker and a lamp. When the attacker turned his attentions to trying to choke Olivia, George was able to overpower him, only to be stabbed again. 'I felt exhausted and could feel the strength draining from me. I vividly remember a deliberate thrust to my chest. I could hear my lung exhaling and had blood in my mouth. I believed I had been fatally stabbed,' he said later. He also told his wife that his thoughts at the time were, 'I can't believe after everything that's happened to me I'm being murdered in my own home.' Fortunately, two police officers arrived on the scene and apprehended the intruder, and paramedics treated George and

Olivia's wounds before they were taken to the Royal Berkshire Hospital in Reading. The pair survived, but George was never really the same again. Many of his friends believe the attack was a factor in the way his cancer spread from his lung to his brain and killed him less than two years later.

Harrison died at the age of fifty-eight, in a friend's house in Beverly Hills surrounded by his wife, son, Ravi Shankar and his family, and close friends from the Hare Krishna movement. Of all the Beatles, it was George who made and nurtured the deepest friendships. One of his last acts was to send a message to the Canadian comedian Mike Myers, who was then filming his Bond movie spoof *Austin Powers in Goldmember*. In this he thanked Myers for the Austin Powers films, which he loved, and told him how he kept a Dr Evil doll by his bed. Dr Evil, of course, was Myers's supervillain character, based on Bond's nemesis Blofeld. 'Sitting here with my Dr. Evil doll... I just wanted to let you know I've been looking all over Europe for a mini-you doll,' he wrote. He then gave Myers – whose parents were both Liverpudlians – advice on pronunciation. 'Dr. Evil says "frickin"', but any good Scouser will tell you it's actually "friggin"', as in a "four of fish and finger pie", if you get my drift. Thanks for the movies, so much fun.' 'Four of fish and finger pie' was a reference to the risqué innuendo McCartney had slipped into the lyrics of 'Penny Lane'. The letter showed that, in the face of death, Harrison had lost none of his lust or silliness.

Harrison was then having difficulty talking. As the writer Ashley Kahn explained, George 'searched for a tool to help him communicate and deflect the seriousness of his situation; being a fan of Austin Powers movies, he found a Dr Evil talking doll to serve as a proxy.' Given his love of absurdity, it seems strangely fitting that the most Bond-like Beatle should end his days with Dr Evil speaking for him.

Fourteen years later, on Christmas Eve 2015, the music of the Beatles arrived on Spotify. A new, younger generation that did not routinely buy CDs or vinyl records suddenly had access to their music, and they took to it in a way entirely unlike the typical reaction to other 1960s bands. It was the 18–24 demographic, and not the Baby Boomers, who were most likely to stream the Beatles. They accounted for 30 per cent of all streams and the 25–29-year-old demographic were second. The tracks that these new listeners chose was a surprise to older Beatles fans. The most streamed of all their songs was Harrison's 'Here Comes the Sun', a song that wasn't even selected as a single back in the day. George may have been overlooked in the band and belittled by John and Paul, but as far as 21st-century music fans go, he wrote the band's most popular work.

This is a reminder that, for all critics have been negative about his songs, there were times when he created something truly universal. True, some of his work could be seen as preachy, hectoring or bitter. But he was also prepared to show his vulnerability, hopes and wit in his music, and when that happened the results were beautiful.

In his final days, he gave his wife and son a message to share with the world: 'Everything else can wait, but the search for God cannot wait, and love one another.' If you can imagine those words coming from his Dr Evil doll, you will know the contradictory soul of George Harrison.

2002: THE FATE OF THE PIXELS

Pierce Brosnan received the call when he was working on a film in the Bahamas in 2004. He was looking forward to making his fifth Bond movie and was thrilled that they were going to make the very first book, *Casino Royale*, which the producers had finally got the rights to after decades of legal issues. Barbara Broccoli had given him a black, leatherbound first edition of the novel. As he told one reporter, 'I would like to do another one, sure. Connery did six. Six would be a good number and then never come back.'

Casino Royale felt like the right step to help ground his character after the wild excesses of his last film, *Die Another Day*. His agents were haggling with the producers over his fee, of course, but this was only to be expected. Brosnan's last film had made more money at the box office than all other Bonds by quite some distance, grossing an impressive $432m. His first three Bonds had grossed over a billion dollars between them, leading to press adverts describing Brosnan as the 'billion-dollar Bond'.

During his tenure in the role Brosnan had been incredibly popular with global audiences. He recalled how, when filming his third film *The World Is Not Enough* in Bilbao, he had crowds chanting for 'James Bond' outside his hotel throughout the night. He eventually came out onto the balcony of his penthouse suite, to huge cheers. He could only compare it to Beatlemania. 'It's like a time warp back in the sixties. This has been gobstoppingly wonderful,' he said. *Die Another Day* received the biggest Bond premiere yet, when the Royal Albert Hall was transformed into an ice palace and the guest of honour, Queen Elizabeth II, was greeted not just by Pierce Brosnan but also by Sir Roger Moore, George Lazenby and Timothy Dalton. When you consider the extent to which film critics had dismissed the Bond franchise as dead in the six fallow years after Timothy Dalton's movies, it was clear that the producers owed Brosnan a great deal.

Then came the call. As Brosnan later told the writers Matthew Field and Ajay Chowdhury, 'I sat in Richard Harris's house in the Bahamas, in this old, faded mansion, and Barbara was on the line and Michael was on the line and they said, "We're so sorry." She was crying. Michael was stoic and he said, "You were a great James Bond. Thank you very much," and I said, "Thank you very much. Goodbye." That was it.' From Brosnan's point of view, his sacking had come as a shock. As he had previously told a journalist, 'The producers have told me that the role is mine as long as I like.'

What had gone wrong? The Bond producers had decided that a radical change of direction was required for the franchise, one which went back to the start and acted as a 'soft reboot' for the films. It may seem strange that such a radical change was felt necessary at a time when the films were more successful than ever. But changing times had thrown up a serious problem which had the potential to destroy 007.

Die Another Day had been criticised on several fronts, as indeed had most of the preceding films. One factor in this was the appearance of Madonna, who played a fencing instructor in the film. Her performance, a little unfairly, led to her winning the Golden

Raspberry Award, or 'Razzzie', for Worst Supporting Actress that year. This was not a new thing for a Bond movie, however. Denise Richards had also won the Worst Supporting Actress for her role as Dr Christmas Jones in *The World Is Not Enough*. In fairness to Richards, it's hard to see how any actor could have made her role as written – a nuclear physicist who dresses like Lara Croft – in any way believable. Madonna's techno theme tune for *Die Another Day* was also widely criticised, but it's hard to see that as a reason to fire Pierce Brosnan.

Others criticised the film for being too cartoony. This had been the intention from the start. Chris McGurk, the MGM executive who oversaw the Bond franchise, said that the studio thought that the previous film 'was a little more plot driven and a little darker than some of the other Bond movies. We wanted to open it up: a little bigger on spectacle and action sequences. We were trying to position the Bond movies in the new age of Hollywood.' *Die Another Day* would become, in consequence, the most ludicrous and fantastical Bond since *Moonraker* in 1979. Both of these films have been much mocked by critics for their excesses, but such ambitious craziness was a box-office draw. *Moonraker*, like *Die Another Day*, was the most successful Bond ever when it was released. Critics and Bond aficionados may dismiss these movies in preference for the more grounded, gritty and Fleming-esque films such as *From Russia with Love, For Your Eyes Only* or *Licence to Kill*, but it's pretty clear from the box-office numbers which films the average ticket-buyer prefers. As McGurk said, 'We were caught up in the idea that Bond had to be competitive with these other big event movies in terms of action and CGI. We were probably all guilty of that.'

Brosnan was unhappy with the direction his final Bond film had taken, complaining that 'In the beginning they were made for adults. Now they're made for kids.' *Die Another Day* featured an under-utilised invisible car, a melting ice hotel, and a villain who wore a cyborg suit that allowed him to destroy anywhere on earth with a powerful space ray. Tonally, it anticipated the Marvel superhero genre that went on to dominate the film industry of the 2010s. Given this, it is possible to imagine how the Bond films would have fitted into the cinema landscape if they had not rejected the fantastical approach and continued along that path. The huge success of the *Fast and Furious* franchise, which got larger and larger as its vehicle-based action sequences became more and more ludicrous, is an indicator of the type of audience it could have attracted. The *Kingsman* franchise has also placed itself firmly into the heightened absurd area that, after *Die Another Day*, the Bond films have kept far away from.

The most common criticism of *Die Another Day* was that there was too much bad CGI. The film was made in the early years of cinema computer-generated imagery, a technology which allowed filmmakers the opportunity to depict action sequences that would previously have been impossible to film. CGI allowed writers and directors to run wild with their imaginations, and it was immediately clear that Hollywood blockbusters would be forever changed by the technology. It made sense that Bond, a franchise which was always attempting to remain contemporary, would experiment with the possibilities. One scene in particular, however, stood out as being particularly unconvincing – an action sequence set in Iceland in which Bond kite-surfed away from a tsunami caused by a collapsing glacier. The film had set up the idea that Bond was a skilled surfer at the beginning of the film, when he is seen riding immense waves at night in order to smuggle himself into North Korea. But although the sequence had been set up in the script as one that should work, the implementation was a different matter.

Much of the CGI in Hollywood movies from the period has not aged well, but this scene was considered laughable at the time. So great was the impact of this sequence that many remember the film as being full of bad CGI, when the great majority of the rest of the effects were achieved with models and practical in-camera stunt work. This one scene managed to tarnish the legacy of the most successful Bond film ever. It caused panicked producers to sack Brosnan, abandon the teen audience and radically reboot the entire franchise. What was it about this one CGI action sequence that caused such a reaction?

Ultimately, CGI threatened the Bond franchise's ability to function as a representation of death. The skill and daring of the stunt teams had kept audiences hooked, knowing that real people were risking their lives – and at times, as we have seen, giving their lives – to entertain their global audience. The moment an obviously CG Bond is seen flying through the air, however, all that collapses. No one, clearly, is in danger. The audience stops caring at that point, unconcerned about the fate of the pixels that dance in front of them. The moment this happens, the franchise is in big trouble. If the stuntmen and women no longer represent death then another sacrifice is called for, or else the franchise is doomed. For the long-term health of the series, that sacrifice demanded the head of Pierce Brosnan himself.

Spy movies in the twenty-first century have tried a number of different approaches to get round the problem of CGI. The *Kingsman* films, as we have noted, have leaned into its possibilities, hoping that absurd wild imagination will keep the audience entertained despite that strange hollow feeling that comes from knowing nothing is really at stake. The *Mission: Impossible* team, in contrast, bit the bullet and took the opposite approach. They put their star Tom Cruise in terrifying situations and made the fact that he did his own stunts a major selling point. We saw clearly that it was genuinely Tom Cruise hanging off the side of a cargo plane as it took off in *Mission: Impossible – Rogue Nation*

(2015), or climbing up the outside of the Burj Khalifa in Dubai, the tallest building in the world, during a tense sequence in *Mission: Impossible – Ghost Protocol* (2011). This approach of putting your star in life-threatening, terrifying situations is only possible because Cruise is the producer of the films, as well as the star. He is in a position in which nobody can prevent him from doing stunts like these. Brosnan's replacement as Bond, Daniel Craig, made a point of doing as many of his own stunts as he could, but there were clear limits as to what he could and couldn't do. 'Of course, I didn't do all the stunts, it's impossible,' he has said. 'I mean, the insurance company won't let me.' There is, ultimately, only one Tom Cruise.

A third approach was favoured by the *Bourne* franchise, the series of films about Robert Ludlum's CIA assassin Jason Bourne. These films avoided CGI altogether – or rather, they avoided anything that the audience would register as CG. Instead, their focus was on a gritty, grounded and believable world where the action sequences were done with as much practical effects work as possible, often filmed with shaky, hand-held cameras and edited with fast, sometimes disorienting cuts in an effort to throw the viewer into the middle of the action. In the months before *Die Another Day* opened, its director Lee Tamahori attended a screening of the first Bourne film with Bond producers Barbara Broccoli and Michael G. Wilson. It made a strong impact on them all. Suddenly, their upcoming Bond film looked old-fashioned. Tamahori recalled that he was explicit about this to the Bond producers. 'I said, "Look, the game's changing fast. You're going to have to rethink this." The writing was on the wall for the end of the franchise as it was then.' After seeing *The Bourne Identity*, the criticisms that followed *Die Another Day* held far more weight with the producers than they might otherwise have done. The attack on the Twin Towers in New York on 11 September 2001 was another factor: suddenly silly fun felt inappropriate, and grim dark realism became more in tune with the zeitgeist.

Most spy films are open about the debt they owe to the Bond franchise. The car chase along the Las Vegas strip in *Jason Bourne* (2016), for example, is a modern updating of a similar chase in *Diamonds Are Forever*. It is tempting to see Jason Bourne's name and initials as a nod to Bond, while the *Kingsman* films feature characters openly discussing how similar they are to characters in Bond movies. But now it was time for Bond to borrow from others. As the franchise was radically overhauled following *Die Another Day*, the style of the Bourne franchise became a guide as to how spy films might react to Hollywood's CG era.

But would this approach sustain the series for long? The *Bourne* franchise lasted for five movies. The first three were hugely successful, but interest in new instalments began to wane and it currently seems unlikely that we will ever see Matt Damon reprising the role again. More grounded stories and hyperkinetic cinematography, on their own, are not enough to sustain a franchise over decades. Ultimately, no one fantasises about being Jason Bourne.

It is worth taking a moment to admire the skill of the Broccoli family here. Their vision and insightful decision-making were apparent when Daniel Craig was announced as the next James Bond – to near universal press derision. Craig was hardly an unknown entity, as his previous films were available for anyone to see, yet professional journalists and film critics simply could not see how he could possibly be right for the role. His longer blond hair during his press announcement seemed to be a problem for many, even though the idea that actors can have different hairstyles in different roles shouldn't be difficult to grasp. In the eyes of many, Craig was destined to be 'James Bland'.

In one of the first examples of press coverage taking its lead from a small number of incensed online fans, an anti-Craig website called BondNotBlonde.com received a huge amount of coverage. 'I am sure that he didn't read it, but it was hard not to be aware. It was all over the place all the time,' recalled Craig's co-star Mads Mikkelsen. 'If I went to work – any kind of work – every day reading in the paper that I am crap at it, that is a hard day.'

'Look, it did affect me, I will not lie to you,' Craig has said, 'It was like, "See the fucking movie and then you can say what you like about it, but watch the movie [before you criticise]." ' The anti-blond people behind the website would clearly not have liked the episode of the 1960s American Beatles cartoon in which the band met the ace British superspy James Blonde. Thanks to his lovely blond hair, all the screaming girls that used to chase the Beatles ditched them for the spy.

After audiences had seen *Casino Royale*, of course, the casting made sense. Industry commentators could now see what Barbara Broccoli had seen years before – that Daniel Craig had what it takes to become one of the great James Bonds. A key influence in convincing Barbara Broccoli that her instincts about Craig were correct was her mother Dana, Cubby's widow, who died at the age of eighty-two shortly after Craig was cast. As Dana said, 'I have a woman's instinct about people. We women don't fall for pretty faces, we want masculine men who are going to protect us forever. James Bond is not politically correct – he's far from that. He has a magnetism, sophistication and earthiness; most women are looking for that all their lives.' As Craig's *Casino Royale* co-star Eva Green described him, 'He's a gentleman and he's strong, and he's not mannered. That ruggedness is attractive and probably quite dangerous. He is sexy and not self-conscious, which is very important for a man.' These appraisals can sound unusual these days, when approving comments about traditional aspects of mas-culinity are rare, and there is never a shortage of people queuing up to tell the Bond producers exactly where they are going wrong.

But Barbara valued her mother's instincts more than the intellect of critics. Here is an example of why the Broccoli family have been able to maintain a film series for sixty years, and nobody else has. They are, ultimately, very good at their jobs.

For the next era of Bond, the approach was to back away from fantastical silliness and instead rely on a strange cocktail of brutality and sophistication. It was an approach that would lead to the most successful era of the Bond movies yet. But it was an approach that jettisoned the young, teenage audience that had always supported the films – and this, in the long term, would have consequences.

2003: COME ON, MR PUTIN!

Vladimir Putin arrived late at Paul McCartney's concert in Red Square, Moscow. McCartney was midway through a performance of 'Calico Skies' with his band when he noticed a disturbance in the giant crowd. A reported 100,000 people had crammed into the historic square in the centre of Moscow on 24 May 2003, to witness the first performance by a Beatle in the former Soviet Union. This took place in front of Lenin's Tomb and the fantastical, brightly coloured domes of Saint Basil's Cathedral. The arrival of their new president was enough to shift the crowd's attention away from the stage. Affairs of state meant that Putin had missed out on hearing songs like 'Jet', 'Blackbird' and a ukulele version of 'Something', but he had made it in time to hear the great bombastic Bond theme 'Live and Let Die'. It was performed with pyrotechnics, fireworks and footage of the James Bond 'gun barrel' title sequence on the giant screens behind McCartney.

The audience greeted Putin like he was the real rock star that evening. He strolled casually to his seat, dressed in an open-necked black shirt and black jacket. Reacting to the furore his presence caused, he lifted a finger and put it to his lips, requesting silence from the cheering crowd. He pointed at his ears and then towards the stage. He made it clear that he wanted them to stop cheering him so that everyone could hear the music being played. As McCartney sang the pro-love, anti-war lyrics about the 'weapons of war we despise', Putin took his seat in a way that was humble but incredibly charismatic.

McCartney had visited Putin at the Kremlin earlier that day, when it was still thought that the President would be unable to attend the evening's concert. Paul and his second wife Heather Mills were met by a general and escorted along miles of corridors – 'It was very Russian,' he recalled. Putin gave the McCartneys a guided tour of parts of the Kremlin and told them the history of the Tsars who were crowned there. Paul sat at a piano and gave Putin a private performance of 'Let It Be'. He asked the President if he had listened to the Beatles growing up. 'Yes, it was extremely popular,' Putin told him. 'It was like a gulp of freedom. Your music was like an open window to the world. It was considered at this time a propaganda of some alien ideology.'

Putin's words chimed with the views of many Russian observers, who have argued that the Beatles not only changed the West, but were also central to the forces that brought about the end of the Soviet Union. As Mikhail Gorbachev has said, 'I do believe the music of the Beatles has taught the young people of the Soviet Union that there is another life, that there is freedom elsewhere, and of course this feeling has pushed them towards *Perestroika*, towards the dialogue with the outside world.' In the words of the Russian author and sociologist Artemy Troitsky, 'The Beatles, Paul, John, George and Ringo, have done more for the fall of communism than any other western institution.'

To credit the Beatles as a significant factor in the fall of the Soviet Union might sound like hyperbole to Western ears, but it is an argument that fits well with communist thought. As Stalin saw it, writers and artists were the 'engineers of the soul'. Here he was quoting approvingly a phrase coined by the Russian novelist Yury Olesha. The Russian revolution had been atheistic, so the Soviet system took responsibility for the state of the soul away from the church and gave it to musicians, painters and writers.

This was significant because Marx had argued that society consisted of two linked aspects, which he called the base and the superstructure. The base was essentially everything to do with the economy, including materials, labour, infrastructure, production and so on. The superstructure was everything else, including the arts, family, law, politics and education. According to Marx, the base and the superstructure were constantly interacting with each other. The way people thought shaped the economy, and the economy shaped the way people thought. In non-communist countries, the nature of power meant that the superstructure was shaped to support the interests of the ruling class, which in turn affected how the daily lives of the workers were structured. The rise of the 'chav' archetype when the demographics of the British 'engineers of the soul' changed is a simple example of this. To avoid this problem, Marx said, it was necessary for the state to use censorship to control how people thought.

Only by managing the superstructure like this would it be possible to create the 'New Soviet Man' that communist ideologies insisted was necessary for the continued success of the revolution. This new Soviet man or woman was a healthy, selfless, enthusiastic Russian worker who was guided by the correct form of communist consciousness. Lenin feared that if the state lost control of the minds of the people, then the base would be altered by the changing superstructure. This could then lead to the collapse of the entire economic structure of the Soviet Union, if no one believed in the system sufficiently to defend it. As history was to prove, he was right about this.

Before the 1917 revolution, the Russian elite had been fond of Western music. Prince Felix Yusupov – who a young Christopher Lee was once fetched from his bed to meet – recalled that a gramophone had been playing 'Yankee Doodle Went to Town' while he was poisoning Rasputin. After the revolution, however, the state saw it as their role to keep the minds of Soviet citizens free from dangerous Western imperial music. When the Beatles arrived on the global stage, it seemed clear to the Soviet state that they were an example of exactly the kind of degenerate Western culture which, if they were not careful, could infect the superstructure of society. They proceeded to crack down on Merseybeat, just as they had previously attacked other unacceptable musical innovations that threatened the consciousness of the New Soviet Man, including saxophones and valved trumpets.

The efforts of Soviet propaganda to undermine the Beatles were not subtle. One Soviet newspaper article labelled them 'Dung Beatles' and included a cartoon that depicted the Fab Four as monkeys. In 1966, a Soviet propaganda film was made that intercut unflattering photographs of the Beatles together with images of the Ku Klux Klan, ecstatic pop fans dancing, burning crosses and images of rural poverty from the American South. The sneering voiceover declared, 'Pop quartet the Beatles. Look how elegant they are! But when they started their career they were performing on stage just wearing swimming trunks with toilet seats on their necks.' This part was true; Lennon did indeed perform one drunken evening in Hamburg with a toilet seat around his neck. 'Then they met a kind fairy – London dealer Brian Epstein,' the film continued, with an unexpected turn into state homophobia. 'This London fairy understood that these gifted guys could be real cash earners. Struck down with psychosis, the fans don't hear anything anymore. Hysterics, screams, fainting people! Demolished concert halls and fights are the usual finale of a concert.' The idea that their music may actually be good is, of course, absent from this narrative. With propaganda films like this played regularly to Soviet citizens, you can see why George Orwell included the idea of a 'daily hate' in his totalitarian dystopia *Nineteen Eighty-Four*.

Beatles music was forbidden by the state. It could not be bought or played on the radio. To the government censors charged with protecting the Soviet superstructure, it must have seemed like they had done their job well. But the music was making its way into Russia regardless, not least on American, British and Japanese radio stations. From these broadcasts it could be taped, and those tapes distributed. In the 1950s, bootleggers had discovered that sound signals could be etched into the emulsion of old X-ray photographs, which then could be distributed as makeshift flexi-disks. These became known as 'records on bones'. The sound quality was often terrible, but a thriving black market sprang up that created these disks on a nearly industrial scale. Old X-rays could be rolled up and hidden from the authorities in your sleeve, which gave them an advantage over real vinyl albums.

In an attempt to crack down on the practice, the state flooded the streets with millions of counterfeit flexis. When played, they contained only strange, scratchy noises and a voice saying, 'You like rock 'n' roll? Fuck you, anti-Soviet slime!' As the Cold War took hold, Nikita Khrushchev declared that the electric guitar was an enemy of the Soviet people. This didn't stop young Russian kids from attempting to make their own. It became widely known that an electric guitar pickup could be made from a telephone receiver, and public telephones across Russia were vandalised by those seeking this vital component.

All types of Western rock music circulated behind the Iron Curtain, but the main focus was on the Beatles – both by the state, and the fans. In Russia the Beatles were known as the 'Bitles', and rock music in general was often called 'Bitles music'. Because the

Beatles were commonly acknowledged as the greatest of all the Western bands, the Russian inclination to support strong leaders gave them an elevated status over their peers behind the Iron Curtain. As the leading Soviet rock critic Artemy Troitsky told the documentary director Leslie Woodhead, 'American rock 'n' roll like Little Richard was way too fast, too violent, too weird. When the Beatles arrived with their beautiful melodies, it was completely different. They had the "something else" factor – the electric sound, long hair, the spirit of freedom.'

As always, it was also a matter of timing. In the early 1960s, the Russian youth could still believe in the rightness and superiority of the communist project. The handsome farm boy Yuri Gagarin had become the first astronaut to orbit the planet, Fidel Castro and Che Guevara were romantic heroic figures in Cuba, and Khrushchev seemed like the right leader to humble the United States. As the 1960s progressed, however, it became increasingly difficult to see the state in the same way, especially after Khrushchev was succeeded by the grey, cautious, inflexible Brezhnev and the Soviet army had invaded Czechoslovakia.

During this period the music of the Beatles was circulating widely, and this made the government crackdown seem ridiculous. The state may have succeeded in convincing people that the music was dangerous if people hadn't heard it, but people already knew and loved it. They knew that the Beatles represented love and life, and by forbidding their music the Soviet state cast themselves in the role of death. The crackdown forced the young to choose between music and the state, and those who had heard the joyful energy of the Beatles knew in their hearts where their sympathies lay. As the late Russian journalist and musician Aleksandr Lipnitsky explained, 'For many years, we were told that the West was an enemy – nothing more. Not our neighbours on the planet, just "the enemy". The Beatles were the first to show us that there was something wrong with what we had always been taught by our Soviet rulers.'

Once people realised that they disagreed with the state over the Beatles, it was no longer possible to see the great Soviet government bureaucracy as infallible or something to unquestioningly believe in. The system was still powerful and frightening enough to continue for a few decades more, but the end was now certain. Without belief in the rightness of the communist party, the system could only collapse. There were other reasons to doubt the Soviet system, of course, and many other causes of this ultimate loss of faith. But repression of the Beatles was an issue that brought this internal conflict into clear focus.

Artists and musicians were supposed, as we have seen, to be the engineers of the soul. But when the blueprint was drawn up by Marxist-Leninist ideology, it only captured a fraction of what the soul was capable of experiencing. If communist ideology had failed to imagine the potential of human imagination and the delights it could create, then its attempts to design a scientific utopia were doomed from the start. How could rigidly defined doctrine balance the interplay between the superstructure and the base when it had no clue what the superstructure was capable of?

For those who were young during the Cold War, who fell for the music of the Beatles and drank in every crackling note smuggled onto discarded X-rays, the idea that they would ever see a Beatle live was unthinkable. Paul McCartney playing in Red Square was therefore an overwhelmingly emotional experience. This was, after all, the very heart of the old repressive regime, where grey, heartless bureaucrats used to watch the passing of missile convoys and parades of Soviet military might. As Troitsky recalled, 'It was a beautiful event. There was a spectacular sunset over Red Square, and the whole thing was like a huge religious ceremony [...] A lot of people my age were standing there, silently crying. It was like one of those huge gatherings on the banks of the Ganges River, a mass baptism.'

McCartney had been unsure how the crowd would react when he played 'Back in the USSR'. It could be seen as something of a joke song. One of the few bands whom the Beatles viewed as genuine competitors were the Beach Boys, and Paul McCartney and Brian Wilson were both competitive people who wanted to best each other. Wilson had huge melodic ability and his band had beautiful vocal harmonies, much like the Beatles. The lyrics of the Beach Boys, however, often revealed an innate belief in American exceptionalism, and the idea of using their unthinking nationalism to mock Wilson's band was something that McCartney was unable to resist. The result was 'Back in the USSR', which borrowed Beach Boys harmonies but twisted the lyrics so that the song praised the beauty of Russian girls rather than American or California girls. To do this at the height of the Cold War when both British and American media portrayed Russia as the enemy was, of course, extremely funny. On this level, the song worked as a good joke. How it would be perceived behind the Iron Curtain was not something McCartney considered when he wrote it.

To the Russian audience poring over forbidden bootlegs etched into X-rays, it was manna from heaven. They already knew, of course, that Ukrainian girls, Moscow girls and Georgian girls were incredibly beautiful, but for a Western Beatle to acknowledge this, and to sing positively about their homeland, seemed like a blessing from beyond. It was a profound recognition that the West and the East were brothers, not enemies. McCartney further enhanced his reputation as a friend to his Russian audience in 1988 when, after *Perestroika* made it possible to release albums in Russia, he recorded an album of rock 'n' roll covers specifically for release in Russia called *Снова в СССР*, the Russian translation of 'Back in the USSR'. It was a huge success, selling more than 400,000 copies in its first year. Enterprising Russians quickly discovered they could make significant amounts of money smuggling copies to sell to Beatles fans in the West. So when McCartney arrived in Red Square and played 'Back in the USSR', in front of the new Russian President and the tomb of Lenin, the audience was ecstatic.

When the character of James Bond was invented, his initial motivation was to fight Russian Intelligence so that the West could win the Cold War. Instead, the Soviet system was fatally wounded by his opposite twin, the anti-establishment youth music and archetype of love. There's not a Hollywood screenwriter alive who would not feel extremely satisfied with themselves if they had come up with this plot. It is not easy to come up with a conclusion this neat and satisfying. This is the point where a good storyteller would choose to end our tale.

But history is not cinema, alas, and there is no place in it for neat endings. The year that Fleming had created James Bond was also the year that Vladimir Putin was born, to a humble family in what was then Leningrad. When Putin sat watching McCartney in that crowd, the West in general viewed him positively. For all that he had been the former head of the KGB, he was then seen as a slightly dull bureaucrat who had been put into power because he had the favour of the oligarchs. It was thought that he was competent and capable of negotiating with these different oligarchs. As he grew in power, he proved able to control and restrain them. To a Russian public who had experienced the economic turmoil and national humiliation of the 1990s, Putin's offer of strength and stability was incredibly attractive.

An oligarchy is a system in which power is consolidated among a small elite group. The Russian oligarchs had risen to power during the huge economic upheavals of the 1990s, following the collapse of the Soviet Union. Private ownership of businesses had been largely forbidden under the Soviet system, but all this changed under a rigged and corrupt system of privatisation overseen by Boris Yeltsin. Where the great state industries had previously been owned by all the Russian people, they now became the private property of a small elite who instantly became incredibly wealthy – especially those who took control of oil, gas and other natural resources. It was a situation similar to the Norman invasion of England in 1066, after which ownership of the land was taken from the Anglo-Saxons who lived there and given to a small group of Norman barons. After obtaining this wealth, the challenge became creating a system that allowed them to keep it. In Marxist terms, the Norman establishment had to create a superstructure that would protect their new British base. Ultimately, they achieved this through control of the law, the military and, in time, the media and education. If the Normans had successfully done this in Britain, then why couldn't the new Russian oligarchs?

Putin was seen in the West as a hard-nosed manager who could deal with the oligarchs and smooth over any disputes that might arise between them. In this he seemed a great improvement on the communist ideologues who had controlled the state during the Cold War and who might have pushed the world towards war for fundamentalist reasons. He had certainly succeeded in charming McCartney, who said he was a 'Nice guy, he seemed very genuine, like most of the people we've met so far. He said he's from a working-class family as we are, he's got those values – no wonder the people like him.'

But as Putin watched the concert, his face remained unreadable and inscrutable. He stayed calm as all those around him shrieked and yelled in delight, even during the mass singalong that marks the end of 'Hey Jude'. Anyone who has been in a huge crowd watching McCartney perform this song will know how difficult it would be to remain still at this point, for the communal singing of the 'Na-na-na-naaas' section would win over even the most committed cynic. Even McCartney on stage noticed the unnatural zen-like calm of Putin at this point, and called out, 'Everybody! Come on, Mr Putin!' But Putin remained still, neither clapping nor singing, with just an enigmatic Mona Lisa-like hint of a smile. No one could know what he was thinking.

The oligarchs were not popular with the Russian people, especially those who moved their money out of the country to the safety of Swiss or other European banks. For a people who had always been able to rely on the state for a basic safety net, the financial chaos and sudden economic inequality of the 1990s was a shock that made the obscene wealth of a few difficult to accept. The oligarchs were seen as part of a system of corruption and criminality. It was necessary, therefore, to shape Russian culture and society in such a way that this resentment did not threaten the oligarchs. One way to help achieve this was the promotion of nationalism. If the people could love Russia and hate foreigners, then they would instinctively side with the oligarchs, because they were Russian too. As we have seen, nothing confuses those who would naturally oppose you as much as adopting their name and pretending you are the same.

There were alternative visions for the future of Russia circulating, overlooked by those in the West. Many seemed too niche, radical or extreme to pay much attention to. One example was a book called *The Foundations of Geopolitics: The Geopolitical Future of Russia*, which had been published six years earlier in 1997. It was written by the occultist Aleksandr Dugin, who had previously embraced Satanism and Nazism, and it featured a 'chaos magic' symbol over the Eurasian landmass on the cover. In the same year he also published an article entitled 'Fascism – Borderless and Red', which heralded the arrival of a new, Russian form of fascism.

It is easy to see how this vision of a new Russia from an extremist fascist could be dismissed as little more than the lunatic fringe by the West. At a time when the oligarch-controlled state was keen to protect themselves by promoting nationalistic feeling in the people, however, it is also easy to see why oligarchs might take an interest. The book has since become influential in Russian military and foreign policy circles. It has been used as a textbook by the Russian military's Academy of the General Staff.

Dugin's book was a strategy for overcoming global US hegemony and Atlanticism in order to refashion the world around a newly resurgent, nationalist Russia that would eventually establish ethnic Russian rule 'from Dublin to Vladivostok'. This was not to be achieved by military might, although it argued that Russia could use its natural gas and oil reserves to bully and pressure those countries which were dependent on them. Instead, it would focus on subverting and destabilising Western cultures internally, in order to weaken and damage them. The idea was to find existing social fault lines and exploit them.

To damage the United States, Dugin wrote, 'It is especially important to introduce geopolitical disorder into internal American activity, encouraging all kinds of separatism and ethnic, social and racial conflicts, actively supporting all dissident movements – extremist, racist, and sectarian groups, thus destabilizing internal political processes in the U.S. It would also make sense simultaneously to support isolationist tendencies in American politics.' The plan for Britain, which it otherwise dismissed as 'an extraterritorial floating base of the U.S.', was that it should be cut off from the rest of Europe 'and shunned'. The book has proved to be a remarkably accurate depiction of how Russia would behave over the following decades.

Putin had been stationed in Dresden, Germany, when the USSR collapsed. He had watched those events, powerless, from the outside, and considered it to be one of the great geopolitical tragedies of the twentieth century. A clue to how he viewed the status of the former Soviet republics, perhaps, can be seen in the way he restructured the FSB, the security organisation that replaced the KGB, at the end of the 1990s. Although the role of the FSB was to provide internal security, like MI5, Putin decreed that it would also operate in Ukraine and other former Soviet republics. Technically these were independent sovereign countries, but that's not how Putin's FSB viewed them.

We can never know, of course, the extent to which Dugin's ideas had reached Putin by the time he sat in Red Square and watched Paul McCartney. But if there was one thing that he had learned from the Beatles, it was that culture could bring down an empire. As Lenin had argued and recent history had demonstrated, the superstructure and the base were indeed connected. Of course, no one believed Russia was capable of producing radical new culture that would destroy the West, in the same way that the Beatles and Western culture had caused Russian people to stop believing in the Soviet Union. But could Western culture be weaponised to attack itself? Was this a method to reshape the world towards Russian dominance, and in doing so help secure the fortunes of the new Russian oligarchy? The collapse of the Soviet Union, if nothing else, had taught the Russians how and why empires collapse. The fatal fault lines are always internal.

McCartney played on, as the sun set in Red Square. Putin sat in the crowd, enjoying the concert on his own terms, feeling no desire to join 100,000 of his fellow countrymen in the 'Hey Jude' singalong.

2008: THE DEATH OF STRAWBERRY FIELDS

The 2008 Bond movie *Quantum of Solace* doesn't get a lot of love from Bond fans. It is overshadowed by the critical acclaim of its predecessor, *Casino Royale* (2006), and the phenomenal commercial success of the film that followed it, *Skyfall* (2012). Audiences weren't expecting it to be a direct continuation of the *Casino Royale* storyline, and parts of it were incomprehensible to those unfamiliar with the earlier film. It was a revenge story about a man who chose not to take revenge, which was a plot that few expected or even recognised. There was also a significant section of the audience who considered *Quantum of Solace* to be a pretty silly title for a film.

Then there was the issue of the editing. A deliberate decision had been made to copy the hyperkinetic, frantic editing of the Jason Bourne films, in an effort to make the Bond franchise fresh and contemporary in the twenty-first century. The second unit director Dan Bradley was hired in part because of his work on the Bourne franchise. The result was, unfortunately, difficult to follow. It was as if the editor knew what was happening in the story but didn't feel like they had to share that information with the audience. Roger Moore was one of those that was unimpressed. 'I enjoy Daniel Craig, I think he's a damn good Bond, but the film as a whole, there was a bit too much flash-cutting for me,' he said in a radio interview. 'I thought *Casino Royale* was better. It was just like a commercial of the action. There didn't seem to be any geography and you were wondering what the hell was going on but there you are, call me old-fashioned and an old fuddy-duddy!' To be fair to the editors they were only given six weeks to cut the film, which didn't give much time for refinement. There remains the hope that the film will one day be recut, at which point its reputation could improve massively.

One of the more memorable parts of *Quantum of Solace* is a Beatles-themed Bond Girl called Strawberry Fields, who works at the British Consulate in La Paz, Bolivia. Fields's mission is simply to ensure that Bond leaves Bolivia on the next available flight but, as the plane doesn't leave until the following morning, she goes with him to a hotel and sleeps with him instead. In a first for the franchise, she immediately regrets her actions. 'Do you know how angry I am with myself?' she asks. Perhaps she knew the odds of a woman living after sex with Bond. He doesn't seem too concerned about her regret, however, and takes her to a lavish party to meet tech billionaires, politicians, Bolivian military officers and various assorted goons and murderers.

The next we see of Fields she is, of course, naked and dead, lying face down on Bond's bed covered in crude oil. The plot justification for this was that it was misdirection on the part of the villain. He was falsely giving the impression that his evil plan revolved around oil, when in fact the precious liquid he was intent on hoarding was water. *Quantum of Solace* is a harsh, brutal, extremely violent film about two damaged people – Bond and the Bolivian agent Camille Montes – who are cut off from their emotions and robotically seeking revenge. A key image is the desert, representing their arid states of mind where no love can grow. All the water has been hoarded by the film's villain, who must be defeated in order to save the Bolivian people, and also to allow Bond and Montes to heal. When Strawberry Fields wanders into this hard, serious film, it is as if she has entered the wrong Bond film by mistake. Fields would have been a hoot in *Die Another Day*.

Fields's pointless death is more upsetting because this promising character never had a chance to shine. But at the point when she was killed off, the likelihood of death for a woman who slept with Daniel Craig's Bond stood at a franchise-high rate of 100 per cent. Every single woman he slept with in his first two films died shortly afterwards. This is something that Judi Dench's M highlights in the film. 'Look how well your charm works, James,' she says, referring to the dead woman. 'They'll do anything for you, won't they? How many is that now?' Daniel Craig's last performance in character as Bond was in a sketch for the BBC charity Comic Relief, in which he was berated by Catherine Tate's character Nan. 'Let's face it, every time you entertain somebody in the bedroom department, next day, wallop, they're dead,' she tells him. At long last, this defining aspect of the Bond character was being publicly recognised and challenged.

It's true, of course, that the men he encounters don't tend to live long either. Bond is death and it's not just baddies who die. The usual rule is that if an ally (other than Q or M) returns for a second film, then they won't make it to the end. Robbie Coltrane's Valentin Zhukovsky, for example, was first seen in *GoldenEye* and then killed in *The World Is Not Enough*. Giancarlo Giannini's René Mathis made it through *Casino Royale* only for his body to be dumped in the trash in *Quantum of Solace*. *Live and Let Die* and *Dr. No* were produced in reverse order to their books, which created a continuity problem – Bond's Cayman Islander associate Quarrel appeared in both books and was naturally killed in the second. This meant that the film of *Live and Let Die* had to create a son for him, called Quarrel Jr, to avoid bringing him back from the dead.

Of all Bond's male friends, it is the CIA agent Felix Leiter who seems the most immune from death. He was originally killed off in a shark attack in the second book he appeared in, as Fleming tradition dictates. But after complaints from Fleming's American agent the scene was rewritten so that this likeable American character survived – although the shark still ate Leiter's right arm and left leg. Leiter was duly munched by a shark on screen in the film *Licence to Kill* (1989).

Still, even if we accept that Bond is an equal-opportunity version of Death, who kills both male and female friends alike, the idea that women must die after having sex is not one that is easy to brush off. Fleming's toxic emotional problems may have been acceptable to the 1950s publishing industry, but they are impossible to excuse in the twenty-first century. One person who understood this was Gemma Arterton, the actor who played Strawberry Fields.

At the time, Arterton was very positive about the role. She signed up to be the face of the Avon perfume *Bond Girl 007*. 'My character's cool,' she said during interviews to promote the film. 'She's funny, and real, and someone you could know from down the road. I'm quite tough – I have to arrest Bond at one point – but I go to bed with him, of course. So it is a good part.' Asked about the film by the *Observer* five years later, she said, 'Yeah, I don't have any shame in that one. That was really a good experience for me.'

Four years later, however, she had started to express regrets about taking the part. 'I don't want to slag off that film, because I really enjoyed it – I was 21, and it was a trip. But would I do it now? No,' she told *ES* magazine in 2017, 'And I am grateful – it set me up... But it sits really badly with me when I make something I'm not proud of, or doesn't say what I want to say.' She expressed similar sentiments at an International Women's Day event in 2020. 'I still get criticism for accepting the Bond film, but I was 21, I had a student loan and, you know, it was a Bond film!' she said. 'But as I got older I realised there was so much wrong with Bond women... My Bond girl should have just said no, really, and worn flat shoes [...] I know I wouldn't choose a role like that now. Because she was funny and she was sweet, but she didn't really have anything to do – or a backstory.' It is fitting, perhaps, that the only Bond Girl who expressed regret about sleeping with Bond on screen has become the actor most vocal about expressing their regret off screen.

In 2018, Arterton attempted to address the problem through fiction. She wrote a short story about Strawberry Fields for the anthology *Feminists Don't Wear Pink (and Other Lies)*. The story was called 'Woke Woman'. It depicted an alternative version of her first scenes in *Quantum of Solace* in which the character of Strawberry Fields was significantly changed. It begins with Fields being woken by her alarm playing 'No Scrubs' by TLC. This is an appropriate choice for the Bond universe. For all its feminist credentials it is a song about refusing to sleep with poor people, and as such is a suitable expression of Fleming-like snobbery. As the short story continues, however, we soon find that we are in a very different world indeed.

Fields immediately dresses differently. She chooses flat shoes and light trousers, instead of the short skirt underneath a trench coat that we see on screen. In the movie, M tells us, Fields 'worked in an office, collecting reports'. In Arterton's story, she regularly fights drug gangs. Arterton describes how Fields has been personally requested by Bond to escort him around Bolivia, and how he makes her feel uncomfortable by staring at her in the taxi. In the film, her job is to make sure Bond leaves Bolivia, and Bond pointedly ignores her on the way to the hotel. Most importantly, Fields in the short story refuses to accompany him up to his room. ' "No thank you," I say. Maybe he is attractive, but he's at least twenty years older than me, we've only just met, he's a work colleague – the list goes on. Plus this man has a reputation. Don't women who go up to his hotel room and sleep with him usually die in some horrific yet iconic way? No, no. Not me.' Instead, they talk about their mutual friend Penny Lane, then Fields has Bond sign the required paperwork and she leaves. She is, therefore, unharmed, and lives to fight crime another day.

When she was promoting her film in 2008, Arterton had described her character with the phrase 'She's not a typical Bond girl', a description used by many different actors over the past half-century. Regardless of how often the female characters were updated, written as being more formidable in action sequences, or played with great confidence and agency, something significant never changed. The need for new actors to insist that their role isn't that of a typical Bond Girl never seemed to go away. There was always something wrong in the power dynamics at the heart of Bond's relationships. It was always the woman who died after sex, and never the man.

What Arterton did when she wrote her story was to reject the set of assumptions that the Bond franchise had been built upon. She offered another way to perceive Bond, and it was not one that many Bond fans would like. Suddenly he was the sleazy office creep, the person that half the staff warn each other about. Arterton wrote her story in 2018, the year in which Paul Haggis, the Oscar-winning writer-director of *Crash* (2004) and the co-writer of *Quantum of Solace*, was accused by multiple women of a series of rapes and sexual assaults. He has denied all accusations.

With hindsight, there is something symbolic about Arterton's reimagination of Strawberry Fields. When Connery's Bond is knocked unconscious after he criticises the Beatles in *Goldfinger*, he comes to and finds that the woman who was in his bed is now covered in gold and quite dead. This woman, Jill Masterson, had become the first woman in a Bond film to sleep with Bond and then die. The death of Strawberry Fields – coated in oil rather than gold – is a clear reference to this key moment, even down to the inclusion of another Beatles reference. Yet after Fields is found naked and dead on Bond's bed, something significant in the Bond world changes. She is not quite the last Bond Girl to die, as Javier Bardem's villain shoots the character of Séverine in *Skyfall*. But Séverine aside, it is striking that for the remaining three and a half films of Craig's run as the spy, no other woman who is romantically involved with Bond is killed. Considering that every woman Craig's Bond had slept with up to and including Fields had died, this was quite a shift.

The societal awareness and changes that Arterton highlighted in her writing had finally caught up with Fleming's demons. Arterton's Bond Girl, the first to experience regret, was the start of a serious change for the James Bond franchise. It is fitting, for our purposes here, that it took a Beatles-themed character to inspire this change.

2012: A GOLDEN THREAD OF PURPOSE

The Opening Ceremony of the 2012 London Olympic Games was not, it is fair to say, what many people were expecting. It was created by the Oscar-winning film director Danny Boyle and written by Frank Cottrell-Boyce. A key inspiration was William Blake's words for the hymn 'Jerusalem'. The opening sequence of the ceremony depicted the tearing up of the pre-industrial 'green and pleasant land' as it was replaced by 'dark Satanic mills'. As Boyle described his ceremony, 'Woven through it all, there runs a golden thread of purpose – the idea of Jerusalem – of a better world that can be built through the prosperity of industry, through the caring nation that built the welfare state, through the joyous energy of popular culture, through the dream of universal communication. We can build Jerusalem. And it will be for everyone.'

As tens of thousands of people in the stadium and hundreds of millions in front of TVs around the world watched, Boyle's ceremony told a story that was not, as had been expected, the saga of the Norman Continuity Empire. Instead, it was the story of the people of Britain. This was a world that included the NHS, the Suffragettes, industrial workers, Mr Bean, the Windrush

generation, children's literature, pop music and the Jarrow march-
ers. The ceremony had a profound impact on the people of Britain;
we were not used to seeing our real story told. We were quite
unprepared for how it would feel when it happened.

A lot of overseas viewers found this quite baffling, especially for
those whose concept of Britain was based on *Downton Abbey*. Some
in the establishment reacted in horror, aware of how threatening
it was. Conservative MP Aidan Burley tweeted that it was 'The
most leftie opening ceremony I have ever seen – more than Beijing,
the capital of a communist state!' and the *Telegraph* fumed, 'The
NHS segment in particular underlined how surprisingly parochial
this ceremony was. The idea of the Health Service as a beacon
for the world is, bluntly, a national self-delusion.' The BBC commentators had to remain polite, but they too reached for words
like 'leftfield' to describe what they were seeing, which indicated
a certain unease. For the great majority of Britons watching, however, the ceremony was spellbinding and powerfully moving, and
something they would never forget. If you were to ask somebody
in Britain about the opening of the 2014 Glasgow Commonwealth
Games or the 2010 World Cup in South Africa, it is unlikely that
they would remember anything at all about them. This is not the
case for what Boyle, Cottrell-Boyce and thousands of volunteers
created in 2012.

For all the exuberant excess and insanity on display, there were
moments in the ceremony that showed restraint and great taste,
and which were remarkably beautiful. The lighting of the Olympic
cauldron was one such moment. Each national team had arrived
with a child carrying a large copper petal, which was then placed
on one of the stems emanating from a large, circular construction
in the stadium. After each of these individual petals had been
lit, they rose up to form one giant flame, as the people of the
world came together through the Olympic spirit. What made

this so extraordinary was the music that was performed at the time. Traditionally, the music played during the lighting of the Olympic cauldron was bombastic and triumphant. In London, however, they undercut the moment with 'Caliban's Dream', a specially commissioned song from the progressive techno band Underworld. This subdued yet haunting song featured a choir of children singing a gentle 'la la la' melody, some whistling, and a vocal by Alex Trimble from the Northern Irish indie band Two Door Cinema Club. The effect was profoundly magical.

The ceremony couldn't ignore the Norman Continuity Empire completely, of course – not least because Queen Elizabeth was due to arrive at the stadium to declare the London Games open. Boyle's solution here was to turn to James Bond. The audience were treated to a previously filmed sequence called 'Happy and Glorious', in which Daniel Craig's Bond travels to Buckingham Palace to escort the Queen to the stadium. The film featured the Queen's own corgi dogs and gave the monarch a scripted line to perform – 'Good Evening, Mr Bond' – which she delivered like a natural. All this was wonderful publicity for *Skyfall*, the twenty-third Bond film. It opened a few months later, almost exactly fifty years after *Dr. No*, and went on to be the first and only Bond film to take over a billion dollars at the box office.

In 'Happy and Glorious', James Bond was shown accompanying the Queen through the corridors of Buckingham Palace to a waiting helicopter. After flying over cheering crowds and several London landmarks, they then head to the Olympic stadium. By making Bond the Queen's bodyguard, Boyle and Cottrell-Boyce had placed the hierarchical head of the Norman Continuity Empire under the protection of that empire's pre-eminent fictitious avatar. It is an interesting question whether Boyle used Bond to protect her, or to protect the integrity of the rest of ceremony from her. As we noted earlier, Elizabeth had been crowned six weeks after

Bond first appeared in print, in Fleming's first novel *Casino Royale*. He had been a reliable and constant presence in her reign ever since, which made him, essentially, the Lancelot of the Second Elizabethan Era.

With impeccable timing, the pre-recorded helicopter trip cut to a real helicopter hovering over the stadium. The camera returned to Bond, coolly looking out of the open helicopter side door at the crowds below. At this point, a stuntwoman dressed as the Queen got up from her seat in the back of the shot and hurled herself past Bond and out of the helicopter. The way the camera remained on Daniel Craig and treated the Queen throwing herself out of a helicopter as a background detail was a masterclass in directing comedy. The best jokes always come out of the blue. No one had expected the Queen's arrival at the stadium to suddenly veer into slapstick.

This was not what overseas viewers had expected from the British ceremony. As the *Guardian* noted, 'In China the state TV commentators did an admirable job of galloping through potted explanations of everything from the industrial revolution to Mary Poppins but appeared to be stunned to near-silence by the parachuting Queen.' Bond then also leapt out of the helicopter, and the crowds in the stadium watched as he followed the Queen in parachuting down towards the ceremony. The punching-brass of the Bond theme accompanied the opening of the two parachutes, which naturally featured Union flags in a nod to Roger Moore's ski jump from the opening of *The Spy Who Loved Me*. Just like that pre-title stunt, patriotism had once again been converted to a punchline. Boyle and Cottrell-Boyce had used the banishing power of laughter to protect their ceremony from being claimed by the powers that be.

The legacy of Ian Fleming made a second appearance during the ceremony, in a sequence celebrating children's literature and the NHS. This section was named after a quote from *Peter Pan*, 'Second to the Right and Straight on Till Morning', in part because Pan's author J.M. Barrie had gifted the copyright of *Peter Pan* to Great Ormond's Street Hospital for Children. In this sequence, the opening scenes of children in bed reading stories while being cared for by nurses was interrupted by the arrival of the Child Catcher, the horrific villain from Fleming's *Chitty-Chitty-Bang-Bang*. This was a children's book about a flying car – Fleming always did like his gadgets.

Fleming had written this book for his son Caspar when he was in Brighton recovering from a heart attack. It had been turned into a film by the Bond producers after Fleming's death, with a script by Roald Dahl. Robert Helpmann's portrayal as the Child Catcher in the movie, as he tempted children into his cage with free lollipops, was later called 'the most sinister presence I have ever seen on film' by Gary Chapman in *The Times*. He became the source of many children's nightmares. This was also his role in the ceremony. The Child Catcher ushered nightmares into the stadium, including Captain Hook, Cruella de Vil and Voldemort. Following the destruction of Blake's green and pleasant land by the dark Satanic mills in the opening sequence, it was a reminder that Boyle and Cottrell-Boyce were not afraid to highlight the darkness they also found in the British soul.

Fortunately, the nightmares were eventually defeated by the combined efforts of the nurses from the NHS and an army of Mary Poppinses. Fleming was politically opposed to the NHS, so he would probably have hated this. It seems likely that he would have been pleased that two of his creations were centre stage during a national celebration nearly fifty years after his death, but they did emphasise that it was the darker side of his psyche that left an impact.

For the grand finale of the opening ceremony, it could only be the Beatles. After the athletes had arrived, the Queen had declared the ceremony open and the cauldron had been lit, there was nowhere else to go except for Paul McCartney. He opened with a snatch of 'The End', to remind us that the love we make is equal to the love we take. He was still determined to keep stressing the central message of the band even half a century later.

The Beatles had been a constant presence throughout the ceremony. They appeared on film singing 'She Loves You' during the celebration of pop music, and the Arctic Monkeys had performed 'Come Together' while illuminated winged cyclists circled the stadium and took flight. During the opening sequence which told the story of Britain, the arrival of a parade of brightly dressed Sgt. Peppers followed by giant floating yellow submarines marked the end of the horrors of the world wars. To end the epic four-hour ceremony, McCartney and his band performed 'Hey Jude' and, despite an embarrassing missed cue at the start, led the entire crowd in a lengthy communal singalong. There was no sign of anyone in that stadium who was able to resist joining in with the 'Na-na-na-naaas', like Putin had in Red Square nine years earlier. Given what Boyle and Cottrell-Boyce had set out to achieve, it's difficult to imagine how their ceremony could have ended any other way.

It's hard, now, to express the transformative effect the ceremony had on the British people. Before the ceremony, cynicism in the media had convinced people that the Games would be a disaster; overly corporate, badly organised and impossibly expensive for a country undergoing the shock of austerity in the aftermath of the 2008 global financial crash. Signs around the Olympic site declaring Orwellian corporate slogans such as 'We are proud to only accept VISA' did not seem compatible with the Olympic spirit. From the reporting of Boyle's plans for the opening ceremony, many were convinced it was going to be a national embarrassment. All this was swept away in the hours between the opening performance of Blake's 'Jerusalem' and the Beatles' 'Hey Jude'. The delight the nation took in the Games that followed, and particularly in the Paralympics, will not be forgotten by those who were there. In recent history, they stand out as golden weeks.

The euphoric national mood that sustained during the Games had to end, however. Sixteen days later, the same stadium played host to the closing ceremony. From the start, it was clear that this was going to be a very different story to that of the opening. The same Shakespeare quotation from *The Tempest* was used at the start – 'Be not afeared; the isle is full of noises'. This quote spoke of the wonders of a dream more real than base reality. The opening ceremony gave these words to Isambard Kingdom Brunel, played by Kenneth Branagh, to announce the dream of the industrial revolution. The closing ceremony, in contrast, gave them to Winston Churchill, played by Timothy Spall, who appeared out of the top of the Big Ben tower. Caliban's words praise the wonder of the strange noises that push us towards our dreams, yet after he finished Shakespeare's quote Spall's Churchill called out 'Stop!' to quiet all the stadium noises. What all this was intended to mean was hard to discern. In the context in which it was delivered the quote seemed to make no sense at all – unless Churchill was being used to tell us that the dream was now over.

Caliban's quote set the trend for a ceremony which seemed intent on robbing literature and music of any meaning. Jessie J arrived and sang 'Price Tag', an anti-wealth song about how money and the pursuit of riches keep us from what matters in life. She perversely performed this while being chauffeur-driven around the stadium in a gold and white Rolls-Royce convertible, as if she did not understand what the words she was singing actually meant. Emile Sande performed her song 'Read All About It', which was about having the strength to speak out, over an unrelated montage of emotional athletes crying. At times, it was hard to tell if this deliberate removal of meaning was intentional, or if no one had really thought these things through. Whatever the explanation, it was clear we were a long way from Boyle's 'golden thread of meaning'.

Despite the fact that the ceremony was directed by Kim Gavin, whose dad was a plumber from Ilford, it quickly became apparent that we were witnessing the Norman Continuity Empire being reinstated as the dominant narrative once again. The story of Britain that the opening ceremony had offered may have been acceptable during the Games itself, but it could not be allowed indefinitely, and it was time to shut it down. It was as if a banishing ritual was being enacted, to dispel the dangerous magic conjured up at the opening ceremony. After Churchill's appearance we had the arrival of Prince Harry, a performance of 'God Save the Queen', and a good deal of flag waving. The following section depicted a monarchist street party, during which the Massed Bands of the Guards Division, with their distinctive red coats and tall bearskin hats, marched around the stadium playing 'Parklife' by Blur.

This reclaiming of the narrative for the Norman Continuity Empire was particularly apparent in the design of the inner stadium where the ceremony took place. If the artist at the heart of the opening ceremony was William Blake, then the artist who dominated the closing ceremony was Damien Hirst. He had produced an enormous version of the Union flag which covered the floor of the stadium, which he called 'Beautiful Union Jack Celebratory Patriotic Olympic Explosion in an Electric Storm Painting' (2012). It was a splodgy, smeared version of the flag – arguably an unfortunate choice, given how many nations refer to this flag as the butcher's apron.

The triangular sections of the flag were large pens, which the athletes of the world were herded into in order to witness the performances to come. To be included in the Olympic closing ceremony, then, athletes from every nation had to physically become part of a huge-scale symbol of the British state. These triangular sections were bounded by rows of volunteers holding hands to form a line that the athletes in their designated part of the flag could not cross. These volunteers were dressed as friendly, comedy policemen and women, with blue outfits and a lightbulb on their helmets. It looked like the world's athletes were being kettled by a police force made up of children's TV presenters. Towards the end of the ceremony, boyband Take That (minus Robbie) stood in the middle of this giant British flag and sang 'Rule the World'. This seemed somewhat opposed to the message of the Olympics. It was, again, another moment that made you wonder if it was deliberate, or if nobody had really thought it through.

Still, the athletes in their designated areas were nothing if not entertained by what followed. The ceremony's theme was 'A Symphony of British Music', and the organisers certainly delivered on this front. The athletes and audience were treated to performances by a lengthy parade of huge-selling artists including Ed Sheeran, the Spice Girls, One Direction, the Pet Shop Boys, Elbow, Ray Davis, Madness, George Michael, the Who, Liam Gallagher, Annie Lennox, Muse, and what's left of Queen.

The 'Symphony of British Music' opened with John Lennon's face looking down at the crowd from giant screens, singing 'Imagine'. The song was then taken up by a children's choir, who wore white 'Imagine' T-shirts as they sang and signed the song. At the same time, a giant model of Lennon's head was constructed in the centre of the stadium, looking up at the sky. 'Imagine' has become something of an institution in the world of Olympic ceremonies, ever since Stevie Wonder performed the song at the 1996 Atlanta Games. It was used by the 2018 PyeongChang and 2006 Torino Winter Olympics. More recently it was played at the opening of the 2020 Tokyo Olympics, where it was performed by artists including John Legend and Keith Urban, and at the 2022 Beijing Winter Olympics opening ceremony. While McCartney performed 'Hey Jude' at the opening ceremony as an expression of British culture, 'Imagine' has risen above its birthplace to become a secular global hymn. When President Trump was defeated in 2020, for example, New Yorkers spontaneously started singing the song when they gathered to celebrate. It fits with the Olympics because it now belongs to the world.

Lennon's 'Imagine' was only one of the many Beatles songs used during the closing ceremony. Russell Brand appeared from a *Magical Mystery Tour* bus and sang 'I Am the Walrus', and George's 'Here Comes the Sun' was performed with Indian musicians. At the very beginning of the ceremony a choir sang 'Because' while the theatrical percussion group Stomp banged stuff, as is their wont. Spelbound, the gymnastic troupe who won *Britain's Got Talent* in 2010, performed to 'A Day in the Life'. Other nods to the Fab Four included newspaper taxis which drove around the stadium, and Eric Idle's performance of 'Always Look on the Bright Side of Life' from the George Harrison-funded and produced film *The Life of Brian*. Had there been this many references to any other band, it would have been remarked upon. But nobody found this many Beatle references in any way strange – such is the extent to which our culture is so deeply soaked in their music, and the extent to which its presence is casually expected and considered normal. It was, however, a sign of how their music, which was once so threatening to the establishment, had now been co-opted to support it. The process by which once radical ideas are defused and absorbed by the powers that be is called recuperation.

Behind the sporting triumphs and the spectacle of the Games, other stories were playing out. In an effort to crack down on the use of banned performance-enhancing drugs, the International

Olympics Committee announced that half of all athletes, including all medal winners, would be tested for drugs. A team of 150 scientists took around 6,000 samples during the 2012 Olympic and Paralympic Games. Competitors from many countries were found to have been illegally doping, and in total thirty-one medals were later rescinded for doping violations. It quickly became apparent that the level of cheating taking place in the Russian team was far in advance of any other country. One such athlete was the female discus thrower Darya Pishchalnikova, who tested positive for the anabolic steroid oxandrolone. Pishchalnikova became a whistle-blower and sent details to the World Anti-Doping Agency of how Russian athletes had to participate in a state-run doping programme. While most international athletes who were caught doping had made the decision to cheat themselves and obtained their drugs through the black market, Russian athletes received theirs from the state.

This was part of an emerging pattern. Seven Russian athletes were suspended from the 2008 Beijing Olympic Games for tampering with their urine samples, and in October 2009 Pierre Weiss, then the IAAF general secretary, wrote, 'This matter of the Russian athletes' blood levels is now so serious and is not getting any better [in fact possibly getting worse] that immediate and drastic action is needed [...] Not only are these athletes cheating their fellow competitors but at these levels are putting their health and even their own lives in very serious danger.' It would not be until 2015, however, that the full extent of the state-sponsored Russian doping scandal became public, and a culture of bribes, cover-ups and corruption at the highest levels of the sport was revealed. By the time the Tokyo Olympic Games took place in 2021, the Russian Federation had been banned from competing.

All this raised the question as to why Russia puts so much effort into cheating at sport and continuing with the practice despite such large-scale opposition internationally. One answer could be because it helps strengthen nationalism at home, to the advantage of the elites and oligarchs. The idea that Russia had got one over the IOC was something that went down well within Russia itself. Russian media pushed the narrative that doping is something that every country does, and that the accusations against Russia were a politically motivated vendetta from the West, who were jealous of Russia's athletic prowess. In November 2017, for example, Putin branded the life bans given to four Russian skiers by the IOC as a politically motivated US plot to interfere with Russian elections. The notion that it is plucky Russia against the world strengthens the 'us versus them' narrative that nationalism relies on.

Perhaps this was the reason why the Russian government did not apologise, as other countries would, when the scale of their doping programme was revealed in 2015. Emboldened by the lack of repercussions for political murders such as the killing of Alexander Litvinenko in London by polonium poisoning, they went on the offensive, with little regard for international reactions. A Russian cyber-espionage organisation called Fancy Bear was tasked with hacks on the IOC and other sporting organisations, and they released the medical files of huge numbers of international athletes. One high-profile victim of the hack was the British cyclist Bradley Wiggins, who had obtained the required Therapeutic Use Exemption Certificates which allowed him to take otherwise banned substances at certain times and under certain conditions. Technically, Wiggins had followed the rules and not done anything illegal, but that wasn't really the point of the hack. Just raising questions about how those rules are interpreted was enough to link Wiggins to the subject of doping scandals. Wiggins was a big name – he had been chosen to ring the giant bell that opened the 2012 Olympic opening ceremony, wearing a yellow jersey signifying his recent Tour de France victory. This guaranteed a lot of media attention, and served to move the focus of the doping scandal away from Russia.

State-sponsored hacking, it seemed, had the potential to be a powerful weapon for the Russian government. Spurred on by their success with sporting hacks, Fancy Bear went on to perform their most notorious exploit. During a 22 January 2016 meeting of Russia's national security council at the Kremlin, Putin had personally authorised Project Lakhta, a secret spy agency operation to support a 'mentally unstable' Donald Trump in the 2016 US presidential election, which would help bring about 'social turmoil' in the US, to Russia's advantage. Fancy Bear then hacked the American Democratic Party, in an effort to help Donald Trump defeat Hilary Clinton in the 2016 presidential elections. Aleksandr Dugin's 1997 book *The Foundations of Geopolitics* had advised that Russia should exploit the cultural fault lines in the West. With the arrival of the internet, there was now an ideal tool with which to do this.

In the 1960s, the time of the Profumo Affair and the fallout from the Cambridge Five Soviet spy ring, Bond fought against Russian espionage. This was the global evil that justified his licence to kill. With the rise of Gorbachev in the 1980s however, the Cold War ended and the KGB and GRU retreated from the West. In the early twenty-first century, as the intelligence agencies focused on Islamic terrorism, Russian espionage had largely been forgotten. This suited Putin perfectly. We relax when the old threats fade away, and fail to notice as new, different threats take their place. As Bond celebrated his fiftieth birthday, few realised that his old enemy had returned, and was prepared to attack us with the most modern of tools.

2015: WHAT IS THE NEW EVIL IN THE WORLD?

The soundtrack to *Spectre*, the twenty-fourth Bond film, was recorded by the American composer Thomas Newman in Studio One at Abbey Road. This was becoming a tradition, for Newman had recorded the soundtrack to *Skyfall*, the preceding Bond film, in the same room. The opening track was *'Los Muertos Vivos Están'*, which translates into English as 'The dead are alive'. This cryptic phrase appeared onscreen, in white text on a black background, at the start of the film. The opening sequence found Bond dressed as a skeleton at the Mexican *Día de los Muertos*, or Day of the Dead, celebrations. The image of Bond as a skeleton loomed large in the background of many of the film's promotional posters and artwork. The film's director Sam Mendes saw this as an intentional nod to the character of Baron Samedi, the vodou loa of the dead, in *Live and Let Die*, the first Bond film he had seen as a child. No other film had defined Bond as death so strongly as *Spectre*. The character of Mr White, for example, explicitly refers to Bond as death when they meet.

Studio One at Abbey Road was also where the Beatles' performance of 'All You Need Is Love' was filmed and broadcast live around the world forty-seven years earlier. Lennon was not singing about romantic love for a partner, as we've noted, but *agape* – unconditional love for all, the highest form of love there is. This was a song about opening yourself up so that you become part of something larger. The theme of the film *Spectre* was a dark inversion of this. It focused on the danger of openness, and the fear and paranoia that can follow.

Spectre was, at the time, the longest Bond film yet. This brought criticism, including from Pierce Brosnan. 'I thought it was too long,' he said. 'The story was kind of weak – it could have been condensed. [...] It's neither Bond nor Bourne. Am I in a Bond movie? Not in a Bond movie?' Of course, no film is too long if the audience are engaged with it. *Spectre* was beautifully shot and effortlessly stylish, with great performances and all the ingredients that you expect in a Bond film – with the exception, perhaps, of humour. With a budget believed to be somewhere between $245m and $300m, it was one of the most expensive films ever made. But it did not hold the audience's attention in quite the same way that *Skyfall* or *Casino Royale* did. The film opened to record box offices, but interest dwindled. It ultimately made over $200m less than *Skyfall*.

For *Spectre*, the Bond producers felt that the time was right to reintroduce the character of Ernst Stavro Blofeld, head of the evil crime syndicate SPECTRE. Blofeld remained dominant in the folk memory of the Bond films, despite not officially appearing in an EON film since 1971's *Diamonds Are Forever*. The problem was that it was the absurd nature of the character that people remembered, with his bald head, scar, white long-haired cat and lapel-less grey Nehru jacket. This was thanks, in part, to the popularity of Dr

Evil, the spoof Blofeld character from the Austin Powers films who became George Harrison's voice on his deathbed.

A character like Blofeld did not seem an ideal fit for the sophisticated, serious tone of the Daniel Craig era, but it is much easier for the general public to grasp a classic Bond supervillain than it is the sort of vague, complex threats that now exist in the real world. Osama bin Laden, for example, was a non-state actor who plotted and executed schemes of destruction on a wildly ambitious scale, much like Ernst Stavro Blofeld, Dr No or Auric Goldfinger. He therefore immediately made sense to people as a villain, without them having to understand the complex history and theology that drove Islamic fundamentalism. Indeed, when bin Laden was believed to be hiding in the Tora Bora cave complex in eastern Afghanistan, the British press invented a vast, sophisticated underground lair for him, of the type that Blofeld would have been proud of. According to an informative illustration of this underground mountain fortress in *The Times*, 'The complex of caves at Tora Bora is carved 1,150ft into a 13,000ft mountain and can accommodate up to 1,000 people.' This would have made the cave complex almost as deep as the Twin Towers were tall, making them a dark mirror of the Twin Towers in the modern myth then unfolding. The caves were wired for light, power and ventilation, *The Times* explained, and included offices, bedrooms and communal areas as well as secret exits and booby traps. It was powered by hydroelectric power generated by mountain streams, and the entrance was large enough to drive a tank in. It was exactly the sort of thing that original Bond designer Ken Adam would have dreamed up.

Or at least, that was where bin Laden was lurking in the imagination of the West. The reality was somewhat different, as a staff sergeant with the US Special Forces division who fought at the Battle of Tora Bora explained. 'With the caves, they weren't these crazy mazes or labyrinths of caves that they described. Most of them were natural caves [...] I know they made a spectacle out of that, and how are we going to be able to get into them? We worried about that too, because we see all these reports. Then it turns out, when you actually go up there, there's really just small bunkers.' It is perhaps a measure of the extent to which the Bond films have shaped our understanding of the world that the idea that bin Laden was a Bond-like supervillain in a high-tech lair seemed plausible, to the extent that a relatively sober newspaper like *The Times* would commission a detailed cross-section of a fantasy fortress.

The enigmatic actor Christoph Waltz was hired to create the modern version of Bond's greatest supervillain. More controversially, Blofeld's backstory was rewritten to make him James Bond's stepbrother. After Bond was orphaned at the age of eleven, this new history claimed, he was adopted by a skiing instructor called Hannes Oberhauser, a character found in the Fleming short story *Octopussy*. To Oberhauser, the strong, handsome Bond was an ideal son, being exceptionally skilled at skiing, mountaineering and – being Bond – everything else he tried. Hannes Oberhauser's real son, Franz, became jealous. He saw Bond as the 'cuckoo in the nest', who was pushing him out of the family group and taking the paternal love that should have been his. This labelling of Bond as a 'cuckoo', as we've noted, neatly echoes the idea that the establishment is also a cuckoo in British culture.

Franz reacted by killing his father, faking his own death, and adopting his maternal family name of Blofeld. He then set up the secret global crime syndicate SPECTRE and used it to take his revenge on Bond. The events of the earlier Craig films were explained as all being part of this process. This meant that Blofeld had been behind the deaths of Vesper Lynd and M, and everything else that had caused Bond to suffer. To many viewers, this did not seem remotely plausible.

In terms of screenwriting theory, all this made perfect sense. It increased the stakes for all the disasters that befall the hero, making events personal and more meaningful. In an effort to match the prevailing trends in blockbuster movies, the Daniel Craig Bond films were reimagined as chapters in a larger story. According to the accepted rules of screenwriting theory, however, Bond films should not work. Writers are taught the necessity of a strong 'character arc' for their heroes. The hero needs to change and grow in a story, the theory goes, and plot events need to drive this change if the narrative is to be engaging and satisfying. In the great majority of Bond films, of course, Bond does not change in the slightest. His 'character arc' is non-existent, and in theory his films should therefore fail. Bond films exist outside the normal rules of cinema, and that includes the world of screenwriting theory. As such, applying its rules is not always wise.

To Bond fans, the revelation that Bond was Blofeld's stepbrother was a terrible idea that should never have made it to screen. Bond had always fought Blofeld because it was his duty, not because of domestic baggage. As heroes go, Bond occupies a unique sweet spot between being a flawed, rounded character who we can believe in, and a blank slate we can project ourselves onto. Here he has much in common with characters from video games, who the player both controls and identifies with. A video game character needs to be distinct and memorable, and can have a complex history, but never to the extent that their motivation and goals differs from that of the player who inhabits them. The fun comes from imagining ourselves to be that character, as they act in the same way we would. When that character's actions are motivated by an implausible personal history that we are unable to identify with, the audience loses its ability to project themselves onto that hero.

We can no longer live vicariously through their actions. Instead, we sit back and passively observe them.

A villain, however, is not a story. The story arises from what the villain does. The first question asked when work begins on a new Bond script is, what are people afraid of now? What is the new evil in the world? By repeatedly asking this question over the last five decades, the Bond producers have managed to keep the franchise relevant, even as Bond himself became an anachronism. For *Spectre*, centralised control of global data was that new fear. As Mendes explained, '*Skyfall* was a post-Julian Assange movie and *Spectre* is a post-Edward Snowden movie [...] The fears that haunted *Skyfall* were to do with hacking and the fears that haunted *Spectre* were to do with surveillance. Neither of them have gone away. Those were things that provided the fuel that drove the antagonist.'

Since the Senate Intelligence Committee report on Russian interference in the 2016 United States presidential election, we have had a greater understanding of the extent to which Russian Intelligence, Bond's original enemy, has been using the internet to interfere in foreign cultures and elections, in order to advance Russian foreign policy goals. We now know that Project Lakhta, the attempt to help Donald Trump defeat Hilary Clinton in the 2016 American election, was ordered directly by Putin himself. Large 'troll farms' of fake social media accounts were established by a group called the Internet Research Agency, who were based in Saint Petersburg. The aim was to actively use the internet to destabilise and weaken the West by aggravating divisions and turning populations against each other – attacking the superstructure, in Marxist terms, in the belief that this will affect the base.

As we've noted, Putin had seen first-hand the effect a foreign culture could have on destabilising a regime. He had seen how the Western culture that the Beatles spearheaded had effectively hollowed out the USSR from within. If culture could do that to his homeland, then it could do it to his foreign enemies as well. Russia may not have been able to create global culture, but they could exploit it, and there were many, readily apparent cultural divides in Western society that they could widen. The internet was the ideal tool for this. According to the *Wall Street Journal*, Russia used the internet to organise at least sixty street protests across America before and after the 2016 election, using both Trump supporters and Black Lives Matter campaigners to inflame social divisions. On occasions it was found that they organised both a protest and a counter-protest at the same place on the same day. Watching the 'enemy' turn on itself like this, from the safety of a laptop in Saint Petersburg, must have been quite a thrill.

It's difficult, of course, to measure exactly how much of an impact all this had on real-world events such as Brexit or the rise of Trump. Russian interference was just one of many factors in deeply complex, highly connected situations. As citizens in a democracy, we feel that responsibility for Brexit or Trump ultimately lies with those who voted for them, as well as with those who stayed at home on election day and didn't vote against them. It's clear, however, that Russian Intelligence saw both the election of Trump and the British vote to leave the EU as major victories in their covert war. According to the journalist Luke Harding, the Russian Ambassador to the UK, Alexander Yakovenko, who returned to Moscow in 2019 after the Brexit referendum, told a fellow diplomat that 'his time as ambassador in London was a triumph. He had smashed the Brits to the ground. "It will be a long time before they rise again." '

It was an irony, then, that *Spectre* not only told a story about the danger of control of data, but was also involved in a real-life example of international hacking. A huge amount of data – the alleged perpetrators claimed that it was 100 terabytes – was taken from Sony Pictures servers in November 2014, and large quantities of this were published on Julian Assange's Wikileaks website. This included an early script of *Spectre*, which revealed that the film's villain was going to be Blofeld, and many emails between the Bond producers and Sony executives arguing about the budget. Sony, we learned, were unhappy that the budget looked set to hit $300m. They repeatedly suggested ways to make the film cheaper, such as using three train carriages instead of four for a fight sequence, and filming certain scenes in London rather than Rome. As Barbara Broccoli said, 'The stuff about us having fights about the budget, well, what's new? We want to put all the money on the screen. We want to deliver the best film that we can. We fight for as much money as we can to make the film. And that's no secret.' The hack led to the resignation of Amy Pascal, the Sony executive in charge of the Bond films, when comments from her personal emails were published concerning President Obama's taste in films. These were widely seen as racially inappropriate.

According to the American government, it was not the Russians behind the hack this time, but the North Koreans. Their motivation was believed to be their anger about Sony's Seth Rogan comedy *The Interview*, which mocked Kim Jong-un and included an assassination attempt against him. President Obama spoke out against North Korean actions and threats and promised a 'proportional response'. The White House Press Secretary Josh Earnest said that the attack was 'being treated as a serious national security matter'. North Korea did not claim responsibility for the hacks, but they did describe them as 'a righteous deed'. A week later North Korea began experiencing a series of national internet and mobile 3G network shutdowns, which lasted hours at a time. The North Korean National Defence Commission blamed Washington for the outages. It also described President Obama as a 'monkey', which gives an indication of the heightened tensions these events produced. This was, clearly, a major deterioration in relations between America and North Korea, which was then undertaking a series of underground nuclear tests in order to develop nuclear weapons. Many feared that the volatile situation would escalate further. The notion that a nuclear war could break out for reasons including a leaked, spoiler-filled James Bond script suddenly seemed horrifyingly plausible.

In these circumstances, the digital paranoia that drove the *Spectre* storyline appeared incredibly prescient. Information, it seemed, did have the power to upend the world order. This was an entirely new form of threat, and one which was difficult for most people to fully comprehend. It felt abstract and invisible, rather like climate change, and so it was difficult to grasp just how serious it was. James Bond was created to fight Russian and other foreign intelligence agencies, but his battle took place in the world of fiction. Suddenly we were in a position where attacks were targeted not at Britain itself, but at its fictions. In terms of international influence and soft power, James Bond had left the page and become a genuine agent on the global stage. He was, however, increasingly being used as a tool not to support Britain, but to attack it.

In 2022, Chinese state media responded to a talk by the head of MI6, Richard Moore, aka C, by releasing a Bond parody film called *No Time to Die Laughing*. This featured James Pond 0.07 and a female British spy called Black Window failing to understand current geopolitical reality. Later that year, when Western intelligence agencies warned that Russia was planning to invade Ukraine, the British foreign secretary Liz Truss claimed that Russia planned to install the former Ukrainian MP Yevhen Murayev as puppet leader of the conquered state. Murayev responded by calling British Intelligence 'more Mr Bean than James Bond' and posting an image online of him posing as Bond in front of the *Skyfall* logo. In Britain, people were generally bemused by these strange reactions. They only really make sense if the overseas view of post-Brexit Britain is acknowledged. The gulf between the competent, powerful image of Britain found in the Bond films and the reality of a country whose influence, reputation and economy has now been significantly downgraded is, to countries unfriendly to Britain, very funny.

While Russian espionage found the internet to be a most effective weapon, it was not against using other, blunter tools to flex its muscles on a global stage. On 1 November 2006 the Russian dissident Alexander Litvinenko was fatally poisoned by radio-active polonium, in a fourth-floor room of the Millennium Hotel in Grosvenor Square, just round the corner from the EON office where the Bond films are produced. Before he died, Litvinenko accused Vladimir Putin of being behind his poisoning, an assessment that the British Intelligence services would agree with. This real-life incident inspired the poisoning of Mr White by radioactive thallium in *Spectre*.

Another approach that Russian Intelligence used was to send agents or go-betweens to befriend British businessmen and politicians, usually through the means of flattery and lavish gifts. There are accounts, for example, of businessmen being offered hugely lucrative preferential access to the sale of Russian gold or diamond mines. The wealth of the Russian oligarchs has opened doors to the highest levels of British business, sport, art and politics. Given the extent to which wealth in Britain has historically originated in India and Africa, it is perhaps unsurprising that the City of London has been comfortable welcoming wealth that was essentially looted from the Russian people during the 1990s. When John Lennon first became rich, he bought Kenwood, a Surrey mansion on St George's Hill. This was the site where, in 1649, Gerarrd Winstanley and his band of 'Diggers' attempted to create a better world by planting crops and living off land that had been 'enclosed' or claimed by local landowners. Such is the extent of Russian oligarch money in Britain that over a hundred of the homes on St George's Hill are now owned by Russians or people from former Soviet states. It is currently impossible to visit this historic site because St George's Hill has become a heavily guarded private community.

Most people would find it extremely suspicious if they were contacted by people linked to the Russian state who wanted to give them compliments and riches. Here Russian interests exploit the psychology of those who attended British public schools. From their perspective, the idea that people would want to flatter and reward them fits so well with their worldview that it does not raise any warning flags. As a result, there is a long history of Russian spies infiltrating the British establishment by complimenting ex-public-school boys. This ranges from using 'useful idiots' to gain influence and connections to full-on recruitment as ideological Soviet agents, such as Old Etonian Guy Burgess and the 'Cambridge Five'.

Vladimir Putin had studied the ineffective international responses to his actions, including the annexation of Crimea and the use of a military-grade nerve agent on British soil to poison the former Russian military agent Sergei Skripal. He concluded that his lengthy covert war had sufficiently weakened and divided the West. He was now in a position, he felt, to invade Ukraine and get away with it. If this was a success, Putin's legacy would be that he was the great leader who expanded Russian power and territory back towards that held by the earlier Russian Empire or the Soviet Union.

On 24 February 2022, the UN Security Council held an emergency meeting to discuss the feared Russian invasion of Ukraine. The Secretary General of the United Nations, António Guterres, was the first to speak. 'If indeed an operation is being prepared, I have only one thing to say, from the bottom of my heart,' he said. 'President Putin: stop your troops from attacking Ukraine. Give peace a chance.' Here Guterres was quoting the slogan that John Lennon and Yoko Ono coined during their bed-ins for peace. The phrase was deemed radical when they recorded it, backed by the likes of Timothy Leary and other counterculture figures. Yet so deeply had it penetrated global culture that there seemed nothing unusual about it being used fifty years later at the heart of international political power. The self-evident rightness of the slogan 'Give Peace a Chance' had, for many in the West, made the idea that a nation could send its tanks over its borders and start shelling civilian populations almost unthinkable. The world didn't work like that, people felt. Not anymore.

When *The World Is Not Enough* was being developed, it originally included a scene in which Judi Dench's M tells Bond that the world has moved on from his day and that he has become a relic. In dialogue cut for being too on the nose, she was going to tell Bond that his problem was he thought that the world was still menaced by evil maniacs holding the globe to nuclear ransom from volcano lairs, when people like that didn't exist. Brosnan's Bond was to reply, 'It only takes one.' In the twenty-first century, we thought that autocratic strongmen evil enough to invade neighbouring countries no longer existed. But, it only takes one. Putin invaded while the UN security council talked. The meeting began in peacetime and ended in war.

Guterres's request that Putin 'give peace a chance' proved to be futile. The soft power of cultural ideas had failed to prevent the hard power of an invading modern army. And yet, Putin's attempts to divide the West through culture had also failed to prevent a reaction of horror to what he had done. The West proved to be far more unified in their response than Putin had expected. Neither did the Ukrainians respond how he anticipated. Like all strongmen dictators who surround themselves with loyalists, he had spent years being told what he wanted to hear until he was entirely deluded about the reality of the world. He thought that his troops would cut through Ukraine and take Kyiv in a matter of days. He hadn't expected hundreds of thousands of Ukrainian James Bonds, both male and female, to step up and put their lives at risk protecting their country from evil.

We're now in a world where ideas, data and arguments are increasingly seen as able to shape geopolitical events. If the Bond myth tells us anything, however, it is that bravery, determination and bloody-mindedness will always remain forces to be reckoned with.

2021: TIME TO DIE

All productions of blockbuster films are difficult, but there were times when it seemed like the twenty-fifth Bond film might well have been cursed. The Daniel Craig Bond films had started strongly with *Casino Royale* but had misfired badly with *Spectre*. When it was announced that Craig would return for one last film, many were sceptical. Could the franchise be salvaged, or was the last wrong turn too serious to come back from? The final Craig movie would be called *No Time to Die*. There was a lot hanging on it.

It was originally announced in July 2017, when the planned release date was 8 November 2019. The following February we learned that it would be directed by Danny Boyle, who had already worked with Craig's 007 – and the Queen – as part of his London Olympics opening ceremony. Boyle was working on a script with his long-term screenwriting partner John Hodge. Boyle and Hodge left the film that August due to 'creative differences', although some thought that those differences were more political. Boyle's film was said to focus on Russian involvement in global politics, which may have been too loaded an issue for the franchise to tackle. Others felt it was Boyle's own politics which made him unsuitable. 'They obviously couldn't take a socialist Bond,' remarked the actor Jonathan Pryce, who had played the villain in *Tomorrow Never Dies*. 'You see, there are the Dannys of this world and then there are people who do the blockbusters.'

Boyle was replaced by the American director Cary Joji Fukunaga and the release date was put back first to February 2020 and then April 2020. At the beginning of March, however, the film became the first major movie to reschedule its release date due to fears that the emerging Covid-19 pandemic might impact global box office. At the time, cinemas in China were closed, and cinemas in Korea, Japan, France and Italy were in the process of closing. The West had been in denial about what was about to hit, but the actions of 007 served as a moment of clarity. Shortly after *No Time to Die* moved its release back to November, almost all other major films followed. Even the cinemas that wanted to remain open had to close due to a lack of major Hollywood films.

When the producers made a last-minute decision to postpone again, and move the release from November 2020 to April 2021, the struggling cinema industry reacted with horror. They had been counting on the guaranteed box-office success of a Bond film after an economically disastrous year. Without this, many thought that cinemas might close and never reopen. The press put the blame for the industry's woes squarely at Bond's feet, and headline after headline declared that it was Bond himself who was killing cinema. The *Guardian* used the headline ' "We've literally been killed by James Bond": Cineworld's final day of screenings', to report on how the Bond delay caused the Cineworld chain to close. The *Telegraph* film critic Robbie Collin wrote an article headlined 'The *No Time to Die* delay is James Bond putting a bullet in his own head', in which he argued that '007 might be responsible for the death of cinema itself.' As Collin explained, 'Simply put, without Bond, there is no obviously navigable economic path that takes the sector through to next spring. Or as one executive at a boutique cinema chain texted me this evening: "We are f—." ' Logically, the idea that Bond alone was responsible for the survival of cinema itself was ridiculous, but the way multiple journalists leaped at this explanation is revealing. Deep down, we all recognise that Bond is death.

As the eventual launch of *No Time to Die* approached, there were many who predicted disaster. The film's budget was believed to be somewhere between $250–300m, and the added costs from the aborted Danny Boyle version, interest payments during the pandemic, and marketing costs in the run-up to previous aborted launches meant that it would need to take two or three times that budget to break even. It did not help that the film was 2 hours and 43 minutes long. Cinemas cannot schedule as many showings for films of that length, and many casual viewers are put off by long movies. Then there was the issue that the Bond audience skewed older than most blockbusters, and it was this older cinema-going public who were proving most hesitant in returning. The general lack of enthusiasm for the previous film *Spectre* did not help matters either.

On top of all this, from a global and international perspective, there was also the matter of Britain's reputation. Englishness had always been a prominent part of the Bond cocktail, and the films had promoted the image of Bond as the avatar of a level-headed, competent and fair country doing its plucky best in the name of the greater good. Brexit had done a great deal of harm to how the rest of the world viewed Britain, however. At the same time that the film finally arrived in cinemas, at the end of September 2021, international newspapers were full of stories about empty shelves in British supermarkets along with panic buying and long queues and fuel shortages at petrol stations. Social media in Europe was full of clips of fights breaking out at the forecourts of British petrol stations, as frustrations about empty pumps boiled over and motorists began attacking each other. Out-of-context footage like this gave the impression of a society close to the point of collapse, and to an overseas audience it was clear what the cause was. Reports that raw sewage was now being dumped into rivers in industrial quantities furthered the impression that the country was falling apart. That British politicians and the press kept insisting that these problems were solely down to Covid-related global supply problems and had nothing to do with Brexit was something that international journalists reported with some amusement.

There was an undeniable air of *schadenfreude* to the international news coverage, as commentators struggled to understand how a country historically seen as sensible and reliable had voluntarily hurt itself to this degree. The cover story of the 17 June 2019 edition of *TIME* magazine, for example, was 'How Britain Went Bonkers'. At the COP26 UN Climate Change Conference in Glasgow shortly after *No Time to Die* was released, Prime Minister Boris Johnson stood in front of the world and made a rambling and often incoherent speech about how the delegates were James Bond, and climate change was like a bomb in a James Bond movie. Whatever charm Johnson may possess in the eyes of the British electorate is often quite invisible to overseas observers, and his speech did not inspire confidence in the UK. That the British people had chosen to elect a man like Johnson made many around the world reassess their opinion of the country. In these circumstances, the idea that a British spy could be relied on to win through against terrible odds suddenly became something of a hard sell. The reputation of Britain was such that Rowan Atkinson's spoof spy Johnny English was now seen as far more realistic than James Bond.

For these reasons, there were many who predicted that *No Time to Die* would be the first Bond film to flop, and actually lose money. Bond's status as the most successful movie character in history was at stake. There are multi-character franchises that have made more money than Bond – most noticeably *Star Wars* and the Marvel Cinematic Universe – but in terms of a single hero who was the focus of the film, Bond was still then number one. But Spider-Man was closing in on Bond's heels. Like Bond movies and Beatle records, Spider-Man was born in 1962, which makes him their peer – or perhaps rival. If *No Time to Die* flopped, and Marvel kept producing Spider-Man movies at the rate they had been doing, Bond looked like he would soon be surrendering his crown as the king of cinematic characters.

A couple of days before *No Time to Die* was released, a magnificent white stag appeared from nowhere and ran through the streets of Liverpool. The stag appeared in the suburb of Bootle, where in the 1950s John, Paul and George used to caddy at the municipal golf course in order to make money to buy instruments. In Celtic folklore, a white stag was seen as a messenger from the otherworld, and to encounter one was a sign of profound change. In Arthurian mythology, the white stag could be pursued but never caught. It represented the never-ending quest for spiritual knowledge. That a white stag should suddenly appear in Liverpool of all places seemed wildly incongruous, and yet also entirely right. Folklorists were horrified, then, when Liverpool Police reacted to the white stag in their streets by shooting it dead. All this was the backdrop to the opening of *No Time to Die*, when cinema goers returned to theatres after a harrowing year expecting to see the always reliable James Bond triumph. Instead, at the end of the film, they watched James Bond die.

For older white males in particular, struggling to understand their place in the twenty-first century, this could only feel deeply ominous. The one fictional character they could rely on, who had been a constant presence throughout their lives, who faced the world as a representation of the vitality and spirit that still lingered in their ancient country, fell in the course of duty just like the white stag of Liverpool. When death himself dies, we are in uncharted territory.

At the start of the film Bond was retired. The codename 007 was now used by a Black female assassin called Nomi. She was confident and capable, although not as fully fleshed out a character as James Bond – the writers didn't even give her a surname. Throughout the film, Bond was openly mocked for the same character traits that had previously been celebrated. Society had changed radically in James Bond's lifetime, and all this was firmly in sync with the current zeitgeist. One reading of the film was that a violent white male like Bond was now redundant in the twenty-first century and had to be put out of his misery. And yet, as unsettling as this was for his long-term audience, Bond's death also felt right in some strange and hard-to-define way. It felt somehow necessary – less of an end and more of a difficult step forward.

In his very first book, Fleming established the trope that after Bond touches women, they die. This was quickly identified as being toxic, and there followed many claims over the decades that the problem was being addressed. Frequently, this meant that the portrayal of women in Bond films was changed to be more powerful or assertive. But the problem, as Gemma Arterton recognised, was that it was not the women who needed to change. The problem was Bond himself. This was the uncomfortable truth that, in the plot of his last film, the Daniel Craig iteration of James Bond finally tackled.

The storyline involved invisible nanobots that were programmed with specific people's DNA so that they would kill that particular person, and that person only. This was a convoluted piece of technobabble easily as absurd as Pierce Brosnan's invisible car, but it served a significant plot function. The story made it explicit that if James was to ever again touch Madeleine Swann, the woman he loved, then she would die. So too would Mathilde, the remarkably well-behaved five-year-old daughter the couple had had together in the years since the previous movie.

This fundamental aspect of Bond – that the women he touches die – had finally been expressed at the level of story. This was significant, because this is the one place where the character of Bond would finally encounter it himself. In this way, Bond was forced by the plot to confront and ultimately accept his toxic nature. His spectre had been brought into the light of understanding. There really was only one way that he could react. He had to sacrifice himself to allow Madeleine and Mathilde to live. The only way that Bond could be a true hero, now he understood who he was, was to annihilate himself in a Royal Navy missile attack.

This was transformational storytelling on a scale no art-house film could hope to match. For sixty years, Bond had marched onwards while those who gave him life fell. He outlived Ian Fleming, Sean Connery and the producers Harry Saltzman and Cubby Broccoli. He persisted as regimes collapsed at the studios of United Artists, MGM and Sony. He grew and evolved over decades in a way that makes it hard for us to define the difference between a work of fiction and something living. James Bond survived in a way that was unprecedented and frankly implausible.

Bond was not an allegory about Britain's imperial spirit, as some have claimed. An allegory is a story with a specific interpretation that comes from the author himself. Bond was a myth, and a myth is endlessly mutable. It can be understood in different and often contradictory ways, always adapting to the changes in society with little concern for canon or established lore. Nothing is more adaptable and capable of survival as a myth. But, as Putin knew, empires fall from within. The only thing that could stop Bond was for him to become self-aware, and sacrifice himself.

The Bond franchise had brought the positive and negative aspects of masculinity, and their seemingly unbreakable marriage, into the light of global attention. This took a long time to process, but that is the speed that profound societal-level change tends to work. Daniel Craig's Bond was always moving towards a modern version of masculinity, embracing age-appropriate relationships and casually hinting at homosexual experiences. Bond did not lead or help bring about social changes in the way that the Beatles might have done, of course, but he did reflect and follow them. He was most explicitly presented as a feminist ally in the 2011 short film *James Bond Supports International Women's Day*, directed by Sam Taylor-Johnson shortly after she finished her John Lennon biopic *Nowhere Boy*. Lennon, of course, was another man who came to understand his own capacity for violence against woman, and who went to extreme lengths to try and escape that aspect of his personality. In this short film, which was narrated by Judi Dench as M, Craig's silent Bond appears first dressed in his usual sharply tailored suit, and then in women's clothes. Craig didn't look hugely comfortable, admittedly, but he did it to help make a wider point about how far we still are from gender equality in the workplace.

Craig's desire to move to a more 21st-century version of Bond was a challenge to more reactionary-minded fans. Many were troubled when he wore a cerise or pink velvet jacket to the *No Time to Die* premiere. The *Evening Standard's* headline was 'The world wasn't ready for Daniel Craig's pink suit at Bond premiere', while the *Telegraph* called his jacket 'controversial'. In the eyes of the *Daily Mail*, the repurposed word 'woke' wasn't sufficient to describe Craig's Bond. Instead, they coined a new, more extreme term: 'Superwoke'.

The issue at the heart of these reactions was one of power. Was Craig's Bond being belittled by wearing pink and sacrificing his life for a woman, or was he growing? For the reactionary and those who find change difficult, supporting the current power status is their default position, because this is how you support the status quo. In this context, the idea of gender equality is not perceived as a victory for women, but a defeat for men. Any sense that a change in masculinity could be positive, and that male identity could be improved by this new scenario, is absent. But as the writer Finn Mackay has noted, 'Masculinity, to put it simply, is whatever is considered appropriate and expected for men in your circle. It is a set of learned behaviours, easily taught and adopted. Acknowledging that these behaviours are learned is not the same as saying they aren't real, or that they don't have real effects, or that they don't form important parts of people's sense of self or identity from a very early age.' From this perspective, to deny the value of masculinity is as wrong as insisting that it is a fixed, unchanging thing.

The American agnostic writer Robert Anton Wilson used to use the terms *neophilia* and *neophobic* to describe our possible attitudes to change. On a societal level, neophilia was a love of the new, which drove our attempts to make the world a better place. The Beatles were a classic example of a group of neophiliacs. Neophobia, in contrast, was a fear of the new based on the grounds that society was fragile and that too much change too quickly could cause collapse. The ongoing struggle between the two outlooks didn't result in a stalemate, but it did mean that when change happened it occurred at a much slower rate than neophiliacs would like. Frequently, change was generational. Often the media's coverage of neophobic reaction can give the impression that change is not happening, or that we are even going backwards, when that is not the case. The long, slow acceptance of feminism into the fictional world of James Bond is as good an example of this as any. 'Bond's been evolving along with all the other men in the world,' remarked

Barbara Broccoli in 2020, 'Some have just gotten there more quickly than others.'

No Time to Die turned out to be a huge hit, of course. Despite the pandemic and other concerns, it took over $770m at the box office, making it the most successful Western film since the pandemic began, ahead of *Fast & Furious 9* and far in advance of other blockbusters like *Black Widow*, *Shang-Chi* and *Dune*. Even with the pandemic, it took more money than all other Bond films except for *Skyfall* and *Spectre*. MGM went to the unusual lengths of issuing a statement after unnamed 'industry insiders' in the press claimed that they still lost money on the film. 'Unnamed and uninformed sources suggesting the film will lose money are categorically unfounded and put more simply, not true,' they said. 'The film has far exceeded our theatrical estimates in this timeframe [...] *No Time to Die* will earn a profit for MGM, both as an individual film title and as part of MGM's incredible library.' When the cinema industry needed a hero to save it, James Bond was there for it, as tradition dictates.

2021: RINGO AND PAUL

When the *Daily Mail* needed a headline to sum up what was most important about the 2021 Grammy Awards, they ran with 'Ringo Starr, 80, looks incredibly youthful as he makes surprise appearance at Grammys to present Record of the Year.' This was perhaps a little disrespectful to the great and the good of the contemporary American music scene, who the awards were attempting to honour. Yet at the same time, the *Mail* had a point. Ringo did look great. 'The legendary drummer looked fabulous with his dyed dark hair and neatly trimmed beard,' the report tells us. There are not many eighty-year-olds who can still get away with dying their hair and beard black. Looking thin, toned and healthy at the glitzy Los Angeles celebrity awards, Ringo had come a long way from the sickly, poverty-stricken Liverpudlian boy who was abandoned by his father and not expected to live to adulthood.

Ringo's appearance was to present the final award, the prestigious Record of the Year. This was won by nineteen-year-old Billie Eilish and her co-writer brother Finneas O'Connell for their song 'Everything I Wanted'. According to the article, the pair 'seemed a little overcome to be on stage with the legendary rock star'. This was not surprising, for Eilish and O'Connell are huge Beatles fan who repeatedly reference them in their work. Eilish wore *Yellow Submarine* branded Beatles clothing for her performance at the 2019 Glastonbury Festival, when she was still only seventeen, and has covered several of their songs including 'Yesterday' and 'Something'. The first song she learned to play was 'I Will' from the *White Album*, when she was about six years old. Billie and Finneas's mother Maggie Baird has said, 'It was actually the Beatles who taught them to write songs.' The importance of the band to this Gen Z megastar illustrates how the Beatles have crossed over to new generations to an extent that no other bands of their era can match.

While Billie and Finneas's interest in the Beatles is not unusual for their age, their love of James Bond perhaps is. The Record of the Year award was the second Grammy that they took home that night. The first was for their Bond theme 'No Time to Die'. Eilish, by some distance the youngest singer of a Bond theme, had actively pursued the Bond gig. 'We have always wanted to do a Bond song. That's a thing that we've always thought about and fantasized about,' Finneas has said. 'At the time it was like, "Are they making another one? Are they going to make another one in a couple years? Let us know who we could tell that we'd love to do that and just make that known." ' Billie Eilish is 'one of the planet's biggest pop stars', according to the *New York Times*, and 'a strong contender for the voice of her generation', in the view of the *Guardian*. When a contemporary artist of that stature takes home two Grammys linked to James Bond and Ringo Starr, it's hard not to marvel at how those two sixty-year-old cultural phenomena continue to remain relevant, and also strangely linked. Eilish would win an Oscar for her Bond theme the following year.

At eighty, Ringo appears as vibrant and active as ever. He continues to write and record, releasing the EP *Change the World* in 2021. There is no pretence that Ringo is a singer or songwriter on a par with John, Paul or George, of course, and no one expects his music to bother the charts. He is already richer and more famous than he could ever have dreamed of. He is simply making music because that is what he loves doing, with no expectation of having a hit. He is, clearly, enjoying his elder years, and it is good to see him so happy and healthy. Meditation and a vegetarian diet, it seems, worked well for him in the long run.

This is especially striking when you look back at footage and photos of him from the 1970s and 1980s, at the height of his problems with drugs and alcohol. Few would have predicted headlines about his youthful appearance in old age back then. Ringo has always credited his second wife, the Russian spy Bond Girl Barbara Bach, with turning his life around and moving him from a self-destructive path to a positive one. For Ringo, Barbara truly was *The Spy Who Loved Me*.

It is rare for anyone to win life's lottery as thoroughly as Sir Ringo Starr has, and even rarer for someone to be in such a privileged position to have so little ill-will aimed at them. Who could begrudge him even a fraction of what he has? This is Ringo we're talking about. If anyone deserves to win life's lottery, it should be someone like him.

In a similar way, life has been good to Sir Paul McCartney. He still has his armour of ordinariness around him, which he uses to protect his self and his sanity from his iconic, legendary stature. He does this by continually presenting as someone domestic, normal and everyday. It's possible to imagine Paul McCartney cooking eggs in your kitchen in a way that you could never imagine Kanye West, Madonna or Mick Jagger. Even his body of work, the cause of his immense fame, doesn't prevent him from losing his grounding. If anyone else had written the list of songs that he has, we would be awestruck about their achievement. But those songs feel like ours, rather than his. They feel like they have always existed and are simply a part of the natural world.

McCartney has not changed his beliefs or his behaviour since he was a critical joke in the 1980s, yet he is now increasingly seen as a national treasure whose fame eclipses that of Hollywood stars, contemporary musicians and even royalty. To the young, the idea that older people once thought of him as a bit of a joke can seem baffling. His commercial success continues. His album *McCartney III* went to number one in the UK album charts on Christmas Day 2020, and number two on the US Billboard chart. His autobiographical book *The Lyrics* was both Waterstones' and Barnes & Noble's Book of the Year in 2021. At the time of writing, McCartney is scheduled to play the 2022 Glastonbury Festival – not in the Sunday afternoon 'legends' slot, which is where much-loved older artists such as Lionel Richie, Shirley Bassey, Neil Diamond or Dolly Parton usually play, but headlining the Pyramid Stage on Saturday night, the most prestigious gig in the British music industry. Usually, only bands at the height of their career can hope to be booked here. For someone who will be eighty years old, and who has been gigging continuously for over sixty years, to be offered that slot shows a level of sustained success without precedent. Billie Eilish, meanwhile, is due to headline that stage on the Friday night, meaning that we should get two Bond themes, 'Live and Let Die' and 'No Time to Die', from the 2022 Glastonbury headliners.

Throughout all this, McCartney appears remarkably unaffected, with little of the preciousness so common with other stars of his stature. Train passengers in Sussex, for example, will sometimes see him on the train up to London, sat by himself without security guards. If you look at promotional photographs of him taken across his career, they are rarely by top celebrity photographers but instead are often taken by members of his family – particularly his brother Mike, first wife Linda or daughter Mary. When you see photos of him at home it is usually in a messy, cluttered, cosy kitchen far removed from the gleaming luxury mansions where celebrities of his wealth are supposed to be found. Speaking with Taylor Swift for *Rolling Stone* magazine – another example of how huge young stars are eager to embrace him – McCartney admitted, 'I don't live fancy. I really don't. Sometimes it's a little bit of an embarrassment, if I've got someone coming to visit me [...] Quincy Jones came to see me and I'm, like, making him a veggie burger or something [...] I'm very consciously thinking, Oh, God, Quincy's got to be thinking, "What is this guy on? He hasn't got big things going on. It's not a fancy house at all. And we're eating in the kitchen! He's not even got the dining room going." ' As he concluded, 'Maybe I should have, like, a big stately home. Maybe I should get a staff. But I think I couldn't do that. I'd be so embarrassed.' McCartney does enjoy fame and wealth, but he is aware that aspects of it can turn you into a monster.

From the seventies onwards, and especially after Lennon's murder, male music writers who tackled the Beatles wrote about the Lennon and McCartney relationship primarily from the perspective of competition. Although they were two ambitious men and their efforts to keep up with the achievements of the other helped them produce their greatest work, there was more to their relationship than competition. People have started to address this issue now, for example in podcasts like *Another Kind of Mind* and *One Sweet Dream*, or in the work of the writer Ian Leslie, who all analyse the couple as a love story. This is generating far more insight into the Beatles story than earlier arguments about who was best. Now that we are moving away from thinking of McCartney simply in terms of competition, our appreciation of him has grown massively. It's also an approach that is more in sync with the younger side of Beatles fandom, if the thousands of works of Lennon and McCartney slash fiction on websites like archiveofourown.org are any guide.

To the emerging generation, the values of home, family and love that Paul espoused from his first solo album onwards, which used to make him a laughing-stock in the eyes of critics, now seem wise, relatable and contemporary. To a generation that looks at the lionised libertine rock stars of yesteryear and mocks them as posturing 'edgelords', Paul McCartney is someone truly impressive. The wider culture has finally caught up with him, and the values that he stood by through thick and thin now seem admirable. A large part of this is thanks to his and Linda's promotion of animal rights and a vegetarian diet during decades when it was the subject of a great deal of ridicule. The establishing of the Linda McCartney Foods range of plant-based foods, at a time when vegetarian choices were far rarer than we are used to now, helped many move away from meat-based diets. Now that climate concerns have created a huge rise in veganism, the McCartneys once again look ahead of the curve. Indeed, for all the cultural changes associated with the Beatles, it may well be in the long run that the most important, on a practical level, could turn out to be because of Linda. Rather brilliantly, she established a factory for her vegetarian food company in the Norfolk town of Fakenham.

As they move into their eighties, Paul and Ringo appear at peace with themselves and their histories. For many, they are familiar, comfortable faces in the media landscape who have somehow managed not to be overwhelmed by the legacy of the Beatles. But that legacy, which was once such a threat to the establishment, has now been safely neutralised. They have both kneeled before the Queen to receive their knighthoods, and the Beatles story is now something that the government is eager to promote. During the 2021 budget Nadine Dorries, the Secretary of State for Digital, Culture, Media and Sport, tweeted a specially prepared budget-branded graphic which used the *Yellow Submarine* font and images from the film. 'Oh! Darling,' she wrote, 'The government has Come Together to invest £2 million into a major new Beatles attraction. With a Little Help from My Friends at @hmtreasury and taxpayers support, we're getting the waterfront development in Liverpool going. That's something to Twist and Shout about.'

For many, this seemed unnecessary. Liverpool already boasts a major Beatles museum in the Albert Dock, a more grassroots Beatles museum in Mathew Street, a rebuilt Cavern club, a Magical Mystery Tour coach attraction, the Hard Day's Night Hotel and National Trust tours of John and Paul's childhood homes. Andy Edwards's statue of the Fab Four in front of the Liver Building is believed to be the most photographed statue in the UK, and the University of Liverpool offers a master's degree called 'The Beatles: Music Industry and Heritage'. The tourist appeal of the Beatles to Liverpool is in no way being ignored, but this wasn't the main reason why the reaction to this announcement among musicians was overwhelmingly critical. They had faced the perfect storm of Covid-cancelled tours, the collapse of physical sales through streaming, Brexit-related difficulties preventing touring Europe, and the closure of many inner-city live venues. The grass-roots music scene was in dire need of help, but all the government was doing was spending millions to help celebrate a band that split up fifty years earlier. It saw British music as part of the heritage industry, not as a living, vibrant expression of contemporary culture. In this, the government is in sync with a music industry that is increasingly focused on exploiting old music, rather than nurturing and promoting new artists. In 2021, for example, 70 per cent of American music consumption was 'catalogue' music, which is defined as music over eighteen months old. That was a 5 per cent increase on the previous year.

The output of the Beatles is now focused on regular box-set

releases which cost over £100 each. One fiftieth-anniversary edition of George Harrison's *All Things Must Pass* came in a wooden crate containing garden gnomes and cost £850. Official John Lennon jumpers from the fashion brand Pretty Green with the slogan 'Working Class Hero' can now be bought for £120 each, presumably by the lower-middle classes. Even a book of Paul McCartney's lyrics had a RRP of £75. There is clearly a market for these things, but we are a long way from the cheap, affordable and democratic nature of the early Beatles singles. Is this, then, the fate of the Beatles – to simply be a heritage industry money-making machine?

It may be that what they created cannot be bottled quite that easily. In Kurt Vonnegut's *Timequake,* he wrote, 'I say in speeches that a plausible mission of artists is to make people appreciate being alive at least a little bit. I am then asked if I know of any artists who pulled that off. I reply, "The Beatles did." ' This is a rare gift that we will always be drawn to.

One day, Paul and Ringo will no longer be with us. The death of David Bowie in 2016 might give us an insight into how the public attitude to them will then change. Bowie's reputation, like that of the surviving Beatles, was primarily based on the work he produced in his early career. While there was a loyal fan base that appreciated and championed his later work, it did not generate the same level of excitement in the wider culture as Bowie had initially, once the hits stopped coming. It was, at this point, easy to take him for granted – a figure that was always there to some extent, welcome but not essential. After he died, three days after the release of his extraordinary album *Blackstar*, the scale of the wave of grief and adulation that followed took many by surprise. It brought the focus on to just how good his initial run of work was, and how important and valuable it was in our lives. On that wave of grief, Bowie was firmly catapulted into the pantheon of true musical visionaries and icons, far above the criticisms of the journalists who dismissed him for decades.

When Ringo and Paul finally die – hopefully many years from now – there is likely to be a similar reckoning. At this point, how much their music meant to people will be clear. Radio and streaming playlists will be dominated by Beatles songs. Younger generations will be exposed to the deeper cuts of their body of work, and many who had taken them for granted will experience that Bowie-style moment of clarity when they recognise just how extraordinary they were. At this point Paul's armour of ordinariness will fall away. We will then finally grasp just how important the Beatles were, and are, as a symbol of love, and the bringers of joy.

As Paul McCartney was about to leave a 2004 interview for *Uncut* magazine, he was asked one final question: was he as in thrall to the Beatles as everyone else? Of course, he replied. 'The Beatles are probably as mysterious and wonderful to me as they are to everyone else. Probably more so. The mystery and the wonder and the magic of it just go on and on. It never stops. Great, isn't it?'

2022: JAMES BOND WILL RETURN

At the end of the credits of most Bond films is the phrase 'James Bond will return'. This has become something of a tradition in itself. Fans find it pleasing, perhaps comforting, and keep watching through the credits in order to see it.

Those fans who saw *No Time to Die* as soon as it opened, or who had managed to avoid spoilers, sat in shock through the end credits, in the aftermath of the death of their undefeatable hero. They did not know if the phrase would appear. For fans of the character of Bond, the words 'James Bond will return' had never been more welcome than when they finally appeared at the end of *No Time to Die*.

But how, exactly, would James Bond return, now that he is dead? Audiences are used to characters being recast. It's happened regularly in the Bond franchise since 1969. It was understood that, although the character on screen looked, spoke and acted differently to when you last saw him, you were supposed to accept them as the same person regardless. Six actors have been James Bond over the years, and Felix Leiter has been played on screen by eight different people. The films repeatedly implied that all these actors portrayed the same character, even when this didn't make sense in terms of Bond's age, or the passing of the decades. Pierce Brosnan examined Q's gadgets from the Sean Connery and Roger Moore eras, for example, while Roger Moore stood by the grave of George Lazenby's wife and Daniel Craig drove a car that belonged to Timothy Dalton. The spell of Bond was such that we happily accepted this.

Seeing Bond die, followed by the words 'James Bond will return', was not a scenario that cinema fans had encountered before. What it meant was not immediately clear. Being recast is one thing, but being recast after characters have been unequivocally killed is quite another. When characters like Marvel's Tony Stark dies, they are not then advertised as returning in the next film. This was different to reboots in which there is suddenly a new Batman or Superman. This seemed closer to the way Doctor Who regenerates. Online jokers mockingly compared it to the resurrection of Jesus.

There is a precedent for what *No Time to Die* did, however, but we have to go back much further into history than the world of franchise cinema. It is an example of what the academic Rogan P. Taylor called 'The Death and Resurrection Show'. Taylor traced the origins of showbiz, and popular entertainment in general, back through time. He went back beyond medicine shows and ancient Greek theatre and found that they originated with the witchdoctors and shamans of nomadic north European tribes. The shaman had the job of maintaining the story of the tribe and protecting his or her people from disease and illness. They did this in the form of a show or performance for their people, who gathered in a dark, smoky tent to watch their shaman re-enact their initiation into the underworld. Here, Taylor argued, are the roots of our modern entertainment industry. Here the tribe would watch the shaman die and be reborn.

There was a point to this. The underworld was a terrifying place of demons and the dead, but the shaman had no choice but to go there because it was also the place where cures for illnesses could be found. To learn those cures required the shaman to symbolically die in the underworld, usually by having their bodies ripped to pieces. The skill of the shaman was to be then reborn, complete with the knowledge of the cure that they had sought. In the shaman's public performances which re-enact this ritual we find the origins of many art forms, including circus skills, stage magic and drama – and also the origins of the narratives underpinning many religions, not least in the death and resurrection of Jesus.

Many centuries later, the central motif of the death and resurrection show – being reborn after being annihilated in the underworld – can still be glimpsed in the evolution of popular entertainment, long after this had become divorced from its original ecstatic element. It can be seen in the importance of the 'hell mouth' in medieval theatre, for example, which is the gateway to the underworld. It was the reason why deaths in Greek theatre had to occur offstage. It still lingers in conjuring tricks such as sawing a lady in half. It is as if the idea of the Death and Resurrection Show is buried deep in our psyches, and we can never quite shake it off.

The ecstatic and healing roots of modern showbiz, in this context, can help explain the mania that surrounded otherworldly celebrities such as David Bowie. The audience recognise that they are not there to simply be passively entertained. They are there to be taken out of their normal lives and, in some way, changed. This is why sick people were taken to Beatles concerts, in the hope they would be cured. This horrified John Lennon in particular, but on one level there was a sort of sense to it. The music of the Beatles affected people on a level far beyond that of simple mindless entertainment; it added something profound to people's lives.

As such, the role it played in our society was not unlike that of the ancient shamans.

Shortly before he died, John Lennon was asked about the possibility of the Beatles reforming. He replied, 'If they didn't understand the Beatles and the sixties then, what the fuck could we do for them now? Do we have to divide the fishes and the loaves for the multitudes again? Do we have to walk on water again because a whole pile of dummies didn't see it the first time, or didn't believe it when they saw?' This answer went far beyond Lennon's infamous earlier remark that the Beatles were bigger than Jesus. As Taylor writes, 'With such an answer there can be little doubt about the sacred and magical context in which Lennon saw his life unfold.'

In *No Time to Die*, the annihilation of James Bond's body in a hellish toxic poison-manufacturing bunker, only for him to then be reborn, was far from the standard scenario of movie franchise reboots. Given that Bond had become aware that his touch kills women and was attempting to find a cure, it works as a re-enactment of the original shamanic death and resurrection show. This suggests that the reborn Bond will be cured of his ailment – that when he returns, he will be wiser and possess the knowledge that he previously lacked.

Given the huge success of *No Time to Die*, there is no doubt that another Bond film will be with us soon – especially after the takeover of MGM by Amazon studios. Whatever direction the producers take, and exactly what this reborn Bond will be like, will be controversial. People are vocal about their opinions, and the level of hate aimed at Daniel Craig for being blond could well be dwarfed by the online arguments that will greet his successor. Barbara Broccoli has repeatedly said that Bond could be any ethnicity, but he has to be male. In the early twenty-first century, this should be uncontroversial. If the part is well cast, modern cinema goers seem as if they will accept Bond as any ethnicity.

Perhaps more controversially, if we assume the chosen actor will be in their early to mid-thirties, then we will be looking at the first millennial Bond. Such a generational leap will unavoidably change the character in interesting ways. When the films moved away from the CG-heavy Marvel-like cartoony action of *Die Another Day* to the more grounded brutal sophistication of the Daniel Craig years, it led to huge success. It did, however, change the demographic makeup of the Bond audience. Teenagers, who had always been a key part of the audience, dropped away. A 2021 survey organised by the cinema chain Showcase found that, with 24 per cent of the vote, 007 was the nation's favourite screen hero. Bond comfortably beat the likes of Superman, Harry Potter or Indiana Jones. But the vote differed significantly according to age. For the oldest category, 65 and over, Bond received 33 per cent of the vote, while 32 per cent in the 55–64 category also put Bond first. In the 25–34 category, however, he received only 14 per cent of the vote, and just 11 per cent of the 18–24s. For Generation Z, Daniel Craig's Bond had strong 'Dad energy', which makes the thought of him as a romantic leading man quite horrific. This is a generation that are only likely to engage with a significantly younger Bond.

In the 2020s, it is clear that the younger generation are not invested in the adventures of James Bond. It used to be that watching old Bond films on Bank Holidays was an unavoidable part of childhood, allowing Bond to continually build new young audiences. This generation have their own screens, however, and are more likely to be in their bedrooms consuming their own media than joining the family around the television. Watching Bond as a father–son activity has ended. Neither has there been another generational jumping-on point, like the Nintendo *GoldenEye 007* video game that made Bond culturally relevant in the 1990s.

When Generation Z mention James Bond, it is often as something to define themselves against. There is a healthy ecosystem of politically progressive podcasters and YouTubers for whom James Bond encapsulates everything they are against. 'Hatewatching' media aimed at successful franchises is common, but this is a subtly different phenomenon to the anti-*Star Trek*, *Doctor Who* or *Star Wars* YouTube channels. Those are usually fronted by ex-fans, who argue that the franchises used to be good but are now being ruined by current executives and showrunners. Anti-Bond media, in contrast, never liked Bond and are horrified that it ever existed. A good example is the *Kill James Bond!* podcast, who refer to Bond as 'British Tuxedo Dickhead'. Their response to *No Time to Die* acknowledged the quality of the cast, designers and director, but concluded that 'the problem is encapsulated in the first two credits of the opening titles – "Albert R. Broccoli's EON Productions presents: Ian Fleming's James Bond 007". The film is a vindication of the *Kill James Bond!* Maxim, which is that you simply cannot make a good Bond movie. It's a contradiction in terms. No matter what you do, if you make it recognisably Bond it will still have the nugget of the racists who invented and popularised him.' Here we are a long way from the *Daily Mail*'s condemnation of *No Time to Die* on the grounds that it was 'Superwoke'.

Generation Z, in general, are deeply unimpressed by the attitudes of their elders. The media their parents and grandparents enjoy, as a result, is treated with great scepticism. It usually contains attitudes that, they believe, belong in the dustbin of history. This is a major problem for Bond. A long-running franchise must attract new generations of fans if it is to continue.

It is possible for twentieth-century franchises to pivot into ones that make sense to an audience raised in the twenty-first century.

When *Star Wars* opened in 1977, for example, the principal cast was entirely white and male, except for Carrie Fisher. It was also concerned with an individual rebelling against an evil parent – Darth Vader was literally the 'dark father' of Jungian psychology. This was a story perfectly in tune with twentieth-century individualism. Now that the franchise is owned by Disney, the cast of new *Star Wars* movies or television series are always reliably diverse. Perhaps more significantly, the plots of current *Star Wars* series like *The Mandalorian* or *The Bad Batch* are about male characters who find themselves taking care of infants and who then strive to become the 'good father' archetype. These stories are diametrically opposed to those the original *Star Wars* told. They have, however, allowed the franchise to make the leap from appealing to twentieth-century individualists to telling stories relevant to the post-individuals of our current time. This is a reminder that such a leap is possible. But not, necessarily, for all characters.

When Sean Connery declined to make any more Bond films, Cubby Broccoli insisted in press interviews that James Bond was a classic character who could be portrayed by many different actors. The examples of similar classic characters he gave were Sherlock Holmes and Tarzan – icons who, like James Bond, lived on beyond individual performances, and who could be endlessly reinvented. While this is still true for Sherlock Holmes, it is noticeably not the case for Tarzan, who is no longer an ongoing media property. The essential nature of the Tarzan character – that an aristocratic white child would become king of the jungle if they were abandoned in Africa – is the product of attitudes our culture now rejects. The Harry Potter director David Yates attempted to restart the franchise with his 2016 film *The Legend of Tarzan*, which included a plot with a strong anti-slavery element and significant roles for African or African American actors such as Samuel L. Jackson and Djimon Hounsou. It was not enough to resuscitate the character, however.

The very essence of Tarzan now looks to us to be fundamentally racist and there seems little chance that such a character could be rebooted in a way that would attract a 21st-century audience. Could this be the fate of James Bond? Could imperialism and misogyny be, as *Kill James Bond!* maintain, so ingrained in his character that he can never be redeemed? Is his fate a relaunch that plays out to an ageing and dwindling audience before he is slowly forgotten?

Such a fate would be out of character. Bond, as we have seen, is death, and therefore the one character who cannot die. Or perhaps we should now say, one who cannot die for long. He is also tradition, and the establishment's ability to 'keep buggering on' is a strong one. But perhaps more importantly, he is a mythic avatar of male fantasy. This element of Bond's makeup is continually changing, and it is these changes which have kept him alive over the past half-century. Men will always need a vision of who they want to be. It inspires them to keep striving to become better than they are. Bond does not represent what men should be, or could be, or need to be. He is instead what some men want to be. He is pure fantasy, and unashamedly so. This makes him ideologically and morally impossible to defend, but also inhuman to deny. Our fantasies may reflect badly on us when they are exposed to the cold light of day, but we still need to explore them, if we are ever to improve them.

The evolution of the character over the years has traced the changes in how men see themselves and their roles in the world, making the films a useful archaeological record of how the attitudes of society have radically shifted over the past half-century. The character as portrayed by Connery, and written by Fleming, showed us how men wanted to be in the pre-Beatle world. We are in the post-Beatle world now. If Bond is to remain successful when he returns, he will have to be in sync with how men today aspire to be. But what, exactly, is a contemporary male aspirational fantasy?

Certain aspects of Bond's historical persona, it is clear, will have no part in this. The next Bond will have an understanding of consent and coercive behaviour that some of his earlier portrayals lacked. Women he touches will no longer die, assuming his trip to the underworld and his death and resurrection show was a success. His relationships may also be more age-appropriate. Bond will still, however, be desired and attractive, and attracted to beautiful people, because that aspect of men has not changed. The typical modern man understands that navigating these territories is more complex now than it was in the late twentieth century. The fantasy is not to go back to how things were but to be good at navigating how things are now. The dream is to do the right thing, and to find that easy. The new Bond, then, should handle current sexual politics effortlessly.

There are aspects of Fleming's Bond that it is time to jettison. In 2021, Changing Faces, the visible difference and disfigurement charity, launched a campaign called I Am Not Your Villain to highlight the extent to which Hollywood uses scars, burns, marks or other facial differences to denote evil. *No Time to Die* was particularly guilty of this, they pointed out, because it had not one but two facially different villains. This was a common trope in Fleming's writings, who frequently used scars, disabilities or physical differences to denote villainy. By the end of the novels it was becoming increasingly absurd – Scaramanga had a third nipple, and Blofeld had no earlobes. This seems like an easy aspect of Bond lore to drop.

Something else that looks increasingly suspect is the double-O programme itself, and Bond's licence to kill. In the aftermath of the Second World War, the notion that the intelligence services needed assassins who could work around the world seemed reasonable, but after seventy years of relative peace that is no longer the case. When governments do authorise murder, such as the Russian poisoning of Sergei and Yulia Skripal in Salisbury, the public reaction is now one of horror. The idea that the British government has the right to kill people is not shared by many, and it gives the Bond franchise an imperialist edge. According to Sir Richard Dearlove, the former head of MI6, 'Assassination is no part of the policy of Her Majesty's Government.' That said, Section 7 of the 1994 Intelligence Services Act allows for agents to commit crimes, presumably including murder, if their actions have been authorised in writing by a secretary of state beforehand. Bond will continue to kill for Britain, of course – the laws of action cinema demand it – but it would perhaps be better to engage more realistically with what this means, and how a perhaps clandestine double-O programme would be regarded by the rest of the intelligence services.

While it is easy to point out what a reborn Bond franchise should move away from, it is more challenging to define where it should go. Here we come back to the idea that Bond needs to be what contemporary men want to be. A definition of what it means to be a modern man living a good life is not something that culture currently gives a lot of thought to.

It goes without saying that Bond's mastery of the material world would remain part of the fantasy, along with his ability to always win. A reborn Bond should also be able to enjoy himself. Daniel Craig's Bond at times made being male look thoroughly miserable. Relationships were stories of deceit and betrayal, and trust and love were out of the question. Being a man, surely, does not have to be this bleak, especially in our fantasies. Bond's licence to kill is a dark liberation, an excuse to ignore the bonds of social expectations and let your inner id loose. It is when we are truly free that we honestly engage with the question of what it is that we want. The desire to behave without restrictions like this helps explain the success of the *Grand Theft Auto* series of video games, which have sold an extraordinary 350,000,000 copies. For all the angst of Daniel Craig and Timothy Dalton, deep down we want to be Bond because we believe the freedom this brings would be fun. This is something that Roger Moore understood.

It helps that 007 was not a treasure hunter and was not driven by a desire for money. When Bond was offered money by his new father-in-law in *On Her Majesty's Secret Service*, he rejected it, saying, 'If you think I'll accept a million pounds from you or from anyone else you're mistaken. I don't want my life to be ruined. Too much money is the worst curse you can lay on anyone's head.' Of course, it takes a certain amount of financial security to think like this. Fleming judged his wealth by those around him and believed that he was not wealthy, even as he was having houses built in Jamaica and ordering custom-made gold-plated typewriters. Bond's attitude is not quite that expressed by the Beatles in 'Can't Buy Me Love', but he did think money was there to be wasted. It has never motivated him. This may be unusual in portrayals of alpha males, but it is in its own way liberating.

Instead, Bond always had a clear, noble purpose. An evil madman was about to destroy the world or, worse, England, and it just so happens that only Bond can stop him. Implausible scenarios like this really simplify the decision-making process. It is always apparent exactly what Bond needs to do next, be that pushing a henchman into a pool of acid or leaping out of a flying plane without a parachute. A sense of purpose is a thing that many are missing and desperately need. Bond, in contrast, is never paralysed by indecision. To never dither is an appealing fantasy.

In the novel *You Only Live Twice*, M writes an obituary for Bond when he wrongly believes he has been killed in action. He ends this with a quote from the American writer Jack London, which he claims represents Bond's philosophy: 'I shall not waste my days in trying to prolong them. I shall use my time.' After Bond's death in *No Time to Die*, Ralph Fiennes's M uses a longer version of London's quote which adds the words, 'The proper function of man is to live, not to exist.' This is, surely, as strong a purpose as any.

An important factor here is that Bond does not see himself as a victim. This feels like it should be an increasingly important aspect of the character, given the extent to which society constantly urges us to define ourselves in this way. This is an issue not necessarily linked to how life has treated us. Donald Trump, the billionaire President of the United States, genuinely saw himself as a victim, while many who have experienced real suffering and terrible abuse do not define themselves in this way. Here straight white males have an advantage, as there are fewer voices in culture attempting to pressure them to define themselves as victims.

To not be a victim does not mean that you become an oppressor. It means that you are able to accept responsibility for your actions and circumstances, and are prepared to resist pressure when necessary. It means that you are willing to stand up and use your voice, even at times when to do so is futile or against your own self-interest. It is to not give in to fear, to act when necessary, and to not be cowed by the realities of the world. This is especially appealing in an era where so many suffer from anxiety. These are usually portrayed as idealised masculine qualities, but they are more universal than that. Greta Thunberg, to give one example, does not act like a victim. In the modern world, this can be enough to mark you out as a hero.

When Bond was born, he personified an aspect of male identity that was prevalent after the war – that of the protector. Men saw their role as being the one to protect their families from external threats. An ability to resort to violence when necessary was part of this, meaning that emotionally, men had to harden and reduce their empathy. The role of protector is an aspect of male identity that is now less necessary. The great majority of men go through their lives without ever having to fight, and those who use violence against others are no longer admired or tolerated. It is a lack of love, particularly in childhood, that can lead to the toxic behaviour and violence that we need to protect ourselves against. Craig's Bond gradually learned that his armour hurt and isolated him, as much as it protected. He came, at the end of a five-film arc, to open himself up, leave himself vulnerable and accept the consequences. This was necessary, he finally understood, even though it would lead to his death.

Love is open, and vulnerable, and impermanent. Death is closed, and isolated, and eternal. For men attempting to fantasise about who they want to be, the question of which to choose might seem a conundrum. But if Bond learned anything in his ritual death and resurrection show, it is that these do not have to be mutually exclusive, binary options. It took sixty years for closed Bond to open. Now that this has happened, we know that going from closed to open is possible, just as it is possible to go from open to closed. It does not have to take decades to make the switch. Just as a reborn Bond should be alert and empathetic enough to navigate sexual politics, so too should he be wise enough to know when his armour is needed, and when it can be laid down.

Here, then, is the idealised fantasy of how modern men could be. They are not motivated by greed, but by a sense of purpose. They are sexually adventurous but not predators. They see themselves as valid, rather than victims, confident enough to be true to themselves and brave enough not to hide themselves away. They know when they can relax and enjoy life, and when they need to harden, stand firm and protect themselves and others. In a very meta-modern way, they are skilled at knowing when they should swing to these extremes. If the Beatles are an expression of 'yes' and Bond is a statement of 'no', they are the ability to choose which is the right response at any given moment. The fantasy of being Bond has always been a desire to be confident, skilled and brave. To make it modern, it needs to also be wise. There is no reason why you can't be emotionally intelligent behind the wheel of a really fast sports car.

Or to put it another way, they need the ambition and mastery of Paul, the bravery and honesty of John, the sense of higher purpose (and great cars) of George, and the ability to enjoy life of Ringo. These were the four qualities which soaked culture so thoroughly that eventually they even contaminated the establishment. As the solo Beatle years show, these individual qualities can be impressive by themselves. But as those solo years also show, it is only when the four are combined that real alchemy occurs. The dream of embodying all four may seem like an overly ambitious fantasy – but it just so happens that being the ultimate fantasy is exactly what James Bond is for.

In the post-Beatle world, this combination of attributes looks like a worthy goal indeed. If Bond can continue to personify the ever-shifting dream of what a good life can be, then there is every reason to think that he will continue. Somewhere between Bond and the Beatles, it seems, there is an identity worth aspiring to.

BIBLIOGRAPHY

Altman, Mark A., and Gross, Edward, *Nobody Does It Better: The Complete, Uncensored, Unauthorised Oral History of James Bond* (Forge, 2020).

Badman, Keith, *The Beatles Diary Volume 2: After the Break-Up 1970–2001* (Omnibus Press, 2001).

Baggini, Julian, *How the World Thinks: A Global History of Philosophy* (Granta, 2018).

Baird, Julia, *Imagine This: Growing Up with My Brother John Lennon* (Hodder & Stoughton, 2011).

Beatles, The, *The Beatles Anthology* (Chronicle Books, 2000).

—, *Get Back* (Callaway Arts & Entertainment/Apple Corps, 2021).

Bramwell, Tony, *Magical Mystery Tours: My Life with the Beatles* (Portico, 2014).

Braun, Michael, *Love Me Do! The Beatles Progress* (Graymalkin Media, 1964).

Brown, Craig, *One Two Three Four: The Beatles in Time* (4th Estate, 2020).

Clayson, Alan, with Jungr, Barb, and Johnson, Rob, *Woman: The Incredible Life of Yoko Ono* (Lume Books, 2019).

BIBLIOGRAPHY

Connolly, Ray, *Being John Lennon: A Restless Life* (Weidenfeld & Nicolson, 2018).

Curtis, Scarlett (editor), *Feminists Don't Wear Pink (and Other Lies): Amazing Women on What the F-word Means to Them* (Penguin, 2018).

Davies, Hunter, *The Beatles: The Only Ever Authorised Biography* (Ebury Press, 2009).

—, *The Beatles Lyrics: The Unseen Story Behind Their Music* (Weidenfeld & Nicolson, 2017).

Doggett, Peter, *You Never Give Me Your Money: The Beatles after the Breakup* (Vintage, 2010).

Field, Matthew, and Chowdhury, Ajay, *Some Kind of Hero: The Remarkable Story of the James Bond Films* (The History Press, 2018).

Fleming, Ian, *Casino Royale* (Jonathan Cape, 1953).

—, *Live and Let Die* (Jonathan Cape, 1954).

—, *Moonraker* (Jonathan Cape, 1955).

—, *Diamonds Are Forever* (Jonathan Cape, 1956).

—, *From Russia with Love* (Jonathan Cape, 1957).

—, *Dr. No* (Jonathan Cape, 1958).

—, *Goldfinger* (Jonathan Cape, 1959).

—, *For Your Eyes Only* (Jonathan Cape, 1960).

—, *Thunderball* (Jonathan Cape, 1961).

—, *The Spy Who Loved Me* (Jonathan Cape, 1962).

—, *On Her Majesty's Secret Service* (Jonathan Cape, 1963).

—, *Thrilling Cities* (Jonathan Cape, 1963).

—, *You Only Live Twice* (Jonathan Cape, 1964).

—, *The Man with the Golden Gun* (Jonathan Cape, 1965).

—, *Octopussy and The Living Daylights* (Jonathan Cape, 1966).

Granados, Stefan, *Those Were the Days 2.0: The Beatles and Apple* (Cherry Red Books, 2021).

BIBLIOGRAPHY

Green, John, *Dakota Days: The Untold Story of John Lennon's Final Years* (Comet, 1984).

Harding, Luke, *Shadow State: Murder, Mayhem and Russia's Remaking of the West* (Guardian Faber, 2020).

Hawes, James, *The Shortest History of England* (Old Street Publishing, 2020).

Hepworth, David, *Nothing Is Real: The Beatles Were Underrated and Other Sweeping Statements about Pop* (Bantam Press, 2018).

Higgs, John, *Stranger than We Can Imagine: Making Sense of the Twentieth Century* (Weidenfeld & Nicolson, 2015).

John, Elton, *Me* (Macmillan, 2019).

Kahn, Ashley, *George Harrison on George Harrison: Interviews and Encounters* (Chicago Review Press, 2020).

Kaye, Lenny, *Lightning Striking: Ten Transformative Moments in Rock & Roll* (White Rabbit, 2021).

Lee, Christopher, *Lord of Misrule: The Autobiography of Christopher Lee* (Orion, 2003).

Lennon, Cynthia, *John* (Hodder & Stoughton, 2012).

Lennon, John, *In His Own Write* (Jonathan Cape, 1964).

Lennon, John, and Ono, Yoko, *John & Yoko/Plastic Ono Band* (Thames & Hudson, 2020).

Lewis, Roger, *The Life and Death of Peter Sellers* (Arrow Books, 1995).

Lewisohn, Mark, *The Beatles – All These Years: Volume One: Tune In* (Little Brown, 2013).

—, *The Complete Beatles Chronicle* (Pyramid Books, 1992).

Lycett, Andrew, *Ian Fleming: The Man Who Created James Bond* (Weidenfeld & Nicolson, 2012).

Macdonald, Ian, *Revolution in the Head: The Beatles' Records and the Sixties: Third Revised Edition* (Vintage, 2008).

Marr, Andrew, *A History of Modern Britain* (Picador, 2009).

McCartney, Paul, and Muldoon, Paul, *The Lyrics: 1956 to the Present* (Allen Lane, 2021).

McNab, Ken, *And in the End: The Last Days of the Beatles* (Polygon, 2019).

Miles, Barry, *Paul McCartney: Many Years from Now* (Vintage, 1998).

Norman, Philip, *Paul McCartney: The Biography* (Weidenfeld & Nicolson, 2016).

O'Dell, Chris, *Miss O'Dell: My Hard Days and Long Nights with The Beatles, The Stones, Bob Dylan, Eric Clapton, and the Women They Loved* (Atria, 2009).

Orton, Joe, *Up Against It: A Screenplay for the Beatles* (Eyre Methuen Ltd., 1979).

Pang, May, and Edwards, Henry, *Loving John* (Warner Books, 1983).

Parker, Matthew, *Goldeneye: Where Bond Was Born: Ian Fleming's Jamaica* (Windmill Books, 2014).

Pring, John, and Thomas, Rob, *Visualising the Beatles: A Complete Graphic History of the World's Favourite Band* (Dey Street, 2018).

Rain, John, *Thunderbook: The World of Bond According to Smersh Pod* (Polaris, 2019).

Richards, Keith, *Life* (Weidenfeld & Nicolson, 2010).

Roberts, Jem, *Fab Fools: The Beatles, The Rutles and Rock 'n' Roll Comedy!* (Candy Jar Books, 2021).

Rosen, Robert, *Nowhere Man: The Final Days of John Lennon* (Soft Skull Press, 2000).

Rubenhold, Hallie, *The Five: The Untold Lives of Women Killed by Jack the Ripper* (Doubleday, 2019).

Sandbrook, Dominic, *White Heat: A History of Britain in the Swinging Sixties* (Abacus, 2015).

Sheffield, Rob, *Dreaming the Beatles: The Love Story of One Band and the Whole World* (Dey Street Books, 2017).

Soocher, Stan, *Baby You're a Rich Man: Suing the Beatles for Fun and Profit* (ForeEdge, 2015).

Starr, Michael Seth, *Ringo: With a Little Help* (Backbeat, 2016).

Starr, Ringo, *Postcards from the Boys* (Cassell Illustrated, 2004).

Taylor, Rogan P., *The Death and Resurrection Show: From Shaman to Superstar* (Frederick Muller, 1983).

Thomson, Graeme, *George Harrison: Behind the Locked Door* (Omnibus Press, 2016).

Turner, Steve, *Beatles '66: The Revolutionary Year* (Ecco, 2016).

Weber, Erin Torkelson, *The Beatles and the Historians: An Analysis of Writings about the Fab Four* (McFarland, 2016).

Wenner, Jann S., *Lennon Remembers: The Full Rolling Stone Interviews from 1970* (Verso, 2000).

Wiener, Jon, *Come Together: John Lennon in His Time* (Random House, 1984).

Winder, Simon, *The Man Who Saved Britain: A Personal Journey into the Disturbing World of James Bond* (Picador, 2006).

Womack, Kenneth, *John Lennon 1980: The Last Days in the Life* (Omnibus Press, 2020).

Woodhead, Leslie, *How the Beatles Rocked the Kremlin: The Untold Story of a Noisy Revolution* (Bloomsbury, 2013).

NOTES AND SOURCES

PART I: INITIATE COUNTDOWN

1945: THERE'S NOBODY TO TALK TO WHEN IT'S RAINING

The description of Ringo's childhood here is based on his own accounts in the Beatles' 2000 book *Anthology*, along with the biography *Ringo* by Michael Seth Starr (no relation) and Mark Lewisohn's epic *Tune In*. For an account of Boris Johnson's description of Liverpool, see Ian Herbert's 16 October 2004 article in the *Independent*, 'In one article, Boris manages to offend an entire city and his boss'. Dave Grohl's comments are taken from HBO's coverage of Ringo Starr's Rock & Roll Hall of Fame presentation.

'The first car that came onto our street...' – Starr, Michael Seth, p.13.
'I wish I had brothers and sisters...' – Lewisohn (2013), p.29.
'the voodoo queen of Liverpool' – Lewisohn (2013), p.33.
'the greatest conception of tempo I've ever heard in my life' – Starr, Michael Seth, p.7.

1952: ALL OF HIS OWN DARKNESS

This account of Fleming's creation of James Bond is largely based on Andrew Lycett's biography *Ian Fleming* and Matthew Parker's *Goldeneye*, as well as Fleming's debut novel *Casino Royale* itself. The letter from Ian to

Ann Fleming which was sold at Sotheby's is quoted in the 12 November 2019 *Times* article by David Sanderson, 'High society and sadism: Ian Fleming's racy letters to Ann Charteris revealed'. The quotes from Tina Beal regarding Fleming at Eton are taken from the special features on the *From Russia with Love* DVD.

'hideous spectre of matrimony' – Parker, p.128.

'I have doubts about their happiness...' – Parker, p.92.

'I loved cooking for you and sleeping beside you...' – Lycett, p.179.

'We are of course totally unsuited...' – Lycett, p.215.

'and please, dear God, help me grow up to be more like Mokie' – Lycett, p.12.

'a quite frightening woman' – Parker, p.8.

'a harsh and often cruel establishment...' – Lycett, p.9.

'his shanks and running shorts stained with his own gore' – Lycett, p.15.

'the English upper crust wants and needs affection...' – Parker, p.10.

'the psychological watershed, the moment when it became apparent...' – Parker, p.211.

'What the hell do they want to send me a woman for?' – Fleming (1953), ebook Loc281.

'Women were for recreation [...] "Bitch," said Bond' – Fleming (1953), ebook Loc304.

'These blithering women...' – Fleming (1953), ebook Loc1044.

'the sweet tang of rape' – Fleming (1953), ebook Loc1684.

'There once was a girl called Asoka...' – Lycett, p.31.

'The bitch is dead now' – Fleming (1953), ebook Loc1912.

'People are islands...' – Fleming (1953), ebook Loc1720.

'It was a room-shaped room...' – Fleming (1961), p.13.

1956: I WOULD HAVE LIKED TO HAVE SEEN THE BOYS GROWING UP

A key source here for the account of Paul and John's early lives is Barry Miles's official biography *Paul McCartney: Many Years from Now*, as well as the *Anthology*. Julia Baird's book *Imagine This* about her half-brother

John Lennon was also hugely helpful and is highly recommended to anyone attempting to understand Lennon's personality. Paul McCartney's explanation of his 'It's a drag' comment is from the April/May 1982 issue of the Canadian magazine *Music Express*, in an interview entitled 'Paul McCartney Wings It Alone'. The *Sunday Times*'s examination of boarding schools was published on 4 December 2021 and called 'The painful truth behind British boarding schools, by *Sunday Times* readers'.

'The streets were thick with snow ...' – Miles, p.6.

'We didn't really know what was happening [...] boys growing up' – Miles, p.20.

'amongst the psychological disturbances ...' Taylor, pp.20–21.

'With the actors and rock stars that I've seen ...' – Lennon and Ono, p.88.

'I felt really angry later on ...' – The Beatles (2000), p.33.

'My mother was a beautiful, vibrant and loving woman ...' – Baird, p.379.

'They've taken my son from me ...' – Baird, p.80.

'The worst pain is that of not being wanted ...' – The Beatles (2000), p.7.

'I lost her twice. Once as a five-year-old ...' – Miles, p.49.

'that was the balance between us: John was caustic ...' – Miles, p.32.

1960: A NOTORIOUS CENTRE FOR PROSTITUTION

Ian Fleming's review of Hamburg's sex clubs is reprinted as Chapter 8 in his book *Thrilling Cities*. The major source for accounts of the Beatles in Hamburg is their *Anthology*. *Ian Fleming* by Andrew Lycett and *Paul McCartney: Many Years from Now* by Barry Miles were also useful sources here.

'She was a big girl with a good figure [...] favourite cities in the world.' – Fleming (1963b), ebook Loc1690-1745.

'We must remember that for a great many of our readers ...' – Lycett, p.374.

'We lived backstage in the Bambi Kino ...' – The Beatles (2000), p.46.

'I grew up in Hamburg, not Liverpool' – The Beatles (2000), p.45.
'It was a sex shock...' – The Beatles (2000), p.53.
'be walking in on each other and things...' – The Beatles (2000), p.54.
'We used to have wanking sessions...' – Miles, p.28.
'The city of Hamburg was brilliant...' – The Beatles (2000), p.45.
'My first shag was in Hamburg...' – The Beatles (2000), p.54.
'In spite of all the things, the Beatles really could...' – Wenner, p.47.

1961: UNASHAMEDLY, FOR PLEASURE AND MONEY

This account of early attempts to put Bond on screen is largely based on the Bond history *Some Kind of Hero* by Matthew Field and Ajay Chowdhury, *Nobody Does It Better* by Altman and Gross, and Andrew Lycett's biography *Ian Fleming*.

'unashamedly, for pleasure and money' – Field and Chowdhury, p.21.
'You don't make a great deal of money from royalties...' – Lycett,
    p.240.
'too much stage Englishness...' – Field and Chowdhury, p.27.
'too English to boot' – Field and Chowdhury, p.51.

1962: GLUTTED WITH THE OVERLOAD OF STUFF

The description of the Cavern is based on multiple sources, including *Anthology* and Mark Lewisohn's *Tune In*. The details about Leslie Woodhead's film and his life as a spy are taken from his book *How the Beatles Rocked the Kremlin*.

'It was a scary moment...' – Woodhead, pp.62–3.
'Driving back to Manchester down the East Lancashire Road...' –
    Woodhead, p.14.

PART 2: DETONATE

1962: BIGGER THAN THE BEATLES

This account of the reaction to the release of 'Love Me Do' is based largely on *Tune In* by Mark Lewisohn. The Tom Holland quote is from Episode 8 of his and Dominic Sandbrook's podcast *The Rest Is History*, 'The Echo of a Coffee House'.

'The Beatles were the first recording artists...' – Lewisohn (2013), p.750.
'We always tried to make every song different...' – Miles, p.482.
'Changing the lifestyle and appearance of youth...' – Miles, p.293.
'I declare that John Lennon, George Harrison...' – Miles, p.346.

1962: SEAN CONNERY (1930–2020)

The quoted reviews of *Dr. No* are from *The Times* on 5 October 1962, the *Guardian* on 6 October 1962, Cecil Wilson's *Daily Mail* review on 5 October 1962 and the *Observer*'s review by Penelope Gilliatt on 7 October 1962. The Barbara Walters interview with Sean Connery can be found on YouTube entitled 'Sean Connery discusses women slapping'. Connery recanted his earlier views about domestic abuse in a 25 June 2006 *Sunday Times* interview with Jason Allardyce, 'Connery: to hit a woman is wrong'. William Gibson's quote 'The future is already here – it's just not evenly distributed' is from the 4 December 2003 edition of *The Economist*.

'We were very lucky in finding the type...' – Altman and Gross, p.40.
'Fleming didn't like Sean Connery...' – Field and Chowdhury, p.77.
'the sexiest devil in the world...' – Field and Chowdhury, p.114.
'frequently placed the onus for a beating...' – Rubenhold, p.274.
'I find that fame tends to turn [...] more attention to character and
    better dialogue' – Field and Chowdhury, p.147.
'It was around the same time as the Beatles...' – Field and
    Chowdhury, p.168.

1963: THERE ARE TRUTHS IN THAT SCREAMING

The toy Aston Martin was named the greatest toy ever in the 6 December 2019 article in *Classic and Sports Car* magazine by Giles Chapman, 'When Corgi struck gold: the story behind the greatest toy ever'. Paul McCartney described the sound of screaming during Beatlemania as sounding like 'a million seagulls' in the 18 October 2021 *New Yorker* article by David Remnick, 'Paul McCartney Doesn't Really Want to Stop the Show'.

'They never ate anything...' – Starr, Michael Seth, p.115.
'Admiral Grove was surrounded by fans...' – Starr, Michael Seth, p.119.

1964: IAN FLEMING (1908–1964)

This account of Ian Fleming's state of mind at the end of his life is based largely on *Ian Fleming* by Andrew Lycett and *Goldeneye* by Matthew Parker. The quote from Ann Fleming's letter to Evelyn Waugh is from the 28 February 2014 *Daily Mail* article by Natalie Clarke, 'Drugs, guns and the torment of his only son: As James Bond author Ian Fleming's life is dramatized, the TRUE story of his family proves just as fascinating'.

'In both cases something undefinable appealed to public fancy...' – Lycett, p.430.
'Probably the fault about my books...' – Lycett, p.289.
'What use is it to me now?' – Lycett, p.440.
'highly intelligent and accomplished, but his emotional age was pre-puberty' – Lycett, p.371.
'You simply never could anticipate how Ian would behave...' – Lycett, p.86.

1964: A FILM WITH FOUR LONG-HAIRED SCHNOOKS

'Goldfinger isn't just big...' – Field and Chowdhury, p.122.
'The premise stands, I think...' – McCartney and Muldoon, p.64.
'Would you rather make a film with four long-haired schnooks...' – Field and Chowdhury, p.82.

'totally devoid of talent' – Brown, p.227.

'bad-mannered little shits' – Brown, p.229.

1965: IT WOULD TAKE TOO MUCH ELSE AWAY

Hanif Kureishi's essay 'How the Beatles changed Britain' is online at the British Library website: www.bl.uk/20th-century-literature/articles/how-the-beatles-changed-britain. The first Paul McCartney quote is from John Harris's 18 November 2021 *Guardian* article ' "Annoying snobs was part of the fun": Paul McCartney and more on the Beatles' rooftop farewell'. James Marriott wrote about the class study in *Sociology* in his 20 January 2021 *Times* article, 'The new elites are working-class wannabes'.

'Look, he can actually write!' – Brown, p.185.

'We're not going to vote for Ted' – Brown, p.325.

'Would the people in the cheaper seats clap your hands...' – Brown, p.324.

'I've got some news for you...' – The Beatles (2000), p.181.

'The Beatles' MBE reeks of mawkish, bizarre effrontery...' – Brown, p.303.

'is, of course, a tactless and major blunder' – Brown, p.227.

'My contribution to the export drive is simply staggering...' – Lycett, p.430.

'We're going to meet the Queen...' – The Beatles (2000), p.183.

'Imagine being brought up like that for 2,000 years!' – The Beatles (2000), p.181.

'always thought of ourselves as posh working class...' – McCartney and Muldoon, p.645.

'There's one moment that I've regretted all my life...' – Miles, p.15.

1965: NOT AS GOOD AS JAMES BOND

'I had electric curtains upstairs...' – Miles, p.256.

'I'd seen the first James Bond film...' – McCartney and Muldoon, p.459.

1965: GREATER THAN THE SUM OF THEIR PARTS

The quote from George Martin is taken from his interview in the October 1968 edition of *Hit Parade* magazine. The reference to the Beatles as the four alchemical elements here is intended as a corrective to an article I wrote for the music website *The Quietus* in 2019, in which I claimed that John was fire, Ringo was earth, Paul was water and George was air. Many thanks to those who wrote to correct me – it indeed should have been Paul is air and George is water. I blame the influence of George's *Cloud 9* album sleeve for my mistake.

1965: THE THINGS I DO FOR ENGLAND

The quote from the late Duke of Westminster is taken from Jill Lawless's 10 August 2016 Associated Press article, 'Billionaire landowner the Duke of Westminster dies at 64'.

'looked at her severely...' – Fleming (1959), p.46.
'Bond loathed and despised tea...' – Fleming (1961), p.33.
'When [the rulers of England] said *England*...' – Hawes, p.183.
'a magic act that owed less to Britain than to Barnum' – Thomson, p.76.
'It didn't worry me that the Empire was crumbling...' – Miles, p.256

1967: WHAT DID HE WANT TO COMMUNICATE?

'When John was tripping...' – Lennon, Cynthia, p.182.
'The creative moment when you come up...' – Miles, p.173.
'I've decided, all the things that we do...' – The Beatles (2021), p.53.
'Is it true there's nothing you can make...' – Davies (2017), p.259.

1967: LARGER THAN REALITY

The best exploration of the Beatles' drug use is *Riding So High: The Beatles and Drugs* by Joe Goodden. The quote from Joe Orton's diary is from his entry for 24 January 1967. McCartney's comments about the *Magical Mystery Tour* film are from his director's commentary on the Blu-Ray release.

'You wake up at night wondering if the whole thing will work...' –
Field and Chowdhury, p.176.
'certainly showed me what was really happening...' – The Beatles
(2000), p.259.
'easily the most amazing new thing we've ever come up with' –
Turner, p.146.
'I enjoyed the fish-and-chip quality of *Magical Mystery*...' – Miles,
p.372–3.

1967: 007 (SHANTY TOWN)

The quote from Ian Rankin is from his introduction to the Bond short
story collection *For Your Eyes Only*.

'that of a Scots laird with his head stalker...' – Fleming (1958), p.206.

1967: WELLES WAS TRYING TO PUT A VOODOO MIND-GRIP ON HIM

Much of the details about Peter Sellers in this chapter is indebted to Roger
Lewis's superb biography *The Life and Death of Peter Sellers*.

'I told him I was making more money in that one film...' – Field and
Chowdhury, p.156.
'benign cheerfulness of Paul, the child-like drollery of Ringo...' –
Roberts, foreword.
'Ian Fleming... he's hysterically funny...' – Lewis, p.806.
'He claimed that Welles was trying to put a voodoo mind-grip on
him' – Lewis, p.895.
'by *Casino Royale* he was pretty much round the bend...' – Lewis,
p.994.
'I myself never met him. Indeed, I shot a scene with Orson...' – Lewis,
p.467.
'walked on to the set and passed [Sellers] by...' – Lewis, p.937.
'the intended manifesto for the film...' – Altman and Gross, p.215.

1968: ON THE BANKS OF THE RIVER GANGES

Filmmaker Paul Saltzman describes the Beatles trip to India as 'a turning point in twentieth-century consciousness' in his 2020 documentary *Meeting the Beatles in India*. Lennon's quote about doing everything they could to promote TM is from that same film. The quote from the *Guardian* is taken from its 28 March 2021 editorial, 'The Guardian view on "post-Christian" Britain: a spiritual enigma'. The list of visual imagery for *White Album* songs is included in *The Lyrics* by Paul McCartney and Paul Muldoon, on p.538. The quote from Ringo about receiving his mantra is from Rob Sheffield's 8 July 2020 *Rolling Stone* article, 'Ringo Starr Celebrates His 80th Birthday with Peace, Love, and Black Lives Matter'. Lennon's quote about the Maharishi being a mistake is from a 14 May 1968 press conference he and Paul gave at the Americana Hotel in New York.

'It was a pleasant afternoon...' – Miles, p.414.
'I thought we should probably have made...' – The Beatles (2000), p.305.
'Look what meditation did for Ringo...' – The Beatles (2000), p.305.
'I still use the mantra...' – Miles, p.396.
'Mardas seems to have taken against the Maharishi...' – Brown, p.452.
'asked many searching [scientific] questions...' – Brown, p.452.
'I said, "Well if you're so cosmic, you'll know why"...' – Wenner, p.27.
'We thought: "They're deliberately keeping the taxi back..."' – The Beatles (2000), p.286.
'whole piece of bullshit was invented' – Thomson, p.139.
'Poor Maharishi. I remember him standing at the gate...' – Miles, p.428.
'I hated leaving on a note of discord and mistrust...' – Lennon, Cynthia, p.210.
'I always do. I always expect too much...' – Wenner, p.28.
'We thought that [the Maharishi] was something other than he was...' – The Beatles (2000), p.286.
'He never said he was a god...' – Miles, pp.428–9.
'This is deference in the extreme' – Baggini, p.11.

'I know John would have a different view [about the Maharishi]
   now...' – Thomson, p.139.
'Oh! My dream's out!' – Baird, p.73.
'Me and John, we'd known each other for a long...' – Miles, p.383.

1968: YOKO AND BILLY

For an account of the arrest of Billy Preston, see Edward J. Boyer's 19
August 1991 *Los Angeles Times* article 'Singer Billy Preston Arrested in
Sex Case'. Lennon's quote about refusing to play to segregated audiences is from the 18 September 2011 *BBC News* report 'The Beatles banned
segregated audiences, contract shows.' For details of the Royal Family's
hiring practices in the 1960s, see the 2 June 2021 *Guardian* investigation
'Buckingham Palace banned ethnic minorities from office roles, papers
reveal', by David Pegg and Rob Evans. For details of Semhar Tesfagiorgis's
case against the casino Aspinalls, see the 15 July 2021 *Guardian* article
'London casino let rich patrons racially abuse staff, tribunal hears', by
Haroon Siddique.

'Rock and Roll was real. Everything else was unreal' – Connolly, p.31.
'*avant garde* is French for bullshit' – Connolly, p.305.
'He had definitely been very lost...' – Lennon and Ono, p.241.
'finally found someone as barmy as I am' – Connolly, p.273.
'I was in shock, operating on auto-pilot...' – Lennon, Cynthia, p.214.
'It's bad enough to be tossed aside by your husband...' – Lennon,
   Cynthia, p.222.
'You had to be in the situation to realise...' – Connolly, p.269.
'We didn't stop to think about anyone else's feelings...' – Connolly,
   p.274.
'George insulted her right to her face...' – Wenner, p.45.
'Yoko just moved in...' – The Beatles (2000), p.308.
'created tension because most of the time...' – The Beatles (2000),
   p.308.
'It was fairly off-putting having her sitting on...' – The Beatles (2000),
   p.310.
'He was used to being a star in his own right...' – Richards, p.403.

'bad enough with four' – The Beatles (2021), p.139.

'sometimes he would get on the rag...' – Richards, p.404.

'respect for human life...' – Fleming (1959), p.136.

'ten-minutes-to-two'– Fleming (1959), p.182.

'and any other Korean firmly in his place...' – Fleming (1959), p.194.

1969: JOHN, PAUL AND JAMES GET MARRIED

'I was an unfashionable woman who married a Beatle...' – McNab, p.61.

'I didn't particularly like the idea of limiting myself to one man again' – Connolly, p.302.

'Do we want to become modern and have a long-haired one?' – Field and Chowdhury, p.185.

'Get rid of the tears...' – Field and Chowdhury, p.200.

'he would no longer be alone. He would be half of two people...' – Fleming (1963), p.281.

'had developed much love, and total respect, for this man...' – Fleming (1963), p.255.

1969: GEORGE LAZENBY'S HAIR

Paul McCartney's quote about the convention of short hair for men is from his interview with Maureen Cleave in the 25 March 1966 *Evening Standard*, 'How Does a Beatle Live? (Part 4, Paul McCartney)'. The *Guardian's* article 'It's *No Time to Die:* But is it time to revoke James Bond's licence to kill?' by Stuart Jeffries was published on 25 September 2021. Lazenby's comments about how Bond is a brute are from the article 'Glenn Takes Flier as Anti-Flight Hero' in the 14 December 1969 edition of the *Los Angeles Times*.

'It is a dirty habit...' – Fleming (1957), p.116.

'thinning margarine-coated hair' – Brown, p.30.

'Doth not even nature itself teach you...' – 1 Corinthians 11:14–15.

'Blofeld's own eyes were deep black pools...' – Fleming (1961), p.48.

'Roger had enough hair to stuff a mattress...' – Field and Chowdhury, p.234.

'People weren't into James Bond...' – Field and Chowdhury, p.203.

'I look around and everyone else has got long hair...' – Altman and Gross, p.255.

1969: PAUL IS DEAD

'We got fed up with being sidemen for Paul...' – Wenner, p.23.

PART 3: AFTERMATH

1970: ANSWER: NO

George Harrison's diary entry for 10 January 1969, the day he left the Beatles, is featured in Martin Scorsese's 2011 documentary *Living in the Material World*. McCartney said that 'the Beatles thing is over' in the 7 November 1969 edition of *Life* magazine.

'got a telegram saying, "You're the best rock'n'roll drummer in the world..."' – The Beatles (2000), p.312.

'I think if George doesn't come back by Monday or Tuesday...' – The Beatles (2021), p.94.

'I've got something very important to tell you...' – Bramwell, p.260.

'But don't write it yet. I'll tell you when you can' – Connolly, p.xi.

1970: MOTHER/LOVE

'A lot of people go to psychoanalysis...' – Lennon and Ono, p.84.

'They cut the therapy off just as it started...' – Wiener, p.138.

'Do you think you're a genius?' – Wenner, p.36.

'I just hate this illusion about George Martin, Brian Epstein...' – Wenner, p.56.

'A lot of people – Dick James and the Derek Taylors...' – Wenner, pp.35–6.

'Dick James and all of them...' – Wenner, p.123.

'I decided I'm sick of reading things about Paul is the musician...' – Wenner, p.87.

'I couldn't be bothered with him when he first came round...' –
    Wenner, pp.133–5.
'as important as anything...' – Wenner, p.14.
'Yoko's *Bottoms* thing is [...] as important as *Sgt. Pepper*' – Wenner,
    p.143.
'took H because of what the Beatles and their pals...' – Wenner, p.16.
'I believe they did love each other, but...' – Pang and Edwards, p.49.
'He wanted me to be Mother, but I wouldn't do it' – Pang and
    Edwards, p.92.
'Julia was very much the girl of John's dreams' – Lewisohn (2013), p.79.
'I was just remembering the time when I had my hand on my mother's
    tit...' – Lewisohn (2013), p.80.
'I always do. I always expect too much...' – Wenner, p.28.
'I mean to sell as many albums as I can...' – Wenner, p.96.
'I think "Love" will do me more good' – Wenner, p.94.
'You chose the word "peace" and not "love"...' – Wenner, p.41.
'said, "Oh Christ, I was stoned out of my fucking mind..."' – Doggett,
    p.151.

1970: THE BEST

Viktor Suvorov's views on the quality of contemporary Russian spies are
described in Luke Harding's 23 June 2020 *Guardian* article, ' "A chain of
stupidity": the Skripal case and the decline of Russia's spy agencies'. The
quotes from John le Carré, Philip Knightley and Adam Curtis are taken
from Adam Curtis's 8 August 2013 BBC blogpost 'Bugger'. For details of
the government report into civil service privilege, see Oliver Wright's
20 May 2021 report in *The Times*, 'Senior civil servants as privileged as
they were 50 years ago.' The quote from Andrei Soldatov is taken from
the 9 March 2022 *Times* article by Tom Ball, 'Putin infuriated by Russian
intelligence failures in Ukraine war'.

'superb [...] The best English cooking is the best in the world' –
    Fleming (1955), p.64.
'Three measures of Gordon's, one of vodka...' – Fleming (1953), ebook
    Loc481.

'the best young publisher in town' – Lycett, p.270.
'without question one of the two or three most brilliant...' – Lycett, p.78.
'seems or seemed to imply a close and valuable link...' – Winder, p.87.
'Their Security Service is excellent...' – Fleming (1957), p.23.

1970: PHIL AND ALLEN

The quote from Leonard Cohen about Phil Spector being the worst person he had ever met is from Spector's 17 January 2021 *Sunday Times* obituary, which also includes details of his treatment of Ronnie Spector. Phil Spector's reaction to McCartney's remix of 'Long and Winding Road' on *Let It Be... Naked* is from Merrell Noden's 2003 article 'Extra-celestial' on p.127 of the *Mojo* Special Limited Edition magazine *1000 Days of Revolution (The Beatles' Final Years – Jan 1, 1968 to Sept 27, 1970)*.

'[Spector] always wanted to work with the Beatles...' – Wenner, pp.101–2.
'That made me very angry...' – The Beatles (2000), p.350.
'I know that Paul was very cross about...' – The Beatles (2000), p.350.
'The music business is about 99 per cent no-talent losers...' – Miles, p.526.
'He knows me as much as you do. *Incredible* guy...' – The Beatles (2021), p.181.
'He was the only one that Yoko liked' – McNab, p.27.
'I didn't trust him and I certainly didn't want him...' – McNab, p.67.
'the biggest mistake you can make' – McNab, p.39.
'I was going through a bad time, what I suspect...' – Miles, pp.570–1.

1971: TO DENY THAT LOVE WAS DESIRABLE

William Blake writes about 'A Hell of our own making' in his epic poem *Milton* (plate 12, line 23).

'"Yeah, I'd probably be interested"...' – McCartney and Muldoon, p.427.
'So, it's come to that' – Altman and Gross, p.307.

1973: CHRISTOPHER LEE (1922–2015)

The quote from photographer Clive Arrowsmith is taken from Nathan Bevan's 23 June 2010 interview for WalesOnline.co.uk, 'How photographer Clive Arrowsmith turned around a botched photo shoot with McCartney'. The details of Christopher Lee's life are largely taken from the updated 2003 edition of his autobiography *Lord of Misrule*. Footage of Lee educating Peter Jackson about the sound a man makes when being stabbed in the back can be found on YouTube, entitled 'Christopher Lee corrects Peter Jackson on set'.

' "That man Scaramanga – interesting!" ' – Lee, pp.237–8.
'It pleased [Fleming] to call me his cousin...' – Lee, p.230.
'I felt I had only to breathe nervously to be beaten' – Lee, p.22.
'Why don't you become an actor, Christopher?' – Lee, p.110.
'has left me with a residue of tension...' – Lee, p.107.
'which had only just been cleaned up, and some that hadn't' – Lee, p.107.

1973: THE PROBLEM IS BOND

The quote from Charlie Higson is taken from Nadia Khomami's 21 September 2021 *Guardian* article 'Daniel Craig has given us "woke" James Bond, says Charlie Higson'. Cary Fukunaga's comments about rape in the Sean Connery era of Bond were reported in Catherine Shoard's 23 September 2021 *Guardian* article 'James Bond was "basically" a rapist in early films, says *No Time to Die* director.' Olga Kurylenko's comments on her character Camille are from the 31 October 2008 *Daily Mirror* article '007 girl Olga Kurylenko is not interested in men'. Léa Seydoux's comments are from her 6 November 2015 interview with Giles Coren for British *Vogue*, 'Léa Seydoux: The Bond Girl Interview'. The quote from Ana de Armas is taken from Sloane Crosley's 18 February 2020 *Vanity Fair* article 'All About Ana'.

'I'd seen Ursula Andress in *Dr. No*...' – Field and Chowdhury, p.263.
'the behind was almost as firm and rounded as a boy's' – Fleming
    (1958), ebook Loc1200.

'hard, boyish flanks' – Fleming (1957), p.91.

'flat and hard at the sides, it jutted like a man's' – Fleming (1957), p.39.

'John's temper could be frightening and at times...' – Lennon, Cynthia, p.25.

'Before I could speak he raised his arm...' – Lennon, Cynthia, p.36.

'not even his wife's battered face could raise a smile...' – Lennon, John, p.18.

'I was just hysterical. That was the trouble...' – Lewisohn (2013), p.245.

'John was true to his word...' – Lennon, Cynthia, p.38.

'Bond came to the conclusion that Tilly Masterton...' – Fleming (1959), p.237.

'Now it may only be a myth...' – Fleming (1965), p.29.

'Coupla lavender boys. You know, pansies.' – Fleming (1956), ebook Loc2185.

'Bill, a pansified Italian, hurried towards them' – Fleming (1959), p.15.

'Bond liked the look of her...' – Fleming (1959), p.211.

'They told me you only liked women...' – Fleming (1959), p.279.

'She was only sixteen at the time...' – Fleming (1956), ebook Loc1002.

'I'm not going to sleep with you...' – Fleming (1956), ebook Loc1016.

'I want it all, James. Everything...' – Fleming (1956), ebook Loc2965.

'like an obedient child' – Fleming (1959), p.278.

'When you look at the early films...' – Altman and Gross, p.633.

'Just another Bond girl. I'm not simply a plastic doll...' – Field and Chowdhury, p.347.

'I've always wanted to *be* James Bond...' – Field and Chowdhury, p.518.

1974: IN THE MATERIAL WORLD

This account of George Harrison is based on Graeme Thomson's excellent biography *George Harrison: Behind the Locked Door*, along with *Anthology*, Keith Badman's *The Beatles Diary* and Chris O'Dell's valuable memoir *Miss O'Dell*. For a useful fact-check about Eric Clapton's on-stage racist rant in 1976, see the 4 December 2020 article by Dan MacGuill on www. snopes.com, 'Did Eric Clapton Once Unleash a Racist Rant Onstage?' David Bowie's 1976 comments about fascism are from an interview with

Cameron Crowe in the September 1976 issue of *Playboy*. Bowie stated that he didn't support fascism in a 29 October 1977 *Melody Maker* interview with Allan Jones, 'Goodbye to Ziggy and all that'.

'Actually, it's about Krishna, but I couldn't say *he*, could I...' – Thomson, pp.177–8.

'At times listening to Harrison's music...' – Thomson, p.152.

'The first George was great fun and loved to gossip...' – O'Dell, p.139.

'weird kind of angry bitterness about certain things in life' – Thomson, p.11.

'After several more requests to "turn the fucking thing up,"...' – Thomson, p.169.

'Pattie and I used to joke that we didn't know if his hand...' – O'Dell, p.188.

'I couldn't reach him' – Thomson, p.167.

'I start beginning to relate less and less to the people I know...' – O'Dell, p.142.

'wanting to be some kind of spiritual being...' – Thomson, p.167.

'They were always holding hands...' – O'Dell, p.123.

'incest' – Thomson, p.255.

'You know, Ringo, I'm in love with your wife.' – O'Dell, p.264.

'Starr was distraught, muttering, "nothing is real, nothing is real".' – Thomson, p.255.

'she got on a motorbike and drove it straight into a brick wall...' – Lennon, Cynthia, p.5.

'I have to tell you, man...' – Thomson, p.256.

'If you want her, take her, she's yours' – Thomson, p.256.

'I didn't get annoyed at [Clapton] and I think that has always annoyed him...' – Thomson, p.256.

'It could have started as a payback day...' – Thomson, p.363.

'someone whose universe is confined to himself' – Thomson, pp.292–3.

'I came home one day from school after being chased...' – Thomson, p.336.

1977: RISKING THEIR LIVES FOR THE AUDIENCE'S ENTERTAINMENT

The quotes from Christopher Wood are taken from the documentary *Inside The Spy Who Loved Me*, which is included on the extra disk of the DVD release.

'I didn't see it as a stunt...' – Field and Chowdhury, p.301.
'I was really daring the devil...' – Field and Chowdhury, p.302.
'I was becoming a drama queen...' – Field and Chowdhury, p.303.
'I got myself together and got my chute on...' – Field and Chowdhury, p.303.
'The stark face I've seen on men returning...' – Lee, p.233.

1980: THE NO-MARK

All quotes from the no-mark are taken from the 2020 documentary *Jealous Guy: The Assassination of John Lennon* by Bill Badgley.

'If everyone who had a gun just shot themselves...' – The Beatles (2000), p.226.

1980: JOHN LENNON (1940–1980)

Details of Ono's business interests in cows are taken from the 9 July 1987 *Los Angeles Times* article 'Yoko Ono, John Lennon Estate Sue IRS'. The quote from Michael Lindsay-Hogg is from Brian Hiatt's 2 November 2021 Rolling Stone article 'Original *Let It Be* Director Defends His Film: "I Don't Care" That Ringo Hates It.' The quote from Sam Havadtoy is from Glenn Plaskin's 6 May 1990 *Los Angeles Times* interview, 'Yoko Ono, a Decade After the "Horrible Thing": John Lennon's widow still lives under a shadow, but, she says, "It's not a bad time"'. The quote from Peter Doggett is from 3 June 2010 entry on his blog, http://peterdoggettbeatles. blogspot.com, entitled 'Heroes & Villains No. 1: Yoko Ono'.

'for the people like me who are working class...' – Wenner, p.92.
'couldn't see a thing and hated wearing glasses...' – Lennon, Cynthia, p.18.

'Oh, I got rid of them. All that *mooing*.' – John, p.137.

'Imagine six apartments...' – John, p.138.

'I don't know what my wife is going to use it for...' – Womack, p.87.

'Stop trying to be nice to the servants...' – Green, p.45.

'They decided upon a story and stuck to it...' – Connolly, p.345.

'Yoko suggested a mistress, because she didn't want to deal with me in bed' – Green, p.36.

'By then I knew that Yoko's suggestions were in fact orders...' – Pang and Edwards, pp.5–6.

'I knew that it was a tradition in Japan for wives of the upper class...' – Pang and Edwards, p.75.

'There was no word from him between 1971 and 1974...' – Lennon, Cynthia, p.247.

'To me he wasn't a musician or peace icon, he was the father I loved...' – Lennon, Cynthia, Foreword.

'Dad's always telling people to love each other...' – Lennon, Cynthia, p.247.

'the feeling in John's voice...' – Lennon and Ono, p.88.

'Throughout his life, John was always...' – Lennon and Ono, p.273.

1981: FOR A TRUE ARTIST THEIR LIFE IS THEIR ART

Yoko Ono's quote about the cover of *Season of Glass* is taken from her sleeve notes for Disc 5 of the compilation boxset *Onobox*. Her quote about being lonely before meeting John is from her Twitter account, @yokoono, on 9 October 2021.

'said that she wanted to bring home to people the reality...' – Lennon, Cynthia, p.275.

'I took one look at her and I thought, "My God, what's that?"...' – Connolly, pp.282–3.

'I often wish my mother had died...' – Lennon and Ono, p.222.

'We were starving...' – Lennon and Ono, p.169.

'I smiled at her, but even though she knew...' – Pang and Edwards, p.19.

'I had a string tied around my waist...' – Green, p.86.

'used to send [John] away on his own so he'd grow up...' – Womack, p.101.

'always asserted herself as an artist...' – Clayson, p.220.

PART 4: GROW UP, 007

1983: A SYMBOL OF REAL VALUE TO THE FREE WORLD

'As I see it, 007 is really a ten...' – Field and Chowdhury, p.377.

'I met him through friends at the American School...' – Field and Chowdhury, p.512.

'The basic material begins to wear thin...' – Field and Chowdhury, p.365.

'The Americans saw a picture on the front page...' – Field and Chowdhury, p.122.

1984: WACKY MACCA THUMBS ALOFT

The comments from Paul Muldoon are taken from Richard Purden's 20 November 2021 *Irish News* interview, 'Paul Muldoon on working with Paul McCartney, bonding over their "similar" Catholic Irish backgrounds and exploring what makes interesting art'. The quote from Michael Lindsay-Hogg is taken from Brian Hiatt's 2 November 2021 *Rolling Stone* article 'Original *Let It Be* Director Defends His Film: "I Don't Care" That Ringo Hates It.' McCartney's 19 October 1984 interview with Barbara Frum can be found in the CBC digital archive titled, 'Talking about the wild days with ex-Beatle Paul McCartney'. The quote from Mary McCartney is from Danny Scott's 26 December 2021 *Times* article 'Paul and Mary McCartney on meat-free life, losing Linda and craving normality'.

'The big thought from me, and from everyone...' – McCartney and Muldoon, p.492.

'you get rid of the hesitation and the doubt...' – McCartney and Muldoon, p.125.

'I used to say, "Oh Dear!"...' – Miles, p.343.

'Some people think that my description of the Maharishi...' –
   McCartney and Muldoon, p.175.
'I'm a bit more purposeful these days...' – McCartney and Muldoon,
   p.197.
'I'm actually quite a fan of "ordinary" ...' – McCartney and Muldoon,
   p.53.

1995: TOO MUCH OF A GOOD TIME

For details of Noel Gallagher's thoughts on his attendance at the Number
10 'Cool Britannia' party, see Nick Paton Walsh's 31 October 1999 *Guardian*
article 'Noel looks back in anger at drinks party with Blair'. For details
of the increase in privately educated musicians, see Liz Thomas's 5
December 2010 *Daily Mail* article 'Public school singers take over the
pop charts: 60% of acts are now privately educated'. For information
about the rise of privately educated actors, see Carole Cadwalladr's 8
May 2016 *Observer* article 'Why working-class actors are a disappearing
breed', and Jemma Carr's 19 January 2021 *Daily Mail* article 'Middle-class
actors and luvvies are more likely to "misidentify" as working class in a
bid to sound "more deserving" of their success'.

'three quarters of the Beatles...' – Weber, ebook Loc2535.
'The reasons were primarily that most teenage boys...' – Field and
   Chowdhury, p.473.
'The Dalton Bonds had not performed significantly well...' – Field and
   Chowdhury, p.479.
'My heart was in my mouth...' – Field and Chowdhury, p.493.
'those sixteen-year-old boys who went and saw *GoldenEye*...' – Altman
   and Gross, p.538.

1999: DESMOND LLEWELYN (1914–1999)

Desmond Llewelyn's quote about being a sentimental grandfather is
from Bruce Feirstein's 23 December 1999 article for *Salon*, 'Desmond
Llewelyn'. The quote from Richard Moore, aka C, is from Tom Newton
Dunn's 25 April 2021 *Sunday Times* interview, 'MI6's 'C': We warned

Putin what would happen if he invaded Ukraine'. The job advert used to recruit the next Q is online at https://www.saxbam.com/appointment/mi6/. Paddy McGuinness described the Aston Martin DB5 as 'the best car in history' in the 21 March 2021 edition of the BBC's *Top Gear*. Details of Llewellyn's tragic death are from the 19 December 1999 *BBC News* article 'Bond actor killed in crash'. Llewellyn's comments about continuing to play Q are from an interview included on *The World Is Not Enough* DVD.

'On the days that he shot, it was wild . . .' – Altman and Gross, pp.585–6.

2001: GEORGE HARRISON (1943–2001)

The main sources for this chapter are Graeme Thomson's *George Harrison: Behind the Locked Door* and Ashley Kahn's *George Harrison on George Harrison: Interviews and Encounters*. The quote from George Harrison describing his attack was from Harrison's evidence at the trial of Michael Abrams, which is detailed in Steven Morris's 15 November 2000 *Guardian* article 'The night George Harrison thought he was dying'.

'with an intensity that was quite rare for George . . .' – Thomson, p.371.
'What I didn't realise . . .' – Thomson, p.156.
'and started playing The Chiffons's melody . . .' – Thomson, p.216.
'Well, that's it [. . .] I'm not a Beatle anymore' – Thomson, p.109.
'typical of a hundred groups in our area . . .' – Thomson, p.88.
'a horror story . . . awful . . . manic . . . crazy, a nightmare' – Thomson, p.85.
'Being in the Beatles was the opportunity of anyone's lifetime . . .' – Thomson, p.85.
'I can't believe after everything that's happened to me . . .' – Thomson, p.387.
'Sitting here with my Dr. Evil doll . . .' – Kahn, p.542.
'searched for a tool to help him communicate . . .' – Kahn, p.542.

2002: THE FATE OF THE PIXELS

This account of the move from Brosnan to Craig is largely based on the accounts in Field and Chowdhury's *Some Kind of Hero* and Altman and Gross's *Nobody Does It Better*.

'I would like to do another one, sure...' – Field and Chowdhury, p.559.

'It's like a time warp back in the sixties...' – Field and Chowdhury, p.531.

'I sat in Richard Harris's house in the Bahamas...' – Field and Chowdhury, p.565.

'The producers have told me that the role is mine as long as I like' – Field and Chowdhury, p.559.

'was a little more plot driven and a little darker...' – Field and Chowdhury, p.541.

'We were caught up in the idea that Bond had to...' – Field and Chowdhury, p.546.

'In the beginning they were made for adults...' – Field and Chowdhury, p.550.

'Of course, I didn't do all the stunts...' – Field and Chowdhury, p.578.

'I said, "Look, the game's changing fast..."' – Field and Chowdhury, p.560.

'I am sure that he didn't read it, but it was hard not to be aware...' – Altman and Gross, pp.631–2.

'Look, it did affect me, I will not lie to you...' – Altman and Gross, p.631.

'I have a woman's instinct about people...' – Field and Chowdhury, p.563.

'He's a gentleman and he's strong, and he's not mannered...' – Altman and Gross, p.630.

2003: COME ON, MR PUTIN!

Paul McCartney's 2003 Moscow concert was recorded for Mark Haefeli's 2005 documentary *Paul McCartney in Red Square*. The quotes from McCartney, Putin, Troitsky and Gorbachev are taken from that documentary. Leslie Woodhead's invaluable book *How the Beatles Rocked the Kremlin* is another important source for this chapter. The English-language quotes from *The Foundations of Geopolitics* are from John B. Dunlop's 31 January 2004 article 'Aleksandr Dugin's Foundations of Geopolitics' in the journal *Demokratizatsiya*.

'Pop quartet the Beatles. Look how elegant they are...' – Woodhead, p.138.
'You like rock 'n' roll? Fuck you, anti-Soviet slime!' – Woodhead, p.64.
'American rock 'n' roll like Little Richard...' – Woodhead, p.25.
'For many years, we were told that the West was an enemy...' – Woodhead, p.92.
'It was a beautiful event. There was a spectacular sunset over Red Square...' – Woodhead, p.150.

2008: THE DEATH OF STRAWBERRY FIELDS

Roger Moore gave his thoughts on *Quantum of Solace* in a March 2009 interview with Christian O'Connell on Absolute Radio's *Who's Calling Christian* show. The initial Gemma Arterton quote can be found online at https://www.mi6-hq.com/sections/girls/arterton.php3. Her *Observer* quote is from Tim Lewis's 12 May 2013 interview 'Gemma Arterton: "Our house was a bit *Ab Fab* at times"'. The *Evening Standard ES Magazine* interview quoted is Jane Mulkerrins's 6 April 2017 feature 'Gemma Arterton on therapy, sacrifice and changing the industry from the inside out'. Arterton's comments at the International Women's Day event were widely reported, for example in Ella Phillip's article for *Harper's Bazaar*, 'Gemma Arterton: "There's so much wrong with Bond women"'.

' "No thank you," I say. Maybe he is attractive...' – Curtis (ed.), p.243.

2012: A GOLDEN THREAD OF PURPOSE

Danny Boyle's quote about building Jerusalem is from page 11 of the London 2020 Olympic Games Opening Ceremony Media Guide. Reactions to the ceremony, including the tweets of MP Aidan Burley, are from the

28 July 2012 BBC News story 'Media reaction to London 2012 Olympic opening ceremony' and the 27 July 2012 *Guardian* round-up 'Olympics opening ceremony: the view from abroad', by Alexandra Topping. Gary Chapman describes the Child Catcher in his 26 March 2005 *Times* article 'Star Choice'. The quote from Pierre Weiss is from the 12 January 2016 *Associated Press* report 'IAAF knew of Russians' rampant doping years before ban: report'.

2015: WHAT IS THE NEW EVIL IN THE WORLD?

The quote from Pierce Brosnan is from Marianne Zumberge's 17 November 2015 *Variety* article 'Pierce Brosnan Criticizes *Spectre*: "The Story Was Kind of Weak" '. The fantasy illustration of the Tora Bora caves was published in *The Times* on 29 November 2001 and captioned 'Bin Laden's Mountain Fortress'. The quote from US Special Forces staff sergeant – who was named only as Jeff – is from his interview for the American PBS series *Frontline*. Details of Russian attempts to divide American society are from Deepa Seetharaman's 30 October 2017 *Wall Street Journal* article 'Russian-Backed Facebook Accounts Staged Events Around Divisive Issues'. For details of the US Government's reaction to the Sony Pictures hack, see Ariana Bacle's 18 December 2014 *Entertainment Weekly* article 'White House treating Sony hack as "serious national security matter" '. North Korea's response to American actions is detailed in the *Guardian*'s 27 December 2014 report 'North Korea calls Obama a "monkey" as it blames US for internet shutdown'. Yevhen Murayev's image of himself as Bond is seen in the *Times*'s 24 January 2022 report 'Kiev puppet is a part of Putin's toolkit in Ukraine, warns US'. For details of the Russian presence on St George's Hill, see Rupert Neate's 28 February 2022 *Guardian* article 'Tensions rise at the £3bn Surrey estate Russian oligarchs call home'. The quote from António Guterres is taken from Julian Borger's 24 February 2022 *Guardian* report 'Moment that Putin thundered to war, drowning out last entreaties for peace'.

'*Skyfall* was a post-Julian Assange movie...' – Field and Chowdhury, p.653.

'his time as ambassador in London was a triumph...' – Harding, p.196.
'The stuff about us having fights about the budget...' – Field and
  Chowdhury, p.653.

2021: TIME TO DIE

Jonathan Pryce's comments are from Sebastian Shakespeare's 24 August
2018 *Daily Mail* article 'Danny Boyle wasn't trusted with lucrative 007
franchise out of fears he'd turn James Bond into a "#MeToo socialist
spy"'. The *Guardian*'s article ' "We've literally been killed by James Bond":
Cineworld's final day of screenings' was written by Archie Bland and
published on 8 October 2020. Robbie Collin's *Telegraph* article 'The *No
Time to Die* delay is James Bond putting a bullet in his own head' was
published on 3 October 2020. MGMs statement about *No Time to Die*'s
profitability is grudgingly reported by Rebecca Rubin and Brent Lang in
their 22 November 2021 *Variety* article 'Covid-Era Conundrum: *No Time to
Die* May Be the Year's Highest-Grossing Hollywood Movie, But It Could
Still Lose Millions'. The *Evening Standard*'s report 'The world wasn't ready
for Daniel Craig's pink suit at Bond premiere' was written by Joe Bromley
on 9 September 2021. The *Daily Mail* coined the word 'superwoke' in
their 1 October 2021 headline, ' "The best Bond in years": *No Time to Die*
is branded "brilliant, epic and awesome" by devoted British fans hours
after cinematic release... yet others claim 007 is "absolutely ruined" by
superwoke spin on the sleuth'. The quote from Finn Mackay is from
their 5 November 2021 *Guardian* article 'What toxic men can learn from
masculine women'. The quote from Barbara Broccoli is taken from Brent
Lang's 15 January 2020 *Variety* article '*No Time to Die*: A Rare In-Depth
Interview with the Keepers of James Bond'.

2021: RINGO AND PAUL

The *Daily Mail* article about the 2021 Grammys was written by Rachel
McGrath on 15 March 2021. The quote from Maggie Baird is from Jem
Aswad's 4 December 2019 *Variety* article, 'Billie Eilish and Her Brother
and Co-Writer, Finneas, Get Deep about Their Music and What's Next'.
The quote from Finneas O'Connell is from Scott Feinberg's 24 November

2021 *Hollywood Reporter*'s article 'Awards Chatter Podcast – Billie Eilish & Finneas (*No Time to Die*)'. McCartney's conversation with Taylor Swift was reported by Patrick Doyle in the 13 November 2020 edition of *Rolling Stone*. The statistics for US music consumption are from a report by MRC Data, 'Annual U.S. 360 Music Report'. The final quote from McCartney comes from his interview with Jon Wilde for the July 2004 edition of *Uncut*.

2022: JAMES BOND WILL RETURN

The comments on *No Time to Die* by the *Kill James Bond!* podcast are from their Twitter account, @killjamesbond, and were posted on 7 October 2021. The comments on assassination by Sir Richard Dearlove – a wonderfully Bondian name – are taken from Ian Cobain's 14 February 2012 *Guardian* article 'How secret renditions shed light on MI6's licence to kill and torture'.

'If they didn't understand the Beatles and the sixties...' – Taylor, p.202.
'If you think I'll accept a million pounds from you...' – Fleming (1963), p.289.

ACKNOWLEDGEMENTS

The author thanks the following kind souls for their generosity to Shelter in deep midwinter:

Claire Beere, Paul Beere, Beat the Drum, Chris Velenik, Dionisio Segovia, Joe O'Mahony, Andy Nash, Dean Bargh, Matt Lunt, Anwen Fryer Burrows, Graeme Rose, Anna Richardson, Judy Mazonowicz, Ian White, Ben Sansum, G.S. Wilkinson, Matt Wilmshurst, Jim Thomlinson, Lisa Crees, Angus Sprackling, Peter Sim, Andy Gell, Helen McIntyre, Donny McIntyre, Tim Holmes, Laura Holmes, Tonie van Ringelestijn, Stuart Betts, Mark Thompson, Tony Summers, Ben Hockman, C.M. Blackmore, Jessica May Escorcia, Holiday Mat, Martin Riley, Andy Morgan-Smith, Fuzzbuddy, Mat, Jocky McSporan, Andrew J. Rosevear, Richard Beckett, Helen Mallon, Sean Beattie, Benny Hollenstein, Cass and Adam, Claudia Egypt Boulton, Daniel Evans, Jeremy Allen, Natalie Galustian, Arthur Pendragon Mitchell-Koeller, Steve Fisher, Jess, Soto and the twins, Patricia Mallon, Ruth x2, John Fillingham, Sean Hannam, Brice Dickson, Katrina Robinson, Richard Gledhill, Frank Goulbourn, Bobby Dalling, Gavin, Erin, Baxter, and Cooper, Andrew Burns, Carl Phillips, Chris Reed, Heather Smith, Dan

ACKNOWLEDGEMENTS

Sumption, Good Cop Bad Cop, Matt Cox, Simon Harris, Stevie Greenaway, Richard Montagu, Sarah Montagu, Dave Carr, Hesham Sabry, Iwan Parris, Rob Manuel, Alex Monroe, Adam Crooke, Jeremy Hassall-Gibson, Keith Ford, Johann Aschenberger, Chris Mellor, MossChops, Jean-Jacques Mugisha, Martin Wellard, Stewart Morris, David John Scott, Harry Freeze, Richard Norris, Pengwern Books, Adrian Raggio, Ed Fagan, Marian Christophers Greaves, Alex Brims, Mark Love, Peter Sims (aka JPGR&B), John Bezzini, Werner, Andy Fish, Huw Maddock, Orlando Monk and Anonymous x5.

The following also deserve huge thanks, for this book would not be here without them: Jenny Lord, Ellen Turner, Ellie Freedman, Kate Moreton, Jo Whitford, Ian Allen and all at Weidenfeld & Nicolson. Sarah Ballard, Eli Keren, Alex Stephens and all at United Agents. Extra-special love and thanks along with medals for bravery go to my beta readers Joanne Mallon, Jason Arnopp, Lia Higgs, David Bramwell and Alistair Fruish. Love also to Isaac, Suzanne, Paul, Patricia, Brice, Helen, Maura, Eric and assorted drinking pals. X

INDEX

INDEX

INDEX